B

For my daughter,
Isabel Rose Baeten Cahoone

Civil Society

The Conservative Meaning of Liberal Politics

Lawrence E. Cahoone

The right of Lawrence E. Cahoone to be identified as author of this work
has been asserted in accordance with the Copyright, Designs and Patents
Act 1988.

First published 2002

2 4 6 8 10 9 7 5 3 1

Blackwell Publishers Inc.
350 Main Street
Malden, Massachusetts 02148
USA

Blackwell Publishers Ltd
108 Cowley Road
Oxford OX4 1JF
UK

Library of Congress Cataloging-in-Publication Data

Cahoone, Lawrence E., 1954–
Civil society : the conservative meaning of liberal politics /
Lawrence E. Cahoone.
p.   cm.
Includes bibliographical references and index.
ISBN 0-631-23204-4 (alk. paper) — ISBN 0-631-23205-2 (pb. : alk. paper)
1. Civil society.   2. Liberalism.   3. Conservatism.   I. Title.
JC337   .C34   2002
300—dc21

2001043206

British Library Cataloguing in Publication Data

A CIP catalogue record for this book is available from the British Library.

Typeset in 10 on 12.5 pt Photina
by Best-set Typesetter Ltd., Hong Kong
Printed in Great Britain by MPG Books Ltd, Bodmin, Cornwall

This book is printed on acid-free paper.

Contents

Acknowledgments

I am grateful to those who have generously contributed to this book, consciously or not, either through their encouragement or critical comments on parts of the text: Peter Berger, Jean Elshtain, William Galston, Knud Haakonssen, Glenn Loury, Bhikhu Parekh, Nancy Rosenblum, James Schmidt, Jack Weinstein, and Alan Wolfe. Their contribution does not, of course, imply any agreement with what follows, either in whole or in part. Lastly, I thank my friends and townsfolk of Lynn, Massachusetts, whose neighborliness helped to inspire these pages.

Above all, civil politics require an understanding of the complexity of virtue, that no virtue stands alone, that every virtuous act costs something in terms of other virtuous acts, that virtues are intertwined with evils, and that no theoretical system of a hierarchy of virtues is ever realizable in practice.

Edward Shils

Introduction

This book is about liberalism, or more broadly, the liberal republican way of politics, and particularly what it became in the second half of the twentieth century in the United States and countries like it. It argues that liberalism has to be seriously reinterpreted to avoid the theoretical and practical liabilities that have become apparent. Many other theorists have come to similar conclusions in the last two decades, but in my view their apples have fallen too close to the tree. A more fundamental critique of liberalism and its dominant versions is required.

Unfortunately, this debate takes place in the precincts of a political Tower of Babel; any contribution seeking to surmount the linguistic haze has to clarify terminology at the outset. In contemporary American political usage, "liberal" usually means the pro-welfare state, high tax, activist government wing of the Democratic Party since the New Deal, which I will call "egalitarian liberalism." This form of liberalism is currently out of favor rhetorically, although it remains popular in practice to all those who benefit from at least some of its policies, which is most of the American population. Despite the "conservative," anti-tax, anti-big government turn in American politics since 1980, the social and governmental institutions created by the egalitarian liberal view remain an essential part of our social and cultural fabric.

But egalitarian or welfare-state liberalism is only one form of a wider and deeper political tradition that has, by dint of age at least, a greater right to the term. Liberalism in this wider sense is the view that political society serves the value of individual liberty, requiring the restraint of forms of power, governmental or otherwise, that would coerce individuals. This liberalism came of age as a variant of modern republicanism, which authorizes and limits political power through the consent of the governed. Some liberals, in the most extreme case, "libertarians," claim that any government or political power beyond that necessary to deter individuals from harming each others' rights is unjustifiably coercive. Because libertarians oppose the welfare state as coercive they are in contemporary politics regarded as "conservatives." This designation retains its plausibility only so long as the debate focuses on the size and role of government. In their basic philosophy, libertarians are liberals – as they sometimes say, "classical" liberals. They join more traditionalist, cultural, and religious conservatives in opposing egalitarian liberalism, but are decidedly non-conservative on other issues, e.g. abortion, drug use, pornography, etc. Egalitarian liberals join libertarians in their concern for individual rights, but regard poverty and the property rights of corporations and the wealthy as threats to those rights requiring government intervention. When the focus turns from economics to civil and personal liberties, egalitarians and libertarians largely agree. And for good reason; they are all liberals.

Many of today's libertarians and egalitarians also share what became in the second half of the twentieth century the dominant interpretation of liberalism, namely *neutralism* or *proceduralism*, according to which government is to remain effectively neutral in questions of substantive morality and the meaning of human existence. Only this neutrality will insure equality before the law – the type of equality on which egalitarians and libertarians agree – and the minimum of coercion. The notion of liberty that informs this view is predominantly *negative* and *voluntarist*; that is, liberty obtains when obstacles to the occasional choices of individuals are absent. Proceduralist liberalism has thus become the prevailing contemporary form of republicanism, the dominant interpretation of what a government of, by, and for the people requires. Not that proceduralism has been without domestic critics or, more importantly, has ever been applied consistently. Americans have never been consistent neutralists, as they have never been consistent egalitarians or libertarians, nor consistent communitarians or individualists. Like most peoples, they have more sense than to be consistent. Nevertheless, liberalism's dominant neutralist self-interpretation has been for half a century a touchstone for Supreme Court decisions and lawmakers' arguments, and remains a powerful player in our political imaginations. It has been, and still is, effective.

But liberalism is today in trouble. Certainly the egalitarian liberalism of the Democratic Party from the New Deal through the 1970s is in trouble in the sense that it is regularly excoriated for bankruptcy, financial and moral. But it is the troubles of the wider and more basic liberalism, the liberalism shared by egalitarians and libertarians, that concern me in what follows. Many of the developed liberal societies of the world, and the United States in particular, are lurching into a future no one can foresee with a long list of chronic social ills to which liberalism seems to have no remedy. We are presented simultaneously with the impression of unprecedented growth and power on the one hand, and incurable social and economic problems on the other, a kind of chaotic stability.

In America there is the commonly cited list of troubles: crime and social pathology, divorce and the destabilization of child-rearing, and a seemingly intractably impoverished underclass. That in the late 1990s the divorce rate apparently topped out, and crime has been temporarily rolled back – at the cost of a huge prison population – does not undo the sense that current social order is hard-won and tenuous in the face of ever-increasing pressures, that in the last third of the twentieth century some kind of social glue was lost, requiring ever new, costly, and only marginally effective bureaucratic forms of putty. Behind these facts is the more amorphous but palpable sense of decline in community, morality, and the value of public life, and the fragmentation of the populace, especially by race. Just as significant is the apparent ineffectiveness of the political sphere to deal with these matters, including the corruption of politics and the indolence of government, leading to a sense of communal ineffectuality that is only papered-over by economic good times. When we add the economic difficulties associated with long-term increases in the cost of health care, social security, decaying infrastructure and education, the looming crises of environmental degradation and energy production, and the chronic insecurity of life in a new age characterized by the post-industrial information economy and the globalization of markets, we are confronted, not only with the fact of a mass technological society coming up against problems novel in human history, but with a public mood and a political system seemingly ill-equipped to achieve the foresight and collective pragmatism necessary to address them. The resurgence of the US economy in the 1990s, like all periods of expansion, made much of this temporarily easier to live with. While we can be grateful for this, we know that, beneath the good times, the ground continues to shift under our feet, awaiting cyclic contraction to make our chronic vulnerability all the more impossible to ignore.

The list of real problems has accumulated simultaneously with the ideological critique of liberalism in the past two decades. In America the conservative spirit, never wholly absent, has been reasserting itself increasingly since the early 1970s, achieving its greatest successes in the presidency of Ronald Reagan and in the Congressional elections of 1994. But these successes are only the periodic ground swells of a continuous and widespread change in American political culture, whereby the rhetoric and some of the principles and practices of egalitarian liberalism have become deeply unpopular, even while the programs it established in its heyday remain generally in force. At any rate, conservatism is back.

Political theory has reflected these popular objections to liberalism. On the one hand, libertarianism has moved from the margins to impact the center, and has even attained some academic respectability. More fundamentally, there have been various attempts to reinterpret liberalism in non-proceduralist ways, sometimes going under the name of "communitarianism," "civic republicanism," and "perfectionist" or "non-neutral" liberalism. These all accept that government and law must promote certain values. The most prominent suggest no radical rejection of liberal policies, no great rollback of individual liberties. But, as I will try to show, any step away from governmental and political neutrality, any attempt to leaven the discourse of individual rights with recognition of either moral limits to those rights or their dependence on a communal background – evident in attempts to limit abortion rights, control technology, promote family values or other particular lifestyles, or to insert moral education into public school curricula – is always a step toward greater social coercion of the individual. That is, all such movements are steps in a traditionally *conservative* direction, despite the desire in some quarters to avoid that loaded term. In this sense, "communitarianism" is simply a kinder and gentler name for conservatism.[1]

I share the concerns of those who object to neutralism. The form of life we increasingly live is one in which *connection*, quasi-permanent relations to others, to place, and to cultural tradition, is increasingly replaced by impersonal functional relations, bureaucracy, and highly impermanent personal relations. This is the direction of technological, social, and economic change. This shift is problematic, not only from the point of view of more traditional community, but for the life of liberal democracy, the experience of a free polity. Our dominant proceduralist talk about politics contributes to this process in two ways, by its valuation of individualism and material progress above all – both legitimate modern goods, I will argue, but only when properly placed in the context of other goods – and by defining the political sphere so as to exclude connection and cultural tradition as legitimate political concerns. Our public discourse about ourselves and our problems has been truncated by a liberal proceduralism that shrinks the debate over the costs of modernization by leaving some of those costs "off the books," non-considerations from the liberal point of view. This does not mean proceduralism does not have virtues. It means that, whatever problems it may have helped to fix in the past, it cannot fix those that increasingly plague us.

However rich and exciting, the current debate over liberalism in political theory is marked by two inadequacies. First, there is a tendency to assume a fairly narrow orthodoxy within which minor disagreements are to be adjudicated. Communitarians, civic republicans and perfectionist liberals attack the concepts and rhetoric of neutralism, but fear to stray very far from neutralist liberal policies. In particular, this means a failure to take seriously the deepest critique of liberalism, that of traditional conservatism. Academic political theory remains decidedly egalitarian and liberal, even if minor flirtations with forms of anti-statism and anti-individualism are now permissible. Conservatives continue to be caricatured as barbarians at the gate, the aim of much contemporary theorizing being not to consider the barbarians' claims but to reinforce the gate. Gate-reinforcing has its place in geo-politics and social life, I agree, but not in theoretical debate. The task of inquiry is not guardianship, but soberly to consider the best arguments conservatism has to offer.

This hesitance to confront conservatism is particularly odd among philosophers. We seem willing soberly to discuss all manner of repugnant views – e.g. of Nietzsche, Heidegger, Sade – as long as their concrete political implications are bracketed. To entertain the thought that there are no ultimate moral rules is standard philosophical practice; but to entertain the thought that limits on abortion rights are legitimate, censorship is tolerable, and nationalism has something to say for it, is for many beyond the pale. Contemporary philosophy is quite willing to speak of the unspeakable, as long as the speech is not political; perhaps this is a sign that many contemporary intellectuals have a politics where their soteriology should be. It seems to me that progress in the current debate requires a frank assessment of the full-bodied form of traditional conservatism in order to set the boundaries within which minor steps in a moderately conservative direction can be adjudicated. In other words, the discussion needs consideration of fundamentals to set the context for melioristic proposals that tinker around the edges of liberalism.

Second, and from the other side, a prominent error of contemporary conservatives is a failure to recognize the realities of modernity. I do not mean to charge them with a failure to accept that modernity is an unalterable fact – although some talk as if they do. Their real error is a failure to recognize the source of those features of contemporary society most repugnant to the conservative outlook. The welfare state, big government, loss of community, excessive individualism, and the debility of moral traditions are not primarily the result of artistic or theoretical or political changes, not chiefly the doing of pointy-headed egalitarian intellectuals or angry levelers from below. Pointy heads and levelers there are; but the question is, how have their policies gained widespread approval from democratic majorities and ruling elites all over the modernized world for generations? Egalitarian proceduralist liberalism is what liberalism came to be under the pressure of real social, economic, and cultural changes. It evolved in response to the new conditions of mass culture, post-industrialism, and technology. The retirement of Ted Kennedy will not lead Americans to give up Medicare and Social Security.

It is certainly true that, as Nietzsche wrote, "No one is free to be a crab," that is, to walk backwards.[2] The current point goes further. It is that conservatives often share with their liberal antagonists a failure to recognize that *conservatism is modern*. Traditionalist conservatism is mainly a product of the eighteenth century, the century of the Enlightenment. Edmund Burke, the godfather of English conservatism, was not anti-modern or pre-modern – although in some places he could be called *non-modern*, someone who recognized that the most important dimensions of human existence are unaltered by modernization. We do well to remember that the "traditional" order Burke defended against French revolutionary ideals was in fact the most progressive and modernized society in eighteenth-century Europe, namely, England. Rather than refusing modernity, conservatism is a different way of handling modernity, and one that is not so antithetical to our contemporary form of political life – as opposed to our political talk – as we usually think. In any event, conservatives must recognize that they, like liberals, are by necessity struggling with the facts of modernity, which all sides at least ambivalently endorse.

In trying to amend these limitations of the current debate, the perspective I will devise is constrained by three commitments, which typically form the basis for the three aforementioned political views, libertarianism, communitarianism or conservatism, and egalitarian liberalism. These views respectively embody the value of individuality and the private life, of the individual's obligations to the community, and of the community's obligations to the individual. That ordering is merely a matter of rhetorical presentation; it does not imply that individuality is logically prior. My task will be to hold these convictions together in balance. What follows below is no argument – that comes later – but a set of promissory notes given in the interest of full disclosure.

First, as an individual, understood in modern terms, I most fundamentally belong neither to community nor state but to myself and a private, local social network, usually of family and friends. Connected with this is the admission that, for the majority of human beings, the meaning of life is achieved in the private sphere of household, family, friends, neighbors, and associates in work. Here is my incipient libertarianism, which expresses the value of self-determination and, with it, the private life (the last of which libertarians do not always honor). Along with this is a negative response both to statism and majoritarianism, that is, a recognition of the costs of collectivist bureaucratic management and intrusive communitarian moralism. Privacy, individuality, recalcitrance, looseness, idiosyncrasy, and wildness are not to be banished by governmental therapy or communal order.

But, second, communities and cultures must be able to preserve and reproduce themselves through time, hence have the right to demand that individuals fulfill obligations that affect the community. This right is buttressed by the dependence of the individual on the community and on culture. The vaunted independence of the individual is exaggerated and overrated by liberals. Such independence as individuals have is communally constructed. Here is my incipient communitarianism, or more honestly, conservatism. Communal demands on the individual are legitimate because: first, the primary end of society is continuance, which can only mean continuance *as that society understands itself*; second, individuality is emergent from community; and third, the political authority of free citizens must express itself in communal self-determination. Democracy as we normally understand it is the formalization of this more basic legitimate power.

Last, communal provision, the obligation of the society to provide for the individual under special circumstances, is a necessary feature of political society, and even more so under modern economic conditions. Here is my incipient welfare or egalitarian liberalism. To allow the innermost destinies of citizens to be destroyed by the lottery of *fortuna* is, where that destruction is avoidable, a violation of the minimal conditions for joint membership in society. Regarding the minimal constituent resources necessary for what most of us consider a meaningful life, individuals cannot be allowed to go without. If they do, then deprived and fortunate individuals cannot regard themselves as members of the same society. And *what society needs above all is for its members to regard themselves as members.*[3]

Now, these three convictions may well seem contradictory. Each of them – individual liberty, communitarian self-determination, and communal provision – taken by itself as the ultimate principle would displace the others. But here I will borrow a page from the conservative tradition: *nothing can be taken by itself*. The attempt to assert one value as ultimate, be it liberty or property rights or popular self-rule or equality or civic virtue or social improvement, as always trumping other considerations, is theoretically soothing but socially implausible. Political association is the endless balancing of a finite set of competing values. This balancing can be, I will argue, morally significant, and not merely an opportunistic or *ad hoc* balancing.

Such balancing is not merely the lesson of sobriety. Its superiority to the assertion of a single ultimate value lies as well in this, that such assertion always proves self-undermining. That is, the diverse values mentioned above are not mutually exclusive, but enter into the conditions for the realization of their apparent contraries. And this fact can serve as the basis for a theoretical rapprochement of the three. *Rapprochement* here means, not synthesis or reconciliation, but a principled cease-fire.

We ought not forget the deep convergence of what might be called the modern North Atlantic political tradition. Libertarianism, egalitarian liberalism, and conservatism – which, to be sure, do not exhaust that tradition – in fact share three notions. First, government is neither sacred nor self-justifying. Governmental power must be legitimated by the relation of government to something outside it in the social sphere, be it the occasional will of some classes, of the people in general, or a tradition of law and custom. Hence office holders, including royalty, can by their actions render their status illegitimate. This is as true for Burkean conservatives as for Lockean liberals.[4] Second, all endorse some form of social equality which government must respect, be it the equality of all individuals before one uniform legal code, or the equal dignity and importance of all classes or Estates. Last and more atmospherically, there is a consistent skepticism regarding governmental dictation of ways of life, culture, *mores*, etc. Now, unlike liberals, conservatives do often condone governmental enforcement of ways of life on recalcitrant minorities and individuals. But even in this case, what is condoned is an enforcement of ways of life whose legitimacy transcends governmental fiat; the government is to administer norms, not invent them. The great fear of the modern North Atlantic political tradition, conservative or liberal, is that something about civil society, be it individual rights or public security or a traditional order, will be violated by political power.

But beyond these obvious historical convergences there are some less obvious conceptual ones. For the stated aims of liberals and conservatives cannot in fact be realized without support by at least some of the values, practices, and institutions typically espoused by their opponents.

Individual liberty is an ultimate value for liberals, not conservatives. But individuality is a communal, cultural product, the result of familial and societal action, as communitarians rightly point out. This dependence does not end with the age of majority. Unless I opt out of society, my adult creativity presupposes a cooperative scheme, not just to support me as I pursue my idiosyncratic aims, but because my aims involve society. Here the "liberal" John Dewey is mostly right: individuality means making an individual contribution *to* society, not the ability to escape *from* society. Take Ayn Rand's fictional character Howard Rourke, the supremely individualistic architect-hero of her novel *The Fountainhead*.[5] It is true, as egalitarian liberals point out against Rand, that Rourke needs society to educate him, protect him, build the roads on which his materials are transported, etc. (Indeed, an architect is, like a film director, that kind of artist utterly dependent on huge sums of other people's money.) But beyond this, Rourke's very aim is to communicate, affect, contribute to society, albeit in his distinctive way. Rourke makes buildings for people to work and live in. This is a supremely social act. The implicit aim – to be sure, not always his "end in view" or conscious aim – is to affect others, and this presumes the maintenance of society, albeit the maintenance of the kind of society that can accept novelty. Without a community and a culture, which, I will argue, means a tradition, there is nothing for the individual to contribute to, making individuality practically meaningless. There would remain only the freedom to be an ineffectual loner, and if this is the only choice available, then it is not freedom at all.

Egalitarians are, as noted, right that liberty and individuality require material conditions for their actualization. The only argument against this notion is the especially libertarian conception of "negative liberty," that liberty means only the absence of interference, versus "positive liberty" or self-determination. But I will argue that this conception cannot stand scrutiny. However laudable the intent of the negative concept of liberty, most famously promoted by Isaiah Berlin as a bulwark against society's potential use of self-determination as an excuse for coercion, it is inadequate. Liberty is at least partly positive, it cannot be conceived in complete distinction from self-determination. Like all other human traits, liberty must be constructed through a process that demands resources, and once achieved, remains dependent on those and other social resources. The problem will be, not to choose negative or positive liberty, but to recognize their balanced necessity for a fulsome notion of freedom.

Now the maintenance of community and tradition does not, by itself, require individuality. That is indeed the danger of communitarianism or conservatism *per se*. There have been communities in human history in which individuality has been, if not absent, then minimal by our standards. But under *modern* conditions, that is, given anything like the conditions of modern liberal republican societies, community in fact requires the creativity and energy that only individual liberty can bring. Modern society not only makes greater room for individuality, it depends on widespread individuality to an unprecedented degree. That is, *departure from tradition is the necessary condition for the vitality of some traditions,* whether creativity flows from lone individuals – which is relatively rare – or from groups who pool their energies to make a distinctive contribution. Most novel enterprises, either in the market or in social reform or in art, are partnerships, cooperative ventures, which break with tradition in some respects while utterly accepting tradition in others. As such they cannot exist without the socialization process; they presume the continuation of the kind of society that can absorb and appreciate their innovation. The maintenance of communal vitality under modern conditions, where progress is an intrinsic and permanent fact, requires individuality. It is the mark of a modern conservatism, which is to say, a conservatism of *our* society and not some bygone world, to recognize this point.[6]

In sketching a political theory of modern liberal republican society that is anchored by these commitments, my argument will make four points, the first polemical, the rest constructive.

First, I will argue against neutralist or proceduralist liberalism, focusing on the work of Robert Nozick and John Rawls; the latter's recent work will be of special concern. Neutralism is inadequate philosophically and politically. It either contributes to chronic social problems or blocks attempts to address them. Most troublesome is its rigid distinction of the political from the social and particularly cultural spheres of life. Its benefits, while significant, can largely be captured by alternative schemes.

Now, as stated, my critical target is proceduralist liberalism and not liberalism *per se*. This may make my turn to conservatism appear unnecessary. For surely there is more to liberalism than neutralism. Many older versions of liberalism are obviously *not* neutralist, and contemporary "perfectionist" liberals have returned to this point. But, I will argue, since the second half of the nineteenth century we can see in the liberal political tradition the same process that can be found in other areas of modern life, namely, a progressive differentiation, narrowing and decontextualization of, in this case, what constitutes "the political." Political theory has become more specialized, purified, and rationalized. Utilitarian, civic republican, and other non-neutralist versions of liberalism lost their grip on the debate in the second half of the twentieth century. Active citizenship, the language of public duty, and the cultural context of politics have been increasingly left behind by the dominant liberal discourse. The sole legitimate concerns of politics tended in the post-World War II period to become rights, opportunity, and prosperity; a good polity is one with individual liberty – for libertarian liberals – or individual liberty plus cash – for egalitarian liberals.

As noted, the anti-neutralist reaction of the past two decades, however welcome, is not non-neutralist enough. Communitarian liberals, civic republicans, and perfectionist liberals typically reject the *language* but not the *policies* of neutralism. They endorse as goods, to be legitimately promoted by government, what neutralism sought to maximize implicitly through procedure. But these "liberal" goods – which turn out to be liberty or individualism, self-rule or democracy, and progress – are not good enough. Any adequate liberalism must assert a substantive account of the good not restricted to these liberal goods. The goods rightly recognized by modern political society are not merely political or economic.

Second, with a number of other recent theorists I will suggest a particular notion of human association that ought to serve as the basis for liberal republican politics. Political society ought to be understood primarily as a civil association or *civitas*. Hence the concepts of law, rights, government, and politics will, in my workshop, be dependent on civil society, rather than the other way around.

Civitas was a Latin term used in ancient Rome for the community of citizens. Only later did it become identified with the *urb* and come to mean city, to which it was, unlike the Greek term *polis*, not originally restricted. Most relevant to contemporary English usage, it unites "citizen" with "civility." The latter does not need to be heard as a synonym for politeness and the refinement of manners. Rather, it refers to the kind of relation, and the kind of order, which is supposed to prevail among those people who share the distinctive human relationship of fellow citizens. I will argue that the core of the notion of civil society is a commitment to the *priority of the social*, the conviction that extant societies gain their norms from within, not from government, Church, or military organizations. To base one's political theory on civil society, then, is to accept society as the source of political norms and institutions, rather than establishing a politics that is supposed to dictate to society.

But in the modern period, starting in the eighteenth century, this notion of civil society received a new impetus. Modern civil society accepts the *spontaneity*, hence the institutional pluralism, of social order. The modern form of social life, which civil society honors as autonomous, is complex and dynamic; this was the insight of Bernard Mandeville and the Scottish Enlightenment. It is linked to the development of commercial or bourgeois society. Socially and politically, rather than economically, this dynamic complexity indicates that in modern civil society, as Claude Lefort writes, "The throne is empty," no one agency, institution, dimension of life, value, or image rules. This curious, liberating, and frightening feature of a "decentered" society, which postmodernists rhapsodize but which is really an eighteenth century notion, is modeled by political liberals in their distinction between public rules of right and private notions of the good, and by economic liberals in their ubiquitous "markets." Each model has its place, but neither is adequate to the reality of this novel form of society in which *there is no whole*, that is, no effective comprehensive doctrine or ruling authority. More precisely, if more paradoxically, in our society every proposed or projected whole must itself be treated *as a part* – limited by the rules of civility and the benefits of pluralism – while recognizing that at the same time the parts only have ultimate meaning and value in relation to proposed wholes. That is, the commitment to the moral value of civil society, hence solidarity, loyalty, and fellow citizenship, itself depends on comprehensive accounts of "the Good." The inability to reconcile this most productive paradox is intrinsic to modern civil society.

Critics of proceduralist liberalism sometimes call for a return to a republic of virtue, a moral community or, using the famous dichotomy of Ferdinand Tönnies, a *Gemeinschaft* of shared traditional morality, in response to purely contractual association, or *Gesellschaft*, of modern liberal society. But civil society is neither *Gesellschaft* nor *Gemeinschaft*, not determined by self-interest or intimacy or affection or community of belief. It rests on the balancing of the three recognitions mentioned above: the quasi-independence of members, the duties of membership, and the rights of membership. Civil association is that political form in which citizens enjoy the bivalent status of *free members*; they are not merely or primarily free, nor merely or primarily members, but primordially both. This civility has not disappeared in modern America; it lives on in many locales. But at municipal, state and national levels – those levels of association most fully affected by modernization, and coincidentally the levels of greatest concern to political theorists and commentators – civility and *civitas* have been increasingly forgotten.

Just as civil society is not "community," neither is it the forum of political participation. Some critics of liberal proceduralism have understandably but mistakenly responded to the apparent individualism, fragmentation, and privatism of liberal society with an *apotheosis of the public sphere*. Thus civic republicanism holds that active citizenship or political participation is the highest good and aim of civil life, and current "discursive" and "deliberative" models of citizenship make public reasoning in speech the center of the *civitas*. In the present perspective, political activity is a tool employed by citizens to create and maintain the civil association. Politics is a means, not the meaning, of civic life. The concept of civil society implies a respect for the private and non-political life lacking in republicanism.

Third, the *civitas* is intrinsically *local*. All non-local forms of political order – which are, of course, legitimate and necessary – are parasitic on local civil association. The contemporary social configuration that most answers to the notion of the *civitas* is the *neighborhood*. I will thus given an analysis of neighborhood as the most basic layer of political society. This will only highlight, and not solve, what is then one of the great and permanent political problems of late modern or "postmodern" society, that the major forces of social and economic modernization work to undermine neighborhood. Locale is at the core of the civic experience, but contemporary society is fundamentally *delocalizing*. This is the greatest dilemma of our political life, and we must find a way to address it.

The primacy of the local civil association reflects what might be called a "populist" streak in what follows, in the sense that the late Christopher Lasch tried to rehabilitate that term in opposition to "progressivism."[7] Populism is not radical democracy in the sense of politicizing all of civic life. American Populism was primarily concerned with the civil association of relatively independent households, whose dignity lies in part in their relative economic self-determination, hence the populist emphasis on "producerism," proprietorship, and "competence." Populism is deeply anti-elitist, but in what I will argue is a *conservative* sense, that is, it sought to unhook local public and private life from their determination by the action of elites, both corporate and governmental. Political action was the tool employed toward this de-linkage, not an end in itself. Populism was further marked, as Lasch insisted, by the historical values of the American lower middle class, the traditional values of pre-industrial farmers and small producers, for whom the promise of American life was neither wealth nor unfettered liberty, but a *dignity* that presupposed and answered their recognition of the limits of social and material "progress." It was linked, in other words, to a kind of cultural conservatism, as its liberal critics have pointed out.

Fourth, in attempting to conceive the relation between the liberal *civitas* and non-political aspects of social life we are led to *holism*, an approach to politics that is at the heart of traditional conservatism. Holism is the meta-theory within which my account of the *civitas* will find its place. It refers, not to the "organic" view of society as a body for which individuals are cells, but to the interdisciplinary view for which the total ensemble of social relations and culture is what matters in political affairs. The politics, social relations, economics, and culture of a human group are interdependent dimensions. Thus politics must be regarded as dependent on non-political social and economic realities, and most especially on culture. The *civitas* must recognize its dependence on inherited cultural ways. This is in direct opposition to the enduring liberal antipathy to culture as the force of tradition, an aversion exacerbated by proceduralism in search of what Rawls in his recent work calls a "freestanding" politics, a politics wholly independent of "comprehensive" cultural views.

The claims of localism and holism can be connected through the insistence that human beings are first and foremost *emplaced*. We are local both in space and in time. We are emplaced spatially or geographically, in social terms within a neighborhood, historically in an inherited culture or tradition. This is not to deny our universality or our individuality; we are indeed in some sense individuals living under universal conditions, but both individuality and universality are emergent from, hence parasitic on, our locality or particularity. Now it is true, as liberals warn in their reflexive distrust of particularity, that spatial and cultural emplacement threatens minorities and idiosyncratic individuals with the prospect of coercion by local majorities. I will argue, however, that the only plausible safeguard for liberty is to work *through* local and cultural emplacement, to seek a balance of cultural values that honors liberty and recalcitrance, rather than attempt to go *around* emplacement, to pretend that the political can operate independent of the cultural and the local.

If we are to call the resulting view liberal, then it is a liberalism that is *civil* and *holist*. Holism shows why proceduralist and voluntarist versions of liberalism are wrong, and why attempts to avoid proceduralism while yet maintaining governmental neutrality regarding all but the implicit values of proceduralism – individual liberty, self-rule, and progress – are inadequate. Individual liberty is one value to be balanced among others, and community self-rule is a means and not the end of the civil association. Civil liberalism legitimates the limited redistribution of wealth and the limited promotion of substantive interpretations of the good life, for the sake not of material *equality*, but material *decency*. A liberalism shorn of proceduralism can meet halfway a conservatism shorn of anachronism, that is, a conservatism that endorses the values of individuality and progress that are part of our modern republican tradition. In short, a holist liberalism and a modern conservatism can converge. And, I claim, they ought.

Such a meeting is not as implausible as may first appear. Despite current impressions, conservatism is by nature non-formulaic. In principle it denies the possibility of deriving politics from a principle. Its main concern is the continued existence of a valued form of life. It may seek to explicate tradition, and to recount its virtues and benefits, but never to *justify* it in the sense of deriving it from the achievements of theoretical reason. Conservatism is in principle obligated to time, to history, in ways that liberalism is not; more the pity for liberalism. It is possible then, within a conservative methodology and anthropology to recognize the core values and practices of modern liberalism as essential to our tradition. *Conservatives are thus required by their own view to endorse liberal institutions and practices where those are part of the traditional fabric of society.* What the conservative must object to in liberal *theory*, as opposed to liberal practice, is the aim of making society *consistently* liberal, of extending liberal formulae to all aspects of social life.

The first three chapters set the stage for the more constructive work of the remaining five. Chapters 1 and 2 present my critique of proceduralist versions of liberalism, while chapter 3 argues that other contemporary versions of liberalism that attempt to ameliorate the problems of proceduralism fall short. Chapter 4 then presents what is most alive and challenging in the tradition of political conservatism. Chapter 5 focuses specifically on recent communitarian attempts to conceive liberty in a way, I will argue, inspired by conservatism yet largely compatible with liberal practices and values (if not liberal theory). Chapters 6 and 7 are my constructive attempt to draw out the notion of civil association as the basis politics; the former is largely historical, while latter introduces my analysis of *civitas* as neighborhood. Chapter 8 turns to meta-political questions that the entire preceding discussion must raise for the philosopher.

Unfortunately, the task of recasting our political discourse is made more difficult by the fact that the primary forum for political discussion – the electronic media and associated major print media – virtually outlaws reasonableness.[8] It is impossible for a media advocate of a policy to say what every member of the audience knows: that while there are things to be said for the policy, there are drawbacks too, even if, on the whole, for the advocate the benefits outweigh the costs. On the contrary, every political advocate must avoid all mention of disadvantages, since such statements provide ammunition for the opposition. The rules of strategic utterance in media politics lead everyone who hopes for success to be as rhetorically intransigent as possible. Indeed, absence of intransigent opposition is taken to be political wishy-washiness. Extreme rhetoric is rewarded, balance is punished. That is the nature of the contemporary game. Everyone knows, and may say in private, that the game skews the truth. But it is the only game in town, and this means that all public political discourse must play by its rules. Hence our political debate takes on the character of a legal contest between advocates – not surprising, given the backgrounds of most political actors – who feel obligated to say anything, short of *discoverable* lies, to sway the jury. Such a system may have its virtues in the courtroom, but in political culture it means the media debate almost never represents what the non-professional audience senses to be the whole, ambiguous and messy truth on an issue. Thus in the name of hard-headed truth-speaking the truth is never spoken. "The Truth is dead! Long live the Truth!" Here one can admire the dictum attributed to the late journalist Lars-Erik Nelson: "The enemy is not conservatism. The enemy is not liberalism. The enemy is bullshit."

But there are hopeful signs too. There are today not a few liberals sick of liberal rhetoric and conservatives cognizant of the need for the civic realm to address its real problems. I believe that conservatism reflects the fundamental political values of most Americans, that is, their deepest values about the proper role of politics in social life. Yet, many of the policies associated with what passes for conservatism, where it merely exchanges bureaucratic control for control by the largest economic actors, find very narrow endorsement. On the other hand, the institutions and practices developed in the name of liberalism, particularly egalitarian liberalism, are widely endorsed by most Americans, and with good reason. Yet the ideology and rhetoric of liberal egalitarianism is at the same time widely resented for its willingness to hand over power to the managerial elite of the bureaucratic state. What many commentators have seen negatively as the ambivalence and apathy of the American electorate in the last decade can be positively viewed as public groping toward a more reasonable political paradigm which it rarely hears from the lips of either its elected officials or its public experts, one that violates the rhetorical formulae that continue to structure our political talk.

Within the literature of political theory, a number of contemporary writers are carving out a space for political thinking in America beyond the Manichean opposition of statist egalitarianism and *laissez-faire* complacency that continue to dominate the official discussion. To take one example, in a remarkable passage William Galston outlines what he believes to be the tenets of an American majority that cuts across class, gender, age, and race. The passage deserves quotation despite its length.

> For there is . . . a contemporary American consensus concerning just principles and institutions. Every citizen is entitled to at least a minimally decent existence. . . . Those who cannot work – either because they are incapable of working or because they cannot find work to do – are to be compensated by the community. Those who can work but choose not to have no valid claims against other individuals or against the community. Above the level of minimal decency . . . individuals are permitted to achieve unequal rewards. . . . The community supervises this domain of competitive inequality by equalizing opportunities to develop talents and by ensuring that the distribution of rewards is governed by task-related factors rather than . . . race, sex, and family background. But it is recognized that this supervision will necessarily remain imperfect . . . because a system of total regulation . . . would gravely impede the ability of individuals to lead their lives as they see fit. . . . Individuals are held to be morally equal, in the sense that membership in the human species . . . suffices to engender certain minimal claims that other members are obliged to honor. At the same time, individuals are naturally

unequal. . . . They enjoy a sphere of privacy within which coercive interference . . . is thought to be illegitimate. They may select and pursue their own plans of life. And they are . . . responsible for the choices they make. But individual freedom is far from unlimited. It is circumscribed by duties both to ourselves and to others.[9]

While not a pollster, I think that one would be hard pressed to find 10 percent of the American public that would not agree to the foregoing, and, just as important, that among no major block of voters – counted by region, race, national origin, sex, sexual orientation, age, income, religion, disability – would the preceding paragraph fail to gain a strong majority. This matters, because it leads one to wonder, whence the fractiousness of our politics, and the allegation of our increasing Balkanism? I think it the nature of our form of political discourse to make problems intractable, to make us seem in greater conflict than we actually are.

This book is the fruit of a hope that we can find a way to think and speak about our politics and society not doomed to a permanent stalemate by the persistence of an anachronistic Manicheanism (which remains in force even as we slap together superficially synthetic phrases like "compassionate conservative"). A different set of categories might allow us to discover that many of our deepest convictions are less remote, less intransigent, less mutually hostile, than we seem to believe. It is a hope that what may be, as in the Galston passage, an actual consensus on certain issues and values can find its reflection at the more systematic and conceptual level, in a shared language and set of ideas that can guide us in political adjudication. For such ideas matter, whenever we talk to each other and seek agreement or compromise on what our shared civic existence is all about.

Notes

1 Certainly some communitarians favor egalitarian policies, the welfare state, etc. One may call this a communitarianism of the left, just as there are more "rightward" or traditionalist forms of communitarianism. But my point is that regarding the broad liberalism shared by egalitarians and libertarians, communitarianism is antiliberal, and thus conservative in that sense.

2 Friedrich Nietzsche, *Twilight of the Gods*, trans. Walter Kaufmann, in *The Portable Nietzsche*, edited by Kaufmann (New York: Viking, 1954), 6:144, par. 43.

3 This echoes the argument of Michael Walzer in his *Spheres of Justice: A Defense of Pluralism and Equality* (New York: Basic Books, 1983).

4 If Lockeans are liberals to start with. At least we may say that most liberals seem to think they are Lockeans.

5   Ayn Rand, *The Fountainhead* (New York: New American Library, 1952).
6   The phrase "modern conservatism" has been used by David Willetts, as we will
    see in chapter 4.
7   See Christopher Lasch, *The True and Only Heaven: Progress and Its Critics* (New
    York: W. W. Norton, 1991), and *The Revolt of the Elites and the Betrayal of
    Democracy* (New York: W. W. Norton, 1995).
8   "Reasonable" in the ordinary, not Rawlsian sense, as we will see.
9   William Galston, *Liberal Purposes: Goods, Virtues, and Diversity in the Liberal State*
    (Cambridge: Cambridge University, 1991), pp. 159–60.

1

Neutrality and Liberty

Proceduralist or neutralist liberalism aims to enforce rules that govern how individuals pursue their goals, without endorsing any particular set of goals. It gives priority in political theory and practice to "the Right," or the rules of association, over "the Good," or any substantive end.[1] While the term 'neutrality' is contemporary in its meaning, the metaphor is as old as John Locke's notion of the political community as an "umpire . . . indifferent and the same to all parties," which served to support the religious toleration Locke famously proposed. Contemporary neutralism purifies Locke's qualified toleration and extends its range of application to morality in general. The current motivation for adopting neutrality is twofold. Ethically, by avoiding the establishment of partisan notions of the Good, a neutralist political theory saves itself unending controversy. Most importantly, neutrality serves to minimize public coercion of individuals or minorities and hence maximize liberty. This liberty is conceived "voluntaristically" and "negatively"; liberty is exhibited by an individual subject's occasional choices whenever there is an absence of interference.[2] The moral and legal limit on such liberty is enforced only when the acts in question threaten to harm others.[3]

Now, one may say that this conception of neutralism is a red herring, that no political theory can be strictly neutral, so that labeling the relevant proceduralist thinkers "neutralists" is holding them to an impossible standard. But this would be an inconsequential terminological joust. Those theories called "neutralist" are effectively, not utterly, neutral; they seek to be as neutral as possible regarding the kinds of value-questions most at issue in real-world politics. That is the only meaning "neutral" can or need have in practice.

I will argue that proceduralist liberalism is mistaken and pernicious; mistaken because it cannot withstand philosophical scrutiny, pernicious because at this moment in history it contributes to persistent problems in liberal society and helps to block their resolution. Not that it is *utterly* mistaken. It is true that any liberal republican polity is committed to procedures and laws that must hold over a pluralistic society whose members affirm diverse conceptions of the Good. Nor is neutralism *entirely* pernicious. I have no doubt it is much better to live in a neutralist polity than in most non-neutralist polities. In point of historical fact, the neutralist view has always had a particular place within the culture of liberal society, balanced and limited by other views and traditions. Proceduralism has served good cause, in part by being saved from the embarrassment of its consistent application. As a result, political societies which allow neutralism to hold sway at some levels of social life at some times can well be better polities than those that never do. But a more adequate conception of liberalism's commitments would be better still.

Before proceeding, some history is in order. While the biography of liberalism is too rich for anything like an adequate presentation here, we need to know something about what liberalism has been if we are to put neutralism and its problems in context.

Early liberalism, or to use J. G. Merquior's term, "proto-liberalism" congealed from the late seventeenth through the eighteenth century around a dominant theme: the reaction against "arbitrary power," meaning primarily but not exclusively arbitrary governmental power.[4] From Locke's *Second Treatise on Government* (1689) to Montesquieu's *The Spirit of the Laws* (1748), the concern of proto-liberals was to limit the inhumane or anti-civil use of such power. This issued in three practical aims: strengthening some form of popular sovereignty; establishing constitutional and legal limits on power, such as divided government; and promoting religious tolerance, to eliminate or reduce one of the primary pretexts for the inhumane use of power. Also, already in Montesquieu we see the historical self-consciousness of this attempt, the belief that such changes constitute *progress*, that despotism is primitive while a free, law-governed society is more advanced. Thus, what I will later call the three canonical values promoted by twentieth century liberalism – liberty, self-rule, and progress – were already present in proto-liberalism in at least a vague form.

Over the one hundred years following *The Spirit of the Laws* a more differentiated notion was worked out, which prepared the ground for the mature liberalism of the mid-nineteenth century. Proto-liberalism came to accumulate a more articulated notion of what a society that is free, humane, and lawful must look like. This political and intellectual process took place simultaneously with massive social changes, especially the emergence of modern commercial and later industrial society. The mature liberalism of the nineteenth century was a political theory for a kind of society which existed only in fragments in the eighteenth century. A series of distinctive elements congealed about the fundamental aim of limiting and humanizing power, in particular, commitments to civil and especially economic liberty, private liberty, collective self-rule, and equality. These elements are part of a family with freedom, toleration, and lawful power; no liberalism can dispense with any one of these. But each can be variously interpreted, the collection of values differently prioritized, not to mention understood through additional institutional or philosophical factors that historically have been crucial for the most prominent forms of liberalism.

Certainly it comes as no surprise that liberalism values liberty. But the prominent concern of eighteenth-century proto-Liberals was with government interference in civil society in general, rather than with the "subjective rights" or privacy of individuals. In early liberalism, religious toleration was the one sphere of privacy that was prominently recognized – and even that toleration was limited by today's standards. The *political*, as opposed to civil or private, rights of the individual were another site of concern, continuous with the republican strand in liberalism. As J. G. A. Pocock has shown, liberalism's concern for non-political liberty competed not only against a feudal-royalist tradition, but against an alternative notion of republican liberty, copied over from Aristotle by the Italian Renaissance, which read freedom in aristocratic, martial, public terms, or as Isaiah Berlin would later put it, as *freedom to* act politically, rather than as *freedom from* political interference. The later developed after the former. Only in the later nineteenth or arguably the twentieth century did the view that an individual's occasional choices were not to be interfered with become the leading edge of liberalism.

But the ground of that eventual liberal commitment was already being laid in the economic sphere in the eighteenth century. Starting with Daniel Defoe's 1704 pamphlet, which insisted that charity harms the poor, through Bernard Mandeville's 1729 slogan of "private vices, publick benefits," and in the Scottish figures of Adam Ferguson, David Hume and above all Adam Smith and his 1776 *Wealth of Nations*,[5] the revolutionary notion of a commercial society was being pounded out.[6] It would reach its mature theoretical conception in the nineteenth century with David Ricardo.[7] Most obvious in the eighteenth century was the novel view that commerce and private interest could be the centerpiece of society. But this brought with it a series of equally revolutionary ideas.

What did a commercial society mean? Certainly it meant that self-interest and even avarice were beneficial. This sent moral philosophers to ask, Can there be a Good society based in material self-interest? Mandeville and the Scots gave the revolutionary affirmative answer. This carried with it the egalitarian consequence that the working and investing classes – those concerned to acquire property, as opposed to those either born with it (the aristocracy) or disbarred from it (the clergy) – are no longer contemptible. This spelled the supersession not only of royalism and aristocracy, but of the moral nobility and martial or heroic virtues of the republican ideal as well. It implied that the goodness of the social whole was not equal to, constituted by, the goodness of its leading (e.g. aristocratic) parts, but rather was a result of the interaction among non-virtuous parts. It meant further that *the ideal society is not the ideal society*, that the best society is one in which human vices were not suppressed but impersonally restrained in a way that led to their own self-discipline towards the common good. The pursuit of true ideality in human society is actually a danger. And it introduced a notion that has a right to be considered *the* mark of modern life, an idea that would still wait two more centuries to be named: the idea of spontaneous or emergent order. The order, even the *good* order, of society need not be the result of design. Thus the eighteenth century turned ideality on its head long before Marx did so to Hegel. The idea of spontaneous order was the proto-Darwinian shock of the eighteenth century. We will return to it later.

The dawning commercial society was thought by many to offer the prospect of international as well as domestic peace. The same virtue has been claimed for liberal democracy. Hence, from Kant's "Perpetual Peace" to the present, liberalism has been connected with the notion of a pacified world where status is measured in money and not force.[8] This should not be taken to mean a world without international conflict or domestic competition. But the understanding has been that commercial agonistics are nevertheless agonistics without what Judith Shklar called the greatest vice, cruelty, or on the international scale, war.[9]

As Habermas has nicely recounted, the concept of a public sphere, a space for private citizens to voice their opinions, was essential to the development of modern liberal republican society.[10] It grew up in the eighteenth century with the rise of the popular press, and a variety of social organizations that served to make what Guizot called "public opinion" a force in the political life of the state. It was not merely the case that citizens were now "free" to write and speak, but that one of the major institutions of society was an on-going public conversation, not in the hands of state, Church, or aristocracy. For us today, a liberal society without such an institution is difficult to imagine.

Based on an inheritance from Herder, in the nineteenth-century German Romanticism had its special impact on the development of liberalism, especially in the work of Wilhelm Von Humboldt. The republican concept of public self-rule was transformed into a concept of the formation and development, the *Bildung*, both of the individual person – for von Humboldt – and of a people or nation – for nationalists like Fichte. John Stuart Mill became the English spokesman for the individualist version. For Mill self-development, while requiring some form of education, was mostly to be furthered by limiting state and community power, whereas in the German case self-development tended to serve as an argument for enhanced state power. Both contributed to the development of an *expressive* individualism, a concern for the individual's right to express him or herself. By the twentieth century, this tendency merged with the rights-based tradition of liberalism, itself narrowed to a concern for subjective or individual rights, resulting in a liberalism increasingly focused on the individual and the conditions required for each individual to pursue its idiosyncratic and "authentic" destiny.

Progress always had some place in liberalism and proto-liberalism, back to Montesquieu, but it was nineteenth century English Utilitarianism that made progress a central liberal notion. Social happiness was to be maximized, educationally, politically, and technologically. Utilitarianism has always read liberalism through progress. Bentham in particular – and, in a different direction, Comte and Marx – expanded the Enlightenment critique of superstition to the belief in a need for scientific social policy. It was easy enough to connect such policy with the economic progress brought by the market, although a permanent conflict was thereby institutionalized between government social planning and the economic liberty of market forces. This, of course, constitutes the most enduring practical dilemma of the liberal tradition.

Now, certainly it is true that equality and liberty, both intrinsic to liberalism, conflict at some point. The excesses of the French Revolution confirmed the Terror of Rousseau's *le volonté genérale* for many. Yet it is also true in practice that one simply cannot have a liberal society without some measure of equality. Liberals agree that equality before the law is essential. But the liberal flirtation with equality goes deeper. Lawfulness itself implies the avoidance of bias in the workings of power, hence equality of individuals and orders – even if in the eighteenth century individuals continued to be understood as intrinsically connected to Estate, class, social role, and natural law. As time went on, the aim of equality was regarded as intrinsic to the limitation on power in a progressively more social, and not merely political or governmental, sense. If the King's arbitrary power is to be limited, why not also the aristocracy's arbitrary power over the bourgeoisie and the peasantry, and then the bourgeoisie's power over workers?

It was utilitarianism and progressivism that formed the fertile field in which the pressures toward equality produced a major change in liberalism in the late nineteenth and early twentieth centuries: the development of egalitarian liberalism. Now, the recognition of the need for poor relief, especially given the dislocation brought by the transition to a market economy, was not new.[11] But it was in the late nineteenth and early twentieth centuries that a line of liberal "progressive" thought arose in which liberals *qua liberals* argued for the necessity of what we today call the welfare state. Through T. H. Green, Hobhouse, and Dewey the betterment of society, understood in a liberal and egalitarian fashion as the betterment of the lives of all individuals, came to the fore, despite its potential conflicts with the liberal concern to limit state power. State power must be used positively to promote individual liberty against the class now standing in the way of popular liberty, the bourgeoisie. Later, under the pressure of a world economic depression, this nascent egalitarian liberalism found its Ricardo in John Maynard Keynes.

But between the world wars this emphasis on equality within the liberal family of commitments produced a reaction. The critique of state power in general and social planning in particular was proposed most famously by Austrian economic thinkers, especially Ludwig von Mises and Friedrich von Hayek, the latter carrying the now oppositionist faith in markets to London and then Chicago. While economic, the libertarian philosophy seemed necessarily deontological, in contrast to the apparently utilitarian framework of progressivist, egalitarian liberalism. The result was the division of the liberal tradition into those opposing state power, and those who saw state power as the weapon promoting the interests of most individuals against powerful economic interests. After the victory of the liberal democracies in 1945, and the unprecedented prosperity of the next two decades, Keynesian liberalism was supreme, if continually in tension with its loyal commercial opposition. Libertarianism seemed to be forced into early retirement during this period of the supremacy of the liberal-democratic-welfare state.

This state received its distinctive theoretical expression only as it began to show wear and tear. In the 1970s and John Rawls' attempt to find a "natural rights" basis for both individual or civil liberty and the welfare state, deontology returned with a vengeance but now on the egalitarian side. Ronald Dworkin, Bruce Ackerman, Thomas Nagel, and others, completed the egalitarian liberal exodus from utility. By this time liberty was conceived, by egalitarian and libertarian alike, as purely a property of individuals; it was understood negatively in civic affairs, as sheer absence of state interference, but positively, by egalitarians, in the context of economics, that is, as requiring material and social conditions. Neutrality became the prime criterion for promoting liberty and limiting state and political power, completing the removal of religious and cultural perfectionism from both the dominant egalitarian liberal view and its theoretical opponent, libertarianism. It was only in the 1980s that a confluence of events – a popular political turn to the right, a growing awareness of the costs and limits of a liberal welfare state, and an inevitable theoretical reaction against the ahistorical form of "high" liberal theory epitomized by the deontological liberals – led to a two-pronged reaction against proceduralist egalitarianism. On the one hand, libertarianism showed that its seeming retirement was merely a temporary leave of absence, and became a major contender. On the other hand, non-proceduralist, perfectionist, and even communitarian versions of liberalism called for a less individualistic form of theory and society.

Thus we stand, roughly speaking. What I hope this historical sketch makes clear is that the following critique is less against liberalism *per se* than what liberalism has become, the contemporary notions I will criticize being in many cases versions of traditional liberal doctrines which, in earlier and less clear, less abstract, less differentiated form, were also less objectionable. It is characteristically conservative to note that progress is not always, well, *progress*. For, forgetting the manifold environmental and social costs of economic and technological development, progress often means the progressive articulation and purification of a phenomenon that might have been better left vague and entwined with the background that birthed it. It is arguable that the more liberalism has purified itself, the more problematic it has become. There is something to be learned from the fact that during the crucial period of 1770–1820, some of the greatest conservatives – I am thinking of Burke and Hume – and some of the greatest proto-liberals – for example, Smith and Constant – were not very far apart. They were part of the same conversation, not, like today, members of warring camps that refuse to learn from one another. Perhaps the earlier thinkers had less soteriological hopes for their politics; proto-liberals could imagine that turning politics into religion would make its conflicts intractable.

Libertarianism

Libertarianism is the current name for the kind of liberalism that holds liberty to be the ultimate political value, demanding minimal government in order to permit its maximization. It is, one might say, the purest liberalism, the form of liberalism that treats society as a voluntary association for the protection of individual liberty, advocating only equality before the law and a solely negative conception of liberty. Historically it remembers Locke with fondness, and embraces the individualism of Mill's *On Liberty*, but in its clarified contemporary form it is really the invention of Friedrich von Hayek. Libertarian economists and social commentators tend to justify their view on a utilitarian basis, namely, that social wealth, even that of the lowest classes, benefits from *laissez-faire*. In what follows, I will ignore such teleological and practical arguments and consider only the philosophical or more precisely deontological argument for libertarianism – that it alone respects individual rights or liberty. For my purposes, Robert Nozick's still incomparable 1974 formulation of libertarianism will serve as exemplar.[12] *Anarchy, State, and Utopia* does not exhaust philosophical libertarianism, but it does epitomize it (despite the fact that Nozick later admitted that his book was "seriously inadequate").[13]

Popular images to the contrary notwithstanding, libertarianism is not a dismal, but a happy doctrine. It enlivens political discussion and clarifies arguments. It takes a simple, clean principle to clear the intellectual palate, and this has been the most salutary intellectual function of libertarianism in the past two decades. It is not immoral, evil, or elitist. On the contrary, it is highly principled, strictly moral, and egalitarian, its sole aim being to reduce coercion to a minimum. Neither is libertarianism stupid. On the contrary, it is especially appealing to smart people concerned with ideas and principles, for whom intellectual consistency is at a premium. When government coercion is proposed on apparently moral grounds to redress unfair or tragic plights, the correct response of the libertarian is the simple ethical maxim I was taught by the non-libertarian nuns of my childhood: two wrongs cannot make a right. The deplorable condition of the poor may not be corrected by the evil of coercing others. Egalitarians may judge this refusal immoral or amoral, but its inspiration and justification is in fact just *differently* moral.

Libertarianism's only problem is that it is absurd. It is too principled to be consistently or generally applied to a human society. Libertarianism is the only living modern political philosophy of which I am aware that believes all normative claims about political arrangements can be derived from a single principle, which need not be compromised or balanced with any other concerns. That principle is individual liberty, or put more opera-tionally, individual rights, which may not be limited or harmed without the consent of the holder except to protect the analogous liberty or rights of others. If, like Ronald Dworkin, one argues that equality is an equally promi-nent liberal value, libertarians point out that this can only mean that all are to be treated equally by law and government in order to preserve their equal liberty. While libertarians do legitimate government coercion in the name of security, strictly speaking this does not mean that they are willing to balance liberty against security, for their concept of security is merely the protection of the liberty of individuals. So liberty is their unquestionably supreme norm. By itself this supremacy of liberty is merely wrong, not absurd; what is absurd is to believe that a normative account of the *polis* can be nothing more than the application of *any* single principle.

Imagine that the invaders are coming over the last hill, intent on carnage, domination, and the obliteration of our liberties. Suppose the only way the majority of remaining citizens can protect the last piece of our territory is to set up defenses on the hilltop property of some citizen overlooking the approaching army. But that citizen denies access to the property, even though he or she stands to lose it permanently if the invaders win. He or she refuses to listen to "reason." Suppose fellow citizens respond, "We would like, under normal conditions, to defend your property rights. But now the existence of our society is at stake, and we need your property, if only temporarily. If we are all alive tomorrow, then we will discuss compensation. We are a bit pressed for time right now. So stand aside!" Is this unjust? Nobody but the property owner in question and libertarians could think so; that is, no one thinks property rights are so absolute that they are to be defended even at the expense of the existence of society, especially given that, with the collapse of the society will probably come the collapse of any ability to defend those property rights.

To respond that many libertarians make exceptions in emergency situations is both correct and reveals the inadequacy of libertarian principle. *For the whole point of libertarian theory is to deny that there can be exceptions.* If libertarianism says only, "Most of the time, under normal conditions, we ought to try to preserve property rights," then only communists would disagree. Outside of crisis situations, the sole limit on the inviolability of property rights recognized by libertarians is the case of monopoly: libertarians deny my right to enter into an exchange which grants me the power to determine the price of a commodity, since this eliminates the liberty of others not to buy from me.[14] Nozick traces this point back to Locke himself.[15] The libertarian claims that this is not an exception to the principle of liberty, though, but rather a condition for it. Fair enough. However, if the libertarian is going to start noting the various conditions that must hold for free exchange to take place, the list of such conditions threatens to become very substantial and very non-libertarian.

There are at least four exceptions to the inviolability of free exchange and property, representing cases in which such rights violate what I will later describe as the necessary conditions of civil association. They are: social survival; scale; goods that cannot be exchanged; and the communal provision of needs.

First, as noted, social survival has to be a more fundamental value than property rights for any society. It must be because continued existence is the first value of any living thing. Society is a living thing, not in the sense of having the kind of unity ascribable to an organism, but as a collection of living things it is itself a living plurality. It is unreasonable to expect anything different. It is also the case, as noted by everybody, that the securing of property rights in a society itself presupposes continued social existence. So the occasional limitation or violation of property rights is the necessary privilege of any society.

Second, scale matters. My home and General Motors cannot, without an impressive leap of abstraction, be drawn under a single category, "private property." This point was made by Hannah Arendt and Michael Walzer among others.[16] Truly private property – of which my home is an example – is indeed a necessary and virtually inviolable conception for civil society, and it is an ancient one. That each family must have a place, with its cherished and necessary physical objects, is a prerequisite for a reasonable human existence. But the vast holdings of a large corporation are no one's domicile and cannot be regarded as "private" in the same sense; they are quite literally *no one's*, that is, they belong to no one – or to everyone, an anonymous network of stockholders, which is the same thing – and those who operate them need have no special identification or connection with their historical missions, their technology, even their region of the market. They no more belong to anyone than does the Registry of Motor Vehicles. Put more broadly, modern capitalism is not about the privacy of property; it is about the *fungibility* of property, the ability to turn labor and resources into more labor and resources. As Arendt pointed out, property in the ancient sense is quasi-permanent, whereas capital is fluid and dynamic. This is not to say that capital ought to be generally under public control, but that it is entirely reasonable to hold truly private property as relatively inviolable while denying such inviolability to the holdings of large corporations.

A further exception is that, as Walzer argues, no one believes that everything on God's Earth may be regarded as property open to free exchange. It is, he insists, an ancient principle that, "The morality of the bazaar belongs in the bazaar. The market is a zone of the city, not the whole of the city."[17] A good example, which Walzer employs, is the Civil War practice of permitting conscripted individuals in the North to buy their way out of the draft, by paying a fee which was regarded by government as more important to the war effort than their actual service. Why, Walzer asks, do we today intuitively regard this as corrupt and unjust? Because it is the invasion of a sphere of public obligation by wealth with its inherent inequalities. Whether or not I may have a Mercedes can rightly depend on how much money I have; whether or not I am required to fight and possibly die for my country ought not. Some things cannot be bought and sold; what those things are varies from culture to culture.

Lastly, and a claim I cannot justify until later, membership in a political society requires that each citizen have available to him or her the resources necessary to dignity, in so far as this is socially possible. That is, what Walzer calls communal provision or welfare is justified by the concept of *member-ship*, and this means taking some of Peter's property, normally in the form of taxes, to give to Paul. That my neighbor's children may die of a curable illness for want of a few thousand dollars, while I build a swimming pool in my backyard for the same amount, means that my neighbor and I cannot regard each other as *members of the same society*, that I feel no more oblig-ation to or connection with my neighbor than if he lived on the far side of the Earth. Such redistribution, of course, the libertarian rejects.[18] I cannot defend it yet; I only mention it here as the final and most controversial limitation on property rights.

As noted, libertarians do admit that some good is to be redistributed by political society, namely, security, or more precisely, protection of liberties or rights. In Nozick's book this admission takes the form of his insistence that the minimal state must protect the rights of individuals residing within its jurisdiction even if they are unable to pay the taxes that support this effort. Why is this so? Why ought anything, including security, be redis-tributed? Nozick gives an answer famously troubling to his libertarian principles, that a moral "principle of compensation" requires that "inde-pendents" must be compensated for group restriction of their risky activi-ties by extending protective services to them. This, I suggest, *ad hoc* device is nevertheless rightly motivated. Principles aside, libertarian and non-libertarian alike would find it intolerable that a group of citizens and police stand by and watch a non-tax-paying resident of the region being raped and butchered by a paying member. In other words, libertarians, being sensible and decent folk in everyday life, cannot tolerate the literal and rigorous application of their own principles.

The libertarian conception of liberty is necessarily negative. Libertarians are bound to reject the positive modifications of liberty that egalitarian lib-erals sometimes employ. They must stick with the view that I have liberty if I am free from interference. As famously distinguished by Isaiah Berlin and before him Benjamin Constant, any positive conception of liberty (e.g. self-determination) threatens to permit communal coercion of the individual in the name of a "higher" freedom. I will criticize the notion of negative liberty later; for the moment what can be said is that negative liberty is an inadequate account of liberty. Libertarianism is wedded to a strict interpretation of freedom as negative liberty, and as such, fails to achieve a sensible notion of its own ultimate value.

On a different score, libertarianism has no conception of the *public* at all. That is, it recognizes only two spheres of action and concern that are relevant to political order: the private, meaning individual, sphere – which in effect includes all of society, conceived as a voluntary association of individuals – and the governmental organization of individuals that has a monopoly on the legitimate use of coercion. Of course this does not mean that libertarians in practice fail to recognize a public realm; it means that they fail to recognize a publicity that is irreducible to privacy. The public in libertarianism is merely a species of private contract, the product of voluntary exchanges, however complex. Related to this, there is no room for *politics* in libertarianism. (Oddly enough, it shares this lack with its ideological opposite, Marxism.) Libertarianism is the attempt to reconceive all human relations on the model of the contract. This is not only undesirable, it is so inconceivable, ahistorical, and abstract as to make one admire its sheer speculative chutzpah. *Anarchy, State, and Utopia* ought to be read, not with egalitarian indignation, but with the same stupefied awe as we may read the metaphysics of Spinoza.

Now, does the rejection of libertarianism, the purest form of proceduralist liberalism, mean that there are no categorical constraints on the organic interest of the society in preserving itself against the non-conforming individual or the burgeoning marketplace? No it does not. But the constraint "Nothing may be done to harm me or any of my rights without my consent under even the worst of circumstances" is too much of a constraint. Nor does the inadequacy of libertarianism mean by itself that socialism, or the welfare state, or any other form of limitation on individual liberty or the free market is thereby justified. The libertarian purification of liberalism has its place in the seminar room, where it serves intellectual clarification, and in politics, where it serves to push against egalitarian institutions. For the present study it serves the further purpose of illustrating what a purified liberalism would mean. But beyond these purposes, it has no application. The phrase "libertarian society" is an oxymoron.

Individuals, Contracts, and Rights

The dominant modern liberal conception of liberty exists not in a vacuum, but as part of a network or family of related notions. Of these, none is more important as background than *individualism*. This is no surprise. The liberalism that has developed since the second half of the nineteenth century, and become dominant since World War II, regards the individual's liberty, life, uniqueness, self-expressiveness, and will, all as among the highest, if not the highest, values in political and ethical life. By no means is liberal society consistent in its application of this rhetoric. But contemporary America is to a large extent, rhetorically and socially, the triumph of this individualism. It would be difficult to find a viable or stable society in human history which more completely grants individuals a role in determining the course of their lives, which denies the hold of family, community, tradition, and state power on individuals, and which celebrates individualism more than does contemporary America.[19]

Minimally, individualism demands that whatever is of ultimate value be a human individual or a trait of an individual, rather than an irreducible trait of a collective. Since human individuals are the kind of things that themselves *value things*, this means that human individuals are to be treated as legitimate judges of what is best for themselves. Now, certainly liberals believe in and value society. They can, if they wish, valorize community; egalitarian liberals do so in the form of economic solidarity. But as liberals they must nevertheless conceive society or community as an aggregate of individuals, whose solidarity is the product of individual choice.

This valorization of individuality is indeed a distinguishing feature of modern Western culture and society. This does not mean that individuality is a modern Western invention. Burkhardt himself argued in his classic analysis of the Italian renaissance that individualism had been seen before in ancient Greece and medieval Islam.[20] What characterized modern Western individualism was the prevalence of such individuals, who did not view themselves or the world as given by tradition, whose life was endowed with meaning by chosen projects rather than by analogy with traditional models. Burkhardt claimed that among the prominent Italians of the fourteenth century "not one of them was afraid of singularity, of being and seeming unlike his neighbors."[21] Along with this went a value on both subjectivity or interiority and objectivism or the cold-eyed evaluation of reality – the two are related – and as well cosmopolitanism. The ideal became *l'uomo universale*, who was simultaneously *l'uomo singolare* or *l'uomo unico*: only the unique and singular individual can rise to the state of being universal. Such a person won the ultimate worldly prize, glory, hence a secular immortality. J. G. A. Pocock argues that this view formed a key philosophical justification of republicanism, which spread from Renaissance Italy, in a modified form, to England.[22] Modern republicanism ascribed to the temporal and local activities of the self a universal significance. The measure of a person was not the embodiment of universal and timeless models *per se*, but how the individual met the times, responded to the needs of the day.

But while it is one thing to honor individuality, it is quite another to make individualism the highest good. The latter view has the effect of, as many critics of liberalism have noted, normatively de-socializing the individual, of making the individual an end-in-itself. Help in this critique comes from an unexpected quarter. John Dewey, a liberal, if a non-proceduralist one, made the crucial distinction between what he regarded as a dangerous and a positive individualism. For Dewey an individualism which makes the individual logically, temporally, or morally prior to society is absurd. "Individuals who are not bound together in associations, whether domestic, economic, religious, political, artistic, or educational," he wrote, "are monstrosities."[23] Whereas an "assured and integrated individuality is the product of definite social relationships and publicly acknowledged functions."[24] Human individuals there are, but they are socially constituted, their own aims and values being almost always social. The idea of a pre- or non-social moral value is impossible. Individuality is not an escape from or independence of society; it is distinctiveness of sensitivity, selection, and contribution to society. Individuality is a distinctive way of being social.

So, individualism, as opposed to individuality, is objectionable at two levels. First, it makes no sense as an ultimate norm, a principle to believe in and guide conduct, either personal or social. No society is free to hold the individual, and not itself, most dear; if it claims to be doing so, it is lying. Society intrinsically requires authority, conformity, and compulsion, each in different measures and in different circumstances. Individuality cannot be a moral norm, just as it makes no sense to assert that *particularity qua particularity* is an ideal or even a value, let alone a moral one. In a moral sense individualism is empty, since it asserts the ultimate value of a *source* of valuing, without saying *what* ought to be valued. Asked for moral advice, the consistent believer in individualism can only say: "Choose. That's my advice." This cannot be our ultimate moral principle, that for the sake of which we live together in society.

Second, individuality cannot be normatively prior to other social values, since it is dependent on them. It is, as we shall see, the strongest suit of conservatives and communitarians to insist that individuality is socially constructed and maintained. If that is so, then even those who value it highly must equally value the maintenance of the social networks that construct it, even if particular individualities threaten those networks. In other words, concern for individuality must recognize the need to temper individuality where it threatens the conditions of its existence. But individual*ism*, which makes individuality the highest value, insists on its trump and refuses the restriction of individuality except for violations of the harm principle (which it understands merely as violations of another individuality).

Liberal individualism has a characteristic account of legitimate human relations, that they must rest on the free choice of individuals, hence on *contract*. Contractualism is individualism's dominant social theory. This does not mean that liberals model *all* personal and intimate relations on contractual relations (although some seem to). It means that one must start somewhere, one must accept a vague conception of human relations at the outset of one's political theory, and for this purpose the contract between independent adults has been privileged, with other modes of relation seen as modifications or special cases. It is so not only for libertarians; egalitarian liberals too regard the contract as a model of freedom. And this is only consistent, for the contract model is simply the social face of liberal individualism, the model of the kind of relation free individuals are supposed to have.

Now it is true that a contract between independent persons is *a* model – not *the* model – of free human interaction. Certainly a society without a large place for such contracts cannot be a free society in any meaningful sense. But most of our most important relationships are most of the time not of that sort, and some are never of that sort, e.g. parent–child, sibling–sibling, friendship, religious fellowship, patriotic attachment to the *civitas*. Others may at one time be contractual, then quickly become some other sort of relationship, for example, a long-term business partnership. Yet others have a contractual aspect which yet cannot account for the ongoing nature of the relationship, for example, marriage. We will return to contract in discussing human dependency. For the moment we can say that what is objectionable here is not contracts but the overweening importance of the contract model in the liberal tradition, its employment as the exemplar of normative human relations.

As individualism receives its social expression in contracts, it receives its political norm in *rights*. "Natural rights" is the name for the principled, pre-conventional, deontological basis of political individualism in the modern West. It is the claim that certain entitlements on the part of individuals, at the very least the entitlement to be free from certain kinds of interference or harm, are normatively pre-civil, that is, morally binding independent of and logically prior to social convention. In contemporary liberal theory, rights have lost their "naturalness" in the seventeenth-century sense, but it remains that case the liberals refuse to accept abridgments of rights, except by other rights. Liberals build rights into the moral self. Thus the transformation of a political issue into a debate over rights makes the issue particularly intimate for us, at least in a civic and political sense. To violate a right is then to violate a *person*, to deny someone their identity. This makes issues particularly intractable: for who would be willing to give up their self?

What is most troubling about such rights is not their assertion or their connotations but their use as ultimate deontic trumps, making even minor violations of rights illegitimate no matter what the context, as when one hears civil libertarians say that *any* restriction on the *most* despised form of speech threatens *all* freedom of speech. The best way to advance any political program is then to connect it with claimed rights. Sometimes our public debates seem to imply that, were something not to concern putative rights and their alleged violation, it would fall outside legitimate political and governmental concern altogether. As a result, many liberals take an account of *rights* to be an adequate account of *right*, at least within the political sphere. This fundamentally personal and yet juridical response to politics, whereby the goal of any debate is to enact a law that stipulates some entitlement whose violation is a violation of some person's moral core, makes political discussion less, not more, productive.

On the grounds of holism, both the holistic understanding of the dependency of individual on society and the holistic rejection of abstract principles, the liberal interpretation of natural rights as individual entitlements that trump all other considerations must be rejected. This rejection need not extend to the very notion of rights *per se*, that is, as entitlements that are presupposed to be binding, nor even to the adjectival prefix "natural" *if* that means that the tradition in question regards such rights as having a supra-conventional validity. For one can accept these points without claiming individual rights as deontic trumps which may never be abridged and which form the ultimate justification for political life. However one respects individual rights, they are merely values which must be balanced with other values, not adequate norms for social life. What is objectionable is not rights, but the philosophy of rights that makes statements of such rights ultimate and adequate as the basis for politics. Even with the political sphere, the philosophy of rights does not exhaust the philosophy of right.

Liberty and Harm

As mentioned, among liberals, libertarians hew most closely to a "negative" conception of liberty. We can trace that conception back to Benjamin Constant. Constant distinguished the liberty of the ancient republics from the liberty of modern republics: the former was public and political, the latter is private and often commercial.[25] Constant made this distinction to support the crucial point that *anachronism can be a crime*. The Jacobins of the French

Revolution had attempted to impose an ancient concept of liberty on a modern commercial society, where it has no place, resulting in bloody tyranny. The modern version of liberty has its limitations, but it is nevertheless appropriate to its age. We can be free, but only as moderns, not ancients. Later in the nineteenth century, John Stuart Mill gave canonical form to the negative notion of liberty by formulating the "harm principle" as the legitimate limit to liberty in a free society.

In his famous essay, "Two Concepts of Liberty," Isaiah Berlin took up this distinction to argue that negative liberty, or "freedom from," simple non-interference, is the true source of modern liberalism, whereas positive freedom, "freedom to" or self-determination, characteristic of democratic majoritarianism, is the dangerous source of totalitarianism.[26] Self-determination can justify collective coercion of the individual in the name of what society recognizes as the "true" or "higher" self, against the individual's false, lower, socially unrecognized desires. If, as in Rousseau, my truest self is in fact identified with the general will or best interest of my community, then Rousseau's chilling admonition that recalcitrants be "forced to be free" makes perfect sense. It is in order to avoid this proto-totalitarian conclusion, suggestive of the Auschwitz slogan *Arbeit Macht Frei* ("Work makes [one] free"), that Berlin famously affirmed that only negative liberty is compatible with liberalism.

There are a variety of ways to object to negative liberty. Charles Taylor has rightly pointed out the incapacity of a purely negative conception of liberty to account for what he calls "strong evaluation," the human agent's interpretive evaluation of its own desires as to their coherence with the self.[27] Gerald Dworkin shows that Mill's own notion of liberty is by no means entirely negative. He argues that there can be, on Mill's account, freedom-enhancing coercion, particularly where the paternalistic authority and the individual coerced affirm the same ends but the later has demonstrably false notions as to how to achieve those ends.[28] But my current point is yet simpler: on logical grounds the concept of negative liberty is not and could not ever be an adequate description of liberty.

To be sure, we want a notion of liberty which at the very least captures that quality we attribute to someone whose shackles have just been removed; and in the same spirit we want to avoid the murkiness of the case in which a person, failing to pursue self-interest while facing no obstacles we can see, nevertheless claims to be an unfree victim due compensation, rather than a weakling or a malingerer. And of course, as Constant and Berlin sought, we want to avoid totalitarian coercion operating under the cover of enhancing citizens' "higher" or "moral" liberty." Negative and positive liberty are inspired by the time-honored models of privacy and political participation. In "private" matters, especially within the household I experience freedom *from* interference or scrutiny, while in the public debate among fellow citizens over what we ought to do, I exercise freedom *to* participate and contribute.

Now, Berlin was aware that this dualism is a highly selective opposition of abstractions; there are many other circumstances and venues for liberty that do not conform to these two models. Their distinction, as abstractions, is justified as long as this is kept in mind. What is not justified is the use of such abstractions *as exclusive norms*, e.g. in the claim that the *only* legiti- mate kind of liberty is positive, or, in Berlin's case, negative. This makes little sense. Even in Berlin's account the horrific consequences of positive liberty depend on a subsequent identification of the true self with the general will, an identification external to the notion of "freedom to," and one which we who wish not to share Rousseauian company need not make.

Simply, pure absence of obstacle is not what anyone means by freedom. On logical or metaphysical grounds alone *simple privation cannot be our whole account of what any norm is.* A purely negative concept of liberty makes liberty a property of an agent, which property is nothing other than the absence of something external to the agent, like the predicates "alone" or "bald." Is "free" really comparable to these? Anthropologically, no one would regard an individual as free if that individual, while facing no exter- nal obstacles to liberty, yet lacked all power or capacity to do. Certainly external obstacles prevent freedom, but so does absence of power, here meant in the most basic sense. A creature without energy, or will, or life, or existence cannot be free. Some element or dimension of potency, power, pos- itive capacity, and hence self-determination is irremovable from our notion of liberty. The problem will be, not ridding our political structure of one or the other concept of liberty, but how to balance these two conceptions, neg- ative and positive, each of which is necessary to an adequate account.

The negative conception of liberty is usually accompanied by a notion of the subject of liberty, that aspect of the person to which "free" is applied. Voluntarism is the view according to which the subject of freedom is indi- vidual will, understood operationally as the occasional choices of the indi- vidual. Thus it is *choices* that are to be protected from coercion, hence as such all choices of all individuals are to be protected equally (although in applying liberal principle certainly the polity and the courts have distin- guished important from trivial choices).

I will suggest that this voluntarism is a recent misinterpretation of what the liberal republican tradition values about freedom. That is, liberal advo- cates have misunderstood, or at least misstated, their own advocacy. While a fuller discussion of liberty must wait until chapter 5, what can be said now is that liberal society need not sanctify occasional choice; what it must value is the uniqueness of individual judgment as it contributes to what it can reasonably regard as a valued existence. That is, liberalism places an ultimate value on liberty understood as the individual's self-determination of a meaningful or valuable life. It can then regard some kinds of choices, which cannot reasonably be understood as such, as not immune to prohibition or discouragement.[29]

Liberalism never suggested, of course, that liberty was to be utterly unlimited. In order to maximize liberty it proposed a minimal limit on freedom, already mentioned, namely the famous "harm" principle. As formulated by Mill, the harm principle is an attempt to say when government or society can intervene in the voluntarist liberty of an individual, namely, only for the purpose of society's own "self-protection."[30] Only threats to harm others legitimate interference. Hence "self-regarding conduct," which affects no one else, can never be interfered with legitimately. Paternalism, or limiting my freedom for my own sake, is never permissible, as least with competent adults. This principle or some reformulation of it is largely shared by egalitarian and libertarian liberals.

What is wrong with the harm principle? Putting aside Gerald Dworkin's aforementioned clarification, nothing; it is, as Charles Peirce said of claims like "nature is orderly," virtually an unavoidable criterion, in the present case valid for anyone who values liberty as a natural limit to public interference in the private sphere. It is enough for current purposes to say that without something like it there can be no liberty. Indeed, it can be argued that this principle is not at all modern, at least in some spheres of life, i.e. in daily domestic and economic life, as opposed to matters of interest to religion and state. It is difficult to find large human societies that have not defined *some* private realm to be at least partly immune to interference, the absence of unwanted effects on others outside the household being one of the marks of privacy (however widely "effects" are then understood). This is to say that most societies have accepted some distinction between the private and public realms.

But as Peirce further pointed out regarding the belief in nature's orderliness, the harm principle is unquestionably valid only as long as it is left entirely *vague*. Any specification of it, particularly of what is to count as "other-regarding" and as harmful, generates trouble. All but the most trivial examples or applications are actually or potentially controversial. What our typical applications of the principle reveal is that, whenever we regard the harm principle as workable, we trade on a background moral account of rights and duties. Without such a background, the principal is inapplicable. We do a disservice to the harm principle if we expect from it an adequate account of human liberty. It can give no such thing. It is merely a conceptual line dividing the concepts of public and private. Its normative use presupposes a common cultural understanding of what constitutes harm, justice, and legitimate authority.

Mill was not unaware of this problem. He declares that I may not be permitted to "harm" others, where harm means "definite injury to definite individuals," and indeed, means the violation of a social duty (perfect or imperfect), and not merely "constructive" injury. But what Mill fails to recognize is that these criteria cannot make any sense without an implicit moral and anthropological theory that allows him to distinguish among all possible forms of harm those that are to be sanctioned. After all, I am harmed if someone defeats me on the basketball court, if my intended falls in love with another, if society does not give me the fame and riches I so desperately want, etc. – indeed, the latter two forms may cause me far greater injury than any theft of property. But no one thinks these can or should be sanctioned. Mill was forced to distinguish, among all the harms I suffer from others' actions, those I have *a right to expect not to suffer*.[31]

Mill makes a perfectly reasonable response to expansive claims of subtle forms of other-regarding harm when he says that if given too much sway they will eliminate liberty altogether. If, to use his example, we accept the argument that my refusal to obey religious dietary laws harms others, and not merely myself, then such an argument can be made for virtually anything I do, and liberty vanishes. We may say that if two males having sex in a private room unobserved by others can be claimed to harm society, then the notion of private freedom effectively vanishes, the Supreme Court in Bowers v. Hardwick to the contrary notwithstanding.[32] But we need not change the example much to generate problems that are harder to ignore. So we may say that individual liberty would indeed disappear if the community sought to prevent me from masturbating in my home with the shades drawn. But as soon as there are other people in the home, like my children, masturbating at the dinner table takes on a different moral aura, even for liberals.[33] The existence of dependants and the sheer presence of others qualify my liberty.

My point is that there is no way to forge a rule of public liberty that is not *cultural*, that does not presuppose both a common morality, itself culturally inherited, and for every test case, a common set of cultural interpretations of the situation, social roles, and practices involved. Mill's harm principle, applied to a traditional society, will not generate chaos and *anomie*; it will generate nothing. It will simply be interpreted in a way that conforms to that culture. Mill would deny that many traditional regulations are plausible interpretations of harm, but he must in the end rest his denial on modern secular, scientific, cultural principles themselves *extrinsic* to the harm principle. As Mill says elsewhere, there is no principle of morality (or politics) which will lead to salutary results if combined with idiocy. Well, absence of cultural literacy, of awareness of local practices and norms, *is* idiocy.

This brings into play an historical problem. Modern societies are characterized by increasing social, economic, and cultural interdependence. There are fewer and fewer areas of life for which no plausible argument can be made that my liberty threatens others, for the simple reason that increasing interdependence is a mark of modernity. In a world in which bad Malaysian real estate loans and the savings rates of Japanese workers affect a Michigan laborer, where second-hand smoke is claimed to be a harm to others, where my personal habits impact insurance payments by my employer and other consumers of my brand of insurance, in which any public behavior is observable by crowded fellow urbanites and, if transmitted into private homes via television, the entire polity, the sphere of uncontroversially self-regarding conduct progressively shrinks.

The best case for the harm principle can be stated simply. Modern government is at least potentially the most coercive force on Earth. The worst cases of government coercion are indeed among the most abhorrent phenomena imaginable, from the various totalitarian slaughters (e.g. Central Europe, the Soviet Union, Uganda, Cambodia, China, the Balkans, etc.) to the treatment of dissidents by Fascist, Communist and authoritarian regimes. Writing in the vein of what might be called a Hobbesian liberalism, Judith Shklar argued, and Richard Rorty echoed, that cruelty is the *summum malum* which liberalism serves to avoid.[34] Cruelty, one might say, is the worst case of, and is made possible by, coercion.

But while cruelty may be *summum malum*, is coercion? This would be difficult to argue. Genocide, torture, political imprisonment and unjust execution, may well be the worst things in the world. But to lasso all forms of public control with these evils is an impressive rope trick. Fines for publishing pornography are not the Gulag. Here the proceduralist civil libertarian resorts to the well-worn "slippery slope," a mantra of liberal public debate, insisting that *any* limitation whatsoever of individual liberty threatens *all* individual liberty. "The purpose of the First Amendment," we hear repeatedly, "is to protect hated speech. Speech that is not hated needs no protection." That is, the principal of freedom of speech is interpreted to mean that the worst possible offense must be given the greatest possible protection. This is an abstraction of the highest order: no context, no consideration of degree, no weighing of positive and negative considerations, only a rule so absolute that it renders inconsiderable all other rules. The merest limit on the worst kind of speech allegedly means freedom of speech *is not*. It is this kind of commitment that gives philosophical foundationalism in general, and doctrinaire liberalism in particular, a bad name. It is precisely the same spirit that animates the claim that no intrusion into property rights can ever be tolerated, that no offense to the Lord can ever be tolerated, etc.

"But what about the slippery slope," we hear again. Well, life is a slippery slope; we have no choice but to try to stand where we think best, despite the poor footing. Even though we all know where the slope ultimately leads.

Spontaneous Order

As we saw, the notion that large parts of social order, even intricate and beneficent or virtuous order, can result from an aggregation of uncoordinated actions comes from the eighteenth century.[35] The stronger claim, which Mandeville and the Scots – most importantly Hume and Smith – also made, was that such order is the *norm* in human society, and consequently the attempt to design usually produces undesirable or evil effects. In the twentieth century libertarians have made this notion a focal study; they can be credited with isolating and naming, if not inventing, the concept. While usually attributed to Friedrich von Hayek and his 1960 book *The Constitution of Liberty*, the term "spontaneous order" was the simultaneous product of Hayek and Michael Polanyi in the 1940s.[36] Both of their accounts, Polanyi's being the lesser known, are illuminating.

For Polanyi spontaneous order is emergent, unplanned order, opposed to "corporate order," the order of central planning. While his concern was with academic and economic liberty, Polanyi drew the concept from physical phenomena, e.g. the equilibrium achieved by the water in a tipping jug. Spontaneous order is the order attained by elements of a system where outside forces have only a negligible effect on the events in question, leaving the determination of the achieved state to the mutual constraints of the elements, given only indiscriminately acting background conditions (e.g. gravity). His point is that a singular agency *could not* determine such a result, or only with far greater use of energy (i.e. if a person were charged to arrange the water molecules in a jug to be level). There is nothing inherently superior about spontaneous order; planned and unplanned order have their "respective proper occasions." Polanyi takes to task even "free-traders" for considering central planning immoral but plausible, including Hayek. Economic planning for a society is simply "impossible in the same sense in which it is impossible for a cat to swim the Atlantic."[37] His argument hangs on the claim that the functioning socialist governments of the world in his day were not in fact centrally-planned; their "plans" were mere aggregates of the spontaneous decisions of agencies within the system in response to their particular environments. The only true example of central planning, he argues, was in the Soviet Union in 1919–21, and it starved five million people. Later, in what the Soviets called their central "plans," the reasons for each point of the plan were in fact local, spontaneous reasons, which did not appear in the state "plan." This was, Polanyi analogizes, like someone observing a hundred chess games who picks one of the players in each game as a member of his or her "team," asks each what the next planned move is, and announces, "Our team plans to move 45 pawns, 20 bishops, etc."

Hayek points out several distinguishing characteristics of spontaneous orders. He notes, like Polanyi, that while spontaneous orders are not inherently complex, "unlike deliberate human arrangements, they may achieve any degree of complexity," thus a level of complexity that no human mind could manage. Further, they are purposeless, that is, the system does not exert a pressure on elements to contribute to an end. His analysis is sympathetic to the traditionalist conservative rejection of principle; Hayek notes his complicity with Oakeshott.[38] His rejection of planning and principle, and his insistence on "particular" or "circumstantial" knowledge is moving in the same direction as Oakeshott's conception of practical knowledge (as we will see later). In his attack on theoretical reason Hayek even quotes Whitehead's remark that "thinking about what we are doing" is usually a hindrance to civilization.[39] None of this means, for Hayek, that the elements of a spontaneous order are anarchic, that they are not rule-governed. Rather they must be governed by certain kinds of rules, purposeless rules that apply indiscriminately to all elements.

This said, it is very difficult to nail down the precise meaning of spontaneous order in its socio-political application. For present purposes, all we need do is clarify the concept with an eye toward the phenomena we are most concerned with. Leaving aside socially uncontrollable, i.e. "natural" constraints, we can distinguish five categories of social constraints on the individual. They are constraints on my action imposed by: (1) enforceable commands, e.g. by government or someone with physical power over me; (2) collective agreement in which I participate, although the outcome of which I may disagree with; (3) the threat of punitive costs intentionally imposed by social equals; (4) the constitution of my self by socio-cultural inheritance; and, (5) the free, self-interested actions of "equals," that is, of other actors without special, socially sanctioned power over me. Those who endorse spontaneous order most completely in the twentieth century, e.g. libertarians, regard the first of these as the great and obvious threat to freedom, and usually amalgamate the second, political agreement, to it, since when I disagree with a democratic majority, governmental force is imposed on me.[40] The most free, the most minimal form of constraint (either minimal in sheer quantitative terms, or in permitting the most important forms of freedom) for libertarians would then be a society in which only the fifth constraint, the unintended consequences of the action of free equals, was operative. What requires clarification is the place of constraints three and four.

Let us start with the "ideal" condition, number five. We must admit that the free acts of others constrain me in all sorts of situations: e.g. if someone buys the house I want, I am not free to obtain it. Libertarians accept that this is the inevitable condition of free equals living together and hence no reduction of liberty. But note two important qualifications. Obviously, the others must be "equals" in at least the minimal sense that the "sponta-neous" decision of the King to behead me can't count as furthering spon-taneous order. Although an individual, the King's authority must be excluded. This is intuitive enough. It raises thorny problems, though, about just which self-interested actions by social actors fall outside the realm of spontaneous order by seeking some "supra-social" form of power over the outcome of interaction. That is, free people acting under only constraint five might freely try to employ constraints one or two as a move *within* their con-straint-five game. So, if a corporation files a lawsuit to inhibit a competitor, we have to decide if that lawsuit represents a "non-spontaneous" attempt to enlist the power of government or law to undermine the social game, or rather a clever "spontaneous" strategy within that game. There has thus to be a presumption of certain rules of the social game, such that when actors seek to go around those rules, even out of spontaneous self-interest, that is *not* a case of free or spontaneous order.

Second, the other actors in a maximally free, constraint-five game must be purely self-interested, so that blocking me from my goals is either an unintended consequence or a secondary effect of pursuing their goals. They cannot be motivated by what Rawls, in describing his "original position," called "envy," the desire of an agent to harm me regardless of whether the agent is benefited or not.[41] A society of mutual adjustment would not be very free if large numbers of its members were motivated primarily to exclude me regardless of their self-interest. That would be a case of the free actors of constraint five-society freely employing constraint three. This is not unusual in reality; citizens boycotting a place of business or shunning a caustic neighbor are examples. Mill himself recognized that a society in which government and law are tolerant but fellow citizens are not is *not* a free society. The difference between such punishment and the first form, that is, direct coercion by threat of violence, is really a matter of degree. What is called "coercion" by libertarians is, after all, only the threat of punishment of a particularly severe form (e.g. jail) by an inescapable agent (e.g. the state). Milder punishments by social equals can be just as effective. Consequently, for an order to be spontaneous in the "pure" sense of only employing constraint five, I must be blocked from my aims only *de facto*, by the choices of others which are not primarily aimed at me. But coercively preventing such group punishment is *itself* arguably a threat to freedom! For in an order operating only with constraint five, social members must presumably be "free" to punish me, otherwise *they* have inadequate freedom. In other words, a "maximally" free, constraint-five system must both *exclude and include* constraint three. And in fact, any society in which even some members share conceptions of the good, hence operate collectively to punish recalcitrants, must muck up the libertarian system.

The flip side of this problem is given by constraint four, the preemptive constitution of the self by tradition, which builds constraints *into the actor*. Deviance is not merely deterred by the prospect of punishment; the ubiquity of social norms and the dearth of opportunity or variety insures that there will be very few deviants. This holds whether the rules that are inculcated attach to persons by virtue of birth ("status") or by virtue of a chosen occupation ("contract").[42] Highly traditional societies are characterized by remarkable homogeneity, yet their order is to a great degree "spontaneous" in the sense of avoiding constraints one and two, but clearly not in the sense intended by Polanyi and Hayek. This is true, however, of all societies in so far as they have traditions, that is, inherited arrangements, for if there are such arrangements, selves will be constructed to conform to them.

The point is, while the ideal sought by the advocates of spontaneous order is tolerably clear in theory, in practice it would have to exclude forms of social constraint that have little to do with government or law. What this means to the conservative is that spontaneous order, if it is to be embraced, must be understood as a matter of degree (just as, we will see, freedom itself must be), operating within forms of non-governmental constraint. The libertarian, the believer in a "market society," the absolute free marketeer, is engaged in a leap of abstraction that ignores the complexity of the constraints on human action. If spontaneous order meant only the absence of a single ruling authority or center that plans a system's outcomes, then modern civil society is unambiguously and in principle spontaneously ordered. But if it means something closer to our idealized notion of a free market, then while it is true to say that modern civil society *has* some such markets, it is entirely wrong to say that society itself is or could be a market or "spontaneous" order. As we will see later, the relation of civil society to spontaneous order is a complex one.

Notes

1 The terminology is inspired by Kant, but was employed first by W. D. Ross. See Ross's 1930 book, *The Right and the Good* (Oxford: Clarendon Press, 1967).

2 Michael Sandel uses "voluntarist" in this sense, to critical purpose, in his *Democracy's Discontent: America in Search of a Public Philosophy* (Cambridge, MA: Harvard University Press, 1996).

3 In theory, the exception to a proceduralist endorsement of a negative view of liberty is whatever is conceptually required for egalitarian liberals to justify government action to restrict the economic liberties of some in order to provide welfare for others. Egalitarians can try to surmount this problem by other means and so remain faithful to negative liberty. We will explore Berlin's distinction of negative and positive liberty presently.

4 See José Guilhermo Merquior's *Liberalism Old and New* (Boston: Twayne, 1991).

5 Daniel Defoe, *Giveing Almss No Charity and Employing the Poor a Grievance to the Nation* (reprint; New York: Johnson Reprint, 1970); Bernard Mandeville, *The Fable of the Bees, or Private Vices, Publick Benefits* (Indianapolis: Liberty Fund, 1988); Adam Smith, *An Inquiry into the Nature and Causes of the Wealth of Nations*, two volumes, Glasgow edition (Indianapolis: Liberty Fund, 1981).

6 Karl Polanyi, *The Great Transformation: The Political and Economic Origins of Our Time* (Boston: Beacon, 1957), p. 113.

7 David Ricardo, *The Principles of Political Economy and Taxation* (New York: Dutton, 1973). Originally published in 1817.

8 Immanuel Kant, "To Perpetual Peace: A Philosophical Sketch," (1795) in *Perpetual Peace and Other Essays*, trans. Ted Humphrey (Indianapolis: Hackett, 1983).

9 See Judith Shklar, *Ordinary Vices* (Cambridge, MA: Harvard University Press, 1984).

10 Jürgen Habermas, *The Structural Transformation of the Public Sphere: An Inquiry into a Category of Bourgeois Society*, trans. Thomas Burger, with Frederick Lawrence (Cambridge, MA: MIT, 1989).

11 Karl Polanyi, *The Great Transformation*.

12 This is a bit unfair, for today there are in fact a family of related views, or libertarian fellow-travelers, who do not fit all of this characterization, e.g. the individualist consent theory of John Simmons, the positive or "project-pursuing" view of Loren Lomasky, the "Aristotelian" libertarianism of Douglas Den Uyl and Douglas Rasmussen, not to mention the objectivism of Ayn Rand. See A. John Simmons, *Moral Principles and Political Obligations* (Princeton:

Princeton University Press, 1979); Loren Lomasky, *Persons, Rights, and the Moral Community* (Oxford: Oxford University Press, 1987); Douglas Rasmussen and Douglas Den Uyl, *Liberty and Nature: An Aristotelian Defense of Liberal Order* (LaSalle: Open Court, 1991); Ayn Rand, *The Virtue of Selfishness: A New Concept of Egoism* (New York: Penguin, 1961). There are a variety of ways of making the libertarian argument; see for example, Tibor Machan, *Individuals and their Rights* (LaSalle: Open Court, 1989) and Eric Mack, "Agent-Relativity of Value, Deontic Restraints, and Self-Ownership," in R. G. Frey and Christopher Morris, eds., *Value Welfare, and Morality* (Cambridge: Cambridge University Press, 1993).

13   Robert Nozick, *Anarchy, State, and Utopia* (New York: Basic Books, 1974). In his *The Examined Life* (New York: Touchstone, 1989), pp. 286–7, Nozick accepts that government performs a legitimate "expressive function," that politics plays an important "symbolic" function in encouraging, expressing, and discouraging ways of life. He leaves it unexplained how much of his earlier view would be invalidated by this new recognition. But we may say that it would have to be an awful lot.

14   The exception is the case of "technical monopolies," monopolies that inevitably arise in a market due to its special character, like utilities. Milton Friedman argued that such are to be operated by democratic government rather than private capital.

15   He calls it the "Lockean proviso." See Nozick, *Anarchy, State, and Utopia*, pp. 174–82.

16   See Hannah Arendt, *The Human Condition* (Chicago: University of Chicago Press, 1958), pp. 58–73, and Michael Walzer, *Spheres of Justice: A Defense of Pluralism and Equality*, pp. 122 and 303.

17   Walzer, *Spheres of Justice: A Defense of Pluralism and Equality*, p. 109.

18   There are exceptions to the libertarian rejection of redistribution; Milton Friedman himself accepted the "negative income tax" scheme in Chapter Twelve of *Capitalism and Freedom* (Chicago: University of Chicago, 1962).

19   Even if some complain that ours is a sham individuality, or one more than balanced by increasing conformity, bureaucratization, etc.

20   Jacob Burkhardt, *The Civilization of the Renaissance in Italy*, trans. S. G. C. Middlemore (New York: Harper, 1958), esp. volume I, part II. Reference is on p. 143.

21   Ibid., p. 144.

22   See J. G. A. Pocock, *The Machiavellian Moment: Florentine Political Thought and the Atlantic Republican Tradition* (Princeton: Princeton University Press, 1975).

23   John Dewey, *Individualism Old and New* (London: Allen and Unwin, 1931), p. 82

24   Ibid., p. 53

25   Benjamin Constant, "The Liberties of the Ancients Compared with that of the Moderns," in *Political Writings* (Cambridge: Cambridge University Press, 1988).

26 Isaiah Berlin, "Two Concepts of Liberty," in *Four Essays on Liberty* (Oxford: Oxford University, 1969).

27 Charles Taylor, "What's Wrong with Negative Liberty," *Philosophy and the Human Sciences* (Cambridge: Cambridge University, 1985), pp. 211–29.

28 Gerald Dworkin, "Paternalism," in *Morality and Law*, ed. Richard Wasserstrom (Belmont, CA: Wadsworth, 1971).

29 Of course, what an individual can "reasonably" regard as a meaningful existence, if it is to be socially judged, makes society the arbiter of meaningfulness, hence potentially coercive. I will discuss this further in chapter 5.

30 John Stuart Mill, *On Liberty* (New York: Penguin, 1974), section one.

31 The only version of the harm principle that might seem to escape this needed background is the admonition against paternalism, the reason being that it concerns the motivation of the interference. In practice, however, almost any interference can be couched in terms that avoid explicit paternalism.

32 In which the Court upheld the right of the state of Georgia to prohibit homosexual acts in private.

33 Indeed, his concern for children led Mill in his final chapter to permit what is, even by today's standards, very intrusive state action: "The laws which . . . forbid marriage unless the parties can show that they have the means of supporting a family do not exceed the legitimate powers of the State . . ."

34 See Shklar, *Ordinary Vices*, and Richard Rorty, *Contingency, Irony, and Solidarity* (Cambridge: Cambridge University Press, 1989).

35 See Ronald Hamowy's, *The Scottish Enlightenment and the Theory of Spontaneous Order* (Carbondale: Southern Illinois University, 1987). See also F. A. Hayek, "The Results of Human Action but not of Human Design," in his *Studies in Philosophy, Politics, and Economics* (Chicago: University of Chicago Press, 1967).

36 Polanyi had used Köhler's term "dynamic order" for the phenomenon of unplanned order in a 1941 essay, applying it to intellectual and scientific advances. Hayek then published a now famous essay in 1945 which insisted on the essential place of knowledge "of particular circumstances of time and place" in economic and social life, a kind of knowledge unavailable to scientific planners (F. A. Hayek, "The Use of Knowledge in Society," in *The Libertarian Reader: Classic and Contemporary Writings from Lao-Tzu to Milton Friedman*, ed. by David Boaz [New York: Free Press, 1997]). In 1946 Polanyi dubbed this "polycentric order," but in a lecture two years later he employed "spontaneous order" for the first time (see Michael Polanyi, *The Logic of Liberty: Reflections and Rejoinders* [Chicago: University of Chicago Press, 1951], p. 154). "Spontaneous order" was then taken up by Hayek in his 1960 book, which refers to Polanyi's discussion (F. A. Hayek, *The Constitution of Liberty* [Chicago: University of Chicago, 1960], p. 160). Hayek's most complete elaboration of the notion came still later in his distinction of "made" and "grown" orders (F. A. Hayek, *Rules and Order*, volume one of *Law, Legislation, and Liberty* [Chicago: University of Chicago, 1973], p. 35).

37 Michael Polanyi, *The Logic of Liberty*, p. 126.

38 F. A. Hayek, *The Mirage of Social Justice*, volume two of *Law, Legislation, and Liberty* (Chicago: University of Chicago, 1976), p. 15.

39 F. A. Hayek, "The Use of Knowledge in Society," p. 223.

40 We should note that libertarians are free to admit that where there must be coercion, e.g. government, a democratic or consensual government is more free than a non-democratic one. While government is coercive, democratic government contains at least an element of freedom. So there ought to be minimal government, but what government there is should be democratic.

41 John Rawls, *A Theory of Justice*, revised edition (Cambridge, MA: Harvard University Press, 1999), p. 124.

42 Henry Summer Maine famously argued that the move from premodern to modern social arrangements is a transition from relations based on status to those based in contract. See his *Ancient Law: Its Connection with the Early History of Society and its Relation to Modern Ideas* (Gloucester: Peter Smith, 1970), p. 165

2

Neutrality and Equality

With respect to the conception of liberalism that evolved from the second half of the nineteenth through the first half of the twentieth, libertarian liberalism is the most theoretically simple form of liberalism. An egalitarian version of liberalism, concretely expressed in the welfare state, can understand itself as liberal in two ways: either it qualifies the value of individual liberty (e.g. property rights) and sheer equality before the law with teleological considerations of socio-economic justice or equality, allowing the former occasionally to be trumped by the later; or it draws attention to the dependence of individual liberty on socio-economic preconditions, which preconditions may require redistribution and so interference in the economic liberty of some. The latter is the most consistently liberal embodiment of egalitarianism, and less open to the external criticism that comes from juggling liberty and equality as competing principles. Thus most deontological egalitarian liberals can be understood as retaining liberty as the ultimate value, but recognizing a more-than-legal equality, some equality of conditions and opportunities, as necessary for liberty.[1]

The recent movement of neutralist egalitarianism was inaugurated by John Rawls' justly famous *A Theory of Justice* (1971). Strategically, Rawls sought to provide a deontological justification of a liberal welfare state in order to avoid the alleged debility of prevalent utilitarian efforts, which had risked majoritarian over-ruling of individual rights. The natural rights of self-interested individuals would now, through an updated Lockean social contract, justify welfare spending. A host of prominent liberals – including Bruce Ackerman, Ronald Dworkin, Charles Larmore, and Thomas Nagel – followed suit.

Rawls' argument is by now more than familiar. Rational, equal, free, and self-interested human beings would choose as the ultimate principles of justice the following two rules: each person must have maximum equal civil and political liberty; and, socio-economic inequalities are just only if all persons have a fair opportunity to occupy the advantaged positions, and the inequalities benefit the least advantaged, i.e. the poor. Persons would chose these principles because, in a hypothetical condition of equality where they could not predict what position they would eventually occupy in society (given Rawls' equality-guaranteeing condition, the "veil of ignorance"), they would rationally prefer a society in which the poor are better off than in any other society, since they themselves may turn out to be poor. Purely rational and self-interested persons would rather live in a society in which people "share each other's fate" than one in which the unlucky are permitted a free-fall into poverty, as in the "natural liberty" advocated by libertarians. In the process, Rawls' "principle of redress" specifically denied that what is morally "arbitrary" can be honored by political society. My inheritance of money, talent, and a secure family are morally arbitrary: I do not "deserve" them, so their benefits can justly be redistributed. In addition, none of my achievements in life can be said to be utterly independent of a social contribution: even if I am a "self-made" entrepreneur my business presupposes an infrastructure of educated consumers, roads, police and fire protection, which was built by society. Thus society deserves repayment. For Rawls within the bounds of political theory I am to be considered a purely moral being, and as a moral being *I owe all* for all I have.

Rather than attempt to add anything new to the copious commentary on *A Theory of Justice*, I will merely situate myself in that literature. Echoing the objections of Michael Sandel and other communitarians, I suggest that the principles of fairness and especially redress are intolerable.[2] Whatever else we might say to defend fair opportunity and the welfare state, we cannot accept the notion that no individual inheritance or accomplishment is rightfully owned unless it benefits society. This is a very narrow and rationalistic form of social theory. It subjects human existence to a thorough moralization, indeed, via a particular morality, that of Kant (at least, in Rawls' truncation of Kant's moral theory). Indeed, the question then arises, Do I have a right to my self, is my self mine? Rawls must answer in one of two ways: either I have no right to my self, and so the self is in effect community property; or my talents, my body, my inheritance, that is, all morally arbitrary and undeserved elements of me must not be parts of my self at all. In the latter case the self has shrunk to my moral rational will, to that part of me which chooses the principles of justice and identifies with them, which is the notion of selfhood in Kant's moral theory. Either conclusion is anthropologically wrong and psychologically impossible.

Not to mention that, if the latter option holds, and if I am only my moral rational will, then I do not need communal provision or the welfare state at all, for my self is independent of such needs; this unwanted conclusion would actually make perfect sense given Rawls' notion of desert. It is in direct conflict, however, not only with his political purposes but with his "thin theory of the good" – the valuation, which must hold in the original position even prior to the selection of the principles of justice, of those things necessary to pursue virtually any form of life, e.g. wealth, income, liberty, etc. – and especially self-respect, which is dependent on material conditions like income. Consequently, there are two incompatible anthropologies in Rawls, a Kantian autonomous moral self, which literally has no desires or needs, and an Aristotelian or Millian self, whose higher or moral concerns, like self-respect, are themselves dependent on the satisfaction of physical and social needs.

Rawls to the contrary notwithstanding, the society of "sharing each other's fate" can be achieved in only two ways: by expanding, in degree, the particular pre-political, familial, neighborhood, community, and cultural ties that do indeed characterize human existence; or by imposing purely political ties at the most abstract and comprehensive, i.e. national or state, level. I will argue later that the former, however difficult and strained, is the more plausible. As Burke claimed, "To be attached to the subdivision, to love the little platoon we belong to in society, is the first principle . . . of public affections. It is the first link in the series by which we proceed toward a love to our country and to mankind."[3] The alternate approach begins by ignoring and supervening the local senses in which humans historically have actually succeeded in coming to share each other's fate, in hopes of universal rather than merely local sharing. Rawls' is in this sense much like the scheme for the communal life of the guardians in Plato's *Republic*, albeit less extreme in its socialism. In another sense, it is like trying to cure tuberculosis by removing the lungs. Rawls is trying to bend Kantianism to utilitarian sympathy. He cannot directly endorse the latter because he is wedded to an individualistic starting point necessary to justify maximum political liberty in his first principle of justice. But, as the apocryphal Maine resident informs the traveler, you can't get there from here.

Rawls is not the only philosopher to offer a defense of neutralist egalitarianism through a systematic thought experiment. While Bruce Ackerman was critical of Rawls for basing liberalism in social contract theory, his own account was similarly based in a counter-factual scenario.[4] In contrast to the historical fiction of the state of nature, Ackerman suggested science fiction: we are to imagine ourselves as occupants of a space ship about to land on a planet where we will henceforth live, with access to a limited supply of a single resource, "manna," necessary for achieving all desires. Ackerman defines liberalism as a particular way of conducting the ensuing conversation about the division of the manna, namely, under the constraint that no justification of a claim to a share through reference to the alleged superiority of one's person or one's view of the Good is permitted. Those who could only justify their claims through such a reference are thereby reduced to "silence," and government must then conclude the adjudication on other grounds.

First, we must wonder, philosophically rather than politically, just what justificatory argument is *not* eventually reduced to silence? The debate about proposals that pass the neutrality test will also be reduced to silence, if opponents refuse to recognize the validity of their arguments, unless endlessly repeating one's position counts as continued discourse. Reasons run out at *some* point. The justification for neutrality itself would be no exception. Absence of novel justification cannot be the criterion that de-legitimates a position.

The political objections to Ackerman's approach are best seen in some of the details of his argument. Ackerman nicely considers something given little attention by Rawls, the obligations of the present community to future generations, which also dovetails with his special concern for genetic and hence reproductive justice. He argues that children can rightfully demand a "liberal" education which does not teach them to adopt any particular notion of the Good. Parents who violate this are acting unjustly. "Parental design" is to be ruled off the liberal agenda. For children may later complain to parents, "What . . . can you say in justification of your decision to shape me in a way that you think good but I [now] think bad? . . . By what right did you assume the power to shape me in the way you thought good?"[5] Later Ackerman accepts that parents can impose discipline in order to discourage their children's aggression against others, but "the parents may not view their initial success [in doing so] as warranting the imposition of more elaborate forms of their favored routine."[6] He goes on to discuss legitimate "guidance," where guidance means factually correcting childhood misunderstandings of social realities, not teaching values.

But in reality all nurturing of children teaches them some account of the Good. The only way a parent can avoid teaching a child that some ways of life are better than others is to ignore the child altogether (if even that would succeed). Further, this teaching always involves spoken or unspoken constraints on the child, that is, coercion. Indeed, it involves *violence* in the sense of the use of physical force on the child – physically restraining a child from running across a busy street is a use of coercive force.[7] I *must* shape my child; not to do so is serious neglect. For *not to constrain* could only mean also *not to enable*. It is entirely reasonable to include as part of this shaping a measure of liberty. Most parents in a modern liberal society would indeed regard it as bad parenting to insist that a child pursue a particular and narrow course of life that the child disliked and for which he or she seemed unsuited. But this cannot mean that the parents ought to provide a "neutral" training that will not in any way restrict the range of ideas of the Good that will be available to the growing child.

In another example Ackerman asks whether infanticide should be permitted. This is, for him, a real question, since infants have no place in discourse, hence no rights under a liberal polity defined by the ability to participate in public reason-giving. Because he is a reasonable and moral individual, of course, Ackerman comes up with two ways of denying the right to kill one's children: first, doing so would deny infertile couples equal access to adoptable children, and second, that simple wanton cruelty is an "unsatisfactory expression of the liberal community's principled agnosticism about the 'proper' relationship between the state and the larger universe."[8]

These arguments are a particularly bizarre case of adding epicycles to a theory innately ill-suited to make normative sense of an area of life central to most human beings, but foreign to the egalitarian discourse model on which Ackerman bases his polity. The evil of my killing my children is not exhausted by the fact that such killing would spoil resources for other adult citizens! But Ackerman's argument is also illegitimate on his own terms. Majoritarian limits on my liberty to kill my children, or litter the Grand Canyon, or buy up wetlands for development, carry with them notions of the good life as much as any other restraint on my freedom. If not, if we are to interpret them as merely "agnostic," then lots of other apparently non-neutral policies are thereby justified by the same "agnosticism." Why not deny abortion rights because fetuses *might* have some value that renders abortion at least as morally dubious as littering? Neutralism was supposed to prevent the polity from limiting my liberty and declaring my notion of the Good inferior to others. If now neutralist agnosticism is supposed to be a justification for limiting liberty and denying me the ability to pursue what I think is good, then just what is neutrality about?

Ronald Dworkin's portrayal of liberalism is distinctive in that he recognizes equality as the dominant liberal value, eschewing talk of the alleged conflict of liberty and equality.[9] As noted earlier, he is in part right in that all forms of liberalism, including libertarianism, value equality of some sort. His endorsement of the free market is also refreshing; for Dworkin the free market is not an unfortunate but a necessary machine of economic growth, but like majoritarian democracy an imperfectly egalitarian institution, some of whose results must be ameliorated.

Dworkin's liberals are committed to treating all individuals *as* equals, that is, with equal concern and respect. Liberalism is neither asocial nor skeptical regarding the Good, it merely endorses equal treatment as the highest political value. Liberals conclude that the only way to do so is for political decisions to be neutral with respect to differing notions of the good life and for the political community to ensure that individuals have access to equal shares of community resources for their particular life-projects. So Dworkin hopes to get both liberty and the welfare state out of equality. To be treated as an equal, I must not be expected to forgo my equal share of resources for the sake of someone else and his or her projects. Dworkin allows that those who increase the sum of social resources by their special projects may legitimately receive more back. But unequal shares of resources are legitimate only if they are the outcome of the members' *choices*, not their *un-chosen circumstances*. As with Rawls, "morally irrelevant differences" like luck, inheritance, gifts, talent, or handicaps may not legitimately affect access to resources.

The problems with this account are instructive regarding the inadequacies of egalitarian proceduralism in general. First, making equality a primary goal of political theory is dubious in itself. Now, egalitarian liberals recognize there are distinctive meanings of "equality," and some, like Dworkin, are willing to depart from strict material equality. Nevertheless, they give material equality enough of a moral standing that any departure from it requires moral justification. Whereas, I would suggest, equality generally speaking is not a worthy political *goal* at all; it is an important *condition* holding over legitimate political goals. Equality in itself is too vacuous to be a goal.[10] If equality were an end in itself, then the various absurdities cited by anti-egalitarians would come into play: we should be willing to dump valuable resources that cannot be distributed equally to all, to cut off the legs of tall people, etc. Of course, no egalitarians take this absurd position, but this merely shows that they implicitly make equality a condition on other ends, not an end in itself.

A further problem hangs on Dworkin's conception of rights. For him rights belong to individuals simply because they deserve equal concern and respect. Rights are indeed trumps over majoritarian interest; if they were not, there would be no point in having them.[11] For to assert an individual's right is to assert that equal concern and respect for that individual is violated by collective utility; utility is perfectly legitimate, but rights are its necessary moral limit. The difficulty is revealed when Dworkin goes on to interpret such rights. If all citizens are to treated as having "equal worth," then, since "no self-respecting person who believes that a particular way to live is most valuable can accept that this way of life is base or degrading," government may not employ any argument to that effect in its decision-making.[12] But this is impossible; government cannot regard as equally valid in all situations patriotism and disloyalty, altruism and selfishness, productive work and idleness, love of learning and love of ignorance, etc.[13]

Violations of rights are, given Dworkin's concept of them, cases of unfairness. Without attempting to be exhaustive, I would distinguish three relevant kinds of unfairness. First is the unfairness that some individuals are uniquely made to bear the *burden* of social practices which benefit others yet without consideration, compensation or consent. This kind of unfairness is, I think, the heart of what Dworkin wants to prevent. Second is the situation in which some individuals, because of their *idiosyncratic notions of the Good*, are disadvantaged by social policy.[14] Third, there is the situation in which some individuals regard themselves as harmed because they are *not benefited* by some social policy while others are.

These are morally distinct cases. We can, if we wish, accept the avoidance of the first kind of unfairness as a limit on inequality while rejecting the second and third as legitimate grounds for the charge of unfairness. For these latter cases, which can overlap, are not necessarily violations of "equal concern and respect." That I am to be treated equally as a citizen by officials and fellow citizens regardless of my gender, class, race, religion, handicap, is one thing. But that I must be treated the same regardless of *my conception of the Good* is another. For, as already said, it is not possible for the polity to be fully "neutral;" some conceptions of the Good will be favored, even if others are permitted. A liberal republican society must be neutral with respect to *some* conceptions of the Good and their opposites, but not with respect to *all* such conceptions. One can claim the later only if one has in mind a very limited range of conceptions of the Good. Regarding the third case, toleration may require that I not be coerced away from my choices, but that does not mean the community is required to benefit me equally with everyone else in all circumstances. Some programs of benefit can and should be equal, but not all can be. Worsening my situation for a reason can be unfair while failing to improve it for the same reason may not be.

Let us take one of Dworkin's examples: liberal arguments for environmental conservation. He rightly denies that, on his definition, liberals can argue that a life lived in touch with wild nature is better than life in a Las Vegas casino. But he then says that the liberal can argue that the over-use of natural resources will make "a way of life that has been desired and found satisfying in the past unavailable to future generations. . . . the process [of consumption] is not neutral amongst competing ideas of the good life, but in fact destructive of the very possibility of some of these."[15] This is an example of egalitarian neutralism trying to smuggle in favorite issues without acknowledging its partisanship. For it implies that it is not after all a violation of neutrality to support the resources necessary for a particular concept of the Good, in order to maintain the possibility of pursuing it. But that would imply that liberals are obliged, not merely to refrain from political endorsement of a good other than equality, but to ensure that *all private notions of the Good remain possible*. That is, like an over-zealous ecologist, government is to make sure that no possible lifestyles become extinct. But of course Dworkin doesn't mean this; he does not mean that the political community must ensure that Nazi memorabilia be preserved somewhere so that American Nazis can worship as they wish. Only *some* ways of life and *some* notions of the Good will be supported in this way. One may agree with Dworkin, as I do, that the American polity ought to act to protect the natural environment. But one must accept that this is a non-neutral, discriminatory, and coercive policy.

As Nozick has rightly objected to Rawls, it is true of Ackerman and Dworkin as well that they set the problem of distributive justice ahistorically, as the problem of how to divide up an already existing set of resources or goods, as if the process of producing such, hence the fact of ownership, had no moral weight. Of course, egalitarians know this is counter-factual, but for normative reasons they accept a counter-factual method, and methods have their consequences. The political problem becomes for them "What share should each have?", making the question, "What is legitimately expected by producers, via investment or labor?" a derivative one. For the egalitarians the attempt to answer the first question must always trump the second. In contrast, both the history of the society and the life-histories of individual members can dictate differential desert and obligation. The theoretical scenario common to these egalitarians is one of the *refugee* or *pilgrim* community, radically understood. We are to develop our normative claims by imagining a situation in which a group of equal citizens must divide up given resources with concern only for short-term future consumption (e.g. survival). Now, when the survivors of a plane crash in the mountains need to decide how to manage until help arrives it makes perfect sense to divide resources either equally or in terms of need, and to dismiss all other considerations. But why ought we regard that imagined situation as determinative for normal social life? Ought we really understand our civil society through the metaphor of *disaster*?

Implicit in all this, egalitarian liberals make distributive justice a purely *moral* problem. As noted, nothing "morally arbitrary" may determine someone's position or share. Differences in resources can only be just if they presume no difference in social birth position and benefit the least advantaged (Rawls), or can be justified without any reference to any notion of the Good (Ackerman), or are due solely to my choices and not to un-chosen circumstances (Dworkin). Even Thomas Nagel, who at least recognizes what he calls the incorrigibility of the "personal" or "partial" viewpoint, hence the impracticality of implementing a pure Rawlsian scheme, nevertheless agrees that all social arrangements must be examined for such moral "arbitrariness." A just, which is to say, equal society "requires abandonment of the idea that there is a morally fundamental distinction, in regard to the socioeconomic framework . . . between what the state does and what it merely allows."[16] Society is "responsible for how things are." It is a mistake to regard economic inequity as "natural," hence not subject to critical examination and governmental reduction. He insists that "*Every* arrangement has to be justified" (Nagel's emphasis). Society must not "permit the distribution of benefits on morally irrelevant grounds;" no arena, including family relations, may escape the moral redistributive effort.[17]

Gift-giving, inheritance, loyalty, and good fortune – be they genetic, familial, or social – are thereby made violations of moral, hence political order. In reality, however, it will always be the aim of a good parent, friend, teacher to generate special advantages for a child, companion, or student. My children have a right to demand that I hold their happiness above everyone else's. Are we to undercut this? Whatever the moral intuitions of the egalitarians, their theory implies that when I go beyond the call of impersonal duty to help someone, I thereby disadvantage others, hence act immorally. This is precisely what Michael Oakeshott, as we will see later, criticized as "rationalism in politics." I would say it reveals an antipathy to political and civil life *per se*: it is the complete reduction of the *political* to the *moral*. Whatever cannot be morally justified has no right to be. Certainly morality is crucial to civic life, but this does not mean that every civic fact can or must "justify itself" before the court of an ahistorical morality. We cannot allow the question, "By what right do you have more than I?", to trump all other questions, to run wild over society. This question stands in the same class with other civically intolerable demands, like, "If you have nothing to hide, you should not resist complete exposure of your private life," and "How can you justify your continuing to live when innocents die?" and "Only those who obey the law of God, who *are right*, have *the right* to live." It is in the very nature of *civil* existence that we *do not ask* each other these questions, that, in Thomas Reid's figure, we do not call civic life before the bar of moral philosophy in this way. As I will suggest, regarding distributive justice the point is not to decide what amount everybody *ought* to have, but only who has *too little* and what we should do about it.[18]

A positive alternative to neutralist egalitarianism is not the job of this chapter. But in summary I may offer a final reason that a neutralist account of distributive justice cannot work. What is just is highly variable, even within a particular society. As Michael Walzer has brilliantly argued regarding distributive justice, distinct spheres of social life entail distinctive distributive rules.[19] They do so because the moral rule for the proper distribution of a good cannot be determined independent of the *social meaning* of that good, which is a cultural matter. Desert, merit, strict equality, need, value, etc., the various principles suggested by competing political theorists, are *all* valid, each in its proper sphere. Injustice (of one kind) results from border-crossings, invasions, and colonizations of one sphere – e.g. needs – by the legitimate principle of another – e.g. wealth. The answer to the question, What do citizens owe one another?, is a *cultural* decision that implies a shared account of the Good, or rather, of goods.[20] Neutralism, by insisting on the division of culture from politics, renders such an account impossible.

Proceduralism Without Foundations

Rawls' 1993 book *Political Liberalism* sought to undermine communitarian and antifoundationalist criticisms of *A Theory of Justice* by recasting the philosophical context of his theory.[21] The new version jettisons Kantian foundations and seeks a basis for liberal neutrality *within* a culture of competing theories of the Good. Rawls abandons any attempt to justify liberalism *per se*; his book aims to clear up the meaning of liberalism for liberal societies. The result is a peerlessly sophisticated rethinking of the basis for the liberal project, and, I will suggest, a remarkably circular restriction of the realm of the political. In attempting to answer attacks on liberal neutralism Rawls exacerbates rather then tempers its deeper inadequacies.

The primary Rawlsian question now is no longer, What is Justice?, but, "How is it possible for those affirming a religious doctrine that is based on religious authority, for example, the Church or the Bible, also to hold a reasonable political conception that supports a just democratic regime?"[22] The answer is that, "rather than confronting religious and nonliberal doctrines with a comprehensive liberal philosophical doctrine, the thought is to formulate a liberal political conception that those nonliberal doctrines might be able to endorse."[23] Differently put, stability is only possible with a liberalism that "removes from the political agenda the most divisive issues . . ." This sounds like a pragmatic argument. Yet Rawls specifically denies that his theory is a merely pragmatic "*modus vivendi*" to which conflicting cultural groups can turn to secure peace. His aim is stability "for the right reasons," a morally justified peace.[24]

He anchors his new non-foundational liberalism with three concepts. The first is *reasonableness*. Reasonable people are those who wish to live together on terms that are fair to others as well as to themselves, and so will not ask unequal sacrifices on the part of others. He writes, "Reasonable persons . . . desire for its own sake a social world in which they, as free and equal, can cooperate with others on terms all can accept. . . . so that each benefits along with others." What Rawls wishes to prohibit is the proposal of rules of association that enforce or favor particular religious or philosophical convictions. Reasonable people do not make such proposals. Reasonableness is tied to modern liberal tolerance as defined by the first principle of justice from *A Theory of Justice*, according to which I propose for myself the maximum freedom consonant with a like freedom for everyone else. Rawls maintains that reasonableness is itself a moral, not merely pragmatic, value, so citizens will not withdraw their support should reasonable liberalism become pragmatically undesirable.

But the meaning of reasonableness is unclear. Putatively I, as reasonable, desire principles and policies that "others can accept." What others "can" accept depends on how thickly we conceive the "others." Majoritarian democracy acknowledges that some people cannot accept almost anything the majority accepts as "fair" terms of cooperation. To be sure, the principle "I, Cahoone, get everything," is out; no one else can agree to that. But why couldn't I say that all fellow citizens *can* accept Jesus as their personal savior, since it is physically and legally possible, hence it is not unfair to establish Christianity? Rawls would object, and rightly. But on what grounds? The only grounds must be that, for example, a Jew cannot, *qua* Jew, accept those terms; that is, cannot accept those terms and remain a Jew (*B'nai Yeshua* to the contrary notwithstanding).

But this means Rawls must have an implicit distinction between which traits of personal identity are to be left untrammeled by public politics – e.g. one's Judaism – and which traits are such that, even if they make it impossible for the person to accept proposed terms of cooperation, the proposed terms are *not* thereby unreasonable – for example, if my wealth leads me to oppose the progressive income tax. This is problematic because Rawls also insists that, as reasonable, we must think of persons merely "as citizens," whom we "don't view . . . as socially situated or otherwise rooted . . . or as having this or that comprehensive doctrine. . . . Accounts of human nature we put aside and rely on a political conception of persons as citizens instead."[25] This is his thin, purely political conception of the subject. But the current example shows that he cannot apply even his most basic conception of reasonableness without a thicker anthropology. There has to be operating behind reasonableness a conception not only of the *citizen* but of the *person* that makes it unreasonable to propose terms of cooperation that differentially disadvantage non-Christians or women or racial groups, but not unreasonable to propose terms that differentially disadvantage, say, the wealthy, or heroin-users, or pederasts.

His second innovation is the idea of an *overlapping consensus* of reasonable comprehensive doctrines. Reasonable comprehensive doctrines are the comprehensive doctrines of citizens who are reasonable. Such doctrines valorize tolerance, fairness, and liberty; that is, they overlap or intersect around such notions. Thus the reasonable Muslim, Christian, and atheist each endorses tolerance on the basis of his or her own privately held comprehensive doctrine. Yet their contributions to public political reasoning will not presuppose their comprehensive doctrines, because each, as reasonable will not propose "private" grounds for social cooperation. While the reasonable Muslim endorses tolerance for Islamic reasons, she will not offer those reasons in public because she cannot expect others to share them, and would not want, say, Christian reasons foisted on herself. This is to say that the consensus among reasonable people is the "module" of reasonableness that obtains within each distinct, privately held comprehensive doctrine.

Rawls thinks there is in fact an overlapping consensus of reasonable comprehensive doctrines, that comprehensive doctrines of reasonable Christians, atheists, Jews, and Buddhists overlap around, jointly but distinctively valorize, liberty, tolerance, fairness, etc. But his examples of such an overlap are few. The main exemplar he offers is itself philosophical; it is a consensus among adherents to doctrines articulated in the history of modern Western philosophy, namely, Locke's deistic justification of tolerance, the moral views of Kant and Mill, and a "pluralist" set of nonpolitical views that also affirm political liberalism.[26] Among these competing comprehensive doctrines he argues that no compromise is required, for they overlap around political liberalism. Then he simply adds to these exemplary comprehensive doctrines "all the historical religions, except for certain kinds of fundamentalism." Excepting this last historical generalization – which, if we were to take it seriously, would significantly water down what is the subject of the consensus – Rawls' example serves to show only that modern liberals, among which are the Kantians, utilitarians, pluralists, and the religious believers commonly met in modern liberal societies, accept modern liberalism. In other words, he defines liberalism in terms of a consensus among liberals.

Now, this charge of circularity would not disturb Rawls, who is not aiming at a non-circular justification of liberalism. True to his notion, Rawls offers no comprehensive doctrine as justification of his account. He insists on what he calls the "freestanding" nature of politics and political theory, denying that a foundation or supra-political justification for liberal politics is either possible or necessary. He responds to philosophical questions with what he calls the "method of avoidance." So the charge of circularity would not bother him. But we ought to notice just *how limited the diameter of this circle is*. Liberalism is defined by the reasonableness that is a module within the comprehensive doctrines of reasonable people. It is indeed true that there is such an overlapping consensus: large numbers of Presbyterians, Jews, Catholics, Muslims, and agnostics in modern liberal societies are indeed modern liberals. But what normative power does this fact have in deciding how to deal with views that are not so "reasonable," that is, not so liberal? We would like to have some normative arguments here, and not merely to perform the trick – the plausibility of which Rawls is probably right to deny – of philosophically convincing antiliberals to be liberal. The real function of such arguments is to convince various kinds of liberals that their version of liberalism is faulty, that their commitment to liberalism is violated by other components of their worldview.

But perhaps the most important of Rawls' new conceptions is the idea, implicit in the foregoing, of *public reason*, or the proper nature and limits of public political discourse. Reasonable citizens will distinguish between their "private" convictions, which they do not propose to see enforced on others, and rules of association that can be justified in public. Public reason is political reason, the kind of reason employed in the political forum, at least under liberal democratic conditions. Politics is not to be conducted under an obligation to the "whole truth," or a full moral theory. "The zeal to embody the whole truth in politics," he writes, "is incompatible with an idea of public reason that belongs with democratic citizenship."[27] The commitment to public reason is thus synonymous with accepting the theory of *Political Liberalism* itself, that liberalism is a political and not a comprehensive doctrine.

It is this notion of public reason that has invited the most critical response, and has led Rawls to re-think his position twice, in the second, 1996 edition of *Political Liberalism* and again in his 1997 essay, "The Idea of Public Reason Revisited." For the exclusion of comprehensive doctrines from public political debate might seem a rather restrictive condition for a liberal public space. Rawls has thus been concerned both to refine the notion of public reason, and to limit its range of application, hence its openness to criticism.

First, Rawls has clarified the restriction that public reason only applies to public debates over "constitutional essentials and matters of basic justice" by saying that this phrase refers to those political rights and liberties that might be considered constitutional and to the justice of the "basic structure" of society. Basic structure means "society's main political, constitutional, social, and economic institutions and how they fit together to form a unified scheme of social cooperation over time."[28] The restrictions of public reason apply only to these fundamental questions, not to any and all topic covered in political debate.

But what would be a political question – in our usual sense of "political"– that did *not* fit this description? Rawls might like to limit the subject matter of public reason to the framework that structures the political process, as in the US constitution. This would be too narrow, however, for then arguments about distributive justice could arguably fall outside public reason. The addition of the "basic justice" of the "basic structure of society" is meant to amend that inadequacy. But this addition makes any restriction vacuous. Almost any particular political question, no matter how local and limited, can easily invoke, in the reasoning used to decide it, some understanding of "society's main political, constitutional, social, and economic institutions and how they fit together . . ." Indeed, our liberal society arguably tends to push all sorts of political issues into that very domain, for example, to resolve disputes by reference to "rights," which are clearly part of the "basic structure."

Most importantly, Rawls distinguishes the realm of public reason from "the many places in the background culture where political matters are discussed."[29] In his new final chapter to the second edition he writes that public reason is carried out by legislators, executives, judges, candidates, party leaders and workers, and citizens "when they vote," although "the ideal of public reason does not have the same requirements in all these cases."[30] He remarks that Jürgen Habermas' apparently similar concept of the public sphere is much broader than his own, since it includes the "background culture" where public reason "with its duty of civility [i.e. fairness] does not apply." Here we see that in determining when the employment of comprehensive doctrines constitutes a violation of the liberal forum, venues for and participants in discourse are more significant than the content or subject matter of discourse. Political liberalism is violated only if comprehensive doctrines are invoked in that portion of political life *where they may generate legal force*. Most recently Rawls has been a bit more restrictive, insisting that public reason is meant to apply only to the "public political forum," which is composed of the discourse of government officials (especially executives and legislators), candidates, and judges. Note that here Rawls does not explicitly include the popular vote for officials.[31] But he adds that while the "idea" of public reason does not apply to the background culture of "civil society," the *ideal* of public reason does. Citizens are "ideally" to "think of themselves *as if* they were legislators . . ." In fact, he claims this is "vital" to the "enduring strength and vigor" of public reason. Citizens have a "moral duty" to follow public reason – not a legal one, because, as Rawls allows, that requirement would be "incompatible" with freedom of speech.[32]

In his discussion of public reason Rawls considers the civil rights movement and abolition. The example is the right one; it hangs like a sword of Damocles above Rawls' argument. For, given Rawls' liberal and egalitarian political convictions, no form of political discourse could be more legitimately a part of public reason than the attempt to gain full political rights for African-Americans. But the rhetoric of the nineteenth century Abolitionists and the 1960s civil rights movement was *explicitly religious and metaphysical*. Martin King Jr. and others argued for black rights on the basis of the Bible, not to mention the Declaration of Independence and the Constitution, documents that are themselves not "neutral" with respect to religion.[33] How can Rawls reconcile his exclusion of religion from political debate with his historical awareness of the crucial importance of such arguments in extending liberalism itself?

His solution in the first edition (1993) was to distinguish religious advocacy for political rights that strengthens public reason from advocacy that does not. An "inclusive" understanding of public reason would permit the former but not the latter; an "exclusive" understanding would permit neither. Rawls supported the inclusive reading. So, civil rights leaders' religious advocacy was legitimate if "they thought, or on reflection would have thought (as they certainly could have thought), that the comprehensive reasons they appealed to were required to give sufficient strength to the political conception to be subsequently realized."[34] Regarding Lincoln's Second Inaugural, with its invocation of divine justice, he opined that it did not violate public reason "as it applied in his day – whether in ours is another matter, since what he says has no implications bearing on constitutional essentials or matters of basic justice. Or whatever implications it might have could surely be supported firmly by the values of public reason."[35] So, a religious or comprehensive advocacy does not violate public reason if its comprehensive rhetoric does not promote any fundamental or constitutional (as we saw, legally forceful) policies that *could not* be supported by public reason. The second edition (1996) renames this the "wide" reading of public reason. Public reason can accommodate any reasonable doctrine "provided that in due course public reasons, given by a reasonable political conception, are presented sufficient to support whatever the comprehensive doctrines are introduced to support,"[36] that is, if the comprehensively supported policy is *in fact* eventually supported by noncomprehensive reasons. Could the Abolitionists and King have fulfilled the wide reading? "Whether they did or not," Rawls intones, "they could have. And, had they known the idea of public reason and shared its ideal, they would have."[37] Rawls repeats this exact formulation in his 1997 essay.[38]

The replacement of the subjunctive "would's" and "could's" of the first edition statement by the second edition's "in due course public reasons . . . *are* presented" is reminiscent of Peirce's notion of truth as convergence: in Rawls, to say today of a comprehensive advocacy that it is politically legitimate to say that it will be given public, noncomprehensive justification, in the future.[39] In the case of abolitionists and civil rights leaders, it is because *we* late twentieth century non-foundationalists can construct non-comprehensive arguments for what their rhetoric advocated that the publicity of their advocacy is redeemed. The earlier use of the comprehensive doctrine was then merely a rhetorical necessity, or at any rate a cultural language irrelevant to the meaning of the policy. *Political Liberalism* is thus the discovery of the true nature of liberalism which prior liberals failed to see, and it finally shows that earlier liberals were justified in their rhetoric. Fortunately for political history, nobody in the 1860s or 1960s realized the inadequacy or irrelevancy of the earlier rhetoric and forbade its employment.

Rawls' account is saved from being a rather remarkable insult to historical political agents only by his faith that they "could" and indeed "would" have given adequate public justification for their reforms under other circumstances. We may wonder, then, how we are to judge such matters in the present, that is, to know in advance which comprehensive justifications will eventually be redeemed? But evidently *fortuna* is with us, for we are privileged to live in that period of time when comprehensive doctrines, especially religious ones, have been more fully dispensed with, enabling us to see the essence of liberalism without the obfuscations of history. It is difficult not to find in Rawls' account both historical naiveté and a chauvinism of the present.

There is in addition an unexpected problem with public reason. While Rawls' framework may seem the apotheosis of neutrality, on at least one famous occasion it appeared to have partisan political implications. In the first edition the normative power of *Political Liberalism* had been famously revealed in a footnote in which Rawls wrote that, starting from three stated "political" values – respect for human life, the reproduction of society and the family, and the equality of women as citizens – "any reasonable balance of these three values will give a woman a duly qualified right to decide whether or not to end her pregnancy during the first trimester . . ." Indeed, he continued,

> any comprehensive doctrine that leads to a balance of political values exclud-
> ing that duly qualified right in the first trimester is to that extent unreason-
> able . . . Thus assuming that this question is either a constitutional essential
> or a matter of basic justice, we would go against the ideal of public reason if
> we voted from a comprehensive doctrine that denied this right.[40]

This seemed to say not only that the framework of liberalism implies the validity of the pro-choice position, but that the pro-life view ought to be excluded from the domain of public reason altogether. Thus some very weighty contemporary political issues would be decided by the allegedly neutral framework.

In the second edition Rawls insists that he never intended the above as an "argument" for the right to abortion (adding somewhat scrupulously that it did express his opinion, "but an opinion is not an argument").[41] The point of that footnote, he now says, was only to illustrate that *if* there is a balance of reasonable political values supporting choice, and none sup-porting the anti-abortion position, then the promotion of the latter position violates public reason. He adds that he is by no means sure that is so; he stands by the hypothetical, even citing a pro-life argument that is, he claims, public.[42] Rawls claims to be, argumentatively (not opiningly) agnostic on which side will win the balance of reasonable views. So he believes that he has now undercut the objection that his "neutral" framework takes sub-stantive political positions.

But he succeeds only to a point. For it is arguable that *comprehensiveness is asymmetrically related to distinctive political positions*, in particular, that various conservative and communitarian political positions are normally tied to comprehensive views in ways that various "liberal" positions are not. If so, then ruling comprehensiveness out distinctively disadvantages non-liberal positions. Oddly enough, then, while Rawls' apparently prejudicial exclusion of pro-choice arguments in the first edition was objectionable, its political prejudices were based in the telling insight that comprehensiveness is not distributed equally across the political spectrum. It is indeed the case that a number of the substantive political positions Rawls happens to hold are less tied to comprehensive doctrines than their political antitheses.

One might say, "Of course, Rawls' doctrine is political *liberalism*, after all!" But here "liberal" is being used ambiguously. It is Rawls' stated aim to produce a political forum that is as presuppositionless as possible – here "liberal" means tolerant and pluralistic – rather than one that justifies a substantively "liberal" view whose validity is a matter for debate within that forum – e.g. the pro-choice position. Rawls can plausibly say that the pro-life policy is not *intrinsically* ruled out by political liberalism. However, what Rawls seemed to say in the first edition, and what he now avoids saying, might indeed be true: it might be that upon a little reflection the arguments against abortion rights would soon have to resort to comprehensive doctrines, e.g. regarding when life begins, the sacredness of life, the limits on autonomy, etc. If a policy, like the denial of abortion rights, cannot be adequately supported on noncomprehensive grounds, then, political liberalism can say, so much the worse for the policy. But the theorist like Rawls would then have to face the fact that his "neutral" doctrine *has partisan political implications*. Consequently, the opposing partisans could rightly object, just as Marxists argued that Locke's "neutral umpire" government was in fact a teammate of the ruling class, that Rawls' playing field is tipped to favor typically "progressive" versions of liberalism.

As a further attempt at reassurance that his framework under-determines substantive political questions, in the later edition Rawls allows that there will be a "family of reasonable political conceptions of justice and this family changes over time. . . . The content of public reason is not fixed."[43] There is a set of "liberal political values" whose distinctive orderings can result in legitimate and even "incompatible" reasonable liberal positions. A definitive list is never given, but at various times Rawls takes it to include: equal political and civil liberty; equal opportunity; social equality; economic reciprocity; the common good; the "primary goods" of *A Theory of Justice* (rights, liberties, freedom of movement and choice of occupation, powers and prerogatives of offices, opportunity, income, wealth, and the social bases of self-respect); appropriate use of argument and evidence; accepting the non-controversial conclusions of science; reasonableness; civility; preserving nature and life, fostering non-human species, and protecting natural beauty where these serve human health, recreation, and pleasure.

Tabling the question of just how all these values qualify as liberal, yet non-comprehensive, we must ask how we can rationally decide among their divergent liberal orderings? For Rawls insists even that in discursive "stand-offs" between distinctive orderings of liberal values comprehensive doctrines cannot be employed.

> Public reason sees the office of citizen with its duty of civility as analogous to that of judgeship with its duty of deciding cases. . . . when there seems to be a stand-off, that is legal arguments seem evenly balanced on both sides, judges cannot simply resolve the case by appealing to their own political views. To do that is for judges to violate their duty. The same holds with public reason: if when stand-offs occur, citizens invoke the grounding reasons of their comprehensive views, then the principle of reciprocity is violated.[44]

What form can rational argument then take in such circumstances? We know what form of argument Rawlsian public discourse rules out; now we must ask what form of argument does it leave in?

First a preliminary clarification is needed. Rawls repeatedly, even as late as 1997, refers to *degrees* of reasonableness within the public political forum. Thus he writes, "Citizens will of course differ as to which conceptions of political justice they think the most reasonable, but they will agree that all are reasonable, even if barely so."[45] But if reasonableness is the trait of a citizen who properly suggests as the conditions for social cooperation only principles that he or she imagines others could accept, what would *more* versus *less* reasonableness be? Rawls seems to flirting with ambiguity by here introducing the usual, non-technical notion of "reasonable" as honoring the overall weight of justificatory reasons or arguments for and against a policy. This is not a trivial confusion. For only thus can he slide from his characterization of a political forum that is reasonable in his technical sense – where no one proposes policies whose only justification must be "private" or comprehensive – to a criterion of what is the *best* or *right* policy *within* that discussion. The better word for the later would be "rational," not reasonable. Having based his own argument on a distinction of the reasonable from the rational, he cannot now try to embed the later in the former, implying that the criterion of tolerance is itself linked to a way to decide *which* tolerant positions are the right ones, even circumstantially. The criterion of what counts as political cannot then be the criterion of what is to count as the politically *more valid* position, any more than the criterion of what counts as art can be identical to the criterion for what is *good* art.[46]

Now, in what we normally think of as "rational" argument, I cannot introduce as the basis for my views considerations that my interlocutors cannot *in principle* be *expected* to share. As suggested earlier, "in principle" and "expected" presuppose a notion of the kind of interlocutor addressed, and the kind of discussion in which the address occurs. For example, in a discussion among contemporary professional philosophers, interlocutors regard each other as more or less free, equal, rational entertainers of virtually any possible belief. Thus in a philosophical discussion I can indeed argue that you ought to accept my religion or my ethical views, if I offer as reasons considerations you might share. I cannot offer mystical experiences that are inaccessible to you, or simply assert my faith, or say you should take it on my authority; those responses carry no weight in such a philosophical discussion.

Rawls is saying that liberal political debate, that is, public reason, is more restricted than this. Why ought it be? Why, in short, is "the citizen" a more cognitively narrow role than "the philosopher?" Here I use the philosopher solely as an example, not in order to argue that the citizen is or ought to be like a philosopher. Why must the rules of citizenship in particular exclude my comprehensive doctrines, even "reasonable" ones? Because I cannot expect you to share my comprehensive doctrine, comes the Rawlsian answer. But this is not so. I do indeed expect fellow citizens to share large chunks of my comprehensive doctrine. Perhaps Rawls means that I *ought not* expect others to share it. But that is troublesome as well, for, to take one example, it would be very difficult, as Michael Walzer suggests, to design any kind of redistributive policy without a "thick" notion of what people typically value in my culture.[47] As Rawls' expanding list of "liberal" political values shows, there are all sorts of things that have to be, and typically are, discussed in politics; when he tries to state those political values, his list threatens to encompass *everything*.

The deeper problem is that, given Rawls' view, how could any proposed ordering of those values be justified, argued for, in public reason? Normally we would discover that these proposed orderings were connected to and contextualized by distinctive comprehensive doctrines held by those that propose them. Here, admittedly, one must not be overly philosophical. It would be silly to presuppose that every person has a *system* of beliefs in a strong sense, such that every more particular belief or value implicates some more general belief, as if everyone were a systematic philosopher. People have numerous collections or coagulations of beliefs which need not be grounded in fundamental beliefs of philosophical generality. Avoidance of inconsistency is important on pragmatic grounds in everyday and policy discourse, but systematicity is usually not. Nevertheless, in many cases people do have general or comprehensive beliefs that support and are implicated in some values and beliefs they assert in public political debate. Their political, and even liberal, views are often contextualized by more general ethical, anthropological, soteriological, and aesthetic beliefs.

For example, suppose someone proposes policies that target children as objects of special concern, policies that implicitly value children more highly than adults. Would such a proposal be legitimate within Rawls' public reason? Someone may object, "You say children deserve special protection, special funding, special tax benefits, etc., because you define the meaning of life in terms of your children. Well this is not a liberal value you can reasonably expect everyone to share." Now, Rawls may well not share the objection; he may accept the proposal that gives children priority. He must, however, object to any comprehensive doctrine used to justify the proposal. But absent any such comprehensive doctrine, the public discussion of the proposal's justification would be in the arbitrary and, from the standpoint of rationality, bizarre situation in which the proposal's advocates can *state* their views but not *argue* for them. Rawls allows in his 1997 essay that there can be "public" arguments for pro-family policies. His examples take the form of consequentialist arguments about the effective reproduction of society.[48] But such a debate would soon naturally turn to more fundamental values regarding the nature of the family and its value beyond mere "social reproduction," which could arguably be accomplished without the family (for example, in Plato's account of communal rearing of the Guardians in *The Republic*).

Simply, it is dubious that there could be anything like what we normally call "political debate" without comprehensive doctrines. This does not mean politics is to be invaded by the foundationalist urges of philosophers, nor that political values are "puppets manipulated from behind the scenes by comprehensive doctrines."[49] One can accept with Wittgenstein that explanations end *somewhere*, that at some point in argument I must simply say, as he famously does in *Philosophical Investigations*, "this is where my spade is turned." But I suggest that in Rawls' forum the spade is getting turned a little early: if my spade is turned by the surface of the soil, then *it does no work*. I can say that I order liberal political values *this* way. Someone asks, Why? Either there is no justification for my ordering, or there is, but the justification is not itself "public" (that is, it is comprehensive). So how can this discussion be rational? Rawls' forum threatens to leave us in the same dialogical position as did the philosophical doctrine of emotivism in ethics, namely, that our political utterances merely express preferences – "I like this" or "I support that" – and nothing more.[50]

What steers Rawls' entire discussion is a rigid segregation of political and non-political life, or more precisely, the realm of political discourse that matters, that holds the legal force to structure social life, from all else. It is possible to reject this segregation, as I do, on positive political, cultural, and anthropological grounds, that is, through reliance on the apparent truth that human beings and human cultures do not and cannot work this way. However, because politics is now supposed to be free of such grounds, Rawls would be unmoved by this retort. He responds to philosophical questions of justification with his method of avoidance. But on logical and internal grounds too Rawls is in trouble.

I said before that *Political Liberalism* is partly determined by a philosophical, and not merely political, reaction against foundationalism. More specifically, it is inspired by the late Wittgenstein. The method of avoidance, for which philosophical questions of certain kinds are to be sidestepped, is a form of Wittgensteinian silence.[51] Indeed, Rawls sometimes employs Wittgensteinian figures, such as: "We cannot ground these principles. . . . With these concepts explanations come to an end; one of philosophy's tasks is to quiet our distress at this thought."[52] Rawls' *Political Liberalism* is in effect a *Wittgensteinian liberalism*.[53] As such, Rawls' methodology is *contextualist*. His aim is to show that the political domain must have a certain structure, like a language-game or a practical-discursive context with its own rules, a structure that neither requires nor is capable of justification on supra-political grounds. His main task is to define the liberal-political language-game, to draw a distinction between that game and culture, tradition, philosophy, etc.; not to justify, but *analytically* to clarify its rules, and then *therapeutically* to prevent philosophy from obscuring them by trying to "ground" them in something outside the political sphere.

But contextualism has two related weaknesses, which are, in the political sphere, devastating. First, let us accept that there is a realm of existence that has its own distinct nature and its own "freestanding" rules; call it "politics." How are we to distinguish this realm? How are we to adjudicate differences of interpretation of it that draw its boundaries and rules differently? A contextualist view must eschew the use of supra-contextual points of reference – in this case, anthropology, social history, etc. What is Rawls' answer to the contemporary non-neutralist liberal theorists who make a substantive theory of the Good intrinsic to liberalism? Rawls makes no attempt to critique such views; he merely proposes methodological strictures which would undercut them. He is right not to attempt any critique of alternative political theories on non-methodological grounds, for he could give no substantive justification of his critique. That inability is the mark of his contextualism.[54]

Second, how are we to determine the proper relationship between this freestanding realm of politics and other spheres of social life? We are not free to avoid this question, and Rawls does not want us to avoid it. For to avoid it would mean two things. First, we would be entirely free to assign no value or importance to the political realm whatsoever. Suppose I invent a game, make up rules, and write a series of books about it. As long as I am consistent, no one can argue with my construction on grounds of truth. But neither does anyone have to pay attention, to take my writings into account, or simply, *to play my game at all*. The comparative judgment of the value of a game can only be made from the outside. But this would, in the present case, mean taking a supra-political view of politics. Second, and particularly in the case of politics, a purely contextual construction would have no right to dictate that other contexts or realms are to be determined and controlled by that constructed realm. My explanation of my game, and my refutation of those who understand my game differently, cannot include a claim that the outcome of the playing of my game ought to determine the outcomes of *other* games, e.g. if I were to say that whoever is best at playing my game ought to be the wealthiest, or most respected, person in society.

But of course, it is precisely the nature of politics, its function and value, to deliberate the rules of, to legislate to, social life. In short, *politics rules*. As soon as the game of politics is recognized to rule other contexts, the contextualist understanding of politics is *dead*. For we can legitimately ask – indeed, we must ask – Why should our social lives be largely determined by rules that are the product of a discussion constituted as Rawls has described? Why ought "reasonableness" be the sole value that governs that which governs – that is, politics? The only way to deny the legitimacy of such a question would be to make politics irrelevant to all of social life; such is the price of a consistent contextualism. But then, of course, the thing thereby theorized *would not be what we normally understand as "politics" at all*. It would instead truly be a construction that had for some reason borrowed an appellation from normal usage – "politics" – but whose meaning or place in social life would not be that of politics. It would be a game that was called "baseball," but was in fact played on a rectangular field with an oblong ball. It would no longer play the role that politics plays in our "form of life," to use another Wittgensteinian figure.

We do, of course, make contextual judgments. When I need to decide which team has won a baseball game I need only look at the score, not at the players' moral character, personal needs, etc. But when I must decide whether or not to attend the game, or to play in it, or to seek a different kind of game; or when the rules of the game are being chosen or modified (to amplify excitement, entertainment, etc.); or in special cases when society must decide whether to permit a game at all (like cock fighting) – in these and other cases, decisions about the game cannot be made solely on criteria *internal* to the game. Likewise, the decisions as to whether to care about politics, to engage in political activity, to value and listen to what politicians say, to modify the rules according to which politics works, to enforce political results on citizens, to obey such results, all necessarily depend on supra-political ends. Hence the rigid distinction of the political from the non-political is self-defeating.

Of course, Rawls' contextualism is in reality determined by ends that transcend it. It is an attempt to devise a purely contextual description of politics as a way of avoiding philosophical and political problems endemic to modern liberal societies while maintaining certain values that have driven the liberal tradition for centuries, in particular, equality and liberty. But in this sense *Political Liberalism* is a peculiar sort of offspring whose claim to title rests on a denial of its own parentage, an indifference to the supra-political doctrines liberalism has employed in the past.

Now, one can rightfully say that the decontextualization of politics is not Rawls' invention, but has always been part of the liberal tradition itself. Liberalism has always sought to make some kind of distinction between the private and the public, the metaphysical and the political, in order to grant tolerance and liberty. True enough. But this liberal distinction was always, and must be, set *within a comprehensive picture*. All such distinctions must be seen as themselves contextualized, that is, conceived and justified against a background view or set of views. As such, in liberal theory the private–public distinction was generally understood to be more permeable than Rawls allows. Rawls has tried to push the distinction of private and political to an extreme that would obliterate the very context that gave meaning to the liberal attempt to distinguish them. The paradoxes and problems of his scheme are inherent in the neutralism it epitomizes.

The Neutrality Pretext

There are three levels of criticism that can be leveled at neutrality *per se*, libertarian or egalitarian. The first is that proceduralist liberalism is not and cannot be neutral regarding all lifestyles or worldviews. As commentators have noted, this is true. Worldviews that would seek to enlist law, politics, and government to promote themselves or the interests of their holders are disadvantaged by neutralism. In the simplest case, liberalism is intolerant of intolerance. This will not cause liberals to lose sleep, but it gives pause to anyone who recognizes that perhaps some things, beyond intolerance itself, ought not be tolerated. At the least, many social members think there are such things, and neutralism puts their views and preferred ways of life at a disadvantage.[55] A corollary to this criticism is the claim that in fact neutralism is meant to promote a particular, modern Western worldview in which some values, like liberty negatively and voluntaristically understood, flourish at the expense of others.

Proceduralists may respond by declaring this critique true but trivial. They may admit that strict neutrality is conceptually impossible. But then, if there really is no such thing as neutralism, there is no point in criticizing liberals for holding that view! Critics of neutralism are thus objecting to an unfortunate *self-description* of proceduralism, rather than to the philosophy and social policies that go under the label. However, the critique of neutralism is not merely a criticism of the accuracy of a self-description. It is the criticism of a description that serves a *normative policy*. Substantive neutrality is in fact used in practice to justify certain policies and defeat others. No political order can be truly neutralist, but an order that seeks substantive or effective neutrality behaves differently than one that does not. And it does so in order to embody as much neutrality as possible, regarding not only religion, but varieties of lifestyles and private practices, philosophical and spiritual conceptions of the meaning of life, etc.

At any rate, merely denying that neutrality is really neutral, while true, does not go very far. The upshot of this first criticism is to ask the neutralist liberal to come clean and announce that he or she seeks neutrality only with respect to *some* notions of the Good, and to say what those are. We might indeed generate a liberal list of ideas of the Good and their contraries toward which government ought to be neutral; government ought to be neutral with respect to Roman Catholicism, sexual orientation, African-American heritage, etc. To establish a complete list of such particulars would require that every item on the list be debated, an admittedly daunting prospect. But trying to avoid that debate by declaring the intention to conduct a public political life in which nobody seeks politically to promote or discourage any notions of the Good, hence ways of life, is utterly implausible. It only becomes plausible when in fact *ad hoc* exceptions are made, and the range of proposed goods is tacitly narrowed. In other words, what is called "neutrality" is in fact neutrality only with respect to a tacit list of ideas of the Good that are controversial in contemporary liberal society.

Second, many critics charge that neutralism or proceduralism is corrosive of various social goods, usually but not exclusively those most of concern to conservatives, communitarians, and civic republicans. These include a potentially long list: patriotism, family, religious belief, community, localism, responsibility, self-sacrifice, etc. If, as these critics argue, neutralist liberal societies contain within themselves powerful forces promoting individualism and secularism, then the goods of community, tradition, and religion are thereby negatively affected. Certainly it would be historically ignorant to lay all the chronic social problems of the American scene at the feet of liberalism or any political view. Nevertheless, along with the development of other social forces, ascendant liberalism ought to admit its powerful role in generating problems, and not merely take credit for its successes. When the holist looks at neutralism in the context of contemporary American society, he or she sees a political view that permits and encourages the development of a form of social, economic, and cultural life in which it is not only possible but clearly more rational to choose primarily self-interested, economically independent, secular, de-localized, individualistic lifestyles. As Sandel has pointed out, liberalism's equality and neutrality systematically disadvantage those who choose to lead lifestyles of dependency, most prominently, those who choose to work in unpaid child care.[56] It is arguable that, given the current rate of divorce, a woman (or a man) who feels the desire to be a full-time parent of small children would be irrational to do so. The rewards of our liberal society almost always lie in the cutting of ties, or the anticipation of the cutting of ties. Neutralism creates an arena of individual liberty in which it is a disadvantage to choose community, connection, and commitment.

Here the neutralist has a characteristic retort. It is that, as neutral, he or she promotes neither individualism nor community, and permits the endorsement of "community"-oriented values as well as their rejection. Neutralism denies responsibility for the secular-individualist-progressivist worldview. In so far as there is a "liberal worldview," while it may indeed have grown up around liberal neutrality like barnacles on a pier, that worldview is simply how free people come to see the world on their own accord.

At this point a third critique, which is a clever version of the second, springs up. It argues that neutralism is corrosive even of the goods it presumably wishes to maximize, that is, democratic participation, autonomy, liberty, toleration, independence, progress, etc. Here is where communitarianism has its strongest innings. For it is impossible to deny that the self is a social product requiring intensive familial and communal action. Just as egalitarians argue against libertarians that liberty has economic prerequisites, communitarians can argue against both egalitarian and libertarian proceduralists that liberty has social and cultural prerequisites. If proceduralist liberalism serves to undermine the processes by which families and communities form the kinds of selves that are capable of self-government, individual self-determination, responsibility, and practical rationality, then we approach the unintended but logically plausible vision of a society in which large numbers of people live without legal-governmental coercion, hence with negative liberty, but without anything we could recognize positively as freedom.

Here neutralism responds with a more sophisticated version of its earlier disclaimer. Following Rawls, it claims to be a merely political doctrine, a view about the shape and limits of political life and discussion which makes no claims either way about the social structures necessary to liberty, rationality, etc. It does not try to deny, as a matter of psycho-sociological fact, the "formative" process required to construct modern liberal individuals. Nor does it affirm responsibility for such formation. Its concern is with the structure of political discourse. What society must or must not be like in order to have such a politics is not its business.

By this point it becomes apparent that implicated in this debate is a *metapolitical* difference between neutralist liberals and their critics. Liberals of most stripes accept a strong distinction between the political and the non-political. Famously the liberal political-legal-governmental sphere is to be unconcerned with religious doctrines, hence permit them to vary without restriction. But neutralism extends this distinction; it insists on the separation of the political from the *cultural*, the largely inherited domain of value-laden interpretive practices and comprehensive outlooks which individuals carry with them as "private" persons. In my terms, it is deeply anti-holist.

The dialectical conundrum here is obvious. The anti-neutralist blames neutralist liberalism for certain social evils. The liberal denies the blame, citing a definitional restriction that liberalism is purely a political doctrine, with no further agenda. Liberalism's conception of the political is such that it can avoid forms of criticism that cite supra-political realities as reasons for rejecting liberalism. A sophisticated neutralism, as in the later Rawls, claims to be a theory of something – politics – and defines that something in such a way that counter-evidence and complaints against the theory are claimed to concern non-political phenomena. It is thus theoretically *self-immunizing*. It draws the limits on politics so narrowly that any complaint against it is claimed not to be a complaint about politics at all, but about social, economic, cultural, or personal problems, and hence irrelevant.

But this self-understanding on the part of neutralism is not entirely frank. While the positive claims of neutralism may indeed make no reference to comprehensive doctrines, the justification of those claims must. That is, why on Earth accept neutralism or liberalism for that matter? The motivation is clear and plausible: to reduce coercion, respect rights, maximize liberty, avoid conflict, promote prosperity, permit self-expression, etc. These are social, moral, cultural, economic, and psychological aims. As argued above, the justification of a context must be supra-contextual. If liberalism seeks to exist in a comprehensive vacuum, then it will have abandoned the comprehensive atmosphere in which its valorization and justification could breathe.

Liberalism in fact cannot live without such air, either in theory or in practice. Yael Tamir points out that anti-nationalist forms of liberalism surreptitiously lean on nationalism to give an account of membership and mutual obligation that their purely legal-political purview could never provide. Liberal states expect and depend on persons born within it to become loyal citizens, and these citizens are granted the political right to exclude other potential members.[57] This is analogous to Karl Polanyi's argument that the extension of market self-regulation to money is self-undermining. For as soon as nations in the 1930s went off the gold standard and endorsed "token money," they implicitly recognized that money is a political, state-issued sign, not a commodity (or backed by a commodity, gold) subject to the market. Likewise, neutralist liberalism implicitly depends on a socio-cultural background that it may corrode, while denying any responsibility for it.

The rigid distinction of the political and non-political permits neutralist theory to ignore the later, to keep the costs of liberal policies *off the books*. The conditions of modern life make this indifference more problematic than it once might have been. For contemporary society has witnessed the concentration of public resources in government and the shrinking of the public non-governmental, non-corporate resources by which civil community can act to solve its problems. Indeed, community itself has arguably shrunk. Increasingly the problems of the public realm can effectively be addressed by no other institution than government, local and non-local. Yet neutralism wants to deny government's use for any aim tied to a partisan conception of the Good. Properly speaking, the neutralist sin is not, as some communitarians have argued, atomic individualism or fragmentation or moral relativism. Rather it is abstraction, or as Rawls admits, "avoidance." It may be that lady justice rightly dons the blindfold when applying the law in court – although even there the metaphor has its limits – but the citizens, the law's makers and executors, and its political theorists cannot take that comfort. They cannot avoid the curse of sight.

Notes

1 The most prominent exception to putting liberty first in principle is Ronald Dworkin, about whom more later.

2 See Sandel, *Liberalism and the Limits of Justice* (Cambridge: Cambridge University Press, 1998).

3 Edmund Burke, *Reflections on the Revolution in France* (Indianapolis: Hackett, 1987), p. 41.

4 Bruce Ackerman, *Social Justice in the Liberal State* (New Haven: Yale University Press, 1980).

5 Ibid., p. 123.

6 Ibid., p. 149.

7 I must say that if the common mantra for denying all use of corporal punishment – that it teaches the child to be violent – is accepted, it ought also hold for *any* use of authority or physical force in child-rearing. When I grab my son's arm to prevent him running across the street, do I teach him that he too can use his superior physical strength to coerce others? When I insist that he attend school, and I teaching him authoritarianism? Parents *must* do things in teaching their children which they cannot permit the children to do to others; if that is impermissible, then child-rearing is impossible. Of course, the mantra to the contrary notwithstanding, most children have little trouble with this distinction.

8 Ackerman, p. 128. Note that the latter holds in Ackerman's scheme only if the aim of infanticidal parents is merely that they *enjoy* killing. The community

may decide that this enjoyment, absent any other reason, cannot justify killing when, for example, putting up the child for adoption would ameliorate any other inconvenience to parents.

9 Ronald Dworkin, "Liberalism" and "Why Liberals Should Care about Equality," in his *A Matter of Principle* (Cambridge, MA: Harvard University Press, 1985), pp. 181–204 and 205–13.

10 The most careful critique of that role of equality in political theory has been given by Joseph Raz. See his *The Morality of Freedom* (Oxford: Clarendon, 1986).

11 Ronald Dworkin, *Taking Rights Seriously* (Cambridge, MA: Harvard University Press, 1977), chapters 7, 11, and 12.

12 Dworkin, "Why Liberals Should Care about Equality," p. 206.

13 See Charles Taylor, "Cross-Purposes: The Liberal-Communitarian Debate," in Nancy Rosenblum, *Liberalism and the Moral Life* (Cambridge, MA: Harvard University Press, 1989).

14 This would include both cases in which the everyone would agree that the holder of an idiosyncratic notion is penalized and those in which it is an idiosyncratic view of the Good that leads the minority to regard itself as penalized under conditions that the majority, given its own view of the Good, does not regard as disadvantageous for anyone, either itself or the minority. For example, if economic policy makes everyone rich at the cost of abandoning traditional forms of life, a minority loathe to give up tradition is disadvantaged under their notion of the Good, but under the majority's notion, which might be indifferent to cultural tradition, they are being equally advantaged.

15 Dworkin, "Liberalism," p. 202

16 Thomas Nagel, *Equality and Partiality* (New York: Oxford University Press, 1991), pp. 99ff.

17 Ibid., p. 118.

18 Not to mention the role of bad luck. It cannot be the fundamental moral obligation of the polity to outlaw bad luck. Not all important determinants of whether a life is a success or not are subject to control. Nagel rightly admits the importance of luck, but then excludes it from consideration.

19 Michael Walzer, *Spheres of Justice: A Defense of Pluralism and Equality.*

20 Walzer in effect makes this argument in his *Thick and Thin: Moral Argument at Home and Abroad* (Notre Dame: University of Notre Dame, 1994).

21 John Rawls, *Political Liberalism* (New York: Columbia, 1993). The second, 1996 edition, also by Columbia, is identical to the first edition except for two additions: a second Introduction, and a new final chapter, "Reply to Habermas." In my notes I will cite the 1996 edition – indicated by the year in parentheses – only when the passage referenced comes from those additions.

22 Rawls, *Political Liberalism* (1996), p. xxxix.

23 Ibid., p. xlvii.

24 Ibid., p. xliii.

25 John Rawls, "The Idea of Public Reason Revisited," *University of Chicago Law Review*, Summer 1997 (64: 765–87), p. 800.

26 Rawls, *Political Liberalism*, p. 145ff.

27 Rawls, "The Idea of Public Reason Revisited," p. 767.
28 Rawls, *Political Liberalism*, p. xliii, n. 7. In my criticism I will leave aside Rawls' unfortunate habit of defining "the social" and "the political" in terms of themselves. The referenced quote instances the former, and elsewhere he typically writes that "the political" dimension of social life includes, first and foremost, principles that "apply to the basic political and social institutions (the basic structure of society)." ("The Idea of Public Reason Revisited," p. 776).
29 By "culture" he means "the culture of the social, not of the political," *Political Liberalism* (1996), p. 14.
30 Ibid., p. 382, n. 13
31 Rawls, "Idea of Public Reason Revisited," p. 769. Regarding popular referendums Rawls simply says that the questions on which citizens vote directly at the state and local levels are "rarely fundamental questions" (ibid., p. 769). While they may be infrequently "fundamental," this is, I think, a large omission on Rawls' part.
32 A host of problems arise here, among which are the clarity of Rawls' own conception – for example, he sometimes treats the "civil" or "civic" as synonymous with his notion of the "public," and sometimes as outside the realm of public reason – as well as the status of an "ideal" for the liberal public forum that would run afoul of its putatively most basic rule, freedom of speech.
33 E.g. "We hold these truths to be self-evident, that all men are endowed by their Creator with certain unalienable rights . . ."
34 Rawls, *Political Liberalism*, p. 251.
35 Ibid., p. 254.
36 Rawls, *Political Liberalism* (1996), pp. li–lii.
37 Ibid., p. lii, n. 27.
38 Rawls, "The Idea of Public Reason Revisited," pp. 785–6, n. 54.
39 Clearly, I am not accusing Rawls of smuggling in truth considerations. It is rather that, as in Peirce, the – here "political" – validity of statements can be assured by subsequent events.
40 Rawls, *Political Liberalism*, p. 243, n. 32.
41 Rawls, *Political Liberalism* (1996), p. lv, n. 31.
42 Ibid., p. lvi, n. 32. Although Rawls does not judge whether the argument can be successful. It doesn't matter, he says, for it is in the "form" of public reason.
43 Ibid., p. liii.
44 Ibid., p. lv.
45 Rawls, "The Idea of Public Reason Revisited," p. 770.
46 The example is Justus Buchler's.
47 See Michael Walzer's *Thick and Thin: Moral Argument at Home and Abroad* (Notre Dame: Notre Dame University, 1994), chapter two. This is based in his earlier *Spheres of Justice: A Defense of Pluralism and Equality*, in which Walzer's basic claim is that the principles of the just distribution of some good must presuppose the social and cultural meaning of that good. Rawls of course disagrees; he has held that only a "thin" theory of the Good, which lists those goods everyone allegedly must want whatever else they want. Here I can only say that it

is not clear that a distributive justice scheme, such as Rawls himself wants to defend, can operate purely on the agnostic grounds he now suggests.

48   Rawls, "The Idea of Public Reason Revisited," pp. 788–90.

49   Ibid., p. 777.

50   Emotivism held that the meaning of any moral utterance is merely an expression of feeling or emotion, such that, for example, "Murder is wrong" has the same logical force as "I find murder repellant."

51   Wittgenstein ended his first book with the view that, "The correct method in philosophy would really be the following: to say nothing except what can be said, i.e. propositions of natural science . . . and then, whenever someone else wanted to say something metaphysical, to demonstrate to him that he had failed to give a meaning to certain signs in his propositions. . . . What we cannot speak about we must pass over in silence." Ludwig Wittgenstein, *Tractatus Logico-Philosophicus*, trans. D. F. Pears and B. F. McGuinness (London: Routledge and Kegan Paul, 1961), paragraphs 6.53 and 7.

52   Rawls, *Political Liberalism*, p. 121, n. 26.

53   That is, inspired by Wittgenstein's late philosophy. A connection to Wittgenstein is also indicated by Rawls' statements of gratitude to his former Harvard colleague, the late Burton Dreben, one of the foremost interpreters of Wittgenstein. No one familiar with Dreben's profound interpretation of Wittgenstein could fail to see his influence in *Political Liberalism*.

54   I should add that Wittgenstein was intensely aware that the philosophical *assertion* of contextualism would be a contradiction. See my *The Ends of Philosophy* (Oxford: Blackwell, 2002), chapter six.

55   As Brian Barry claimed in "How Not to Defend Liberal Institutions," in R. Bruce Douglass et al., *Liberalism and the Good* (New York: Routledge, 1990).

56   See Sandel, *Democracy's Discontents: American in Search of a Public Philosophy*, pp. 111–15. A similar point, although without the antiliberal conclusion, is made by Susan Moller Okin in her *Justice, Gender, and the Family* (New York: Basic Books, 1989).

57   Yael Tamir, *Liberal Nationalism* (Princeton: Princeton University Press, 1993), ch. 6.

3

Beyond Neutralism

In the past two decades some political theorists have rejected neutralism while nevertheless maintaining most of the policies associated with it.[1] They acknowledge that liberalism has an account of the Good, hence neutralism was mistaken as a self-description. The goods which these "non-neutralists" now acknowledge were implicit in neutralism itself, and in the historic achievements of liberalism. These writers are in effect *affirmative*, rather than neutral, liberals. Their views can be divided into three types, according to the three chief ends found in liberalism, two political and one socio-economic.

The most obvious candidate for a substantive end for liberalism is *individualism* or *individual liberty*. One can argue whether negative liberty in fact counts as a substantive good or goal, but affirmative liberals are free to employ a positive notion of liberty, like autonomy. There are also ends which are in effect collective names for a society of autonomy or individualism: pluralism or diversity. These are natural allies of individualism, self-expression, and autonomy.[2] The second candidate for the chief end of liberalism is *self-rule*. Despite the potential conflict of liberalism and democracy, liberalism as we know it always exists in a partnership with democracy, as the term "liberal republicanism" implies. Liberal republicans can make self-rule a central good, as long as it is conceived in ways that make it compatible with individual liberty. So, for example, some theorists emphasize the process of political decision-making in which each member has equal rights and liberties to contribute. Finally, a third good endorsed by affirmative liberals is *progress*, which is necessarily connected to increased material prosperity, although it may include moral progress, reform of institutions, intellectual growth, etc.[3]

In contemporary political theory there are a rich variety of conceptions that embody these three kinds of goals in different ways and with different constraints. Some argue for individual autonomy, or for expressive individualism, or for the maximization of each individual's chance to live an "excellent" life. Some find a form of democracy that is particularly sensitive to liberal demands for procedure, thereby endorsing a "discourse" theory or "deliberative democracy." Others promote a "civic republic" focused on the inculcation of the virtues of citizenship. Some are primarily concerned with a community of moral values, others with a community of mutual recognition.

I will suggest that these attempts to repair neutralist liberalism by non-neutral means are welcome but inadequate. Most are subject to three overlapping biases that are particularly widespread and troublesome in contemporary political theory: a liberal fear and devaluation of democracy; an overly philosophical notion of political virtue; and the apotheosis of the public sphere. The first two tendencies are typically conjoined, resulting in a conception of citizenship that is highly philosophical and anti-democratic. The third gives the public, and especially political, domain virtually transcendent importance, devaluing the "private" life of personal aims, domicile, familial relations, neighborhood, and friendship. But more generally, while affirmative liberals may be literally non-neutralist, they are not non-neutralist enough. Their accounts of the Good are too narrow. For they take as the goods to be endorsed by the liberal polity only "liberal" goods, that is, the political goods of individual liberty and self-rule, plus the socio-economic good of progress. They have taken as the proper ends of the liberal polity the defining features of liberalism itself, *rather than the goods of the society and culture the polity serves* – as if aestheticians believed the only proper subject matter of art were art itself. The ends of politics need not be political. Goods other than individual liberty, self-rule, and progress are legitimate objects of communal promotion, both for intrinsic reasons and because without them the liberal goods are impractical or unintelligible. The liberal goods obtain within the context of those *non-liberal goods*. Still, the affirmative liberal positions I will criticize are in fact fellow travelers of mine; I share their concerns. My aim is to redirect and re-focus their critique of proceduralist liberalism.

Individuality and Freedom

Three different forms of affirmative liberalism promoting the good of individuality can be seen in the work of George Kateb, whose individualism emphasizes self-expression, Martha Nussbaum, for whom liberalism seeks to promote each individual's chance of living an excellent life, and Joseph Raz, for whom autonomy is the positively conceived end of liberalism.

For Kateb liberalism exists to maximize the chances for individual self-expression and pursuit of a distinctive way of life.[4] He correctly identifies a strain of the Romantic, nineteenth century liberal tradition, particularly in the work of Emerson and Whitman, that has been powerful in American culture. This is a romanticism that insists on rights-based democratic procedures as the necessary institutional womb from which a truly democratic culture of individualism can be born. Kateb's work is a refreshing exception to the apotheosis of the public realm I will describe. His unique achievement is to recognize the possibility of an "impersonal" and ego-transcending individualism, for him the highest type of the "culture of democratic individuality." Those who pursue individuality to its heights, he argues, discover the beauty in everyone and everything, recognizing the self as a creative project whose inner "infinity" can never be fully known. The ultimate democratic experience is in effect to see that one's self is a *demos*. Thus the journey into the self leads to the discovery of equality and community. Kateb believes that this experience, while realized by the few, is "latent" in every democratic individual.

However, short of this transcendent individualism, regarding the quotidian individuality most evident in democratic society, Kateb leaves the ends of the individual indeterminate. Outside its most mystical heights, Kateb's culture of individuality is virtually without content. That is, individualism under-determines most of what counts as the major decisions in life, personal or political. Logically his individualism certainly does reject slavery and conformity, but on intrinsic grounds any other kind of life could be chosen. In other words, transcendent Romantic individualism suffers from the same problems as any other view which makes individuality or liberty the ultimate end of human society. More problematic, such individualism is inevitably hostile toward convention and thus ordinary life. True, Kateb remarks at one point that "ordinariness becomes troubling only when it is rooted in unreflective conformity."[5] But his characteristic tone is revealed in his fear of "superstition," and derogation of "identification with any role or set of conventions." In the simply "unironical" performances "known as social life" he discovers "grotesque solemnity."[6]

Of course, individual self-expression is one of the things that can give life meaning. It can also take meaning away, as when my attempts at self-discovery lead me to destroy the connections I later discover to have been crucial to my self. Many people, perhaps all, under conditions of freedom will develop the hope or need for self-expression at some times in some respect. But only for the few does that value come to outweigh all others, leading them to burst the bonds of social convention. Most people in liberal societies, no differently than non-liberal societies, want and need to conform and be contained within a stable, socially recognized lifestyle. Liberalism has no business in dissuading persons from such conformity. The Romantic cult of the individual is a respectable but marginal member of the liberal family of ideas, and serves its purpose if it remains as a possibility that some individuals may choose. As Nietzsche wrote regarding "free spirits" like himself, "There actually are things to be said in favor of the exception, provided that it never wants to become the rule."[7] A functioning liberal republic can certainly stand a few mystical individualists, but not too many.

One can say in defense of Kateb's individualism that to promote individual liberty and self-creation is to inhibit forms of coercion so as to allow that some will *choose* convention, dependency, permanent binding relations, etc. What the emphasis on individuality then must mean is that convention, dependency, and permanently binding relations are valuable in so far as they are reflectively, self-consciously chosen. That a person never considers leaving their home, locale, spouse, shows a lack of individual liberty; that she considers it, but *chooses not* to, is consistent with the individualist ideal. Kateb's individualism is thus highly cognitive and reflective. In order to transcend conformity I must know *why* I do what I do. Self-knowledge is the key to individuality.

Can we really accept such a cognitivist, or one feels, philosophically biased view of what makes human lives valuable? Do great humanitarians or morally noble individuals chose their values, or rather feel compelled to honor a moral call they have never questioned? Could Mother Teresa have thematized and criticized her deepest moral presuppositions, and their contraries, and consciously affirmed the first in a fair contest of the two? If she was unable to do so, was her life less admirable? On the contrary, was it a condition of her moral greatness that she was *unable* critically to question her commitments? There are both kinds of persons in the world – those whose virtuous action is a kind of conscious choice, and those whose virtuous action is the unreflective application of a compulsory moral sense resulting from childhood training, innate disposition, or we know not what – but I think there are far more of the later. Is self-reflective choice even the necessary condition for a high level *individuality*, let alone moral greatness? Are idiosyncratic, creative, iconoclasts typically the most self-aware persons, or are they more often driven by impulses and an inner sensibility they themselves do not understand? It is by no means clear that self-consciousness is the key to either goodness or individuality.

Martha Nussbaum's account of "Aristotelian" liberalism makes the aim of civil life the development of the background conditions in which individuals may fulfill their potentialities.[8] Her liberalism is openly anthropological; it attempts to describe the universal features of an excellent human life, a "thick but vague" account of the Good. She rightly draws the conclusion that if we are to avoid neutrality, yet remain liberal, we must go about the difficult task of spelling out the liberal goods. Her turn to world literature, rather than rational choice theory and economics, as the place to find such universal goods is insightful.

Nussbaum's is first of all an individualist account. While she endorses many goods, all are individual goods. Even though some of these goods involve others, they remain possessions of individuals. Presumably this is part of what makes her account an Aristotelian "liberalism." The *telos* of liberal society is for Nussbaum the provision of a context that encourages excellent individual lives. One may say she has one meta-good, self-actualization, the achievement of such a life. Government is to insure that the resources necessary to this achievement are available to each individual.

Her individualism is also reflected in the goods included and those left out. If we are to hazard an account of the Good based on cultural history and anthropology, then it is a bit odd to leave off the list, as she does, *family*, and in particular, *reproduction*, as well as *religion*. These are at least as common and as central to cultural descriptions of the good life as some of her listed goods; world mythology hardly suggests otherwise. One suspects that to include family and religion is intolerable for Nussbaum for reasons of liberal toleration; presumably she wants to privilege neither heterosexuality nor theism.[9] Nevertheless, if one is going for the dominant goods in most human cultures in history then child-rearing, blood relations generally, and religion certainly loom at least as large as her seventh good: "Being able to live with concern for and in relation to animals, plants, and the world of nature."

My objection is a twofold complaint against, first, her particular list of goods, and second, the underlying notion that the human good is the *individual* good, the achievement of self-actualization or individual life-paths. In each case she has remained a liberal, which was no doubt her intention. But the preservation of the society and its historical institutions, which is the actual context of individual life-paths, is at least as important as her individual goods. Now, one could say that, to promote individual fulfillment is, if that fulfillment actually does require historical institutions, to promote the latter as necessary means. That is, Nussbaum's individualism might favor the historical institutions that I favor; it would be up to the individuals. But the point is that for Nussbaum the value of objects, institutions, and traditions is only that which individuals grant. Whereas, I would say, individuals only know what to grant through the transmission to them of a social and cultural tradition, whose institutions need to be supported *a priori*, so to speak, with respect to individuals.

It so happens that there is an alternative contemporary political theory which, while it makes autonomy the highest liberal good, denies neutralism, the priority of rights, and accepts to some extent a communitarian anthropology. For these reasons Joseph Raz's account of liberalism in his very sophisticated *The Morality of Freedom* might seem to avoid many of the criticisms made here. This impression would be, up to a point, correct. Raz first of all denies that "rights" can be the basis of liberalism. Second, he accepts that a non-neutralist or perfectionist account of autonomy is the only plausible notion of liberty. Third, he explicitly denies individualism, that individuals are the sole bearers of value.

Nevertheless, by making autonomy the core liberal commitment Raz is left with two choices: either liberalism is a name for the view that autonomy is *an* essential component of the human good, so that political decisions must take autonomy and the autonomously chosen nature of other goods into consideration; or liberalism makes autonomy *the ultimate* human good that can be recognized politically, hence autonomy trumps all other considerations. Even granted his openness to a non-individualist conception of autonomy, the latter would again make individual liberty the ultimate good. If the former is the case, then this indeed is a kind of liberalism that is generally *compatible* with what I will later call holism, although by itself it is incomplete in that it does not specify other goods. But in other ways Raz continues to put autonomy first. His notion of a life as one's "free creation" is not essential to liberal republicanism, nor is it, as I will argue later, plausible.[10] Raz correctly admits the possibility of limiting that autonomy where its results are morally bad, thereby accepting a non-coercive perfectionism, but still leaves autonomy as the decisive political value.[11]

Discourse, Deliberation, and Recognition

The ideal of political participation is currently promoted by different colors on the political spectrum. Those who emphasize the power of popular will used to be dubbed "participatory democrats," associated with left in the 1960s and '70s. The past two decades have witnessed the development of a more procedural version of this view focused on discourse and deliberation, on the nature of the self-ruling community's internal communication practices. This approach has been especially associated with the work of Jürgen Habermas. A third view, civic republicanism, the tradition of ancient political liberty and the virtues of citizenship, is today experiencing a revival. The three views share the ultimate value of self-rule, but with distinctive accents. The first is decidedly democratic, perhaps even populist; its adherents read their liberalism through their democracy. The second are liberals who are able to define liberalism through communication practices, hence a procedural version of democracy. The third emphasizes the need to educate individuals to be citizens, the inculcation of civic virtues, which presumes communal intervention into individual life, hence is arguably more "conservative." We will turn to populism and civic republicanism in later sections; for the moment, discourse is our subject.

Jürgen Habermas is the father of contemporary accounts of discursive and deliberative liberalism. Habermas has always been concerned to find a way out of the apparent irrationality of all norms, the fear that in late modern society a purely logical and instrumental conception of rationality would become ubiquitous, to which both Max Weber and the German Frankfurt School theorists Max Horkheimer and Theodor Adorno had succumbed. His aim was to preserve the normative possibilities of "emancipatory" reason. Inspired partly by American pragmatism, Habermas claimed that discursive communication, in which all people engage at least part of the time, reveals an intrinsically normative character. Participants necessarily presuppose the distinction of rightness from power, the freedom of participants to speak, the willingness and ability to accept superior reasons, etc. The basic insight is that rationality, freedom, and morality are indeed bound together as Kant claimed, but the activity in which they are so bound is the intersubjective practice of "communication oriented to achieving consensus," or discourse. Normative rationality is intrinsically social, but not conventional. In his *Theory of Communicative Action* (1981 in German) Habermas presented a critical theory of contemporary society which argued that modernization has led to the "colonization" of citizens' communicative rationality by the instrumental rationality of money-and-power bureaucracies.[12] Later, Habermas sought to fashion a "discourse ethics," a rational criterion for ethical decision-making taken from the normative structures of discourse. The aim of discourse ethics, developed not only by Habermas but by Thomas McCarthy, Seyla Benhabib, and others, is first of all to justify the rationality of moral claims, versus naturalism (which denies that moral norms transcend natural processes) and emotivism (which denies the cognitive status of moral claims). Such rationality consists in arguments to show that a proposed norm could be accepted by all those affected by the norm (could obey "principle U" or universalizability).

This principle is an unavoidable, pragmatic-transcendental presupposition of rational discussions oriented toward achieving agreement or consensus; participants must presuppose it. The discourse constraint (principle D) then holds that only those norms are valid to which all concerned could agree as participants in a practical discourse.[13]

In a later essay, Habermas claims that the discourse model stands between the liberal conception of democracy as insuring individual rights to bargain for interests and the republican model of democracy as the expression of a community of substantive morality.[14] Whereas liberalism makes discourse the legitimation of political power, and republicanism sees discourse as the constitution of society, for Habermas discourse alone can make power moral. Habermas criticizes the republican view for its reliance on *presence* – most famously in Rousseau's direct democracy of the general will – and *action* – Habermas insists that "only the administrative system itself can 'act'." He argues that the discourse conception alone yields a "decentered" conception of politics, permitting a variety of "public spheres" for the rationalization and criticism of social structures. He writes:

> deliberative politics remains a component of a complex society . . . the discourse-theoretic reading of democracy has a point of contact with a detached sociological approach that considers the political system neither the peak nor the center, nor even the formative model of society in general, but just one action system among others.[15]

Benhabib has clarified the discourse model in interesting ways.[16] She portrays it as a joint answer to the question of democratic legitimacy and the rationality of ethical decisions, acknowledging that questions of economic welfare and collective identity are another matter. Legitimacy and rationality of the polity's decisions are attained "if and only if" what is called the "common interest of all . . . results from processes of collective deliberation conducted rationally and fairly among free and equal individuals."[17] She rightly rejects the "methodological fiction of an individual with an ordered set of coherent preferences." Importantly, she admits that the conditions of deliberative democracy "under-determine" practical rationality. Thus the majoritarian opinion has a merely "presumptive claim to being rational until shown to be otherwise."[18] She acknowledges that the conviction that the results of open, reciprocal deliberation will be more legitimate and rational than other decision-making methods (e.g. the practice of leaving discourse to "experts," especially lawyers) is a "wager."[19] Like Habermas, rather than conceiving of discourse as a single all-inclusive forum she correctly regards it as a name for what occurs across an "interlocking net of . . . multiple forms of association . . . a medium of loosely associated, multiple foci of opinion-formation . . ."[20] This deliberative model, *contra* Rawls, puts the public sphere *in* civil society. Benhabib accepts, with Kenneth Baynes, that the "normative constraints on discourses" are subject to "recursive validation" within discourse: nothing is *a priori* off the table. To the liberal fear that discourse may overturn individual liberties, she writes that the normative rules of the game (of discourse) can be contested within the game, but only "insofar as one first accepts to abide by them and play the game at all."[21]

Amy Gutmann has offered a related approach, called "deliberative democracy." With Dennis Thompson she proposes that democratic handling of deep and controversial moral problems, absent moral foundationalism, need not abandon the hope of a morally valid resolution.[22] Neither a proceduralist nor a neutralist refusal to employ substantive moral views, nor a constitutional establishment of constraining values or rules that are off the political table, is necessary. Once basic liberty and basic opportunity for every member is accepted, and the values governing democratic deliberation – reciprocity, publicity, and accountability – are in place, citizens can bring their full moral views into the public arena and come to respectful provisional decisions regarding their moral disagreements that are more than a *modus vivendi*. There is much to admire in the relative evenhandedness and inclusiveness of Gutmann's and Thompson's discussions of a wide variety of contemporary moral dilemmas. They consistently admit the moral downside of the views they advocate; a rare virtue in political debate. The need for "respectful accommodation" is undeniable for any politics in a civil society. They correctly insist that liberal democracy cannot be neutralist. It must promote "substantive" moral principles.

One of these, Benhabib points out, is the moral commitment to "egalitarian reciprocity."[23] It is arguable that egalitarian reciprocity, as embodied in communicative action, exists in all human societies in some "isonomic" social contexts in which participants understand themselves as equals (e.g. peasants chatting on the way to town). The argument would then be that such reciprocity becomes the norm of social relations generally, as well as the systematic basis for political authority, only in modern liberal democracy. In this sense, as Dewey had claimed, liberal democracy is the actualization of a form of life latent in earlier hierarchical forms of social life. It is the shift of egalitarian communication from local, non-official, non-political venues in pre-liberal societies to the center of the social and political stage.

We may mention here a related notion of community: the idea of a community constituted by *mutual recognition*. Its source is Hegel. Previewed by the famous master-slave dialectic of his early *Phenomenology of Spirit*, in the third and final volume of his Encyclopedia, the *Philosophy of Mind*, Hegel conceives of the achievement of mutual recognition as a necessary step in gaining self-consciousness. Universal self-consciousness is achieved "in the shape of reciprocity," whereby each individual in the formerly unequal relation of master and slave now becomes aware of its own freedom by setting aside its own "unequal particularity," seeing itself in the other, and knowing the other likewise sees itself in oneself.[24] Mutual recognition delivers community.[25] The substance of all ethical life, whether in the form of family, civil society, state, friendship, love, etc., lies in this reciprocity. The urge for recognition, one might say, is the democratic or egalitarian version of Machiavellian glory, the secular political goal *par excellence*. Yet it holds out the promise of an egalitarian community of individuals, where the individuality of each is not merely permitted but recognized, without regard to social hierarchy. The liberal democratic recognition of each is the egalitarian version of the recognition sought by the aristocratic political actor.

The discourse, deliberative and recognitive viewpoints exhibit a variety of merits. But they also employ a common set of presuppositions that skew their accounts of civic life. First, they make moral–political life cognitive or reflective and rational; it is a matter of deliberation and reflection. Second, their egalitarianism requires that differential obligations, identity dependent on role, kinship, and station, what Nagel calls "partiality," must be secondary.[26] Third, the ethical–political event is understood as *presence*, actual interaction, in which the proximity to an other makes me present to myself. It is this powerful notion of ethics and politics as an *authentic meeting*, a rendezvous of consciousnesses, that has had the most lasting impact. It implies, as Charles Taylor points out, a "communitarian" conception of the self as formed through interaction.[27] Fourth and last, the discourse and deliberative views make *talking* the essence of civic relatedness.

Benhabib's cautions to the contrary notwithstanding, there is a tendency among the discourse theorists, out of a German idealist inheritance, to make "rationality" and "rightness" synonyms, such that justifying the *rationality* of a group decision is tantamount to justifying that it is the *right* decision. Now, rationality for Habermas means, in this context, communicative rationality, and this means *reason-giving*. But how to arbitrate what counts as a reason? The sensible response would be to accept that the arbitration of what counts as a reason can only occur within discourse itself. Let us presume that the discourse theory accepts this view. But reasons stop somewhere. How, on what basis, can discourse at any moment endorse a standard of rationality by which one proposed argument is judged more rational than another?

Benhabib, we have seen, explicitly denies that any issue, including the procedural rules of the political discussion, are off the table *for* that discussion. She only stipulates that any anti-liberal view must present itself in that forum according to its rules. But is that fact necessarily transformative for the anti-liberal views? Certainly such groups can enter the forum in good liberal form, then liberally express views whose aim is to dismantle the liberal forum; the mere fact that the expression must take a liberal procedural form does not dictate liberal content. This was precisely the situation of Weimar Germany, in which National Socialists self-consciously made use of liberal freedoms they then eliminated upon gaining power. And if Benhabib means by the procedural rules of the forum the discourse ethical principles, according to which proposals can only be made if they "could" be accepted by all members, then we are back to Rawls, and the problem of how "thickly" to conceive those members. For, what does it mean to say that all participants "could" agree? This "could" would be wholly indeterminate except for the notion of rationality: people must be able *rationally* to agree. Here we run into the same problem we found in Rawls, namely, the ambiguity of what "rationally" could be expected to be "public" grounds for group, political decisions, versus what must remain private. If actual consensus were the only way to show possible consensus, then we would be in trouble, because the chances of unanimity among "all those affected" on important political issues is nil. Discourse theorists know this, which is why the subjunctive "could" is used. We are thereby returned to the necessity of a thick conception of the person in order to give this rational "could" force. But this would threaten the allegedly non-partisan nature of the appeal to discursive procedure.

Like Rawls, Gutmann and Thompson deny that any "comprehensive" moral views have a place in deliberation.[28] Fundamentalism, which Gutmann elsewhere takes to imply an assertion of the superiority of one's views without accepting the need for either rational inquiry or public justification, has no legitimate public role. She feels able to argue that democracy ought to fund artwork that violates common non-political values. Democratic humanism "resists the view that parents . . . may invoke their parental rights . . . to prevent exposing their children to ways of life or thinking that challenge their personal commitments."[29] She accepts the Deweyan view that democracy is continuous with education and both are continuous with philosophy; that is, democratic values, the value of education, and the value of philosophical reflection do not conflict. In effect, the "open" deliberation that includes all views turns out "rationally" to come down on the side of certain characteristically liberal egalitarian views, and to exclude comprehensive views that would reject the former.

Benhabib recognizes that Habermas' discourse rules presuppose an Enlightenment conception that all speakers of natural language could in principle be part of a rational discourse. This implies the exclusion of, for example, children.[30] I would press further. "All those affected" by a policy decision is potentially a much larger set than the class of potential contributors to public speech. The latter excludes not only children, the seriously retarded or emotionally disturbed, and those with certain kinds of communication disorders, but also the yet unborn and the already dead. Further, some speak and deliberate better than others, especially if deliberation is understood as reason-giving. Walzer says of democracy, that it implies rule by politicians, hence, the best speakers.[31] Discourse theory strengthens this hold of the most talented in discourse. Now, my point is not the silly one that discourse is illegitimate because insufficiently inclusive. It is rather the sobering one that this most inclusive procedure is still not utterly inclusive. No procedure could be. But that may mean, the procedure *by itself*, without additional constraints, is not yet an adequate picture of a free *polis*.

Most basically, is *talking* the essence of a liberal republican society? Is speech what makes our society liberal? Notwithstanding Habermas' criticism of republicanism, discourse theory shares with most contemporary forms of republicanism the view that it is the political process itself, understand as verbal political interaction, which makes the good *polis* good. Now, there is no doubt that free participation in political life, and political discussion in particular, is a necessary condition of liberalism. But is it the sole or even the chief condition? Are the problems of liberal society to be solved by more and better talking? This would be a rather bald form of political "phonocentrism."[32] I would argue that the tolerant living-adjacently of neighbors in civil society is more definitive, and important, for liberal republicanism than verbal political activity.

What of the apparently wholesome commitments to mutual recognition and egalitarian reciprocity? There is nothing wrong with these notions *per se*. But recognitive community by itself is less a solution than a restatement of the problem. Like the Kantian notion of duty and Mill's harm principle, recognition merely serves to reorient our discussion without deciding the most pressing problems. For the crucial question is: recognition *as what?* The relationship I will call civil certainly implies a kind of mutual recognition, namely, mutual recognition as neighbors or potential neighbors. But it is not recognition of me in my particularity, either my bio-cultural identity – e.g. gender, ethnicity – or my idiosyncratic uniqueness, my particular, historical self. That kind of recognition is too much to ask of the *civitas*. In her recent study of associations Nancy Rosenblum points out that it is part of the function of voluntary associations to fill the identity gap that must exist in the civil association.[33] The later requires a degree of abstraction from, irrelevance of, indifference to, identity in the full sense. A liberal republican *polis* in particular requires that we ignore and be indifferent to a wide rage of personal differences, a willingness to demand not more, but *less* of others![34] Part of the "less" is a willingness *not to require* that fellow citizens respond to what I regard as my full individuality. Civic recognition involves a willingness to forgo greater and more "authentic" demands for recognition. Voluntary associations then serve as the supraintimate way to get recognition while preserving equal citizenship. Thus the politics of recognition is either not enough or too much. Recognition is not all I owe my fellow citizens, and a politics that prizes recognition too highly demands too much of civic life, that is, its demands would, if carried out, turn civic life into something uncivil.

Likewise egalitarian reciprocity *is* an aspect of community.[35] But it shares with discourse and recognitive community the privilege of *presence*, of the *authentic meeting*, as the model for citizenship. This is too much democracy, too much community, too much reciprocity. We are also liberal, and civil, in that large majority of our lives where we are not attending the forum. Civil society presupposes that the *civitas* is as well the arena for private life, the arena that leaves a large chunk of each citizen's existence outside the meeting house. Simply, the achievement of normatively adequate representation, participation, and discursive deliberation, and the enforcement of egalitarian reciprocity, while to some extent a part of a good liberal republican *polis*, are not sufficient to it. Like civic republicanism, the discursive–deliberative perspective makes the political process the glue to hold society together. A good procedure is a good thing, but still not good enough.

Another version of the discursive–deliberative model might seem still closer to the affirmative liberalism I will endorse. Stephen Macedo argues that liberalism depends on the inculcation of certain kinds of virtue and character, and constitutes its own version of community, centered in the process of public political deliberation; liberalism is not compatible with just any mode of life or worldview. He denies that liberalism can tolerate a very strict distinction of public and private morality; "liberalism requires that all private commitments have a certain form and fall with a certain range."[36] The language of "right prior to the good" is more trouble than it is worth. Macedo rightly insists that liberalism does itself no favor by trying to hide this fact, that "reticent liberals" who promote neutralism serve to undermine liberalism's public self-justification. Their reticence is, he interestingly suggests, a strategic silence that hopes to gain popular support by hiding liberalism's real commitments. Macedo carefully works out the virtues and practices that he thinks liberalism needs.

What he offers is essentially a perfectionist form of discourse theory. For Macedo the highest good of liberalism is *public justification*. It is literally an "end in itself."[37] This naturally brings with it a commitment to rational deliberation, public reasonableness, impartiality, tolerance, etc. Such deliberation is like philosophical inquiry in being ever incomplete. Thus, "At the point at which argument is closed, public reason is transformed into public dogma."[38] Echoing Rawls' claim about the judicial attitude proper to citizens, he claims that kind of public deliberation found in Supreme Court decisions is the epitome of liberal political life. The liberal community is a community of constitutional interpreters. Accordingly, he insists that the reflective capacities of the liberal citizen require a "distance" from his or her background, history, and interests. This requirement is not ambiguous: "We must be able to imagine ourselves without the commitment being reflected upon if we are to test it by a public liberal standard of justice; we might be morally obliged to revise or renounce any commitment."[39] He takes the point far enough that he claims it holds for private as well as public morality, since "the liberal virtues are at once political and personal, civic and private."[40] Consequently "liberal citizens ought to adopt a 'judicial' attitude toward their own projects, viewing them impersonally . . ."[41] The rational, free, deliberative self must be capable of, and practiced in, viewing itself and even its ultimate values "impersonally," or as Nagel would say, "impartially."

Macedo valiantly struggles to square this notion with what he admits to be the "situated" nature of the self; he feels the pressure of the communitarian and republican critiques. But it turns out that his situated-ness places no limits on self-reflection and self-revision. The liberal attitude is one of self-criticism and "falsification" or readiness to change fundamental values. He acknowledges that I cannot reflexively pick up my character collectively by, so to speak, its own beard, but insists that no item in my self is immune distributively to thematization and revision – "I cannot choose my character . . . but I can shape and revise it piecemeal."[42] Characteristically, he makes this disconnection from any particular community or commitment the enabling condition for social justice. For we ought to sympathize universally with all fellow citizens regardless of the substance of our choices, through the mere fact of the burden and glory of choice. He even quotes Oakeshott's metaphor about "men sailing a boundless and bottomless sea" without harbor or destination, but then applies it – unlike Oakeshott – to personal rather than political life.[43] Value pluralism and incommensurability, as offered by Berlin, is the "normal" liberal attitude. This inner plurality "allows the reflective self to maintain some distance from any single end.

. . . For liberals, the capacity to choose is more basic than what is chosen. . . . Liberals forsake all-enveloping memberships in particular, homogeneous, local communities. . . ."[44] He admits that this may entail some degree of "alienation," and "superficiality."[45]

This conception of the citizen is both narrow and implausible. To claim that the liberal democratic citizen must be capable of changing any element of his or her self, through critical self-reflection, and maintain "distance" from every commitment, is at best a merely metaphysical posit, devoid of evidence, and impossible to imagine in general practice. It is a conception of the person that might fit a few academics and intellectuals, if that. At the very least one must say that, if the neutralist conception of the self is wanting, this virtue-conception of liberalism mirrors, rather than repairs, its failings.

Philosophy Against Democracy

A point that has emerged repeatedly in the foregoing deserves separate emphasis. The contemporary individualist and deliberative–discursive conceptions of liberal democracy share a bias in favor of critical self-consciousness. They are deeply Socratic. They hold that it is an important value for individuals, acting on their own and participating in the forum, to know themselves, indeed, to be able to critically revise themselves. What lies behind this commonalty is first of all an ideal of *emancipation*, but one conceived as hinging on a critical spirit: freedom is the result of rational self-awareness. Benhabib, echoing Habermas' conception of a "moment of unconditionality" contained in "ideal speech situations," writes that:

> False needs would . . . be viewed as those aspects of inner nature which resist verbalization and articulation. . . . In the communicative ethics model . . . the emphasis in . . . on the dynamic and logic of those blockages – on those silences, evasions, and displacements which point to the presence of an unmastered force in the life of an individual.[46]

"Unmastered force" means something in me that makes me or determines me but which I can neither critically examine nor control. To claim that the presence of such "unmastered forces" undermines autonomy is to presuppose too metaphysical a conception of freedom.

Notice that not only does the discursive–deliberative view make rational speech and public deliberation the essence of the liberal republican experience, granting them dominance over the private and non-political life, but with Kateb's individualism, they curiously make public life sound like what philosophers do for a living. The public realm is identified with the philosophical, since philosophy epitomizes what is alleged to be the essence of public political life, i.e. reason-giving in speech. This makes for some dialectically strange bed-sharing. The work of Leo Strauss is anathema to most liberal theorists. A brilliant and idiosyncratic twentieth century political philosopher, Strauss was an elitist for whom philosophical reflection was the highest of human activities, and one to which the many can never aspire.[47] At one level of his thought he hoped the philosophers would educate the "gentlemen" who would wield influence in a republican society; here philosophy does have an important role to play in the *polis*. But, at another level, the real philosophers privately know that philosophy undermines all beliefs, and so is dangerous to the polity. Thus philosophers in their true, "esoteric" work must be protected from the polity, as the polity must be protected from them.

Certainly the esoteric claim separates Strauss from the liberals under discussion. The liberal view holds with Mill and Dewey and to some extent the Encyclopedists of the Enlightenment, that public culture and politics need philosophy and ought to become philosophical. Their position accords with the stated position of Socrates in *The Republic*: Until the philosophers become rulers, or rulers philosophers, there will be no justice in the city. For the discursive–deliberative theorists, there will be no justice until the citizens, or their various stand-ins, reason with each other like philosophers. But this means that, like Strauss, the individualist and discursive liberals maintain that philosophy is the highest activity, or is essential to what is highest. They are not elitists in that, unlike Strauss, they extend philosophy to all. But, I would argue, the really anti-elitist position would be still different: it would deny that non-philosophical public discourse is inadequate, that the citizen needs the philosopher to train him or her in critical thinking, that, absent such training, popular thought is dangerous.

This Socratic concept of the citizen valorizes a very particular personal style as the ultimate norm for humanity. It is neither necessary nor particularly appropriate for liberal republican society. In contrast, the civil society I will propose accepts with William Galston that "liberal freedom means the right to live unexamined as well as examined lives . . ."[48] And not merely the "right." The philosophical habits of reflection, distance, skepticism regarding loyalty or patriotism or community, and above all, the commitment to the power of reason-giving in speech, are *not* the highest virtues for the political community, even if it is liberal. The public good, like the private good, hangs on all sorts of character traits and values that have been inculcated through a non-philosophical process of training. Talking and reflecting are not the essence of life in a liberal republic, nor are they the essence of the moral life.

Good intentions to the contrary notwithstanding, much of the thought we have examined in this chapter is imbued with a deeply *anti-democratic* spirit. Presumably this is the result of a confluence of a proceduralist liberal fear of majoritarian injustice to minorities and individuals, the remnants of a critical–egalitarian liberal animosity toward average apolitical Americans, and a cultural opposition to local rural and suburban life, which in America are usually not hotbeds of ethnic pluralism or cultural innovation. Consciously or not, this liberal bias is heir to Richard Hofstadter's influential critique of American Populism as jingoist.[49] One finds again and again that references to populism or democracy or localism must immediately be followed by guarantees of minority rights, as if democracy and popular will are unfortunate necessities with no moral standing of their own. There are historical reasons behind this. Neutralist liberalism evolved in the decades following the Holocaust and during the American civil rights movement. Unfortunately, the result is that among many contemporary liberals any mention of local democracy or populism or the concerns of Americans outside cosmopolitan centers immediately raises the prospect of lynching African-Americans and gassing Jews. There has been as well a strong, linked tendency of egalitarian liberals since the 1960s to distance themselves from, in Christopher Lasch's terms, the petty bourgeois and working class values of earlier, union-oriented and class-based liberalism, tied as they typically were to a quasi-Victorian work ethic, as well as family and community loyalty. For many liberals of the late twentieth century these came to be seen as the concomitants of jingoism and racism. Galston has argued that the egalitarians' overweening concern with the least advantaged tempted them to "a systematic effort to discard, as morally arbitrary or irrelevant, precisely those features of human life on which the claims, and the self-respect, of the working class rested."[50]

In the aforementioned affirmative liberal schemes, as in their neutralist counterparts, the mundane projects of most citizens, which are neither projects of self-creation nor philosophical self-questioning nor rational discourse, have little place. Most of what constitutes *living* for most social members has little place. I do not claim these theorists are hostile to ordinary living in these United States. It is simply that the maintenance of civil society – the domicile, family, local institutions, workplace relations – are not issues for them. They may simply assume that such things will take care of themselves, or that the best way to guarantee their survival is to free individuals or the discursive community to secure them. I will suggest that our perspective needs to be grounded instead in an understanding of what it means for citizens to *live together*, lest we design solutions to our perceived crises that tread on the mechanisms that will inevitably subtend, and survive, our solutions.

The deliberative and discourse theorists, seeking to avoid a fully neutral and abstract version of liberalism devoid of any kind of social interaction or community, have devised a version of democratic self-rule that is particularly congenial to proceduralist liberalism. A bit of the appeal of civic republicanism and popular democracy is thereby proceduralized and drained off. In this way democratic *will* is replaced by a commitment to a democratic *reason*. This is a liberalism that is unabashedly political in the positive or affirmative sense of locating the heart of liberal polity in political participation, in the maintenance of institutions of political interaction. But at the same time these are to be controlled, normalized, by reason, whose procedures are then spelled out in various ways. This is why law and especially juridical rationality becomes the *locus classicus* for this kind of political theory.

Now, one might say this is in fact a sensible way to bridge liberal concerns for individuality and limits on the political with the democratic commitment to popular rule. The conservative perspective I am advocating certainly accepts that our political tradition is both liberal and democratic and that these two potentially conflicting strains need to be balanced. But a distinction needs to be drawn here between *balancing* and *synthesizing* liberalism and democracy. To balance the two is to hold them together and negotiate conflicts, trying to avoid giving too much to either side. To synthesize them is to try to find single, integral political form that is both liberal and democratic. This latter is what the discursive-deliberative model seeks to do; it endeavors a democracy which has been strained through a philosophical conception of rationality. In contrast, the perspective I will offer accepts that our liberal republican, North Atlantic political tradition is a holistic amalgam which cannot be fully articulated and rationalized as a set of principles. The attempt to synthesize is too monolithic and idealistic; the attempt to balance, on the other hand, accepts the complexity of our inheritance.

Civic Republicanism, Participatory Democracy, and Popular Equality

Civic republicanism, which has returned in recent decades as a response to the apparent privatism of liberal society, is not new. On the contrary, it is arguably the most ancient concept of a free and non-tyrannical, or civil, politics, and formed the model against which liberalism had to define itself in the eighteenth and early nineteenth centuries. J. G. A. Pocock has shown that liberalism, with its acceptance of a commercial society, representative democracy, and its "modern" notion of liberty as private (in Constant's sense), emerged not effortlessly but through a hard-won battle against not only monarchy but the revived ancient tradition of the republican city-state, which was transmitted from the Italian Renaissance to England and the Americas.[51] Republican thought was a means of finding universal and timeless validity in the particular, local, and historical life of society, a life to which the Christian era, building on ancient philosophical notions, was in theory indifferent. For medieval Christianity, the realm of meaning is not of this world, and may be contacted only by means of grace, devotion, and perhaps contemplation, but not worldly action. Worldly affairs are not the domain in which the meaning of existence is to be hammered out. The vagaries of fortune make all such corruptible in the extreme. Machiavelli and the Italian Renaissance, trading on ancient political notions, then made a startling turn. The worldly life is a stage whose prizes may indeed be cor-ruptible, but the memory of the achievement of those prizes is not. A man's eternal virtue is constituted by the way he meets the test of his time. *Fortuna* was to be, not transcended, but met in the existential, unpredictable space of action – beyond, to an extent, law, custom, and reason. In modern England commerce, property, and material construction took the place of ancient and Renaissance martial and statesmanly activity, forging a bour-geois, hence "liberal," version of freedom. Contemporary civic republican-ism seeks to revive the older, public spirited notion of citizenship, a kinder, gentler form of the martial tradition.

Hannah Arendt is its strongest representative in twentieth-century political theory.[52] Decrying the modern subordination of the political to the economic that is common to bourgeois liberalism and Marxism, Arendt called for a reinvigoration of the ancient conception of political life as the truly human dimension of the active (as opposed to the contemplative) life. Only in public deeds and speeches, which are memorialized by "work" or the creation of enduring meaningful objects, can identity be forged and immortality be attained. To subordinate politics to economics, the "private" realm of mere necessity and metabolic consumption that renders all persons equivalent, is to deprive the active life of any potential for meaning. Arendt certainly did not want a literal return to the ancient model, predi-cated as it was on slave labor and the exclusion of women from the public domain. For her, the self-ruling democratic community of equals, most purely embodied in revolutionary people's councils, captured the ancient republican essence.[53]

Michael Sandel, earlier associated with communitarianism, is best understood as a perfectionist and a republican. He insists that the defense of rights must presuppose a notion of the Good.[54] His historical account of American democracy takes liberalism to task for choosing to respond to the pressures of the growth of capitalism by turning to the power of centralized government as a counterweight, rather than to empowering local civic self-determination.[55] The nineteenth century American concern for economic independence, the hope of becoming a producer and not merely a consumer and employee, has become virtually a lost ideal. Sandel sees neutralism as a political artifact of the attempt to make the federal government the safeguard of each individual, the later conceived, as in late capitalism, on the model of the consumer-client.

Sandel moves further from proceduralism than do most of the aforementioned affirmative liberals. His concern for localism and his advocacy for the community's legitimate interest in the "formative" project, the task of fostering the development of virtues and skills, fly in the face of more procedural conceptions. Typically, a high percentage of citizens – higher than in non-republican societies – must acquire a relatively high degree of self-control and capacity for rational deliberation, willingness to engage in public discussion with others, willingness to submerge self-interest at least part of the time, tolerance of divergent beliefs, a distinction between private and public morality, not to mention knowledge of political procedures and civic history, etc. So, commitment to self-rule and participatory democracy lead to a belief in legitimate state and community interest in the formation of character, education, and the development of certain virtues.

Despite the anti-democratic spirit of much recent theory, a few proponents of democracy remain. The most forceful recent presentation of participatory democracy by a political theorist is Benjamin Barber's *Strong Democracy: Participatory Politics for a New Age*.[56] Barber's neo-populist endorsement of local and neighborhood political action, his insistence on distinguishing the everyday political activity of citizens, which often fails even to be called "politics" by those who make politics their profession (as agents or observers), and his recognition that limits on government and negative liberty are inadequate bases for liberal republican society, are congenial to the position I will advance.

But there are problems too. First, Barber and Sandel seem reticent to admit that the turn to local democratic control will necessarily mean at least a potential loss of individual liberty. Berlin was right, after all, that democracy need not respect individuals. In Sandel's case the endorsement of the formative project makes this all the greater, for such formation is made possible by practices and institutions imposed by some citizens, perhaps the majority, on others. Civic republicanism has to accept that it diminishes voluntarist liberty; participatory democracy must recognize its conflict with individuality. But second and more fundamentally, along with Arendt we can question their valorization of political activity. Is political activity properly the polity's highest value? Are the self-governing community's virtues and practices really what is missing in and needed by the currently liberal society? Is the self-governing community enough of a community?

These thinkers make self-government central in three different ways. First, they claim that active participation is the necessary condition for a free society. This claim is highly plausible. No liberal republicanism can dispense with it. Second, especially for Arendt, self-rule is constitutive of the very meaning of human existence, that is, it is an intrinsically valuable sphere of action. This is utterly resistable. Why ought we accept this arguably Greek premise? Our modern tradition is equally heir to a Judeo-Christian heritage for which politics is intrinsically corrupt. Political action can plausible be *a* meaning of life, but why *the* meaning? Third, political participation provides community otherwise lacking in liberal society. But is political community, a community of political action, the kind of community we are lacking? There are many forms of association possible and actual in our society, some of which may be on the decline and in need of promotion. One can argue that political participation manifests community only if the citizens thereby interacting already share traits, concerns, values, or purposes which fuel, but are not provided by, political action. The turn to political participation puts the cart before the horse. I will argue later that from the perspective of civil society, active self-ruling is a means and not an end. The end of the *civitas* is *living*, not ruling. Democratic or republican politics serves, and does not constitute, civil society.

Related to the participatory democracy of those like Barber, in the last decade the historian Christopher Lasch attempted to rehabilitate American Populism, which he saw as a counter to what he regarded as the unfortunate direction the left took in the second half of the twentieth century.[57] Less concerned with promoting political participation, Lasch's primary aim was to recount the development of rational scrutiny of everyday or "common" life by the growing institutions of capital and government, which "progressively" hand over the management of life to "experts."[58] Misunderstood as anti-feminist, conservative nostalgia for the "traditional" family and social authority on the order of, say, Allan Bloom, Lasch's analysis is in fact closer to that of the Frankfurt School theorists, Adorno and Horkheimer, and not unrelated to that of Foucault.[59] It is in his late book, *The True and Only Heaven: Progress and Its Critics*, that Lasch comes down squarely on the side of Populism and against American Progressivism. The later, he argues, encouraged the substitution of systems of expertise for the competence of the people. Populism was a movement of proprietary democracy, that is, a democratic movement of low-income producers to enable them to better control the economics of their lives. Populists linked democratic activism to work, proprietorship, and its manifold responsibilities. They emphasized producerism and independence, the value of the family and locale, and the moral status of work. Like Sandel, Lasch recalls the now virtually forgotten "producerist" and "free labor" movements of nineteenth century associated with names like Orestes Brownson.[60]

Lasch claims that Populism reflected the values of the pre-New Deal American petty bourgeoisie of farmers, tradesmen, artisans, small proprietors. While admitting its characteristic vices, Lasch bemoans the inability of today's cultural critics to recognize the virtues of this class, "its egalitarianism, its respect for workmanship, its understanding of the value of loyalty, and its struggle against the moral temptation of resentment." Other values, which the left has typically failed to see as values at all, are "its moral realism, its understanding that everything has its place," its sense of shame and guilt, and above all, its sense of limits.[61] These petty bourgeois values are clearly an obstacle to progress, a fact not lost on Progressives. Rather than seeing in them the moral resources for economic change, the left-Progressive response was to critique the language of limits and competence as blocking revolution. Their thought was embraced by the growing managerial class of experts to whom the operation of social institutions has increasingly been given over. Lasch attacks this "new class" of placeless, loyalty-less management most vehemently in his last book, *The Revolt of the Elites* (a paraphrase of Ortega y Gasset's 1929 *Revolt of the Masses*). Finally, Lasch was one of the few social critics to connect this line of thought to the critique of *careerism*. He wrote, "Careerism tends to undermine democracy by divorcing knowledge from practical experience, devaluing the kind of knowledge . . . gained from experience, and generating social conditions in which ordinary people are not expected to know anything at all."[62] He distinguished careerism from a high value placed on work, devotion to productive activity, which he took to be central to the American notion of dignity.[63]

Lasch refers admiringly to the work of Mickey Kaus. Using a phrase congenial to the current volume, in *The End of Equality* Kaus calls for a "civic liberalism." Kaus attacks what he calls "money liberalism," which wants to establish equality of wealth as the only means to equality, in favor of a civic liberalism that recognizes equality is primarily civic and not economic, and so tries to limit the sphere in which inequality of wealth matters.[64] This strategy is certainly welcome. For example, Kaus insists that as part of welfare reform jobs, not merely funds, must be provided, because he correctly points out that no one can have equality in America who does not have a job, paid or unpaid. The social and civic stigma of joblessness is powerful. Being a respected citizen in America means having work to do.

However, Kaus goes too far in his search for equality, repeatedly suggesting civic projects for no other reason than that they promote equality, like national service. He disparages suburban life because it is for him synonymous with class-segregation, calling for tax incentives and zoning laws to class-integrate residential areas. With a quasi-religious zeal he pursues *egalité*, trying to ferret out inequality in any dark corner of the polity. He wants to forge social conditions that keep anyone from "pretend[ing] to any fundamental superiority." Kaus is against meritocracy, for meritocratic spheres will result, he reasonably believes, in the inheritance of class. Indeed, the more the market is seen to be "fair" – based on merit – the "greater the threat to social equality."[65] He proposes instead that we expand the public sphere, the area of life in which equal dignity is accorded regardless of material inequality: "The idea . . . is that the public sphere will eventually have the sort of primacy to which religions have aspired."[66] Kaus supports the military draft, as a "class-mixing institution."

This is too much. It is deeply undermining of private life and individual liberties. Americans have a right to object to policies that seek to increase the burdens of their lives, especially when these are offered for the paternalistic purpose of *re-educating* them. Kaus has moved into social engineering. He fails to accord sufficient weight to balancing distinctive and legitimate values; equality wins out all the time. Kaus leaves the reader feeling that his ideal society would be the waiting line at the Registry of Motor Vehicles, which is a class-indifferent experience. Kaus is led to this in part because he confounds equality with *commonalty* and *interaction*. He is entirely right that civic equality is largely distinct from material equality. But he strays into asserting that egalitarianism can only be fostered if people actually live in the same place, do the same things, interact with each other across class lines. And since their spontaneous behavior and the development of class distinctions in America do not naturally accomplish this, people ought to be forced into interaction. Of course it is government that must do the forcing.

Americans believe in equality more than most humans. But very few make an argument that the reasonable and moral way to deal with misfortune, which is a bad thing, is to actually increase it so no one fails to be disadvantaged. Making society generally *worse* cannot be the right answer to any problem. Improving the conditions of the unfortunate is morally required, even on conservative grounds, if the improvement is not too costly; but making life worse for everyone else is equality gone mad. And how are we to keep people, as Kaus wants, from "pretending" to superiority? Only a Jacobin could design a policy to prevent this, an impression fostered as well by Kaus' bizarre attempt to make public works the sacrament of a civic religion. The point that there must be spheres in which citizens are equals, and some in which they actually interact as equals, is well-taken. But making the public sphere into a transcendent, ultimate goal is not *civil* equality.

Populist egalitarians like Lasch and Kaus correctly turn our attention to the realities of local civil society, and the self-determination of average citizens. The limitation on their approach is twofold. Negatively, they fail to admit the costs of equality. Like republicans and democrats, I fear the populists imagine that no increased limits on individual liberty attend their policies. In reality, a step toward community, equality or democracy is a step away from individual rights-guarantees. I am willing to take that step; their silence suggests that they believe they can take the step with one foot but keep the other in the same liberal place. Positively, they take as their proposed value something public and political. Enhancement of local self-rule, which I will agree is desirable, is by itself inadequate to solve the problems of contemporary liberal republican society. Likewise, making citizens interact, increasing their public involvement and equality, is insufficient. This is a well-meant mistake. Higher involvement, interaction, political power without some shared set of goals, goods, or ends, is increased activity without purpose. What is needed as well is a recognition of the substantive goods, including non-political goods, built into civil society and characteristic of the culture that informs civil society. As the *Reason* of the proceduralists and discourse theorists was not enough, neither is the *Will* of the democrats, republicans, and populists. There must be, in addition, the *Good*, or goods, the toward-which of reason and will. Self-rule and the equality of self-ruling citizens by itself is inadequate as an account of the goods intrinsic to modern liberal republics. Thus it fails to recognize that, given other goods, democracy is sometimes to be balanced and restrained by those other considerations.

Moral Community

Although the post-World War II call for lost community in America began with Robert Nisbet's 1953 *The Quest for Community*, communitarianism as a movement in political theory and social criticism perhaps should be dated to the work of Sandel, Alasdair MacIntyre, Amitai Etzioni, and Robert Bellah in the early and mid-1980s.[67] They made "community" a prominent name for that which liberal theory had neglected and liberal society undermined.[68] Properly speaking, communitarianism is less a political position than an anti-individualist anthropological claim, namely, that community and tradition are logically prior to and constitutive of individuality. Regarding its political consequences, matters are less clear. As Charles Taylor has pointed out, communitarian anthropology and communitarian policy are separate.[69] Communitarians can go on to accept or reject self-government, participation in politics, or individual rights, prayer in the schools, redistribution of wealth, gun control – anything you like. They can recommend policies that are only marginally distinct from Rawls', or turn to a premodern, pre-democratic polity, or anything in between. In most cases, their endorsed policies diverge only a few degrees from those of egalitarian liberals.

Not to mention – although critics often have mentioned – the term "community" is used in utterly various ways. When a commentator speaks of a contemporary "search for community" the term has a rather different connotation than in referring to the "legal community" in New York City. Etymologically, community is the commons, fellowship, and in one of its Latinate connections, the realm of *com-munis*, or shared obligations. In contemporary social and political theory the term is marked by the common translation of Tönnies's famously dichotomous title, "*Gemeinschaft und Gesellschaft.*"[70] Tönnies was willing to make this opposition rather stark. For him *Gemeinschaft* or community applied to all primordial, intimate, "organic" forms of association, whereas *Gesellschaft* or society referred to a historically more restricted associations of strangers based on consent, a "mechanical" structure.[71] While current communitarians do not import all or even most of this description, it remains the case that "community" carries with it a strength of connection that "society" does not. It is almost inevitably a warmer term than, for example, civil society. And it is virtually normative. As Tönnies wrote, "the expression 'bad *Gemeinschaft*' violates the meaning of the word."[72]

The most consistent proponent of communitarianism as a viewpoint on policy, not just anthropology, is Amitai Etzioni. In his hands, communitarianism is a above all a call for a moral revival in American life. The need for this revival is the decay of a sense of moral obligation to family and society, which has been undermined by a combination of economic change and the cultural-political mania for individual rights. Etzioni calls for "a moratorium on the minting of most, if not all, new rights."[73] He wants to make communitarianism a "third" force in American political thought, neither market-libertarian nor welfare-statist. In many cases Etzioni's recommendations are entirely in accord with a revision of liberalism that seeks to interpret individuality and liberty less rigidly than proceduralism has.

Nevertheless, Etzioni's moralism is discomfiting. This may seem a strange objection; things being what they, more morality is almost never a bad thing. The contemporary American scene appears not to be an exception. Nevertheless, in the current climate, the largely wholesome call to moral obligation still misses the mark.

First, in some ways we continue to be a very moralistic society. The call to moral responsibility and sensitivity to various dangers (violent crime, drug abuse, child abuse, sexual harassment, etc.) have so increased in the past two decades that it is easy to cite absurd horror stories of children being suspended from school for taking aspirin (in a "drug-free zone") or kissing ("creating a hostile work environment"). Our public discourse can be brought to a standstill for months or years by the allegations of a public figure's infidelity. It appears that our media culture is capable of maintaining ultra-sensitivity to morally questionable public behavior and speech, simultaneous with a major breakdown in the sense of many personal obligations. We seem most "moral" when it counts least; we are too busy complaining about sex in the White House or worrying about discrimination to play with our children. Perhaps we think we can make up for concrete and daily moral failure by speaking more loudly about morality in public. Certainly Etzioni would object to such priorities. Nevertheless, the call to moral obligation *per se* needs to be sharpened by analysis.

Second, it is my belief that the apparent absence of a vibrant moral culture, as charged not only by Etzioni but by many others, is, to the extent it is true at all, conditioned by social changes that make moral renewal difficult. In the contemporary world it is harder to find where and how more traditional moral practices and thinking are to be applied. Etzioni is right that shifting social coordination and control from civil structures to law and government, especially national government, is morally speaking a losing proposition. Nevertheless, if civil and local social structures are *unavailable*, there is little choice in the matter. The older system of moral inculcation, social monitoring of behavior, personal connections to local others, neighborhood stability, the rewards for good as well as punishments for bad behavior, are for many Americans no longer intact. For example, in a highly mobile population fewer people have permanent connections to local others, leading them to neglect public duties. It is not enough to call for a change of heart, as Etzioni does – although, to be sure, change of heart is nothing to scoff at. We may have to recognize that we live under social conditions that have permanently dislodged older forms of moral control, and thus increased the percentage of citizens who feel unbound by civility under normal conditions.

Third, Etzioni fails to admit the limits of community, in particular, he fails to recognize that community is *local*. He writes that, "Communitarians are concerned with maintaining a supra-community, a community of communities – *the* American society."[74] Even further, his Communitarian platform continues, "*Our Communitarian concern may begin with ourselves and our families, but it rises inexorably to the long-imagined community of humankind*" (his emphasis).[75] I think this makes little sense. If "community" implies come concrete connection not captured by "society," then there can be no "global community." Even the "we" of American society as a whole, the extent to which America can be a mega-community, will always be dominated, I will argue in the following chapters, by media culture and legalism. To protect substantive moral community means protecting *localism*. And protecting localism will inevitably mean granting local majorities some greater power over local individual liberties. This means that community has its costs. The conservative accepts this fact, but it is not clear that Etzioni does.

Lastly, Etzioni does not attend sufficiently to the cultural requirements of the form of moral community he calls for. It is difficult to imagine the level of individual commitment to the common good he would require without, for example, shared metanarratives, either religious or nationalistic. These are not necessarily objectionable for a conservative, but they would constitute a substantive communitarian admission. Mere exhortation to care more for "we" than for me will not do the job. For caring about "we" is indistinguishable from caring about the cultural values that "we" embody. If I am to care in a personal way about my polity, my polity must stand for a way of life that embodies, at least partially, my own deepest sense of meaning, which again can mean coercion or discouragement of behavior.

The Apotheosis of the Public Realm

Just as individualist and discursive–deliberative versions of liberalism share a Socratic bias, the discursive–deliberative, democratic, populist, civic republican, and communitarian versions share an *apotheosis of the public realm*. They over-value political or public or common life – the last meaning for them what is held in common, rather than what is distributively common among citizens – which they take to be the moral glue that will hold together a liberal society. Society needs more solidarity than neutralist liberalism recognized, they agree, and that solidarity will be provided by active participation in community, interaction among social classes, face-to-face presence in the political forum, direct communication among members, etc. The glue of the public realm is public action directed toward the public realm.

We may notice its activist tenor. What constitutes political society is the socially-regarding actions – "deeds and speeches," as Arendt put it – of citizens. Citizens are to be present to each other, meet face to face, talk, participate, interact, etc. Philosophically this is an inheritance of what I would call the *idealist cult of activity*. The notion of mind as essentially active, as that which constructs reality, is an inheritance of German idealism starting with Kant (or, if you wish, Leibniz). Present in Hegel's notion of mind and in the Marxist focus on labor and production, it has had a significant role in political theory, right through the activist republicanism of Hannah Arendt, who replaces Marx's labor with her own neo-existentialist notion of action. This focus on action, and in particular on construction, tends wherever it appears to devalue merely cyclic, repetitive life processes. It tends to conceive of civil society as something the citizens are always in the process of making, building, re-establishing, investing with their energy, as if, like a city held aloft on a column of water, it would collapse if there were a drop in pressure. It is a politics of intensity and improvement. It is tailor-made for progress. In this view the mere living together of citizens in their mundane experience is not especially important in the maintenance of civil society; it is the merely raw material for the deliberation and manipulation that is politics. For much of that quotidian experience is "private" in the broad sense of being concerned with personal gain, family survival, recreational enjoyment, and local social networks of friends and nearby residents.

It is understandable that political theory, in trying to repair the seeming self-interestedness and individualism of some forms of liberalism, would turn in this direction. But to use Stephen Holmes's figure, this is a case of choosing the wrong antonym.[76] What will repair the excessive individualism and public neutralism of proceduralist liberalism is not cathecting public life as that-for-which we live together in the *polis*, as the moral justification of the fact of social existence, but a recognition of the processes and preconditions of that sheer living together which *is* the *civitas*. Social existence does not need a moral justification; it is the *source* of all such justification. Political activity cannot and ought not constitute the meaning or value of life for more than a small minority of citizens, e.g. politicians, whether elected officials or professional activists or political journalists.

For most citizens life is outside the forum; the forum serves, but cannot replace, that life. I will claim in chapters 6 and 7 that this life outside the forum is "civil society": a social overlap of private networks and interests living in relative harmony with limited guidance and without a declared *telos*. Any such *telos* would function as a call to whip civil society into shape, to increase its uniformity, as in what Michael Oakeshott will call an "enterprise association." We will see that certain forms of group enterprise are indeed justified and essential to civil society; but only those forms that serve to return us to the condition of civil society. To hope for a deliberative, activist, participatory project that will tie us all together is to work *against* the true spirit of civil society. That spirit is not salvational: if civil society is properly conceived it cannot constitute the meaning of anyone's existence. The association of citizens remains such only as long as it renounces being anything "more." But then, it is already quite a lot.

Progress

Our third liberal good, progress, would seem to have a more ambiguous theoretical status within liberalism than liberty and self-rule. One might imagine that it is a fundamental value for utilitarian versions of liberalism only. And there is ample evidence that progress of some kind – e.g. material and technological – is at least temporarily compatible with authoritarianism and totalitarianism, even if today, at the beginning of the twenty-first century, it seems that the most reliably progressive societies over the long haul are in fact liberal. Furthermore, on logical grounds alone progress is distinct from the other liberal values mentioned in that it is always relative to some other value; one could have progress in social order and stability, progress in religious devotion, progress in health care, progress in technical fields, etc. To make individualism or self-rule ultimate values is also to endorse progress in achieving those values.

Let us start with the easy cases. Certainly one can argue that liberalism increases social happiness, in part through economic, scientific, and technological progress. Utilitarianism must endorse such progress, as it arguably increases general happiness. But utilitarianism must then accept, as deontologists rightly note, that any prohibition against violations of individual liberty or democratic procedure can be only a contingent, secondary principle; if collective prosperity or happiness is maximized by such violation, then it is to be permitted. Utilitarian liberals like Mill believed that as a matter of fact such violations – of individual liberty, anyway – will not bring social happiness in the long run. This is the line the consistent utilitarian liberal must take: liberal rights and procedures are constitutive of the society of maximum happiness or well-being.

John Dewey, who respected Mill very highly, has a double right to being regarded as the archetypal philosophical progressive, both because of his association with the movement of that name, and in the centrality of development or progress to his thought. His conception of progress was broad: he sought moral, aesthetic, and political as well as scientific, economic, and technical progress. And it was a utopian conception. I mean not that he failed to see the costs of progress, but that his notion of growth or progress was intrinsically normative. Developments whose costs are excessive count as insufficient progress for Dewey. For example, an economic gain that came at the cost of lessened freedom or aesthetic deprivation would turn out *not* to be a case of progress; Dewey demanded that progress in science, technology, and industry be combined with progress in aesthetic experience and democracy and morality. This is in part because Dewey's very notion of development implies that progress is caused by the widening of possible interaction of diverse elements, be they experiences, ideas, cultures, persons, or styles of life. That is, the most complete and various interaction is the womb of all growth and development.[77] A democratic, egalitarian, participatory politics is then for Dewey the actualization of the innermost possibilities of human experience.[78]

Non-utilitarian liberals would seem not to endorse progress in this way. But while the place that progress has in their views is different, the commitment is nonetheless characteristic. Progress shows up in four ways. First, all liberals endorse progress with respect to their stated ultimate norms, e.g. rights, welfare, individualism, political participation, etc. In practice one normally sees deontological liberalisms referring to progress as desirable with respect to their ultimate ends, that is, progress in the achievement of equality, rights, opportunity, justice, etc. This is as true for neutralists as for affirmative liberals. By itself this would be trivial, but second, for almost all of the foregoing moral-political values, progress in other and more "material" respects – e.g. scientific, economic, technological, etc. – is a necessary prerequisite. I mean this in a narrow and specific way. Egalitarian liberals must favor economic growth to better the condition of the poor and scientific and technological progress to ameliorate disease and handicaps and other "morally arbitrary" disadvantages. Democratic and even republican political participation is enhanced by communications technologies. Third, in fact the only kind of society we know which has embodied these liberal principles is modern, progressive society. That is, in a more generic way, the values of neutralist and affirmative liberals seem only to be achieved in materially progressive societies. The society of limited government, liberty, democracy, discourse, etc. is in fact also the society of science, technology, and high per capita GNP. Even for deontological liberals, *prosperity matters*. If it is immoral to cut up social wealth unfairly, thereby insuring undeserved misfortune for some, it is also immoral to endorse policies that lead to misery. If it is immoral to distribute resources unequally so that my child dies from lack of medical treatment, it is also immoral to fail to invest in medical research that would have found the cure for my child's illness. At any rate, no one thinks equal poverty and fair misery is a bargain. So utility, maximization of average well-being, increasing net or average prosperity, ought to matter and matter *morally*, even for deontologists. Failure to progress can be evil.

Behind these particular uses of progress in liberal theory there is a fourth and more amorphous employment. Modern liberalism shares with much of modern life an implicit soteriology, a notion of *salvation* or *redemption* through progress. Liberals of all stripes have been drawn to progress as *metanarrative*. Liberalism has regarded itself as the proper culmination and sublation of earlier political history; this is as true for libertarians as for egalitarian and affirmative liberals. And the achievement of the liberal program, for all of these versions, is never fully accomplished. For liberals the good society always in progress, whether the progress be the overcoming of prejudice and racism, the improvement of the quality of life, the elimination of moral arbitrariness, the overcoming of tradition and superstition and provincialism, the achievement and diffusion of emancipation, or the development of a common and good life. This is, of course, no surprise. Liberalism is a child of modernity, and modernity tends to regard the meaning of current experience, social conditions, and life itself to lie in what they lead to, in an improved future state of the political community or mankind as a whole. This is the sense in which the notion of worldly progress has replaced religion in the minds of many secular intellectuals. Lasch referred to it by quoting Hawthorne: liberals, having lost an older Heaven, regard progress as "the true and only heaven," the only heaven that is left.[79] This perspective is connected in its own way with the idealist cult of activity mentioned above.

Nevertheless, progress cannot be the highest good, and for three reasons. One reason deontology well-knows: there must be rules governing the treatment of individuals and minorities as we march forward. The second reason society knows well too: progress has costs, and so must be managed and limited. But third, as Lasch argued, progress inevitably requires political power to devolve to expertise and the collective management of enterprise. It requires bureaucracy and rational management.[80] It requires that we volatilize tradition, which means not only cultural values but inherited institutions and practices. It can thus become *uncivil*. In particular, when progress becomes the ultimate value, the non-progressive is inevitably devalued. This means that those areas of human existence that are merely "vegetative" or "metabolic," cyclic, repetitive and relatively un-improvable aspects of life – certain features of child-rearing, garden-tending, feeding, love-making, recreation, "idle talk," etc. – tend to drop out of our conversation of what "matters," what is "at issue," what is "hot."[81]

The conservative tradition finds this notion of progress a dangerous form of idolatry, the investing of properly religious and transcendent meanings in political and social life. Civil society is particularly endangered by the flood of salvific passions, by the attempt to make it the ultimate meaning of human existence. For civil society primarily concerns those metabolic processes of mere living together, without extrinsic aim or improvement, that are most refractory to progress. This is Oakeshott's famous figure: the ship of civil association is aimless, without a destination, other than keeping afloat. My point is not to prevent or devalue progress, but to insist that the value of progress must be gauged with respect to an understanding of human social life that values the non-progressive as well. While we ought to be free to pursue unending improvement in some dimensions of social life, we ought also to be free to excuse ourselves at least partly from the march of Progress, and subsist in the quiet life of the present bequeathed by the past. We may see that this is, indeed, the core of our civil existence. The notion of the *civitas* cannot be tied to progress, even if the sensible *civitas* will, under modern conditions, be concerned to progress.

Thus, while progress is, like individuality and self-rule, a legitimate and intrinsic value of modern liberal republican societies, nevertheless, like individual liberty and self-rule, progress is *a*, not *the*, value of such polities. It must therefore be balanced against yet other goods; it can be trumped. When it becomes the ultimate good it violates the conditions of civil society.

Toward a Holist Liberalism

It is time to suggest an alternative. By *holist* liberalism I mean a liberalism that is explicitly non-neutral, one which claims that liberalism must by nature endorse a substantive account of the human Good. Holism thus far travels alongside the affirmative liberals recounted above. But it takes two further steps. First, that account must be *plural*; there is not one ultimate end or value of the liberal republican *polis*, but several. This means they can compete and conflict, and there is no *principle* that determines which ought to trump on which occasion. Second, unlike the versions of affirmative liberalism explored, the account of the Good must be *supra-political* and *supra-liberal*. That is, it must accept that the goods for which a liberal polity legitimately strives are *not* restricted to individual self-determination and self-government or participation, nor to those goods combined with progress. Holistic liberalism endorses an account of the Good that cannot be reduced to the minimal goods to which the republican tradition has been reduced by the dominant liberal political theories of the last half-century.

In effect, this means I will endorse what is today called *perfectionism*. The term is unfortunate. First, the polity is not in the business of "perfecting" anything; the idea of perfection is intrinsically uncivil. To a conservative, perfection is for the next world. Second, there is no implication that the goods supported by the polity can be simultaneously maximized, or define some particular, narrow form of life. The holism I will endorse is perfectly compatible with the "incommensurability" of ultimate goods claimed by Berlin, Larmore, and Raz. To accept plural and non-political goods that are not homogeneous entails that the goods must be *balanced*. There will be no hierarchy among these goods, and so the balancing act is one that cannot be dictated by formulae. This can only be accomplished by practical reason, *phronesis*. And practical reason cannot be conceived as operating but against a background of inherited cultural practices and interpretations.

Stephen Salkever claims that liberalism has an historical commitment to three goods, liberty, self-rule, and material prosperity.[82] According to his pluralism, there is no lexical ordering, no hierarchy, among these three goods. Indeed, Salkever points out, the neglect of any one leads to serious problems for a liberal society. This means that sometimes a degree of liberty and/or of self-rule is legitimately sacrificed by liberal societies for greater prosperity or quality of life. What in the work of many theorists is a non-political concern for prosperity or quality of life, is recognized by Salkever as an intra-political norm, along with liberty and democracy. He goes on to describe how such a balance must be struck through public debate.

A more elaborate account of the liberal Good comes from William Galston. He explicitly claims that the highest good is not individual liberty, negative or positive, nor self-rule, nor minimal coercion, nor self-actualization. Rather there is a finite plural set of goods that all are legitimately taken into account as "liberal purposes." Galston faces the necessary consequences of this claim: such demotion of liberty to one among a number of concerns means that coercion is legitimate to a degree a neutralist would reject. He denies that "the uncoerced pursuit of the bad enjoys priority in principle – that is, in every case – over the coerced pursuit of the good."[83] There are goods – virtue, responsibility, communal prosperity, etc. – which can legitimately compromise or trump liberty, self-expression, individualism, and self-rule depending on the circumstances. Government must promote certain lifestyles over others, in addition to occasionally coercing individuals in cases where both the egalitarian and libertarian versions of liberalism would recoil. For example, Galston accepts voluntary non-denominational prayer in public schools. He even accepts that certain beliefs must be encouraged in the populace for which truth-governed inquiry, e.g. philosophy, can find no ultimate justification.[84] With all this I am in agreement.

By calling for a holist liberalism, I am suggesting that plural, supra-political non-neutralisms, like Galston's, should become more explicit about their theoretical basis: they are accepting the *embeddedness of politics in culture*. This is to accept that: (a) the political order is only part of a larger set of relations that constitute society, other orders including – although not limited to – the economic and the cultural; (b) the constitution of the political, and of the person as political (the citizen), cannot be strictly distinct from the other orders of the whole; and, (c) liberty and self-government are two among several ultimate goods for a liberal society, all of which have a claim on social decision-making, hence which require an endless process of balancing. No one value in principle trumps all others.

Holism is a characteristically conservative doctrine. Consequently, a holist liberalism can find common ground with conservatism. But the conservatism that can attend this rendezvous must be a *modern* conservatism, that is, a traditionalist or cultural conservatism that accepts essential values of modernity – among others, individuality, self-rule, and progress – along with a variety of social and political institutions to which liberalism has contributed, as constitutive for our tradition. The result is a version of liberalism that neither rejects those typical liberal virtues anachronistically, as with some conservatives, nor embraces them in an un-contextualized form, as proceduralist and affirmative liberals have been wont to do. To specify such a view requires that we explore two topics in the remainder of this book: the methodological and anthropological resources of conservatism; and the concept to which a holist liberalism or a modern conservatism must turn in understanding the basis and chief concern of politics, namely, civil society.

Notes

1 My chapter title is paraphrased from George Sher's *Beyond Neutrality: Perfectionism and Politics* (New York: Cambridge University Press, 1997).
2 This natural alliance depends on the kind of pluralism or diversity; that is, a pluralism or diversity *of what?* A pluralism of communities, not individuals, or of individuals whose identity is internally related to ethnicity, gender, etc., is threatening to liberalism, and needs a special justification.
3 While it is true that only utilitarian versions of liberalism can endorse progress as an end in itself (e.g. the increase of general happiness), we shall see that progress is inevitably valued as well by deontological liberals, in practise and even in theory.
4 See George Kateb, *The Inner Ocean: Individualism and Democratic Culture* (Ithaca: Cornell University Press, 1992).
5 Ibid., p. 258.
6 Ibid., p. 97.
7 Friedrich Nietzsche, *The Gay Science*, trans. Walter Kaufmann (New York: Vintage, 1974), sec. 76.
8 Martha Nussbaum, "Aristotelian Social Democracy," in R. Bruce Douglass, Gerald M. Mara, and Henry A. Richardson, *Liberalism and the Good* (New York: Routledge, 1990).
9 While family and child-rearing are not restricted to heterosexuals, there is enough of a tie between both and heterosexuality, I imagine, for Nussbaum to want to exclude them.
10 Joseph Raz, *The Morality of Freedom* (Oxford: Oxford University Press, 1988), p. 412.
11 I might add before ending this section that pluralism, the view that differences among citizens are a chief political good for their own sake, suffers from the same problems as views that make individuality or liberty the ultimate good. This is to be expected, given that versions of pluralism put forward within the liberal tradition are almost always individualist. Individual liberty always makes for some increase in pluralism or diversity. But the notion that diversity, difference, or plurality, is good *per se* was not intrinsic to proto-liberalism. It presumes a Romantic, nineteenth century inheritance that may run counter to what the self-ruling community takes to be its needs at any particular time. It is true that the *possibility* of diversity, difference, and plurality is essential to liberal civil society in the sense that it would be a violation of liberty to enforce certain kinds of homogeneity. Civil tolerance will likely lead to some kind of diversity; but how much and of what kind is highly contingent. Is this a cause for disappointment? It is to some. Our culture may value diversity, and as such diversity may be legitimately promoted. But that is the value-commitment of a particular culture *enforcing* its cultural beliefs, not restraining them. "Deep" diversity is not an intrinsic good of liberal republican or civil society as such.

12 Jürgen Habermas, *Theory of Communicative Action*, trans. Thomas McCarthy (Boston: Beacon, 1984, 1987).

13 Jürgen Habermas, "Discourse Ethics: Notes on a Program of Philosophical Justification," in Habermas's *Moral Consciousness and Communicative Action*, trans. Christian Lenhardt and Shierry Weber Nicholsen (Cambridge, MA: MIT, 1990), p. 66.

14 Jürgen Habermas, "Three Normative Models of Democracy," in *Constellations: An International Journal of Critical and Democratic Theory*, 1, no. 1, 1994.

15 Ibid., p. 10.

16 See especially Seyla Benhabib, *Critique, Norm, and Utopia: A Study of the Foundations of Critical Theory* (New York: Columbia University Press, 1986). Most provocatively, she criticizes Habermas' earlier work as continuing a version of the philosophy of consciousness, in its employment of the "work" or "production" model, part of the Marxist legacy. See p. 344ff.

17 Seyla Benhabib, "Deliberative Rationality and Models of Democratic Legitimacy," *Constellations* 1, no. 1, 1994, pp. 30–1.

18 Ibid., p. 33.

19 Ibid., p. 49, n. 22.

20 Ibid., p. 35.

21 Ibid., p. 39.

22 Amy Gutmann and Dennis Thompson, *Democracy and Disagreement* (Cambridge, MA: Belknap, 1996).

23 Seyla Benhabib, "Liberal Dialogue Versus a Critical Theory of Discursive Legitimation," in Nancy Rosenblum, *Liberalism and the Moral Life* (Cambridge, MA: Harvard University Press, 1989), p. 150.

24 G. W. F. Hegel, *Philosophy of Mind: being part three of the Encyclopaedia of the Philosophical Sciences*, trans. William Wallace (Oxford: Clarendon, 1971), para. 436.

25 Ibid., para. 435: "the master's self-consciousness is brought by the *community* of needs and the concern for their satisfaction existing between him and the slave . . ." (Hegel's emphasis).

26 Thomas Nagel, *Equality and Partiality* (New York: Oxford University Press, 1991).

27 Here are the seeds of what is today called the "politics of recognition," the "identity politics" of competing cultural groups, as Taylor has noted. Now I do not mean to shackle the Hegelian tradition with all that goes under those loaded terms. Hegelian reciprocity is attained through renouncing particularity; in the master–slave struggle, Hegel's slave does not demand to be recognized in her ethnic or gendered identity. Further, mutual recognition is for Hegel only the *beginning* of ethical life, not its ultimate goal. We know that his understanding of the *sittlich* nature of that life implies that, however universalized is our recognitive reciprocity, the concrete obligations of ethical life are particular to social role. See Charles Taylor, "The Politics of Recognition," in Amy Gutmann, *Multiculturalism: Examining the Politics of Recognition* (Princeton: Princeton University Press, 1994).

28 Gutmann and Thompson. *Democracy and Disagreement*, p. 92.
29 Amy Gutmann, "Undemocratic Education," in Rosenblum, *Liberalism and the Moral Life*, p. 79.
30 Benhabib, *Critique, Norm, and Utopia*, pp. 306–7.
31 Walzer, *Spheres of Justice*, p. 304.
32 I wish to steal this term but leave behind its elaborate deconstructive baggage. The point will only be that to define liberal republican society as a form of talking and listening is excessively narrow.
33 Nancy Rosenblum, *Membership and Morals: The Personal Uses of Pluralism in America* (Princeton: Princeton University Press, 1998).
34 Ibid., p. 354.
35 Note that reciprocity and mutuality do not by themselves imply equality. As Karl Polanyi pointed out, reciprocity is not the property of modern democracy. Indeed, it was *more* crucial in premodern and tribal societies; whole "primitive" economies and social orders were operated on the basis of the gift-exchange. Feudalism itself was a system of reciprocal obligations among unequals (see Karl Polanyi, *The Great Transformation*, p. 48ff). Neither, I should add, does equality imply reciprocity or mutuality. The point is, these are distinct concepts.
36 Stephen Macedo, *Liberal Virtues: Citizenship, Virtue, and Community in Liberal Constitutionalism* (Oxford: Oxford University Press, 1990), p. 64.
37 Ibid., p. 59.
38 Ibid., p. 58.
39 Ibid., p. 246.
40 Ibid., p. 276.
41 Ibid., p. 274.
42 Ibid., p. 223.
43 Ibid., p. 227.
44 Ibid., p. 239.
45 Thus Macedo writes: "Liberalism holds out the promise, or the threat of making all the world like California," ibid., p. 278.
46 Benhabib, *Critique, Norm, and Utopia*, p. 338.
47 Strauss will be discussed more fully in my final chapter.
48 William Galston, "Civic Education in the Liberal State," in Rosenblum, *Liberalism and the Moral Life*, p. 100.
49 See Richard Hofstadter, *The Age of Reform: From Bryan to F.D.R.* (New York: Knopf, 1955) and *The Paranoid Style in American Politics and Other Essays* (Chicago: University of Chicago Press, 1979).
50 He continues: "Rawls severed the connection between the willingness to produce and the right to consume; he replaced claims based on achievement with those based on bare existence; he dismissed, as unrelated or even hostile to the conduct of our public life, the claims of particularity and of religion." This was arguably connected to the decline of the Democratic Party until at least the Clinton realignment. See Galston, *Liberal Purposes*, pp. 161–2.

51   See J. G. A. Pocock, *The Machiavellian Moment: Florentine Political Thought and the Atlantic Republican Tradition*.

52   See Hannah Arendt, *The Human Condition*.

53   Hannah Arendt, "The Revolutionary Tradition and its Lost Treasure," in *On Revolution* (Westport: Greenwood, 1982).

54   In the second edition preface to *Liberalism and the Limits of Justice*, Sandel voices a fear that communitarianism implies majoritarianism and conventionalism, hence the inability to critique majority notions of the Good. But his anthropology remains communitarian.

55   See Sandel, *Democracy's Discontents*.

56   Benjamin Barber, *Strong Democracy: Participatory Politics for a New Age* (Berkeley: University of California, 1984).

57   In the last decade of his life, Lasch endorsed Populism as an apt expression of his critical hopes for American society in two books, *The True and Only Heaven: Progress and Its Critics* (1991) and *The Revolt of the Elites and the Betrayal of Democracy* (1996). His interpretation of the Populist movement refers especially to Lawrence Goodwyn, *Democratic Promise: The Populist Moment in America* (Oxford: Oxford University Press, 1976), and *The Populist Moment: A Short History of the Agrarian Revolt in America* (Oxford: Oxford University Press, 1978).

58   As Elizabeth Lasch-Quinn correctly describes in her Introduction to Lasch's posthumous *Women and the Common Life: Love, Marriage, and Feminism* (New York: Norton, 1977), p. xii.

59   As I argued in my *The Dilemma of Modernity* (Albany: State University of New York, 1988), and as Lasch confirms in the Introduction to *The True and Only Heaven*, pp. 28–9.

60   See Michael Sandel, *Democracy and its Discontents*. Both Lasch and Sandel have a connection here with the social critic Ivan Illich, for whom the great sin of modernity is undermining independence. See for example, Illich's *Toward a History of Needs* (Berkeley: Heyday Books, 1977). As a modern citizen, Illich quips, when confronted with a government cutback in health care that causes my mother to be released from the hospital, instead of learning how to care for my mother, I learn how to picket the state capital.

61   Lasch, *The True and Only Heaven*, p. 17.

62   Ibid., p. 79.

63   See Lasch, *The Revolt of the Elites*, p. 22. I do think that Lasch valorized work too highly, as opposed to the domestic and local public spheres. As Elisabeth Lasch-Quinn wrote of her father, who continued working through an ultimately fatal illness, "That my father chose to work until the very end, to carry on the normal activities of life . . . is a measure . . . of his belief that meaningful work is inseparable from life itself. . . . For the first time I fully understood . . . just how liberating and exciting it is to lose oneself completely in the task at hand . . ." This is fine for some, but not for all. Related to this, at one point Lasch insists that luxury is morally and democratically repugnant (as we will

see Mickey Kaus do in a moment). In my view, he has gone a bit too nineteenth-century-Protestant here, in the sense of *innerweltliche Askese*.

64 Kaus' argument is based in Walzer's distinction among spheres of justice.

65 Mickey Kaus, *The End of Equality* (New York: Basic Books, 1992), p. 48.

66 Ibid., p. 162.

67 Robert A. Nisbet, *The Quest for Community: A Study in the Ethics of Order and Freedom* (San Francisco: Institute for Contemporary Studies, 1990), orignally published by Oxford University in 1953, later confusingly reprinted as *Community and Power*, then still later returned again to the original title. See also Robert Bellah, Richard Madsen, William Sullivan, Ann Swidler, and Steven Tipton, *Habits of the Heart: Individualism and Commitment in American Life* (New York: Harper & Row, 1985); Alasdair MacIntyre, *After Virtue: A Study in Moral Theory* (Notre Dame: Notre Dame, 1981); Amitai Etzioni, *The Spirit of Community: The Reinvention of American Society* (New York: Simon and Schuster, 1993); and Sandel's *Liberalism and the Limits of Justice*.

68 Although MacIntyre's explicit concern is tradition, not community. His work was nevertheless regarded by many as a primary inspiration for communitarianism.

69 Charles Taylor, "Cross Purposes: the Liberal-Communitarian Debate," in Nancy Rosenblum, *Liberalism and the Moral Life*.

70 Ferdinand Tönnies, *Community and Society*, trans. Charles Loomis (Lansing: Michigan State University Press, 1957).

71 Notice that Tönnies's employment of "organic" and "mechanical" is precisely opposite to Durkheim's. Durkheim made traditional society "mechanical" (functionally identical, repetitive roles) and modern society "organic" (functionally differentiated, interlocking roles). See Emile Durkheim, *The Division of Labor in Society*, trans. W. D. Halls (New York: Free Press, 1984).

72 Tönnies, *Community and Society*, p. 34.

73 Amitai Etzioni, *The Spirit of Community: The Reinvention of American Society* (New York: Simon and Schuster, 1993), p. 4.

74 Etzioni, *The Spirit of Community*, p. 160. Etzioni's emphasis.

75 Ibid., p. 266. Etzioni's emphasis.

76 Stephen Holmes, *The Anatomy of Antiliberalism* (Cambridge, MA: Harvard University Press, 1993). Holmes ascribes this mistake, of course, to antiliberals, some of whom I will defend.

77 Although I would correct his claim by saying that it is the womb of *certain types* of growth and development, e.g. of artistic and intellectual, and not others, e.g. child-development; we cannot presume that maximum diversity is the proper growth medium for every kind of thing at every phase of its growth.

78 Modern society does seem to presuppose this "Great Confluence," as Theodore Von Laue called it, in which all elements – people, ideas, materials, nations – are increasingly thrown into interaction with each other. See Theodore von Laue, *The World Revolution of Westernization: The Twentieth Century in Global Perspective* (New York: Oxford University Press, 1987).

79 Ernest Gellner referred to the demise of Marxism, itself the most "progressive" of political doctrines, as "the second secularization."
80 See Lasch, *The True and Only Heaven*.
81 "Idle talk" was one of Heidegger's categories of inauthentic existence in *Being and Time*.
82 Stephen Salkever, "'Lopp'd and Bound': How Liberal Theory Obscures the Goods of Liberal Practices," in Douglass et al., *Liberalism and the Good*.
83 Galston, *Liberal Purposes*, p. 87.
84 See Galston, "Civic Education in the Liberal State."

4

A (Post)Modern Conservatism

In what follows I will unfold the conservative challenge to liberalism. If, as I argued earlier, many thinkers at different places along the political spectrum can be seen to be moving in a conservative direction, we may learn most about this direction by examining a full-bodied traditionalist conservatism. But at the same time I will be distinguishing what I take to be the defensible core of conservatism from its anachronistic and objectionable features. The goal is a *modern conservatism*, distinct from any defense of the *ancien règime*.[1] Indeed, accepting the terms of the age, we might employ the label "postmodern conservatism." This may sound utterly oxymoronic. We must first of all remember that historical conservatism was an Enlightenment movement, and that Burke's conservatism served to defend an English social order that was at the time the most modern society in Europe.[2] Conservatism calls us to value our traditions, to be sure, but *our* traditions are both modern and, in the present case, American. There is something about modernity that rejects tradition; but modernity has its own traditions too. And if "postmodern," alternately burdened by proponents and buffeted by opponents, is understood minimally, it indicates not the end of the modern era but a significant contemporary discontinuity with what we could call the principles under which modernity came to be.[3] Suffice to say that I wish to describe what I take to be the living core of conservatism in the contemporary age.

Given the demise of Marxism, conservatism is the chief contemporary form of anti-liberalism, hence is a main target for liberal critique. Stephen Holmes includes in the antiliberal camp writers that I have occasion to rely upon, like Alasdair MacIntyre and Christopher Lasch.[4] Thus his critique may be seen as an attack on some of the views expressed in this chapter and the next. As a prefatory note, I will respond to a central criticism.

Holmes makes an important point that conservatives cannot lay all of the problems of modern liberal societies at the door of liberal political ideas. We must distinguish liberal *politics* from liberal *society*. Holmes takes anti-liberals to task for discovering Lockean "atomistic individualism" behind all current social problems. Now, while he is right to resist such conflations, the anti-liberal argument is not always so simplistic. Liberal theory is not to blame for all the ills of liberal society, but neither is it utterly blameless. Locke knew all about families and dependence, but he claimed we will only see the world aright and come to the correct normative views if we think of society as a voluntary association of individuals. Deontological liberal theory makes justice rest on the acceptance of rules that would rationally have been chosen by purely self-interested, asocial individuals. This approach is not without *some* social consequences. It would be absurd to deny that political liberalism is individualistic in *any* significant sense, to deny that it exerts a pressure in that direction. Is it the sole source of our cultural and social predicament? No, but it is an important piece of the puzzle.

Returning to our task, we need to gain some indication of the meaning and breadth of "conservative." An ahistorical gloss on the term is clear: conservatism seeks to *conserve*. Certainly we cannot take this meaning too rigidly; conservatism doesn't want to conserve *everything* and not everyone who wants to conserve something is a conservative. In a particularly bizarre case, the remaining Stalinists in contemporary post-Soviet Russia have sometimes been labeled "conservatives." But there is something to this admittedly perverse usage, which explains its existence. To respond to situations of change by asserting the value of old institutions and practices is in a meaningful, albeit historically and locally relative, sense to be conservative.

Sometimes what gets labeled as conservative in the modern, liberal republican West is any form of politics that attempts to preserve the remnants of a pre-democratic, pre-individualist, traditionally authoritarian, perhaps religious, social order. In other words, a conservative is whoever is *not* a modern Western liberal. But that would presumably include virtually all forms of political order in human history! All that would not be conservative would be modern liberal republicanism, and perhaps ancient Greek republicanism (despite its slavery and traditionalism). So, while it is true that conservatism has something anti-individualist and anti-democratic about it, this global characterization helps us little.

A different approach is to see how the term evolved in the tradition in which we are now speaking. Here the field is significantly narrowed. Conservatism in modern Western political theory emerged in the late eighteenth century, the century of Enlightenment, primarily as a response to the French Revolution.[5] It is a defense of a family of older orders in the face of something new. Conservatism is thus part of the modern critique of modernity. It has many variants, which cannot be reviewed here. All I can offer is a brief account of the distinctions among some major historical sources of conservatism, with the aim of distinguishing the English conservative tradition from others, in preparation for the examination of Burke's views in later sections. Note that some of the following thinkers could as easily be labeled liberal; the late eighteenth and early nineteenth century was a time in which the distinction between liberal and conservative was being invented, hence many of its most important thinkers are refractory to those labels.

For the darkest and most intransigent form of conservatism we must go to the European Continent. For Joseph De Maistre (1753–1821), the father of French conservatism (he was a Savoyan writing in French), human reason and liberty are sharply circumscribed. The order of human society is based in the *mysterium tremendum et fascinans*. Awe, in its negative and positive forms, terror and blessedness, are the warp and woof of that order. We can see this in his famous description of the figure of the executioner, which must be appreciated despite its length.

> A poisoner, a parricide, or a blasphemer is thrown to him; [the executioner] seizes him, he stretches him on the ground, he ties him to a horizontal cross, he raises it up: then a dreadful silence falls, and nothing can be heard except the crack of bones breaking under the crossbar and the howls of the victim. . . . He is finished: his heart flutters, but it is with joy; he congratulates himself, he says sincerely, *No one can break men on the wheel better than I.* He steps down. . . . He sits down to a meal and eats; then to bed, where he sleeps. And the next day, on waking, he thinks of anything other than what he did the day before. . . . He is not a criminal, yet it is impossible to say, for example, that he *is virtuous, that he is an honest man, that he is estimable,* and so on. Moral praise cannot be appropriate for him, since this assumes relationships with men, and he has none. And yet all grandeur, all power, all subordination rests on the executioner: he is the horror and the bond of human association. Remove this incomprehensible agent from the world, and . . . order gives way to chaos. God, who is the author of sovereignty, is the author also of chastisement: he has built our world on these two poles . . .[6]

This is deeply anti-humanist. De Maistre's is not an amoral realism; it is not Machiavelli, it is Freud, Sade, and Kafka. The executioner is not a pragmatist, nor the servant of pragmatists; neither he, nor his masters, understand or control the forces they unleash. The foundation of human life and society lies in incomprehensible, natural or God-decreed forces. All great things are beyond human control. Humans play their parts in the cosmic drama unconscious of the meaning of their roles. Reason is a puny, threatening device. The world into which God has plunged us for His inscrutable reasons is evil and man is evil *whenever he is himself*; he is good only when he gives himself over to a higher power. To blunder into reform is not to undo the ultimate order, for that is impossible. It is rather to unleash unanticipated consequences which will follow with the surety of a mechanism.

It is useful to distinguish De Maistre from Hobbes. De Maistre is on some issues actually more "liberal" than Hobbes. Political forces, hence the Estates, must be balanced. Even the king may not reinvent society. De Maistre admired Burke, and even Hume's ethical and political works (while despising his epistemology and skepticism regarding religion). Like Hobbes, rule must be by law, not whim. Both accept that will, not reason, is the basis of political authority, and that political authority is the basis of society. Civil association is based in a supra-civil and amoral power. But for Hobbes the acceptance of this power is rooted in the rational self-interest of individuals. The supra-civil authority is not mysterious; the will on which society is based is not a metaphysical will like Schopenhauer's. Hobbesian pessimism sees human beings as acquisitive, rapacious, greedy, and maleficent, but not irrational or unconscious. This is the sense in which Hobbes straddles the liberal-conservative distinction: the power and aim of government is essentially conservative, and may limit liberty as it sees fit, but the justification of that power is rational, individualistic, and self-interested, hence "liberal." De Maistre's justification of power, on the other hand, presupposes a human nature that is not transparent to itself.

The German response to the Napoleonic era brought something special to conservatism: nationalism. Its philosophical roots can be found in Herder's philosophy of culture, and in aspects of Kant, particularly those entailed in his admiration for Rousseau. Rousseau was the great patron of radicalism, left and right. His ideal of self-determination found its way into Kant's notion of autonomy, and thereby into German philosophy.[7] In his *Addresses to the German Nation* (1808), Johann Gottlieb Fichte (1762–1814), adapting Herder, made national culture the core of the Rousseauian-Kantian self, and the nationalist tradition was off and running.

Fichte's passionate addresses to his fellow Prussians immediately following Napoleon's conquest called for a cultural, not a military, answer to the French. Germans must return to their true selves, their authentic, distinctive culture. The means is to be education, the education of the spiritual man, for the *inner* man must rule the outer man, the spiritual interiority of Germans must remake the superficial, material, outward structures of social life (which to Fichte were the primary concerns of the French). As with Herder and later Wilhelm von Humboldt, language is the mark of the original nature of a people, by which its way of life and view of the world is expressed. Fichte claims that to speak another's language is to receive the "flat and dead history of a foreign culture,"[8] to think "second-hand." He regards the authentic *Volk*, the continuous cultural-spiritual life of a people in its Fatherland, as the medium of eternity, which gives immortal significance to the work of the individual German.

> So long as this people exists, every further revelation of the divine will appears and takes shape in that people in accordance with the same natural law. . . . This, then, is a people in the higher meaning of the word . . . the totality of men continuing to live in society with each other and continually creating themselves naturally and spiritually out of themselves, a totality that arises together out of the divine under a certain special law of divine development. It is the subjection in common to this special law that unites this mass in the eternal world, and therefore in the temporal also . . .[9]

At the same time, Fichte's nationalism is not entirely ill-liberal. He defended the rule of law; arbitrariness of government cannot express the spirit of the nation. He endorsed republicanism and popular sovereignty, indeed, he believes that Germans are *the* intrinsically republican, egalitarian nation, unlike the hierarchical French. That language and action, which, unlike contemplation, are bequeathed to all as the media of authenticity makes this egalitarianism possible. Indeed, in a sense it would be accurate to deny that Fichte's nationalism is conservative at all. For while he calls for a return to the authentic, his interests are idealistic, utopian, and futural. Germany is called upon to create a new society, albeit one that more truly expresses its traditional nature. Property, distinctions of rank, and all institutions are to be subjected to reform. Nationalism in Fichte is self-consciously progressive and innovative. But its aim is to capture the essence of a particular cultural tradition, against the cosmopolitanism of the Enlightenment, and to this extent it is conservative.

Remaining in Germany for the moment, we move to the most influential philosopher of the nineteenth century. Of Hegel it is perhaps more true than of any other philosopher that one can find almost anything in his work; his thought has inspired conservatism, liberalism, communitarianism, statism, and Marxism. In the present context I only wish to list the elements of the moderate conservatism that can be and has been found in Hegel.[10] To do that we must briefly review three different political Hegels and the texts in which they are rooted.

The dialectic of Lord and Bondsman in the *Phenomenology of Spirit* (1807) is central to Hegel's doctrine of the social basis of self-consciousness, for the slave must pass through his dependence and fear to be recognized by the master, and thus recognize his own freedom and consciousness. Freedom is the core of Hegel's admiring view of modernity and modern politics, and as such the Lord-Bondsman discussion is basic to egalitarian and Marxist interpretations of Hegel. But in at least two respects the *Phenomenology* gives comfort to conservatives. First is the social evolution of self-consciousness. Immediate self-awareness, which was arguably pre-supposed by epistemology since Descartes, is primitive and undeveloped. True or free self-consciousness, hence "Spirit," can only emerge through social relations. Second, Hegel famously attacks what he regards as the Enlightenment's abstract, un-contextualized conception of freedom and equality, and blames the excesses of the French Revolution on it. James Schmidt nicely clarifies the Hegelian and Burkean responses to the Revolution: "For Hegel, the French Revolution inaugurated a new age. . . . While Burke saw the disaster of the Revolution to lie in its forgetting of the lessons of the past, for Hegel, its disaster lay in its failure to find an institutional form adequate to the principles on which the present rests."[11]

Hegel's ways of constructing this "institutional form" of modern liberty is the source for the communitarian Hegel. In the third and final volume of his Encyclopedia, the *Philosophy of Mind* (1817), Hegel conceives of self-conscious freedom as emerging from, as we saw, mutual recognition. Universal self-consciousness is achieved "in the shape of reciprocity," whereby each individual in the formerly unequal relation of master and slave now becomes aware of his own freedom only by setting aside its own "unequal particularity" and seeing itself in the other, while knowing the other likewise does the same.[12] The substance of all ethical life, whether in the form of family, civil society, state, friendship, or love lies in this recognitive community.

It is the *Philosophy of Right* (1821) that carries the most conservative Hegel. In it much hangs on his distinction of *Moralität*, or abstract duty, from *Sittlichkeit*, customary moral life. The former must inevitably be contextualized by the latter; a community of custom is the concrete embodiment of ethical life. Ethical life places the individual within family, then civil society, and lastly the state as the objectification of the notion of Right (*Rechtstaat*). Civil society mediates the private and public spheres – or rather, the most private with the most public sphere. The ethical supremacy Hegel grants to the State, hence its moral non-neutrality, is anathema to liberals. Most disturbingly for liberal social critics, in the notorious Preface he denies that the function of philosophy is to change society. Social history evolves according to its own reasons: "What is rational is actual and what is actual is rational." Philosophy cannot instruct the world as to what is ought to be, since it comes "too late." Famously, "When philosophy paints its gray in gray, then has a shape of life grown old. . . . it cannot be rejuvenated but only understood. The owl of Minerva spreads its wings only with the falling of the dusk."

A similarly complex relation to conservatism is evident in the work of Benjamin Constant, one of the inventors of the term "liberal" in its modern usage.[13] As we saw in chapter 1, Constant criticized those who sought to apply ancient "public" liberty to modern politics. As a critic of anachronism, Constant might seem antithetical to Burke, the champion of tradition. One might imagine that Constant sees modernity while Burke does not. But this would be overstated. Constant praises tradition, even remarking that,

> if I found a people who, having been offered the most perfect of institutions, metaphysically speaking, refused them in order to remain faithful to those of their fathers, I would admire this people, and I would think it happier in its feelings and in its soul under its faulty institutions, than it could be made by all the proposed improvements.[14]

He joins Burke in his admiration for civil society and for localism, against the homogenizing power of the modern state. "Variety is life," Constant writes, "uniformity, death." We must remember that the anachronism Constant attacked was that of the French Revolution, whereas the English tradition that Burke defended served as Constant's model of a modern free society. Furthermore, note that, while Constant deserves a place in the liberal pantheon, he endorsed constitutional monarchy, accepted limits on freedom of the press and suffrage, and rejected natural rights. The liberalism of Constant and the conservatism of Burke are not so very far apart. They differ less on the political forms they approve and condemn than on their names for the evil they jointly opposed in the French Revolution.

At this point we may say a few words about the distinctive nature of the British political tradition. The unity of that tradition, whether conservative or liberal, English or Scottish or Irish, from Hobbes through Locke to Hume, Smith, and Burke is the characteristic fear of what Locke called "enthusiasm." Presumably the Puritan revolt served as an inoculation. This is the genius of the British tradition, whatever its limitations: *a religiosity that fears religious excess.*[15] But it characteristically found such enthusiasm not only in the passionate solidarity of groups stoked by divine inspiration, but also in the utopian fervor of intellectuals.[16] Philosophy itself is suspect. This is a hallmark of the Scottish Enlightenment, and it is crucial to the history of conservatism. Thomas Reid formulated his "common sense" philosophy in a way congenial to the modern conservative:

> the votaries of . . . Philosophy, from a natural prejudice in her favour, have endeavoured to extend her jurisdiction beyond its just limits and to call to her bar the dictates of Common Sense. *But these decline this jurisdiction*; they disdain the trial of reasoning and disown its authority; they neither claim its aid, nor dread its attacks. (my emphasis)[17]

This opposition to philosophy is evident in Hume, whose political essays were influential.[18] Hume based his political analyses on his account of English history, by which he opposed common interpretations of English government. For Hume that government's legitimacy was based neither on Lockean social contract nor on its antiquity, but on its *utility*. British governance evolved accidentally through a variety of strategic moves by various parties and is maintained because it is beneficial to society. Hume had no patience for the social contract theory of Locke, which he regarded as a philosophical fancy; here one can see the continuity between Hume's epistemology and his politics. Thus Hume also disagreed with Burke, who accepted both the factual antiquity of the English constitution, and the legitimacy conferred by it. However, while Hume denied that antiquity or tradition legitimates government *for him*, that is, philosophically, he saw that it did indeed legitimate government for common people. It was evident that tradition was part of what made a particular political form serve social interests. Hume accepted conventionalism, that social opinion is the sole source of legitimacy. For Hume there could be no philosophical politics, that is, no supra-conventional, normative justification of the forms of a polity. Like Reid, who he otherwise ridiculed, and like Burke, Hume saw philosophy as a social danger when it is practiced, as it often is, wrongly.

In general, for English conservatism reason is limited and founded on what is greater or more fundamental than reason. But, versus De Maistre, what is greater and more fundamental does not contradict reason, as the reasonable recognize. *Contra* Hegel the real is not rational, but neither is it irrational. The relation of reason to what is greater is the relation of *part to whole*. There is no reason to believe that this part is antithetical to the whole; on the contrary, one presumes it was designed or evolved to serve or conform to the whole. But neither can the part presume to encompass the whole. The microcosm does not capture the macrocosm. Ideology, theoretical reason, and philosophy threaten society when they presume to critique society by their own invented standards. The result of this largely Scottish view is a politics that is pragmatic rather than ideological. But pragmatism must be pragmatism for the people in question, and each people has a tradition and hence standards of legitimacy and of right. Hence this is a pragmatism that does not abandon morality. Likewise, politics is to be rooted in civil society, which is regarded with respect by English proto-liberals and conservatives. For Locke, Hume, Smith, and Burke, political power is distinct from civil society. Power does not *make* society; rather, it serves it, and society, as reasonable, knows this. Hence society does not call for politics to remake the world. As we will see, when Burke asserts the legitimacy of traditional authority he characteristically insists that the people endorse that authority and wish for no other. Compared to De Maistre, English conservatism is a conservatism of light and optimism, not darkness and pessimism; compared to Fichte, it is a conservatism of confidence, not fear of inauthenticity and self-pollution.

Conservatism, *Ancien* and Modern

Drawing on that English tradition, we may say that what is called liberalism and what is called conservatism are not analogous forms of political theory. Liberalism can fairly be described as a normative theory that explicitly endorses a set of political policies, e.g. claims about the ultimate value of liberty, popular sovereignty, constitutionalism, rights guarantees, and more controversially, distributive justice rules. Liberals typically announce moral principles – deontologically, about rights or equality, or teleologically, about happiness – and derive from them a set of justified political and social arrangements.

Conservatism rejects this approach to political thought. With only vague exceptions, conservatism is *not* tied to the universal advocacy of particular policies. Strictly speaking, it is neither a theory nor a doctrine, and this will have its joys and sorrows for any application of conservatism.[19] Conservatism is a *method*, an attitude toward whatever topic draws our attention, and how such ought to be treated by the inquiring mind. The conservative typically applies this attitude to two things which generate political implications. First is the nature of the political dimension of human existence and its relations to other, non-political dimensions of that existence, particularly, social relations, economy, and culture. Thus conservatism always entails an account of society and the proper place of politics in it. Second is the question of what human beings are like. Thus conservatism always has an anthropology. While we cannot present a list of essential conservative "doctrines" or "policies," we can describe four fundamental commitments or beliefs characteristic of conservatism.

The most basic is this: *endurance is validity.* What endures, in so far as it endures, is valid. This is not to say that *only* what endures is valid, nor that everything that endures is valid *simpliciter*, for the conservative need not deny that there are other, sometimes conflicting, standards of validity. Simply, when the conservative sees a social arrangement that has been standing for a long time, he or she concludes, like the ecologist, that there are probably good reasons for its continued existence.[20] The conservative's initial response to what persists in existence is to honor it. This means the conservative, within limits to be spelled out later, honors tradition. Tradition, from the Latin *traditum*, is simply what is inherited. The conservative is keenly aware that the bulk of the conditions of any individual or social existence are inherited from the past. We might say the conservative accepts the medieval principle, *esse qua esse bonum est*, being as being is good, as long as being is not understood as *presence*. The conservative sees, or more accurately, *feels* the weight of endurance, the *wherefrom* of the present, which promises its continuance into the future. The present is the moving face of the past as it becomes the future. One might say in contrast that the liberal tends to *see* – not feel – sheer presence as *posse*, possibility. For the liberal, the *sui generis* nature of sheer presence, its ahistorical givenness to (one suspects) vision, is a readiness to be formed into a future which *need not* be continuous with the past.[21]

Such conservatism has been ridiculed by liberals as unsophisticated, brutish, the relic of a less developed mentality. This criticism is *correct*. The acceptance of the validity of what endures is literally primitive. At the most basic level of our experience, we accept the world as given, and – here is the philosophically more interesting point – *valid as given*. Conservatism is a reflective assertion of that primitive response to the world that does not fully distinguish *is* and *ought*, or existence and validity, to which we learn to find exceptions, but we can never get fully past or live without. However much we subject some areas of experience to criticism and reform, acceptance forms the indefinite dark background that permits the critical spotlight to volatilize some patch of foreground. That which is critically examined floats on, and its criticism is made possible by, a sea of acceptance. Without this acceptance, we would be forced to put every item and facet of experience before constructed principles of judgment, whose own validity would be open to question. Conservatism is the articulation of a basic, pre-theoretical human attitude that all of us share. It is, one might say, the "natural attitude."[22]

This also defines the conservative attitude to change. Conservatives are famously un-fond of change (unless of course the change is a reaction that returns society to the *status quo ante*). The future raises for the conservative a worry, namely, will the gift of the past endure? The conservative is concerned that the future be continuous with the past, which is to say, with what is *best* in the past. But this concern does not fuel simplistic opposition. Burke famously warned that, "A state without the means of some change is without the means of its conservation."[23] It is the bending tree that survives the storm. But beyond this pragmatic wisdom, conservatism holds that there is no such thing as *total* change or *utter* novelty. Social tradition is complex; any change takes place against a background of persistence. The aim is to navigate the tides and currents and, as Oakeshott says, stay afloat.

Second and just as important, conservatism accepts *holism*, or that the total ensemble of social relations and culture is what matters in human affairs. This has two distinct sorts of implications. The more familiar is anthropological: conservatism accepts that the human self cannot be understood independently of its social embeddedness and cultural inheritance.[24] We will postpone this important side of conservatism until the following chapter. Less familiar are the methodological implications. Politics, understood as a realm of concern distinct from economics, culture, and social relations is always an abstraction, circumstantially legitimate depending on its purposes, but potentially dangerous and ultimately invalid. We may legitimately use such abstractions as long as we recognize them as such.[25] In the contemporary world, where nobody thinks economic matters are politically irrelevant, this holism especially signifies the relevance of culture to politics. John Gray's term for this is the "primacy of cultural forms," the view that "neither market institutions nor political institutions can or should be autonomous in regard to the cultures they serve."[26]

Having opened the door of politics to culture and social life and denied theoretical simplifications, the conservative recognizes that many distinctive values place legitimate demands on political decision. No one value can "trump" all others. While refractory to many current depictions of conservatism, it is nonetheless true to say that conservatism is inherently *pluralist*. John Kekes expresses this value pluralism by enumerating what he regards as the "political" conditions of citizens leading "good" lives, including civility, equality, freedom, order, prosperity, welfare, etc. He insists that conservatives take all of these factors into account, privileging none, rather than declaring with liberals that some one or two (e.g. freedom or equality) trump all others.[27] Holists are condemned to an endless balancing act.

One consequence of holism is that what endures and is valid *cannot be adequately summarized by stated principles*, or more precisely, formulae. The institutions, practices, habits, and principles of a society are not reducible to the last of these. Consequently, *incoherence* or conflict of principles, within limits, *is not a disqualification of validity*. This becomes in the mouths of some conservatives a critique of theoretical reason wherever it attempts to state norms that political society ought to obey. This was the heart of Burke's reaction to the French Revolution. To be sure, he objected to the particular principles the revolution endorsed, but this was inseparable in his mind from its over-reliance on principle *per se*. (Here it should – but unfortunately cannot – go without saying that "principle" is not identical to "morality." Traditional conservatives are not amoral followers of *Realpolitik*.)

Conservatism is thus critical of a prominent tendency of politics and political thought since the eighteenth century – one crucial to what came to be liberalism – namely the belief that reason, in its *theoretical* employment, can discover the truth of universal, hence supra-cultural, ahistorical, articulated moral principles (e.g. of equality, natural rights, and popular sovereignty) which alone provide the legitimacy of political institutions, and to which social and political arrangements ought to conform. Conservatism rejects this, *even where it accepts the legitimacy of the institutions and practices thereby evolved*. Conservatism's enemy in this sense is the *hubris* of modern political theory, evident in various movements, sometimes liberal, sometimes Marxist, sometimes Fascist. It is the attempt to remake society on the basis of formulae, explicit rules that declare the fundamental norms for social life. It is this that, consciously or not, informs and unites the diverse brands of conservatism active in American politics, from the religious right to libertarianism, in their suspicion of government itself. Conservatism is not, despite current rhetoric and the politics of a militant extreme, intrinsically anti-government; it is certainly not anti-authority. But it is circumstantially opposed to modern government, because it happens that, especially in the modern state, there is no power on Earth more likely to attempt to remake society on the basis of principle than government.

Here we must briefly deal with an intra-conservative argument. Conservatism has a *goal*, namely, to preserve society, which means preserving the good things of society. The most systematic British conservative of the twentieth century, Michael Oakeshott, claimed that conservatism is not teleological, that it refuses to yoke society to a *telos* or goal. Oakeshott famously says that the aim of the ship of society is to stay afloat, not to go anywhere in particular. But, of course, staying afloat is a kind of goal, and may require much activism, especially in a storm. Oakeshott would deny that staying afloat is a goal in that it is not "substantive." Fair enough. But conservatism is a historical response to the attempt to yoke society to some other, more substantive goal, and much may be required to un-yoke society. Conservatism thus has its own goal, which is to return society to its intrinsic "goal," *goal-less endurance.*

This clearly means that conservative government must as far a possible preserve life and prevent misery. Some contemporary conservatives may already hear in this formulation the thin end of the wedge of activist government, which they wish to reject, most emphatically in the redistributive policies of the welfare state. Their hearing is still good: the wedge is there. But it is unavoidable, since the preservation of the good is inseparable from the conservative's primary concern. Widespread death or misery is nothing but the impending collapse of society, and no government but a tyranny can be indifferent to it. Extreme government *disengagement* is as much a mark of tyranny as extreme government *involvement*; only a tyrant can fiddle while Rome burns.[28] Conservatism does not accept a back seat to liberalism in opposing tyranny, and this includes opposing the *tyranny of indifference*. The current hostility toward government of some who go by the name "conservative" threatens to turn conservatism on its head when it passes from antipathy toward over-large, over-interfering, ideological, formulaic government to an antipathy toward *all* government *per se*, an antipathy for which there is only one name: anarchy. Nothing could be more oxymoronic than *"conservative anarchy."*[29]

This double commitment to governmental limitation and governmental activism does introduce a tension into conservatism, namely, the tension of preventing death and misery beyond some level without recourse to means that would undermine the traditional institutions and practices that as well support other social goods. *But living with tension is precisely what conservatives are happy to do.* For the conservative, conflict among a system's principles is insufficient reason for rejecting it, or even for correcting it, if the correction is particularly costly. Life is tension; the peaceful consistency of the grave will come soon enough. For the conservative, the dream of tensionless existence is rather motivation for that modern form of political death-in-life, totalitarianism.

Thirdly, conservatism accepts the *finitude* of the human realm. The reader may recognize in talk of finitude the pessimistic conception of human nature characteristic of some conservatives, a conception that has sometimes been used to justify authoritarianism at the expense of individual liberty. But this link of conservatism with pessimism is resistable. Conservatism is perfectly compatible with idealism and optimism as long as they are limited; indeed, the conservative must remain suspicious of those excessively dissatisfied with the ubiquitous limitations on human life.[30] Certainly this acceptance of finitude has nothing to do with an existentialist or anti-religious stance.

There are two related aspects of the conservative attitude toward human limits. First, conservatives accept the contingency and imperfection of human beings and human society, which is to say, they accept that such are incompletely corrigible by human attempts at control.[31] This is connected to the critique of rationalism; just as theoretical reason is limited, practical reason is limited. Second, in particular, personal restraint, especially of appetite, is essential to both the individual's prospects for a happy and moral life, and the survival of a good society. This is the kernel of truth in the charge of pessimism: human being has a rapacious side that cannot be excised or fulfilled, but only restrained. The expansion of appetite threatens society. Happiness and morality presuppose an acceptance of the imperfections of worldly life, a willingness to enjoy the limited goods of society. Positively put, conservatism enjoys the good things that are available; as capable as the next philosopher of the imaginative sublation of mundane particularities, the conservative refuses to regard *something* as *nothing* because it is not *everything*.[32]

Conservatives are thus anti-utopian. Utopianism is, to borrow the terminology of Michael Walzer, the *tyranny of political power* over the diverse spheres social and personal life.[33] At the minimum, conservatism accepts that the first order of civic and political business is to avoid the *summum malum*, the greatest evil, not to seek the *summum bonum*, the greatest good. In this sense – and only in this sense – the conservative can follow Judith Shklar's "liberalism of fear."[34] The avoidance of utopianism demands that limits be placed on the political and governmental sphere. Hence the conservative does insist, like the liberal, on some kind of distinction of political and non-political life, although we will see that this distinction must be porous for the conservative. More expansively: conservatives regard *idolatry* as a political sin. The attempt to make the real ideal is idolatrous, and as the ancient Hebrews repeatedly learned (hence repeatedly failed to learn), idolatry can have serious costs.

Now, commitment to the validity of what endures, to holism, and to finitude do not by themselves specify any particular political order as superior. To be sure, some forms of order, like totalitarianism, are thereby ruled out. But there are many political traditions in the world that are holist in their appreciation of finite social goods. To refer to a problem we will examine later, these three commitments would be consistent with conventionalism, the view that the validity of a political order is relative to the agreements or shared beliefs of members, making very different forms of order equally valid. But the fourth and last conservative commitment prevents this. Modern conservatives are committed to the universal validity of a particular form of order, regardless of history, tradition, or culture, namely, that of modern *civil association*. I am claiming – and it is both controversial and a philosophical problem for conservatism to so claim – that conservatism is committed to the ahistorical validity of modern civil society as a model of political arrangement.

As I will argue later, civil association is an association of primarily (not exclusively) independent households equally obliged by a single set of morally significant, primarily (not exclusively) procedural rules. Its associates, that is, citizens, enjoy the bivalent status of *free members*. Civil society famously protects liberty in the sense of preserving the relative independence of the citizen and his or her holdings within a moral association. It further expects citizens to be related through *civility* – which does not mean that civility is the only mode of their relation. To accept the primacy of civil association is to ground politics and government in civil order, rather than the other way around. Thus politics and governance are bound, and limited, by the end of serving civil society. For the purposes of this chapter all that is necessary is to say that modern conservatism is philosophically *realist*, as opposed to relativist or conventionalist, in endorsing a particular form of political order emphasizing the relative independence of households established by quasi-procedural rules of civility.

Given that conservatism is bound to take into account all saliencies and not cut through social reality with a formulaic scythe, it may seem that the conservative's task is rather vague. If it is conservative to accept liberal practices and values when they are intrinsic to the social and cultural order, exactly what does the conservative distinctively stand for? Pragmatically, it is to oppose the attempt to *make liberalism consistent*, to apply the abstract principles of liberalism to every facet of society. However far liberal principles are entrenched in contemporary American society, they continue to subsist cheek by jowl with non-liberal attitudes, institutions, and habits. The conservative respects this inconsistency and will not carelessly or ideologically tinker with it. The conservative enemy is not all liberal institutions or practices, but the liberal attempt to reform all of society according to political principle, the fantasy of ideological consistency, which does in fact haunt the imaginations of many liberals, leading them to hunt out ever new areas for "chronic reform."[35] This is the invasion of civil society by the *teleological*, the yoking of social life to rational aim.

In closing this section I will venture a contentious and doubtless unwelcome observation: some of the most important non-political philosophical advances of the last half-century are conservative in implication, including some which liberal philosophers themselves endorse when turning their attention away from politics. I refer to two advances in particular: the belief that meaning, hence mind, is social, rather than the property or development of subjectivity; and the refusal of philosophical foundationalism. The dominant subject of Western philosophy in the twentieth century was language, and it issued in the dominant view of mind and meaning since the last mid-century, evident in approaches as different as ordinary language philosophy, hermeneutics, pragmatism, structuralism and post-structuralism, that the human mind or self is intrinsically linguistic, hence logically dependent on and derivative of social and cultural forms.[36] In other words, the individualist anthropology that liberals accept in their politics has done very poorly in other domains of philosophy during the past half century. Likewise the belief that a complex domain of human socio-cultural practice can rightly be conceived as the application of universal, supra-cultural normative principles capable of justification by a supra-cultural reason has been under attack from all sides. These developments buttress holism and serve to undermine the philosophical rationalism that typically subtended liberalism. Of course, the connection between such holism and concrete political issues is highly mediated; nothing said here implies that recent philosophy of language or methodology *necessarily* leads to a conservative political stance. My point is only that between the meta-theory of conservatism and the meta-theory of liberalism, the mainstream of twentieth-century non-political philosophy has tended, perhaps despite itself, toward the former, not the later.

Oakeshott on Principle

As mentioned, the heart of Burke's attack on the French Revolution was his critique of a politics based in theoretical principle. But it is Michael Oakeshott who provides the most principled attack on principle. I will use "formulae" for what Oakeshott calls the "principles" appealed to by "ideology" or "rationalism," the especially modern habit of substituting theoretical and "scientific" reason for practical and historical wisdom as the guide for conduct.

For Oakeshott, principles in the guidance of human action, political or not, are "abridgments" of practices, the later being inculcated through training. The abridgments are inadequate for guiding behavior; at best they can serve as convenient starting points for a teacher or a practitioner trying to introduce novices to the practice, or a short-hand means of communication among practitioners. They are rules whose application requires *phronesis* or practical wisdom, which itself can only be got through long experience. Thus, to use a favorite example, one cannot learn to cook by learning a recipe; if one could, then any novice capable of reading could equal any accomplished cook. Rather, the recipe is adequate only to someone already possessing the practical skills of cooking; in anyone else's hands the results will be uninspiring. Cooking is a practice. For political "rationalism," in contrast, *the recipe is served*, the abridgments are taken as the essence of political activity, so that to act on political principle is to act with political virtue.

According to Oakeshott, there are two prongs to the modern flight from practice, theoretical and technical. On the one hand rationalists believe that the theoretical abridgments grasp the essence of traditional practices; on the other, when it comes to application of theory, they understand the residuum of "knowing-how" to be nothing more than technique, which, like the theoretical abridgment, is independent of social and cultural context. Theory and technique are teachable in non-practical ways, each can be gleaned from a textbook, each is an abstraction from practice. Society ought to be remade – already this can only be believed by a rationalist – to accord with principles whose validity can be discovered in ahistorical philosophical argument, through the use of techniques applicable regardless of the history of the society in question. The result is that, having arrived at principles through a kind of political *mathematics*, the model for the job of application is *engineering*.

This is a deep criticism not only of liberalism, but of the very occupation of the political theorist. For much of what we call political theory or political philosophy is an attempt to determine from one's armchair what the ultimate principles of a polity ought to be, culminating in advice to politicians as to what direction in which to steer the state. For Oakeshott this entire enterprise is wrong-headed. He defines politics as nothing more specific than "attending to the general arrangements of a collection of people who, in respect of their common recognition of a manner of attending to its arrangements, compose a single community."[37]

Rationalist principle often leads to expanded government, for such principle is almost always the justification for social reform through government action.[38] Such reform usually involves the imaginative and practical reconstitution of society into what Oakeshott calls an "enterprise association," an organization in service of substantive purposes, in which government serves as manager of the enterprise. While this takes different forms at different times and places, it typically leads to governmental adoption of the maximization of the common good as its *telos*, transfer of political and governmental power to "experts" who claim special knowledge necessary to coordinate that enterprise, and governmental expansion. Oakeshott's most sustained object of criticism is the habit of treating society as an enterprise association. Expanded government is an evil, not only because it is the primary modern vehicle of formulaic reform, but because this expansion is normally at the expense of indigenous social and cultural mechanisms which have been heretofore performing the needed service. Hence the expansion is an insult to the society it claims to help.

In David Cronenberg's film *Dead Ringers* a psychotic gynecologist designs a bizarre examination tool, and is stopped by colleagues just before he inserts it into one of his patients. He says afterwards, thoughtfully and chillingly, "The instrument is right. It's the body that's wrong." It is *this* attitude which conservatism was born to fight. Now, in a sense the psychotic was right. The body is "wrong;" it is imperfect, it gets sick and dies. But it is the only body we have, and the only sensible approach to life is to enjoy the goods it offers. A certain kind of tampering with the body (e.g. artificial organs) will lead to medical advances, longer life, less suffering. So, the liberal, futurist attitude, the dominant attitude of modernity does in fact benefit us. But so does the conservative attitude, which calls us to honor the given. The radicalization of the liberal approach is that of the psychotic gynecologist; the radicalization of the conservative approach is the refusal to change at the cost of everything good. Each side has its vice. When to conserve and when to critique the status quo is the task of *phronesis*, practical wisdom. So one might imagine that political wisdom is the *phronesis* to know when to be a conservative and when to be a liberal. But here the conservative says, with justification, *that* is what I have been saying: the ultimate wisdom is one which cannot be rule-determined. The abandonment of formulae means the turn to *phronesis*.

Burke and Equality

Essential to the liberal republican tradition we hold dear is the notion of equality, at the very least legal equality – for all liberals – and stronger notions of equality of opportunity or possessions – for egalitarian liberals. We may as well take the bull by the horns and see how the canonical conservative, Edmund Burke, objects to this pillar of our politics. The point will not be to defend Burke in the sense of showing him to be right, but to show that he, hence the conservative tradition, is less objectionable than is usually thought.

To begin with, Burke's classic *Reflections on the Revolution in France* (1790) was a critique of modern republicanism. He accepted royalism, aristocratic privilege, and rejected democracy and even equality before the law as usually understood. Nevertheless, Burke's conservatism is a rather "liberal" one. He supported revolution against authorities that he regarded as having acted illegitimately, in the cases of Ireland, the American colonies, and the English "Glorious Revolution" of 1689. For Burke, that government which violates a people's traditional rights is illegitimate. Burke's favors restrained, limited government. He is, after all, an English conservative, which is to say, a conservative in that Western European society which, prior to *declaration* of the Rights of Man, most fully acknowledge those rights in *practice*. It was his historical role to give a critique of a particularly radical (some would say, "illiberal") version of liberalism – the French Revolution – in favor of a particularly liberal form of royalism.

Burke's position on equality is as simple to enunciate as it is complex to understand. He writes that all citizens have "equal rights, but not to equal things." As with everything in Burke's *Reflections*, this must be seen as a polemical opposition to the principles of the Revolution, in particular, the interpretation of *egalité* through *fraternité*. French revolutionary equality meant the relation of brother to brother, a metaphorical family relation that, in this understanding, overrides differences due to social status. Burke wants to say that the classes of society all are to be treated with respect and dignity, all are to have their interests (that is, their *true* interests) taken into account by government, but the rights and duties of those classes are different. The dignity of the servant does presuppose that the servant be treated as a citizen and not a slave, that government is the servant's government as well as the gentleman's government, but not that the servant has the same legal status or political role as the gentleman. Burke's notion rests on a moral conception of "stations" in social life, with corresponding rights and duties.[39] For Burke, the having of rights and duties is equal, but the rights and duties thereby had are not. If you will, this is the Supreme Court's decision in *Plessy* v. *Ferguson*, the doctrine of "separate but equal," albeit applied not to races but to classes or stations. Yet it would also be unfair to accuse Burke of rejecting legal equality altogether. He recognized some forms of legal equality of all social members, regardless of station. Burke is an English nationalist, despite his Irish origins, and as such inherits the egalitarianism common among modern nationalists.[40]

There is indeed something in Burke that can rightfully be called a *conservative egalitarianism*. It was Burke who was, as Habermas rightly points out, one of first modern Western political writers to make note of public opinion, writing that, "In a free country every man thinks he has a concern in all pubic matters . . . They are curious, eager, attentive, and jealous. . . . there is often more real public wisdom and sagacity in shops and

manufactories than in the cabinets of princes . . ."[41] It is rightly conservative to see in each human being, of whatever station, the same perennial
issues being worked out, the common problems of sickness and health,
family and enterprise, love and loneliness, faith and despair, and to refuse
to allow the embroidery of the highly positioned to distract from the fundamentals. It is quite true that in a hierarchical society the unperceptive
members of the elite may then feel that they *are* the state, that the brain *is*
the organism, and they are right to the extent that the brain's unique function is to command the rest. But the sagacious have always recognized that
the brain will not do very well if it ignores the needs and offends the dignity
of the hands, feet, and bowels. This is an implication of finitude. It is characteristic of the genuine conservative not to be too dazzled by elites except
insofar as they exhibit qualities that contribute to social life, either in a practical or in an imaginative sense. There is a fine line here that the conservative walks. The embroidery of the great is good in so far as it endows life
with meaning for all, granting pride in his Englishness to the dustman who
gazes on the Queen, but only as long as she is accepted as *human*. If the
refinement is a pretense of infinity, or supra-human status, then it is an idolatrous debasement of all other citizens whose recognition of finitude is
thereby ridiculed.

What above all determines Burke's "equal right, but not to equal things"
is his acceptance of a social, not political, notion whose rejection is as
crucial to the development of modern republicanism as any notion of rights
or equality. The essential distinction here between the Burkean or *ancien
règime* view, and the modern republican view, is less a political norm than
a disagreement over the referent of 'society.' Burke accepted the doctrine of
isonomia. For him English society was in effect *several societies*, several geographically coextensive social orders. Within this collection of orders two
distinct forms of equality could exist: each member of a social order could
be held to account to the same law as every other member of that order;
and each of the orders could be given equal consideration, equal dignity, by
the governance of the whole, which applies the law as a whole, albeit dis-
tinctly in each of its orders. Burke accepts the view that the individual must
in fact live within an association characterized by legal and civic equality;
there must be, if you will, a dimension of my social existence, a level of my
social involvement, that is characterized by equality. But Burke did not
regard *the state* – the autonomous polity, in this case England – *as one society*.
Within each social order legal and civic equality must reign, but for Burke
the relations between these societies were not to be equal.

In this context, the distinctive achievement of modern republicanism is
less the invention of human dignity or equality or reciprocity or democracy

– all of these had existed earlier at various places and times – than the interpretation of the entire state as one society, requiring that intra-mural, isonomic equality be extended homogeneously to all citizens.[42] Now the
nobles, the royals, the clergy, the merchants, the peasants and laborers are
all citizens of the same social order, all equal before the same set of laws,
granted entry to the same political forum (in theory) as individuals. This
entails the distinction of the civil-political citizen from his or her socio-
economic role or station, so that in the forum and before the court, the
lady and the washerwoman stand face to face with equal rights and duties,
however different their destinies are in socio-economic life. The distinction
between Burke's conservatism and the modern republican view hangs less
on novel political ideas, and more on a shift in the conception of society that
brought with it a change in how equality and rights were applied. And it is
a change that a modern conservatism must not only accept, but assert as
essential to limits on political power, to combating idolatry and false elitism,
and to a respect for civil society.

More generally we may ask, exactly in what does the sin of anti-
egalitarianism or elitism consist? Whenever I say that there are moral
values or standards of excellence I thereby say that those who meet the
standards and embody the values are *better* than those that do not. Whenever I want to educate or improve myself I admit that I am not good enough,
and that some people are better than I; this is the motivation for making
myself better. Plato, Nietzsche, and Ortega y Gasset are all right in believing that the denial of elitism across the board and the assertion of universal substantive equality is a rejection of all attempts at education, and
ultimately of any meaning we might ascribe to human existence. If everyone deserves a prize, the prize is no prize.

Of course, this only serves to redirect the question from the misleading,
"Is elitism defensible?", to the more realistic, "*About what* may we be elitists?" To decide that some people's vote is worth more than others, or some
people's lives, or some people's freedom, is a rather different matter than
deciding that someone's talent is more valuable than someone else's.
Burke's elitism does extend into realms that ours does not, for he is an elitist
about political power, legal status, and rights. What this shows is that, here
too, his political elitism is determined by a logically independent sociological view, namely, that he *does not differentiate* the legal-political realm from
the cultural, social, and economic realms of life as we do. That is, he is a
holist of a pre-modern type, anachronistic from the perspective of a modern
conservatism.

We should note two other forms of elitism with which conservatism
is sometimes, but I will argue, unnecessarily linked. Some "perfectionists"

have claimed that the norm according to which the social whole is to be evaluated – its incipient, if unrecognized aim – is to manifest some value which only a minority of citizens can achieve or embody.[43] The purpose of a society is to be the womb or audience of a few artistic geniuses, the army for a great conqueror, the labor pool for the captain of industry, the guardians for the philosopher in her study, etc. Almost no one today accepts this view, conservatives included. But a diluted, pragmatic version can sometimes be heard mixed in the conservative stew, in an impatience with novel demands on the part of previously undemanding parts of society. The implication allowed by some conservatives is that society can only function if some people settle for less and do not make the claims on the polity made by other groups.

Now, the conservative is right to say that the good things of life are distributed unequally, that nothing can ever reverse this fact, and so those who are unlucky should be prevented from harming the rest of society out of resentment. Even if strict economic equality and equality of social status were achieved – which is, I suggest, as impossible as it is undesirable – there will still be somebody who climbs out on a ledge with a high-powered rifle because of suffering more than his or her share of misfortune in love, if nothing else. This resentment, or what some call "egalitarian envy," the desire not to improve the lot of the unfortunate but simply to worsen the lot of those more fortunate, has no moral standing.[44] However, when the previously ignored or disenfranchised seek a share of the pie, rather than the destruction of everyone else's share, this caution does not apply. And here we must admit that the impatience of some conservatives with those newly unwilling to take a back seat is an acceptance of an *ancien* elitism which denies equality before the law. This is another part of Burke's view which a modern conservative cannot accept.

Burke and Democracy

Our idea of equality is linked to the notion of popular sovereignty, the foundation stone of modern republicanism. Popular sovereignty asserts that all legitimate political authority rests on the consent of the governed. We may ask, however, just what is the consent of the governed, what are the strict criteria for the presence of popular sovereignty? In particular, one may ask in what time and place has government *not* governed with the consent of the governed, except immediately preceding revolt and governmental collapse, or succeeding conquest? Except for empires ruling distinct local populations, government and its forces are inevitably dwarfed by the population of any society, which cannot be subdued if it is not willing to be subdued.

All government, with the exceptions noted, is therefore by consent *in some sense.*

The question becomes, What constitutes consent? If a government eliminates all rights of election, public speech and assembly, it can make the people's attempts to form and evidence dissent very inefficient and costly. It can ensure that only a small minority of the most aggrieved and courageous, or if you will, the most political, will act. On the other hand, if mechanisms for the expression of dissent are intact, then average people may dissent while continuing their private lives, and oppositionist minorities can use the political process to try to gain recruits and influence. The relevant distinction is not that of "explicit" versus "implicit" consent, but rather presence or absence of institutional spaces in which consent and dissent can form and play a public role. In modern liberal republicanism, the people are not merely *permitted* to exercise power or express dissent, they are *asked for* their consent. Prospective governors must present themselves to the people, and try to convince the people to choose them over others, and the procedures of election must invite the people to play a fully public role. The formation of public opinion and consent is institutionally recognized and promoted.

Burke agrees that government rests on consent, and even that, in a sense, the King is the servant of the people. He writes, "In effect, to follow, not to force, the public inclination . . . is the true end of legislature."[45] But he regards the people's consent as given by their enjoyment of protection by law and government, denying that regular elections are right or desired by the people. The people, after all, wish to feel that their government has a dignity that rests on more than a contingent, occasional choice, even their own. For Burke, awe matters. Modern liberals will find this an obvious ideological support for the interests of the powerful. But we ought not be so quick. For our vaunted political equality is in fact not so equal. Differences in social status can be only partly segregated from the realm of political power. Modern republicanism can indeed count the vote of Bill Gates and the homeless woman equally, but it cannot rule out the former's greater ability to affect the electoral process, or political power in general. The Estates are still with us, albeit in a new form. Democratic political equality is permeated and pushed and pulled by the status distinctions among citizens. Is the liberal democratic arrangement made *absolutely* superior by the fact that I have one vote out of a hundred thousand in deciding whether I will be ruled by a millionaire Democratic attorney or a millionaire Republican land developer?

Strictly speaking, "self-government" is a misnomer. It is a romantic overstatement of the relation of people in contemporary democracy to governing. It could hardly be otherwise. To govern is to direct, to control. The people cannot control, because "the people" are plural and never understandable as one person, with one mind, one will, one many-handed body. This is simply a matter of population size and social complexity. Even if the riders on the bus tell the driver where to turn, the wheel is in the driver's hands; a dozen hands cannot hold the wheel, much less a hundred thousand or three hundred million. Even the classic eighteenth-century democrat Jean-Jacques Rousseau advocated only popular vote on the proposals of the legislator, not collective administration of the law. Collective legislation or "direct democracy" cannot occur in a society larger or more complex than is politically embodied in the New England town meeting. In so far as it is plausible in a large, complex society, self-government can mean this and no more: that government power and its office-holders are open to public inspection and subject to replacement through regular elections; at the local level collective decision on policy and law is possible; at state and national levels referendums are possible; public political discussion and expression are in principle open to all; many citizens do so participate, most marginally, but others as fully as their interest and resources can carry them; and government is in fact responsive to popular opinion whose formation is encouraged by a network of institutions (a free press, universal education, etc.). Not to mention that liberal democracies, like the American system, were constructed to limit self-government at the same time that they sought to open up a space for it, through the balance of governing powers, and constitutional rights guarantees, not to mention arcane mechanisms like the electoral college. Advocates of self-government may well say that this is all they ever hoped for. But then this should not be called *self-government*, which could only mean that the government and the people are identical, which would be to say that there is no government.

There are two aspects to Burke's denial of popular election. One has to do with time, hence the concept of action. In requiring that consent be explicit and openly requested, popular election requires there be *a moment* of active decision. All voting citizens must act as one, at the same moment, in public (albeit secret) decision. This momentarily forges the society as a collective actor, and hinges governmental authority on this moment-ous decision. Burke objects to what this implies about the institutions of society, that their existence can hinge on a moment in time.

The second concerns will, and the distinction, already mentioned, between constitutional and occasional will. Constitutional will is expressed in the fundamental rules of the association, the form of a society's political life, rules that are not to be changed without altering the fundamental character of the association. Occasional will is the ruling will of the moment, be it that of the people or the elite. Burke regards the constitutional will as the true will of the people, as opposed to the occasional will. Here there is a comparison with, of all people, Rousseau. For Rousseau distinguished between the will of all, or the majority will at any one time, and the general will, which is the true will of the people, whether they know it or not. Rousseau, like Burke, denied that the occasional will of the people ought always to be regarded as their true will. Burke takes that true or constitutional will to be given by the accretions of the past, hence law and tradition, whereas Rousseau, by not specifying the source at all, leaves it to the judgment of the future (or the mysterious will of the legislator). At any rate, for Burke the present moment has only limited authority over the past; or rather, it has authority *because of* the past.

With Burke, conservatism does indeed distrust democracy where it makes the present will of the people so important that the past will of the people is lost. But we must clarify: the conservative position, as I am developing it, is that the great danger to the polity is not the occasional will of the people, but *all* occasional will, *whether of the majority or of the ruling elites*. Conservatism need not be starry-eyed about elites. To regard any one piece of society or social life as transcendentally valuable or infallible is a violation of conservative holism and finitude. The question is, which strains the conservative's credulity and trust more: power to the elite or power to the people? The true conservative answer is to limit the power of each. For the conservative's faith is in the whole, not in any part. The "people," which means the majority at any moment, are not the whole. Indeed, the totality of all living citizens are not the whole, for the dead and the unborn are present in the form of the lasting institutions and practices bequeathed by the former for the benefit of the latter. Of course, occasional will must in some sense rule; no constitution is a sufficient guide to particular situations, especially in a modern and hence changing world, and so must be subject to occasional will. But the notion of constitution, the acceptation that there is a distinction of constitutional and occasional will, must never be threatened.

Here we must admit that many conservatives since Burke have railed against the mob. Fair enough; no one wants ochlocracy. But some conservatives have followed too closely the spirit of their birth-class and attacked all movements in the direction of universal suffrage, all forms of democracy, as "leveling." Many of these remarks betrayed a simple fear: if the masses have power they will seize the property of the rich.

From today's perspective, that is a very *un*-conservative fear. It betrays an anticipation that, absent governmental legislation and the use of force, society will run amok, no other strictures will restrain the majority of citizens. I see no reason to believe this. Some citizens are held in check only by explicit law and force; but they are a relative, albeit potentially troublesome, few. The fear of chaos is not conservative, for the conservative knows that social reality has enduring substance independent of government. If institutions have done their work, most citizens can go quite a distance with local self-restraint alone. Chaos is to be feared precisely where traditional social and civil mechanisms of order have been supplanted by governmental, technological, or corporate change, which then prove inadequate. Regarding America, the point can be made rather simply: *the people are not levelers*. Strict egalitarianism has had very few supporters in American history. Or we may put this pro-democratic point, for the sake of argument, in elitist terms: If a nation's elite has so ignored the material and moral state of the majority of citizens that without a gun to their heads the masses will destroy society, then the elite has utterly failed. To hold the dike against a few, or more than a few in very bad weather, is one thing, but to conceive the central task of governance as dike-holding is to imagine most citizens as devoid of restraint, which is to say, devoid of responsibility, socialization, and culture. This pessimistic and vacuous anthropology is not conservative; if it were right, it would simply mean that there is in fact nothing to conserve.

What balance should then be drawn? One tactic is to insist that no one gets the undisputed upper hand. Generally this domestic balance-of-power view is good conservatism, just as it can be good liberalism, with respect to the liberal concern to limit power. But while wise as a rule of thumb, this answer is too formulaic, for some one party may at any moment be right in its assessment, and society benefit in the long run from that party's being able to enforce its will. While it is true that no one has a monopoly on being right, at any time *someone* may be right, and it is the mark of the superior political system that it most frequently puts those who happen to be right on a particular question in the position to be heard and followed. How can a system be arranged such that it is more likely that the party which we will eventually judge to have been right gets the chance to influence or direct governmental policy? The Burkean view was that we should rely on the historical expertise of an inherited ruling class, hedged about by limiting powers. The modern liberal democratic retort is *not* merely to let "the people" decide; that is our rhetoric, not our reality. In practice, the liberal democratic way is to create an open culture of discussion, with widespread higher education and social mobility, in which elites dominate but are plural (there is a business elite, a government elite, a scientific–academic elite, etc.), porous, constitutionally limited, partly meritocratic, vulnerable to pressure from below, and compelled to appeal to the people, who can choose among them. The effect is to discipline the elites, that is, to secure a *democratically-vulnerable elitism*. Again, this is different from Burke's system, but not as different as our political "principles" indicate.

Progress

Modern society is, as we have seen, intrinsically progressive. Conservatism's relationship to modernity is naturally of special concern. I have argued that conservatism is not anti-modern, but a different way of being modern. Let us explore this a bit further.

First, conservatism need not be anti-scientific, anti-philosophical, or opposed to the critical spirit. The conservative does not particularly object to asking the question "Why?" about anything and everything in the world, including social traditions. But the conservative does object when that "Why?" question is informed by a certain tone of voice so as to say, "It is the primary mark of intellectual sophistication to understand that nothing need be as it is, that our inherited social ways, which the average fool takes to be eternal, unchangeable, and valid, are in fact merely contingent historical constructions from which the advanced mind can liberate itself so as to see them as the supra-structural consequence of some historical, psychological, biological, or economic infra-structure, hence open to any imaginable reform." The conservative does not recognize such "liberation" as either possible or desirable, or as granting license to modify enduring ways.

Conservatism's goal is to preserve society and, indistinguishably from the former, the good things of society. A modern conservatism recognizes progress in many of its forms as a characteristic good of our society. But modernity is marked not only by progress, but by Progress, a certain spirit or ideology which we might call Progressivism (if we may steal the name of the political movement). This ideology impresses some people with the vision of complete fulfillment, total possibility, the avoidance of all necessity, the complete volatility of the given. While a modern conservatism accepts, given proper caution and critique, the society of improvement and its undeniable gains, it deeply opposes this ideology.

Oakeshott is again the key figure. To regard social life as progressive requires the attitude of the engineer, which is precisely what rationalism brings to politics. Oakeshott's most famous declarations against what he alternately called "ideology" and "political rationalism" are in fact attacks on the notion that politics is supposed to serve progress, e.g. his remark about sailing without destination. Less often quoted, but perhaps even more direct, is this:

> And the more thoroughly we understand our own political tradition . . . the
> less likely we shall be to embrace the illusions which wait for the ignorant and
> the unwary: the illusion that in politics we can get on without a tradition of
> behaviour, the illusion that the abridgement of a tradition is itself a sufficient
> guide, and the illusion that in politics there is anywhere a safe harbour, a
> destination to be reached or even a detectable strand of progress.[46]

To many this is absurd. Certainly our politics has progressed! The modern conservative will indeed applaud the expansion of the franchise, the empowerment of ethnic minorities, women, the handicapped, etc. But this is an *expansion* of civil society to include previously excluded citizens, not an *improvement in* civil society. For how can civility *progress?* Only in the sense of strengthening it, extending it maximally; not in the sense of making it "better." Given the conservative identification of the political with the civil, a "politics of progress" would have to mean progress in civility. And this makes no sense.

Conservatism honors what it regards as timeless facts. In *this sense* – and not necessarily in others – it is, not anti-modern, but *non-modern*, that is, it rejects the notion that the most important things to be taken into account in the human condition are those that are historically novel. Human individuals at all times and in all places need and rely on certain things. Besides the physical supplies of food, clothing, and shelter, there is the integrity of the self, the family that forms and, traditionally, remains as the permanent network for the self's adventures, and the various levels of social order and cultural life that are the context for human families living together, including some form of governance. These social groupings of selves and families have their own timeless necessities, e.g. authority, law, adjudication of conflict, shared cultural understandings of life. While the institutions of social life vary, *institutions there must be*. Finally, politics and government have certain timeless values dictated by their function. As I will claim later, good (which is not to say, legitimate) government in any time and place must at the least avoid conquest, prevent among its citizens widespread premature death and excessive misery, and pursue its ends without recourse to tyranny, corruption, the intentional punishment of the innocent or the intentional reward of the guilty.

But we might press the conservative here that, even if the progressive attitude is dangerous, it is also the mother of invention. People who insist that all is possible, that there is no necessity to limitation and suffering, sometimes perform a service as well as a disservice; the denial of impossibility is an attitude that often accompanies the greatest innovations. There is an apparent dilemma here embodied by Bernard Shaw's line that reasonable men adapt themselves to their surroundings, whereas unreasonable men demand that the world adapt to their own requirements – and that, consequently, progress is made by the *un*reasonable. We must admit that the selective bracketing of what appears to most people as inevitable is the prerequisite for creative innovation.

The conservative does not deny this, but reminds us of two things. First, the changeable always stands against a background of what is at that moment unchangeable, especially in the realm of the human spirit, that is, of culture and hence society. This need not dampen innovation, but it does deny the speculative halo surrounding some innovators (or their interpreters) by which they turn their innovative spirit and courage into the assertion that *everything* is changeable. It is not innovation, but *heedless* innovation, not the innovative spirit, but the grand *rhetoric* of innovation, that is objectionable to the conservative. Second, without an acceptance of limits nothing can be contained, including the human self. Within this world, *to be something* is *to be limited*; not to be limited is to be *nothing*. Any particular proposed change may have merits. But the conservative insists that those merits will be judged with inherited standards, and further, whatever the merits of particular reforms, the rhetoric of total possibility is both wrong and socially destructive.

Thus, conservatives utterly reject progress as a metanarrative. They cannot believe that progress can solve the basic problems of human life, or provide the ultimate meaning of either human existence or social goodness. Endless improvement is not the ultimate criterion of either the good human life or the good human society. To accept progress as the *ultimate* order of value is to deny human finitude. The common liberal habit of, while ostensibly refusing all metanarratives, nevertheless tacitly accepting the theodicy of the eventual arrival of the Ideal Society as justifying one's existence and one's politics, is for the conservative a dangerous and idolatrous transfer of religious, soteriological hopes from their proper, other-wordly object to the political engineering of civil society. Conservatism thus speaks up for the vegetative or metabolic, the meaning of a realm of acts that are "going nowhere," which were traditionally valorized by a non-temporal horizon of meaning, usually divine and/or socially permanent. Civil society, the civil experience of living together, is one of those non-progressive realms, which politics, for the conservative, exists to preserve, not improve. Unfortunately or fortunately, the mundane complexity of civil society, its non-progressive and "nothing-too-much" character, is difficult to abridge for a placard or a sound-bite.

In *The Captive Mind* Czeslaw Milosz described the scene of a World War II Russian train station. In the midst of the "vast ugliness" of the building, adorned with monumental depictions of the saints of History, a building that both in its architecture and its manner of utilization functioned to dwarf the human beings that passed through it, Milosz witnessed a transient Polish family huddled in a corner. The mother pulled out tiny teacups, obviously the treasured last remnants of a petty bourgeois domestic life, to pour tea for the children. Why did these teacups matter, Milosz was compelled to ask himself, when the whole world was poised on destruction, when the greatest ideals of Equality and Revolution were hanging in the balance? The family could never, Milosz mused, explain or justify their customs before the court of Reason. Those customs were part of what made life meaningful for them within a keen sense of the limits of human existence. But it is in the name of this, in Milosz's words, "stammering and mumbling" humanity, indistinguishable from the imperfect institutions that have supported it throughout our historical memory, a humanity that cannot give an ultimate explanation or justification of itself, that the conservative speaks. Conservatives must mumble, as humanity must always when trying to express its deepest feelings.

The Market

This topic is as muddy as it is crucial. Received wisdom regards liberalism as a two-faced coin, one picturing political and personal rights, the other property rights and capitalism. As we know, changing terminology has left us with radical free marketeers or libertarians, labeled "conservative," while "liberalism" is attacked as the theory of the egalitarian welfare state and nothing else. We might imagine that since liberal republicanism grew up intrinsically intertwined with the market, traditionalist conservatism, which is hostile to neutralist liberalism whether libertarian or egalitarian, would be no special friend to the market. After all, capitalism is not famous for conserving anything. Burke lamented that the French Revolutionaries had torn the "decent drapery" from royal personage; Marx saw that capitalism had torn the "sentimental veil" from traditional familial and social relations. The canonical conservative and the arch-revolutionary thus had similar worries about the fabric of modern life.

But this imagination is, of course, not true. Even given the divergence of contemporary cultural conservatives and libertarians over personal liberties and the welfare state, they both love the market. Perhaps we could take this conservative affection as pragmatic, the choice of the lesser of two evils, rather than a principled commitment. Given the choice of socialism and the market, the conservative may rationally choose the market as the lesser of two evils, because arguably, at least in the modern Western context, it permits greater continuity with tradition than do command economies.[47]

But there is more to the connection of market and tradition than either contingent political alliances or the lesser of two evils. The advocates of the market and the advocates of tradition have been an item from the start: Adam Smith and Edmund Burke each deeply approved of the other's work.[48] Of course, Smith is no libertarian in the modern sense of insisting on utter neutrality of government and law, and we cannot expect contemporary libertarians to feel comfortable with Burke. Still, Burke approved the free market and harshly criticized government interference. He regarded himself a convinced Smithean.[49] He even accepted what is for us the draconian version of this thesis; in the great English debates over poor relief Burke argued that the poor must be allowed to starve.[50]

But as noted in chapter 1, the political–economic question of whether and how to interfere with the market is but one piece of a much broader debate by which the eighteenth century confronted, and created, modernity. Smith's analysis was part of a century-long discussion of realism versus idealism in social philosophy concerning the question, Can a good society be compatible with, or indeed, be derived from, interest or avarice? The modern answer is a very anti-traditional yes. In this context, both Smithean "liberalism" and Burkean "traditionalism" are modern, anti-utopian, and anti-classical. Mandeville had put it in its baldest form: private vice is, by "paradox," productive of social good. A society of interests can achieve a moral balance, in its way superior to ancient "republics of virtue." Most fundamentally, as explored earlier, this analysis implicated the notion of society as spontaneously ordered.

Now, the conception of spontaneous order is in a sense highly attractive to the traditionalist conservative. It is, as Ronald Hamowy recognized, central to Burke and carries the conservative implication that rationalist social reform is to be treated with skepticism. Spontaneous order is in fact arguably the common theme running through two notions crucial to modern society, both born in the eighteenth century: the free market and civil society. The conception of civil society, beginning with Adam Ferguson, is a conception of unplanned society with a relatively high degree of independence from religious, aristocratic, or governmental designs. Burke's concept of tradition, while it certainly ascribed the legitimacy of civil structures to their history, nevertheless is primarily a name for the unplanned ongoing structures of society: tradition *was* civil society in a largely non-progressive world. And as we will argue later, the market is the economic face of civil society, while civil society is the society that has markets. The connection of tradition to civil society and civil society to market is the mediated source of the conservative's admiration for markets.

The modern conservative does not doubt that form of human interaction through contract, provoked by capital investment, that we call the free market, is both an embodiment of a kind of liberty, and a remarkably free way for the economic activity of a society to be regulated. This description is, however, an abstraction, as are the notions of a completely voluntary and informed choice among equally available options, economic activity independent of social order and cultural tradition, and a market free of pressures from monopoly, oligopolistic collusion, and "extra-economic" factors. A society without a substantially free market cannot have sufficient liberty; nevertheless, no human society can tolerate the ubiquity of the market. Hence the market, itself a social construction, cannot tolerate it either. As Karl Polanyi showed, the market itself presupposes, not only a political-legal framework, but that the fundamental resources of land, labor, and currency cannot be *entirely* subjected to the market.[51] Even within the sphere of economic activity the conservative recognizes the reality that there are few truly "free" or "wide open" markets. There are existing economic practices and institutions and corporations and their owners and entrepreneurs and the employees of both. Each makes a furrow in the ground, taking up space (capital investment, market share, physical and labor resources), altering the ground on which any future activity may occur. The most dominant and stable corporations form a background structure. There is always structure; there is never a *tabula rasa*. It is very difficult to sustain the claim that structure has come from chaos; it is rather that the kind of structure we call a market economy is particularly open to inputs from an indefinitely large number of sources, hence to unplanned change. Agreements freely engaged can occur at any time and can create or add to structure. But it is misleading, a kind of reversion to the idea of a state of nature, itself a very un-conservative concept, to imply that the existing economic order can be understood *simply* as the result of free, individual agreements, absent all normative social or culturally-induced constraints. No one authority is in command, that is true. But each moment is the furrow of the past, a realm of necessity in which freedom must wend its way, and the dominant players influence all that happens.

In short, conservatism must embrace the free market, but like statesmen embracing, with a wary eye. A less circumspect embrace is evidence of a lapse into theoretical reason. As David Willetts suggests, "Conservative thought at its best conveys the mutual dependence between the community and the free market," and, he also makes clear, the tension between them.[52]

A society without markets *cannot* be free. Socialism – which is to say, a fully implemented socialism – is *de jure* incompatible with a free society. But it is also true that a "society" that is all markets is *no society*. Civil society has markets, but is not itself a market and cannot conceive of itself as a mere framework for markets. Capitalism is *de facto* a condition of a free society under conditions of modernity; the connection of free market with liberty is contingent. Such contingencies are, of course, of primary importance for the conservative. The point is that the free market is a crucial but volatile constitutive part of civil society whose present configuration must be constantly observed as to its compatibility with other institutions and practices that the conservative values. Conservatism is barred from economic idolatry. It is *socius*, not *oikos*, that is its worldly love. So by all means, two cheers for the market. But only two.

Transcendence

Is conservatism necessarily religious? Must it root the social world in the sacred? Many liberal critics of conservatism, and many of its supporters, would answer in the affirmative, the former with a sneer.

Burke considered religion crucial to society, and regarded the institution of the Church as both socially and politically indispensable. But it is in another, not explicitly religious, discussion that we can perhaps best see the role of the sacred in Burke. In one of the most famous passages of *Reflections*, Burke expressed his horror at the French mob that in the Fall of 1789 took the Queen into custody, simultaneously dragging through the mud two pillars of cultural heritage, royalty and chivalry. Burke not only asserts that traditional values and hierarchies are essential to society, which could be a merely pragmatic claim. At least as he presents himself in *Reflections*, Burke was a true believer; he held the royal personage in awe. The Queen was not a *mere* person. His eloquent discussion of chivalry is a wonderful portrayal of the importance of the "drapery" of cultural tradition, without which the human being becomes a bag of organs, bones, and water.[53] This tradition held certain persons sacred. The sacred, the mythical, the religious, the transcendent, are for him the anchors of cultural and political tradition.

To be fair, we must remember that the sacral nature of the royals did not drive Burke to ignore their legal and political responsibilities. While Burke refuses to say that the King is subject to the law, nevertheless the King may not abuse the traditional rights of the people. Such abuse legitimates revolution for Burke. What is sacred for Burke is God, God's Church, and the tradition that he believes honors and is rooted in both. He is not an ancient

Egyptian: The royals are sacred only *semiotically*, by reference to or in representation of something higher, and remain so only as long as they uphold their customary place and duty. But still, for Burke, some points within the socio-political order touch the supra-human, thereby obtaining in two registers, a kind of "double aspect" theory, and this helps to anchor the former.

The problem is that modern thought can be not inaccurately claimed to have dispensed with such, even limited, awe. From Marx to Adorno and Horkheimer, this has been one of the common features of many accounts of modernity, that the modern subjection of everything to rational inquiry and the demand for rational justification is incompatible with belief in the sacred. If so, and if conservatism needs something to be sacred, it would seem at some level to be non-rational and premodern. This problem is a deep one, extending beyond the quasi-sacral nature of authority in Burke, for it is embedded in holism itself. If culture, which throughout history has included reference to the transcendent, is tied to politics, then politics is necessarily open to the transcendent. It can thus be argued that liberalism shares at least this much with radical versions of the Enlightenment, that culture is illusion, hence reason and culture are antagonists. Conservatives cannot accept that view. We cannot engage this issue adequately here, but a few preliminary remarks can be made.

One negative constraint on the kind of sacredness and its relation to the political that the conservative must endorse is that *the sacred may not be political*. That would be idolatry. The order of human discourse and decision about society, and government, its agent, cannot be sacred. The sacred must be beyond human control. Here again our difference with Burke is most determined by a changed conception of society; for modern liberals and conservatives alike, those who staff government are *us*, part of one society, not a distinct order. Thus a sacred conception of political authority, either of the government or the people, is ruled out by a modern conservatism. Government and people can serve the sacred; indeed, for the conservative, they must. But the conservative cannot believe that we can embody the sacred by our acts, by reform, by fidelity to the ideal. The conservative must walk this line: society and hence political decision is constrained and justified by a relation to the sacred, but human nature is marked by finitude, so the real can never be ideal. Whether one emphasizes the baseness of the real or its connection to the ideal is less important than asserting that the real is valuable in reflecting and pointing to an ideal which it cannot embody.

We may advance cautiously by suggesting that one cannot be a conservative without *piety*. The conservative must revere something about social arrangements and the human condition. What is revered may be so indirectly, of course, as conforming to something transcendent. But some goods and forms of beauty must be so compelling that the conservative will sacrifice him or herself for them. Something must be ahistorically more valuable than either the self or the present, hence the occasional will of either self or society. The notion that "nothing is sacred" is, if not inconsistent with the intellection of all conservatives, inconsistent with their practice.

Nevertheless, I will suggest that conservatism is not intrinsically theistic, certainly not intrinsically Christian. I believe that a modern American conservative who is Christian, upon meeting a Hindu religious conservative, and an English non-religious conservative, and discovering that many of their views were common, would regard them as fellow conservatives. Most Americans of conservative temperament would be ultimately more comfortable with religious Hindus as neighbors than with European–Americans who have sublimated the religion of their grandparents into careerism or hedonism. Divinity is not logically necessary to the conservatism sketched in this chapter; a non-theistic view would serve just as well. If someone wishes to say that a non-theistic view will ultimately prove inadequate to justify or make sense of conservatism, then I can only say that this leads to the deepest of all philosophical conversations, and would take some time. I do not believe the task of defining conservatism, nor any political task, can be tied that tightly to such an ultimate metaphysical question. And I believe it is conservative to think that it cannot be.

To clarify, let me distinguish the *ultimate*, the *transcendent*, and the *mythical*. The ultimate is the first or final, the foundational or comprehensive. An assertion of ultimacy is a claim to non-relative logical priority in the systematic ordering of judgments. Ultimacy is the rejection of philosophical contextualism or relativism. Myth, including religion, *names and narrates* ultimacy, and does so in valuative terms that are continuous with normative human experience. The transcendent is an unconditioned existence, something that is not solely historical or human or open to our control. Claims about transcendence are ultimate. But one can make ultimate claims that are not about the transcendent.

Now, modern conservatism is necessarily ultimate and sometimes transcendent; it regards its fundamental commitments as ultimate philosophical truths in a realist sense, and some understand these as referential to what is beyond human control and historical change. But it is *not* mythical, it refuses to endorse a *particular narrative* of transcendence for society, which endorsement it would regard as intolerant. Conservatism is a social and political, not a salvific view, even if it recognizes the connection of society and salvation or ultimacy. This refusal to narrate the transcendent is part of conservatism's distinction of real and ideal, and its honor for civil society. The point is that conservatism is explicitly ultimate and transcendent, but its public or political employment of the transcendent is *vague*. This is how conservatives tolerate, not through neutrality on the question of transcendence, but, if you will, through public vagueness regarding the *name* of God. Liberals and conservatives thus employ distinctive strategies for relating politics to ultimacy. Liberals lean on ultimacy through an official non-transcendent story, that is, an *immanent political myth* of progress and liberty. They have their own heroic story of individuality and democracy and progress, but the values that give the story its ultimate meaning are worldly and immanent. Modern conservatism contacts ultimacy via a non-political, ultimate transcendence that is left vague.

Each position must engage in a kind of dance at the edges of its discourse. I recommend the conservative steps. They mark the transcendent, but refuse its political actualization. Liberals ostensibly refuse to worship, but in fact bow to the god of Progress. Refusing explicit reference to transcendence, their subtext is full of faith. From the conservative viewpoint, the liberal's immanent mythology is dangerous and idolatrous, for it believes there to be no legitimate reason for dissent from its non-transcendent ideals. Liberalism believes no objection to it could be "reasonable." The liberal tolerates those from other cultures as long as they accept that their culture has only limited, relative truth, and swear a loyalty oath to neutrality and tolerance. In contrast, the modern conservative says to someone from another culture, "Although my complex tradition includes both civility, which leads me to treat you with humane respect, and a recognition of the value of traditional life, which leads me to honor your faithfulness to your own ways, I nevertheless assert my own tradition's ultimate rightness. I hope we can find common ground at some important level, with respect to whatever purposes lead us to interact. I have faith that we will."

The conservative is content to live in the tension of such contingencies. The discontinuity with the ideal tinges the conservative appreciation of the human, political condition with tragedy or comedy, as one prefers. The conservative insists that the civil realm is moral and represents the divine, but that Heaven is elsewhere. The liberal, engaging in a kind of negative theology, says there is no Heaven beyond the just *polis*, then expects the *polis* to be a (neutralist) Heaven. The liberal makes tolerance the ultimate law that will bring Heaven on Earth, the conservative endorses it as, in effect, the humaneness and humility the absence of Heaven dictates. One is led here to think of Robert Bolt's screenplay for David Lean's film *Lawrence of Arabia*, the story of British officer T. E. Lawrence leading an Arab revolt against the Turks during World War I. In it, an American journalist, hungry for quotes that would satisfy his readership's jingoistic desire to imagine the European

Lawrence as a civilizing influence on the Arabs, asks the Arab Prince Faisal whether his army's benign treatment of captured Turks is due to the influence of the English colonel. "With Colonel Lawrence, mercy is a passion," the Prince acknowledges, "With me it is merely good manners. You may judge which motive is the more reliable."

The Conservative Paradox

Conservatism faces a paradox. For it is committed to conserve the ways it has inherited, even in the face of principled incoherence, within limits. But what if that very inheritance is substantively *liberal*, that is, anti-conservative? Modern conservatives, I claim, accept those liberal practices, institutions, and values that are essential to our society. But where should this acceptance stop? Must a twenty-first century American conservative seek to preserve affirmative action and oppose welfare reform? Of course not, one may say. But then, which era's policies are those to be conserved or recovered? Some say the *laissez-faire* of the nineteenth century, others the classical period of the American founders, with its ideal of a republic of self-governing virtue. But why stop there? Why not the *ancien règime*, Burke's England? Why not some combination of royalism and theocracy, as in the Ultramontanism of Lamennais?

This question opens a series of difficulties that stem from conservatism's core commitments, difficulties we can only acknowledge, not resolve. Conservatives have a special problem: they admit that *time and place matter*. The policies a conservative approves must differ not only from place to place – i.e. cultural tradition to cultural tradition – but from time to time within any given tradition. A policy which a conservative disapproves in the year one, might ten years latter, precisely because of the victory of anti-conservatives who imposed a wrong-headed policy, be for the conservative irremovable without unacceptable damage. Once the wrong road has been taken, the best way out may not be to go back to the right road, but to find a way to live with the problems of the wrong road. The conservative is not a hypocrite; rather, she loves her flesh-and-blood society more than she loves principles. If my brother has stupidly or even immorally picked a fight with a gang, then my task is to fight with him, to defend his safety in this wrong-headed venture, at least for the time being, rather than attempt a public moral analysis in the midst of a brawl, the practical effect of which would be to stand by as my brother is beaten. I can always give him a brotherly thrashing after we get home. This is to recognize that for conservatism loyalty to the preservation of existing community is a legitimate competitor to deontic rules for the mantle of right, or better, loyalty to the community and to deontic rules cannot ultimately be separated.

Conservatives are thus in the position of having to endorse some liberal practices and policies. The modern conservative must then draw a distinction between liberal *theory* on the one hand, and the *institutions* and *practices* evolved by liberalism on the other. It is possible circumstantially to accept much of the later while rejecting the former. The conservative must accept structures that keep society going – depending on how well it is going – even while objecting to the reasoning that led to their establishment. This is the conservative's lot, a consequence of the fundamental conservative distinction between theory and practice. The conservative may not be doctrinaire, nor happily watch society crumble from the ivory tower of knowing that he or she was right all along. Poor conservatives – condemned to be reasonable.

But this ability raises paradoxical problems. It may give the appearance that being a conservative has no content, that the conservative can endorse virtually any policy proposed by liberals. One can state certain meta-limits on conservative acceptance, to be sure; as noted above, the conservative must oppose the liberal attempt to make the manifold spheres of social life consistently liberal. But beyond this, what *a priori* policy commitments does the conservative have?

Conservatism is an Enlightenment European tradition with, as I have claimed, a commitment to a particular and definite form of political association, modern civil society, hence to a high degree of individual liberty, to the rule of law and not persons, to the equal moral worth of all citizens, to property rights, to the responsibility of government to the welfare of all orders of society, etc. As such, a self-consciously modern conservatism stands for the preservation of the messy family of practices, institutions, and traditions of our liberal republican *civitas*, and opposes any rationalist ideology that would clear-cut that mess in service of utopian neatness. But beyond this we cannot say. We cannot draw in advance a theoretical line that says, "This is that essential part of our nature and interests which we cannot compromise even on pain of extinction," whereas, "That part is open for negotiation." We must draw that line anew in each generation, which means interpreting who we are, have been, and can stand to be.

Even more daunting might seem the question of conservatism's philosophical justification. How can conservatism justify its own validity? Given that, as holist, it appears to rest the validity of political norms on culture and history, is the conservative driven ultimately to relativism? It is true that conservatives necessarily open themselves to the threat of relativism in a way that deontic and neutralist liberals do not. Fortunately, my task in this chapter is one of definition and not proof. We shall see how conservatives may best endure this threat in our final chapter.

Notes

1 David Willetts has similarly employed this term in his *Modern Conservatism* (London: Penguin, 1992). By it he means to refer to the "new" English conservatism of the post-World War II period. But he also uses it in a normative sense, as I do, to indicate a contemporary, versus an anachronistic, conservatism. Thus his conservatism endorses a limited welfare state, and embodies a permanent dialogue between markets and tradition, two forces conservatives approve but which also conflict.

2 As James Schmidt indicates, there is not one but a family of Enlightenments. If the eighteenth century created modernity, it also initiated its critique. It is very hard to find arguments in recent debate over the "critique of Enlightenment" and "postmodernism" that were *not* prefigured in that century. See Schmidt, *What is Enlightenment? Eighteenth-Century Answers and Twentieth-Century Questions* (Berkeley: University of California Press, 1996).

3 I would suggest that philosophical and social versions of postmodernism have something to learn from Charles Jencks' characterization of architectural postmodernism. Postmodern building, for Jencks, exhibits "double-coding," the inclusion of non-modernist signs within a modernist idiom. What makes current society and culture postmodern, in this sense, is not that it abandons the modern, but that it includes modern, premodern, and other elements without gagging on their apparent contradiction, e.g. exploding functionalist social organization peppered with traditionalist metanarratives.

4 Stephen Holmes, *The Anatomy of Antiliberalism* (Cambridge, MA: Harvard University Press, 1993). I must say that Holmes' extremely negative portrait of Lasch is a bit of a puzzle. Lasch was an American historian concerned with social criticism, not a political theorist. Indeed, it is not at all clear that Lasch was a political anti-liberal in the sense of the other writers Holmes targets, especially if one accepts Holmes' own distinction of liberal society from liberal political theory. Lasch's is almost entirely a critique of the social and cultural world that has grown up in the twentieth century around liberal politics, not of liberal politics itself.

5 The term "conservative" as a name for a party or coherent view appeared in English only in the 1830s during the debate over the Reform Bill.

6 Joseph De Maistre, *The Saint Petersburg Dialogues* (1821), First Dialogue, in Jack Lively's edited, *The Works of Joseph de Maistre* (New York: Macmillan, 1965), p. 192.

7 See Nöel O'Sullivan, *Conservatism* (New York: St. artin's Press, 1976).

8 Johann Gottlieb Fichte, *Addresses to the German Nation*, trans. R. F. James et al. (Chicago: Open Court, 1922), p. 63.

9   Ibid., pp. 134–5.

10 In a sense, this is Charles Taylor's Hegel. See his *Hegel* (New York: Cambridge University Press, 1975), and his essay "Hegel's Philosophy of Mind," in *Human Agency and Language*, volume one of *Philosophical Papers* (Cambridge: Cambridge University Press, 1985).

11 James Schmidt, "Introduction" to *What is Enlightenment? Eighteenth Century Answers and Twentieth Century Questions*, p. 22.

12 G. W. F. Hegel, *Philosophy of Mind*, par. 436.

13 See Benjamin Constant, *Political Writings*, ed. Biancamaria Fontana (Cambridge: Cambridge University Press, 1988). The term *liberale* was actually used before Constant by Spanish opponents of the crown in the first two decades of the nineteenth century.

14 Constant, "The Spirit of Conquest and Usurpation and their Relation to European Civilization," *Political Writings*, p. 75.

15 Certainly Hume is excluded from this.

16 This distinction is what Edward Shils wants to capture in his differentiation of "primordial" and "sacred" ties, the later of which fuels "ideology." See Shils, "Primordial, Personal, Sacred and Civil Ties," *British Journal of Sociology*, VIII, n. 2, 1957.

17 Thomas Reid, *An Inquiry into the Human Mind on the Principles of Common Sense*, in *Inquiry and Essays*, edited by Ronald Beanblossom and Keith Lehrer (Indianapolis: Hackett Publishing, 1983), p. 7. It should be noted that, as I have discussed elsewhere, Reid's common sensism is closely related to a number of contemporary philosophical movements that attempt to drastically limit philosophy's scope, including postmodernism, the work of Richard Rorty, etc. *On this point*, these movements are conservative, that is, consistent with the conservative methodology. Whether postmodern philosophy is conservative in other respects is another matter. This allegation of conservatism is not novel. Jürgen Habermas, attending to a different implication of postmodern thought, long ago called the French postmodernists the "Young Conservatives" (see "Modernity versus Postmodernity," a 1981 *New German Critique* essay, reprinted in Joseph Natoli and Linda Hutcheon, *A Postmodern Reader* [Albany: SUNY, 1993], p. 103).

18 See David Hume, *Political Essays*, edited by Knud Haakonssen (Cambridge: Cambridge University Press, 1994).

19 There are few traditionalist conservatives today who are also philosophers. One is Roger Scruton, whose *The Meaning of Conservatism* (Totowa: Barnes and Noble Books, 1980), is perhaps the only current "systematic" treatment. The quotes around 'systematic' are to indicate, as Scruton recognizes, that conservatism by definition cannot constitute a system. Ironically enough, that indicates its unrecognized currency. For a recent American formulation see John Kekes, *A Case for Conservatism* (Ithaca: Cornell University Press, 1998).

20 While I admire Torbjörn Tännsjö's attention to this fundamental attitude of conservatism, and his iconoclasm in separating conservatism from what he

calls "right-wing" politics, he is mistaken to interpret the conservative tradition as nothing more than the assertion that whatever is a "well-established fact" is valid. A narrow focus on this notion then leads him to the view that communism can be conservatively defended. This is too extreme; it empties conservatism of any relation to a form of life. See his *Conservatism for Our Time* (London: Routledge, 1990). Not to mention his unlucky, in hindsight, anachronism: he regarded Gorbachev as the embodiment of his view.

21 I think there is a connection, admittedly resistible, between the alleged ocularism of modern Western consciousness and the liberal concern for a "vision" of the future, as there is a connection, likewise resistible, between conservatism and feeling, meant here in both the senses of tactility and affect.

22 I use this Husserlian term advisedly, for its sense is not so far from what Husserl meant. John Kekes thinks of conservatism in the same way, as "a natural attitude," albeit without the Husserlian connection. See Kekes, *A Case for Conservatism*, pp. 5–6.

23 Edmund Burke, *Reflections on the Revolution in France* (1790), ed. J. G. A. Pocock (Indianapolis: Hackett, 1987), p. 19.

24 Notice that this holism is distinct from *organicism*, the view that society is to be understood on the model of a single organism, hence in a collectivist manner. Society is not an organism, but it is a whole. Not all wholes are organic. Holism insists that the parts of a whole cannot be, nor be understood as, fundamentally independent of each other.

25 While holism can refer to the interdependence of social members, it primarily concerns the interdependence of spheres or functions of social life, i.e. the political, economic, and cultural.

26 John Gray, "The Undoing of Conservatism," in *Enlightenment's Wake: Politics and Culture at the Close of the Modern Age* (London: Routledge, 1995), p. 108.

27 Kekes, *A Case for Conservatism*, p. 24.

28 Or, to use a twentieth-century example, like Stalin calmly compose a work on linguistics while German forces threatened Russia.

29 Conservatives could, I suppose, be called *theoretical* anarchists in the sense that they can live with principled incoherence; but social anarchy is quite another thing.

30 We should remember that Oakeshott's early, non-political work developed a Bradleyan idealism.

31 See another version of the same point in Kekes, *A Case for Conservatism*, chapter two.

32 This apparently unsophisticated acceptance is, on the part of the best conservative thinkers, a sophisticated dualism of practical and theoretical reason, by which a supra-mundane perspective is employed – either through a positive conception of an ideal world or, more negatively, a recognition of the existential limitations of the real world – but segregated and controlled by a practical wisdom that recognizes that the primary worldly aim is preserving those goods that are plausible or actual.

33   See Walzer, *Spheres of Justice*, p. 316.

34   Judith Shklar, "The Liberalism of Fear," in Nancy Rosenblum's *Liberalism and the Good Life*. Where the conservative breaks with Shklar is the point at which the mere possibility of coercion leads the Shklarian liberal to refuse the community and governmental power that, when controlled properly, are necessary to the pursuit of good.

35   The phrase is Roger Scruton's.

36   The connection with Wittgenstein is also made in Charles Covell's *The Redefinition of Conservatism: Politics and Doctrine* (New York: St. Martin's Press, 1986).

37   Michael Oakeshott, "Rationalism in Politics," in *Rationalism in Politics and Other Essays* (Indianapolis: Liberty Fund, 1991). In his famous liquid metaphor: "In political activity, then, men sail a boundless and bottomless sea; there is neither harbor for shelter nor floor for anchorage, neither starting-place nor appointed destination. The enterprise is to keep afloat on an even keel . . ." ("Political Education," in *Rationalism in Politics*, p. 60).

38   But it need not. Certainly libertarianism is a prime case of political rationalism.

39   It so happens that the eighteenth-century republicans who invented America, along with the majority of other political theorists of their century, accepted an analogous notion of rights as embedded in stations, versus the "subjective" notion of the rights of persons *uberhaupt* and without corresponding duties, which is a much more recent idea. See Knud Haakonssen, *Natural Law and Moral Philosophy: From Grotius to the Scottish Enlightenment* (New York: Cambridge University Press, 1996).

40   See Liah Greenfeld, *Nationalism: Five Roads to Modernity* (Cambridge, MA: Harvard University Press, 1992).

41   Quoted in Habermas, *The Structural Transformation of the Public Sphere*, p. 94. The original is from *Burke's Politics: Selected Writings and Speeches of Edmund Burke on Reform, Revolution, and War*, edited by Ross J. S. Hoffman and Paul Levack (New York: Knopf, 1949); p. 119.

42   This view arguably was, and is, common in small segmentary or tribal societies, but not in the large agro-literate polities that have dominated civilization for the last few thousand years, including medieval Europe.

43   Note that this meaning of "perfectionism," employed by Rawls for a position he rejects, has nothing to do with "perfectionist liberalism," a non-neutralist liberalism that affirms an account of liberal goods. An exemplar of the perfectionism here referred to would be Nietzsche.

44   See Gonzalo Fernández de la Mora, *Egalitarian Envy: The Political Foundations of Social Justice*, trans. Antonio T. de Nicolás (New York: Paragon House, 1987).

45   Hoffman and Levack, *Burke's Politics*, p. 106.

46   Oakeshott, *Rationalism in Politics*, p. 66.

47   It is arguable that some non-Western people have at least temporarily perceived command economy and the rejection of economic individualism as less jarring

to their traditions in some sense than full-blown Western capitalism (as noted by Peter Berger). Presumably this depends on many factors, including the nature of the historical, cultural tradition, and the rapidity with which market changes threaten to impinge on it. The faster the transition to capitalism, the more likely capitalism will be experienced as a seismic dislocation and socialism as a soothing constraint.

48 See Donald Winch, *Riches and Poverty: An Intellectual History of Political Economy in Britain, 1750–1834* (Cambridge: Cambridge University Press, 1996).

49 Ironically, as Donald Winch confirms, about the market Smith was the realist, Burke the formulaic idealist. Winch suggests a number of reasons for the differences, placing Burke's religiosity high on the list. But it seems to me that other differences are more important. Smith, the economist, is an empiricist about the market; Burke is an admiring but more distant politician. Burke is concerned with sheer maintenance through "circulation," whereas Smith aims at growth and hence progress. Burke's main fight was against popular egalitarian "frenzy," which he opposed even at the cost of being less reasonable and nuanced than Smith. More broadly, as Charles Griswold's recent study shows, Smith's complexity as an economic and a moral philosopher was great. It is hard to doubt that it was greater than Burke's. See Charles Griswold, *Adam Smith and the Virtues of Enlightenment* (Cambridge: Cambridge University Press, 1999).

50 See Burke's "Thoughts and Details on Scarcity." We should recognize that this issue was more complicated than we today might credit. Like other opponents, Burke argued that relief would only result in greater poverty; the urge to cure suffering would, in the new market society, make more suffering. This point, made originally by Daniel Defoe in 1704, became the crucial bone of contention in Burke's time and for the next half century in England. The, if you will, less humane view was in fact the more modern; it was at least half-right in recognizing the new world. Others argued for relief on a more traditional basis. As Karl Polanyi shows in his *The Great Transformation: The Political and Economic Origins of Our Time*, both sides were right and both were wrong. The introduction of the market for labor created great suffering among the poor, but the Speenlanham Poor Relief law of 1795, which granted relief in addition to wages up to a minimum income, made for even more. The absence of incentive not only led to the fall of the productivity of laborers, but worse, it encouraged employers to lower wages, government making up the difference. So wages were generally depressed and poverty increased dramatically. As Polanyi put it, no one yet understood what a market society was to mean, and how rightly to limit or interfere with it.

51 Karl Polanyi, *The Great Transformation*, ch. 6, 11–12.

52 Willetts, *Modern Conservatism*, p. 182. Willetts' balanced discussion of this issue deserves reading.

53 One of the measures of the difference between conservative and libertarian is the remark of Tom Palmer, who, in an otherwise very useful bibliographic essay on libertarian sources in Boaz's *The Libertarian Reader*, considers this section of the *Reflections* "an embarrassment to Burke's memory." It is, from my perspective, no such thing. See Boaz, p. 452.

5

Another Liberty

We will now pursue a view of human being and of liberty that is suggested by the conservative tradition and recent communitarianism. We must lay down the outlines of what another, less liberal liberty might mean.[1] This task is hampered by the fact that there is not a generally accepted, fulsome conception of liberty among conservatives. While conservatives have offered telling polemics against liberal concepts of liberty, they frequently offer as alternatives merely negations of the liberal concepts. One conservative claim about liberty is clear enough; famously the conservative wants to endorse a liberty that is not "license." It is connected to the old doctrine, evident in Hobbes, of *silentia leges*, that liberty is the silence of the law. While a negative claim, we can wring something positive from it: liberty by definition must be lawful, its scope is defined by law. This implies liberty must be embedded in a context of norms, rather than being the ultimate norm of our politics. Conservatives deny that individual freedom is the highest social or political value, that it can trump all other values. This is not merely because other goods are equally valued, but also because liberty, as embedded in normative social contexts, cannot be expanded to the point that it threatens the social conditions that make it possible in the first place. Furthermore, liberty is something achieved. It is not a "natural" or pre-social trait which civil society ought subsequently to recognize. Roger Scruton can rightly say that "Individual freedom is the great social artifact which, in trying to represent itself as nature alone, generates the myth of liberalism."[2] The conservative finds it odd that many neutralist liberals theorize as if their ultimate end of social life, liberty, were something that arrives effortlessly at the age of full citizenship, or, with egalitarian liberals, at the age of citizenship plus cash. For conservatism the free self is socially constructed. So rather than forming a novel conception of liberty itself, the conservative account of liberty tends merely to contextualize it. In the present chapter we will try to do more; after putting the self in context, we will try to characterize liberty itself, albeit minimally.

Liberals sometimes, and perhaps most consistently, conceive of liberty as purely negative, as Berlin suggested they ought. But both those liberals who leave neutrality behind, and, one suspects, even neutralists outside the methodological abstinence of theory construction, employ some more-than-negative conception of liberty as motivation for their theories in the first place. After all, the more negatively we conceive liberty, the harder it is to justify the *value* of liberty. Why ought we ensure the widest possible "absence of interference" in human action? Like anyone else, when liberals do think about liberty's ultimate value, they tend to conceive it through two conditions of human experience: *latitude* and *propriativity*.

My acts first of all occur in the context of latitude, a range of possibility. Latitude is a matter of discontinuity, looseness, the disconnection of things. It is a social and a natural consideration. It is not solely negative, but it is, we might say, easy to ignore its positive aspects. The increase of latitude requires both the negative process of lessening coercion, hence the range and/or intensity of unwanted consequences to my choices, and the positive process of increasing opportunity, capacity and social complexity. But all of this is discontinuous with the act of choice itself; it sets the stage for a "free" choice, but says nothing about the constitution of that choice. Latitude concerns the *possibility* of liberty. Propriativity, on the other hand, is a matter of the *actualization* of liberty. It is a psychological or anthropological consideration. It claims freedom is present when choice is continuous with the self, "proper" to it, ap-propriated by it, hence characterized by "mineness."[3] This self can of course be variously understood. While one can grant another person latitude, that is, reduce coercion or provide resources or opportunities, no one can be *made* free in the sense of mineness. Someone can give me, or give me back, a thing that is mine, but no one else can make an *act* mine.

The differential recognition of these two traits has led to three distinct notions of liberty. First, when latitude alone comprises freedom, freedom is understood as *independence*. This implies the absence of coercion or dependence on external forces, and can be applied internally, that is, within the self, to indicate the absence of compulsion or internal coercion. This is the negative conception of liberty. Second, when mineness alone determines the concept of freedom, freedom is understood as *authenticity*, as pertaining to what is proper to, what belongs to, the self. When a decision, action, or a form of life is held to be continuous with or expressive of who and what I am, the decision or act or life is held to be free. It is a positive conception in Berlin's sense. The third notion, the result of trying to synthesize latitude and mineness, is *autonomy*. Autonomy both says that my act or decision must be independent of external – or sometimes as well, certain internal – conditions, and that it must be mine, caused by or expressive of my true self. Given the way the distinction of positive and negative liberty is typically drawn, autonomy is a positive conception. But as noted earlier, even in Berlin's account autonomy acquires antiliberal meaning only if combined with secondary notions, e.g. the identification of the "true" self with the General Will, the nation, the will of the Party, etc.

Each of these three concepts of liberty has its virtues, but also its vices. While authenticity has had a place in the liberal tradition, especially in "Romantic" liberalism, Berlin's admonitions against it have been taken seriously by proceduralist liberals. As a result, the dominant notions of liberty for liberals are independence and autonomy. We will explore these now, and leave authenticity, which has an interesting place in conservatism, for later in this chapter. My point will be that independence and autonomy, while capturing legitimate aspects of what must count as liberty, when taken by themselves and out of context, are parodies of liberty.[4]

Independence

The use of independence entails perhaps the most vexing problem of liberty: the requirement that coercion, dependency, or more broadly, *necessity* be absent from choice. Independence is the antonym to dependence, obviously, but dependence exists in a series with necessity, coercion, compulsion, etc. Independence is the conception of choice as non-dependent, hence non-determined or uncaused. Most reliably, the absence of necessity refers to external necessity, outside the self. Freedom here means the absence of "obstacle" to the self's potential choices, absence of coercion or other forms of countervailing force. We all agree that in some crucial sense the slave, the woman with a mugger's gun at her head, the prisoner, and the torture victim suffer from unfreedom (although we will see that even this most reliable, intuitive version of the independence thesis is already troublesome). But the more well-known troubles arise for the other fork in the conceptual road, namely, if we wish to consider obstacles *internal* to the self among those obstacles which must be absent for freedom to be present.

For certainly there are conditions of the person, barring physical or mental incapacity, which count for us as diminishing independence or freedom. Shall we say that the person driven by uncontrollable passions or addictions or inherited and unquestioned traditions is unfree, in effect, coerced from the inside? If we restrict our concern to external coercion we arrive at essentially the position of negative liberty; freedom from interference and independence of external sources of determination are virtually synonymous. Even in the most abstemiously negative versions of liberty, one can usually find covertly operating a notion of liberty as independence not only from external coercion, but also tradition, inculcation, prejudice, biological or psychological compulsion, etc. The reason is simple enough: there is a vast region of historical human life in which one cannot find, in the most obvious sense, a gun to the head, but of which both liberals and conservatives would want to say that freedom was limited or absent. What then can be the criterion for distinguishing "true" independence or freedom from the cases in which people act unfreely but without the pressure of cold steel?

Now, presumably just about all of my traits which could be expressed in, or could proximally cause, my choices are themselves caused. Many of my desires and personality traits are due to genetic inheritance and to the conditions of my upbringing, not to mention the manifold effects of experience. In other words, much of what I bring to a moment of choice, even if external necessity is at the moment "absent," is nevertheless caused by factors that, even if internal, are yet necessitous. The only way to avoid this is to claim that those traits of myself that cause my action are themselves uncaused. This is very difficult to argue, for it requires putting either my choice or the motivations or personality structures that cause it out of continuity with all other necessitous spacio-temporal events. We are familiar with philosophical positions that resort to a metaphysical dualism to support this discontinuity, whereby mind and nature constitute discontinuous orders. Kant's transcendental philosophy asserted a methodological dualism: we must act as if our acts are free, hence discontinuous with natural causation, although we cannot know this to be true (knowledge for Kant being limited to deterministic appearances). Habermas, who considers himself a "post-metaphysical" thinker, must speak of a "moment of unconditionality" in human affairs, that unconditionality being freedom. But if this is so, it is difficult to see how free decisions can then re-enter the world, either in order to link up with motivation or in order to be efficacious. If discontinuity "liberates" it must also trivialize, or deny the choice a place in the ongoing causal developments of the world.

What is trailing us here is no less than the metaphysical issue of freedom versus necessity. This unwieldy problem shows up, not only in the macrophilosophical question, Can there be freedom in a necessitous world?, but in the ethical–political question, Is *this particular* choice a free or a necessitous one? To think of freedom as independence is to wave the flag in front of this metaphysical bull, to take on the burden of finding the non-necessitous. The difficulty does not disappear when we forget about the muddy psychology of internal necessity and turn to external sources of coercion. For it is very hard to find actions that are not conditioned by external necessity as well as internal necessity. Wherever there is what is ethically recognized as a "free choice," it is typically entangled with vines of necessity without as well as within.

For even the gun to the head is not unambiguously the ultimate example of coercion, since I can refuse my assailant's demands; sometimes people do. There is indeed a sense in which, like Epictetus the Stoic, a slave may still be "free" to defy the master, although the cost of defiance is very high. Coercion in the purest sense would have to be neurological or physical manipulation in which the body of the victim is forced to move in the desired ways. Such manipulation approaches the case of simple physical assault, which is telling, for if the other can make my body move directly, without the mediation of my will in any sense, it becomes difficult to call that movement an "act" at all, let alone *my* act. That is, coercion in the purest sense never coerces me to "act," to "do" something; such coercion is all *undergoing, not doing*. As soon as we say "I was coerced into *doing* X" we have moved into a more ambiguous case.

My claim is not that human acts are never coerced. It is entirely legitimate to call the gun to the head or the slave threatened with punishment cases of "coercion," otherwise we would simply define the term out of existence. The point is rather that necessity is always a *matter of degree*. Virtually every act is the response of the human individual or group to sets of pressing circumstances, revealing sets of opportunities for possible response, each of which comes with some burden or cost. A "free" or "uncoerced" act cannot mean one in which no necessity or coercion is present, for there is virtually no such thing. If we are to use these categories, a free act must be one in which the necessity has left ample socially recognizable options, the costs associated with each option are not very high, and/or have not been intentionally and directly imposed by others.

The trouble does not end here. Hannah Arendt makes the point that freedom is not temporally continuous, but *interstitial*. Freedom obtains only in initiating action, in beginning a project.[5] Freedom obtains at the junctures in one's life where major decisions are made, offices chosen, obligations incurred or refused, etc. Such choices are made under manifold pressures, with a knowledge that options are limited. But every option is itself a sequence of necessity, hence makes me "unfree." Am I free when I get up with the baby at three o'clock in the morning? No, I *must* get up. But long ago I arguably did choose to undertake these responsibilities. So we say that getting up is "freely chosen." Apparently we want "free" to be a trait unlike, say, "happiness," which we accept as a fluctuating property; I can be happy in beginning a project, and unhappy later, without anything much happening. But we want to ascribe continuity and integrity to the "free" self, so we avoid saying that while I freely chose to have children, now that I have them I am no longer free.

Despite the absurdity of his conception of absolute freedom, Sartre makes the very insightful point that freedom is self-undermining. This comes out most clearly in his dramatic version of the Orestes myth, *The Flies*.[6] Orestes must decide whether to remain in Argos and avenge his father's murder, or live the life of a wandering aesthete. Sartre nicely contrasts the feeling of "lightness," of possibility that lies before Orestes when he contemplates the latter choice, as he is urged by his Tutor (presumably the voice of the non-existentialist philosopher). To stay in Argos is to decide to be his father's son, to take up the fixed identity and burden of his blood station in life. This free act means giving up freedom as possibility and instead taking on a finite identity with a permanent burden. But Orestes, unlike his sister Electra, *becomes himself* under this burden, while it crushes her. This is not merely to say that freedom is a trouble from which modern humans are, as Eric Fromm asserted, tempted to "escape."[7] It is that freedom can be two utterly different things. Not yet acted upon, in the contemplation before the choice, it is possibility, hence lightness, the absence of necessity. But the choice itself is the acceptance of necessity, burden, and the restriction of future choice.

We sometimes feel most "free" when we have nothing, because "having" normally entails responsibilities, demands, sequences of necessitous actions. In the words of that other dialectician, Kris Kristofferson: "Freedom's just another word for nothin' left to lose." (This is revealing, even if balanced by Kristofferson's next line, which states the other side of the modernist conundrum: "But it's nothin' if it ain't free.")[8] Having nothing is poverty, whether material, social, or psychological. On the other hand, many things of value that I have come to treasure were either forced on me, the result of accident, or chanced upon while I was responding to some other demand. Would I have written this book if I had never been in need of a job, hence become a professional philosopher? If I had been sufficiently handsome and wealthy, so that I might reasonably have anticipated endless possibilities for sex and social adoration throughout my life span, would I have married and produced children, a course in life partly motivated by a desire to create a sphere of reliable personal recognition and intimacy in an otherwise anonymous world? What is there that I have ostensibly "chosen" which was not tailored by necessity? Simply, *did I choose this life?* Well, at particular moments under distinctive pressures of necessity and given available possibilities I made choices – some which I knew to be life-shaping, but many more either undramatic, or momentous without my knowing it. That collection of moments, embedded in ongoing processes, has led to this life. But I certainly did not rationally consider all possibilities and choose *this life* as this particular totality of actualities (personally, to the extent that I can imagine what the term actually would mean, I shudder to think what kind of life I would have "freely chosen.")

The problem of the notion of freedom as independence is that while freedom and necessity may be antithetical conceptually, they are intertwined in reality. Utter necessity, the absence of possibility, and utter possibility, the absence of necessity, are asymptotes that are rarely reached in human experience. Every choice and judgment takes place in a situation of mixed necessity and possibility, and every necessity brings possibilities, and every possibility brings necessities. Differently put, freedom is not the absence of constraint, it is the *constrained selection of constraints*. So, independence of a mundane sort, the denial of freedom in the prison cell or crack den, is fair enough, but a wider and more general use of independence is always problematic.

Autonomy

When liberals reach for some more positive conception of liberty, they frequently turn to autonomy. Autonomy is linked to independence – an autonomous choice must be independent – but autonomy goes further to posit a relation between the choice and the self. If an independent choice is one *not* caused by the *not*-self, an autonomous choice is one caused by the self. For philosophers Kant's idealization of autonomy as rational self-legislation has been widely influential. Robert Pippin is in large measure right that the notion of self-legislation is one of the key images of Western modernity.[9]

We should note from the outset that autonomy is a metaphor. *Autonomos* is the state of being a law unto oneself, or a law-giver to oneself. It was taken originally from the field of politics, where it referred to the self-governing territory. To speak of the autonomous individual, then, applies the idea of *nomos* or social convention, versus *physis* or nature, to the decisions of the individual. With it go the notions of sovereignty and power. Kant's version is the most famous. In his case, the self that gives laws to itself is essentially rational, and rationality contains within itself an ultimate valuation of rational nature itself. Since this is the same for all rational actors, the rational self is supposed to be universal. But, absent Kant's conception of a universal, ends-bearing reason, this notion devolves into the following: what gives validity to the act is my choice. Where the act is the affirmation of a rule or principle or value, we then say that what makes the rule, principle, or value valid or binding is its having been chosen.

Now, if autonomy is supposed to mean simply the level of self-controlled deliberate action by an individual unafraid to disagree with majorities and authorities, all as defined by a particular culture at a particular time, then there is no objection to it. But if it means something more than this conventional, intra-cultural notion, something philosophical, namely the condition of being purely self-determining, then it is deeply problematic.[10]

The first objection to autonomy is a matter of domain of application. In reality, the normative force of "having-been-chosen" holds only for a certain class of human acts, like promises or contracts. The binding nature of the promise or contract often does obtain only if, and because of, my affirmation or choice.[11] But this is not the case for other acts or choices. Nobody in fact regards only those laws as binding which have been chosen by the individuals to which they apply. One might almost say that such an idea is the cancellation of the very notion of law as a social norm, which implies a rule that binds independent of the choice of individuals. What saves Kant, and Locke, from that conclusion is that they accept, again, a concept of reason and the self which makes the I which chooses the law essentially identical to every other I, and hence makes the "choice" of law actually a *discovery* of law, a natural law not *produced* by convention or choice. Only that controversial addition mitigates the subjectivism that would otherwise attend the concept of autonomy.

Furthermore, the concept of autonomy, and by osmosis liberalism as a whole, has been heavily invested with a *cognitive* bias. Autonomy is a free choice determined by law, and law is understood to be something cognitively grasped; it cannot be spontaneous nor determined by character or instinct or desire. It is represented in the mind by a concept. Freedom is then necessarily tied to consciousness, self-consciousness, reflectiveness, the ability to discern within myself my true motivations, presuppositions, habits, and their possible sources of compulsion. The presupposition works both ways: freedom is understood to imply self-consciousness and self-consciousness is understood to imply freedom. Some writers make these biconditional traits the very basis for human dignity.

For liberals who follow the highly cognitive path of autonomy, when I merely continue a tradition or process that I did not initiate, it becomes difficult to call those actions free. They are more comfortable if I become explicitly conscious of other options, am subjected to a cosmopolitan education, or suffer a dark night of uncertainty and doubt, and then consciously reaffirm my tradition or practice in the face of options. Only if I say "I don't have to do it" can we reliably attribute autonomy to my doing it. But as we saw, "have to" is ambiguous. It is almost always relative to other processes or conditions that the self affirms, or is unwilling to go without. The slave does not "have to" obey the master if the slave is willing to suffer and die. I "can" leave my wife if I am willing to live without my children.

It is on this cognitivist–rationalist notion of autonomy that communitarianism has focused its attacks. In his *Liberalism and the Limits of Justice* (1982), Michael Sandel claimed that neutralist liberalism is committed to a conception of freedom that requires a self logically prior to, and therefore able to choose among, its ultimate ends. He argued that this presupposition is nonsensical, since choice must be guided by logically prior ends, so *some* ends must be prior to or constitute the self and guide its freedom to choose. Such ends must be acquired without choice from community or tradition.[12]

Some liberals have responded by limiting the liberal presupposition so as to duck under Sandel's critique. Of course, they admit, community or tradition may have been historically responsible for the creation or inculcation of values which the individual never "chose," but liberalism merely requires that the individual *could* subject this heritage to conscious criticism. Liberalism does not presuppose an "empty" self uninformed by constitutive motives, community, and tradition, but a self which can nevertheless thematize, rationally criticize, and change any particular piece of its constitution. In a careful reaffirmation, Yael Tamir and Will Kymlicka, each of whom has tried to interpret liberalism as amenable to cultural identity, insist that all that must be avoided by the liberal is the idea that cultural membership or identity "determines" life. This means it must be possible *distributively*, not collectively, to thematize and change any component of the inherited self. As we saw Stephen Macedo claim, every self-constituting end must be "revisable." As Kymlicka puts it, "Liberals . . . insist that we have an ability to detach ourselves from any particular communal practice."[13] Hence "no end or goal is exempt from possible re-examination," and so we are not "trapped by out present attachments . . ." Even this apparently measured rhetoric tends to become expansive. Thus, Kymlicka continues, the liberal "desires a society that is transparently intelligible – where nothing works behind the backs of its members."[14] As Avishai Margalit writes, "Every human being has the radical possibility of starting life anew at any moment irrespective of his life's previous course."[15]

This is absurd. If the notion that no part of the self is unrevisable is a descriptive claim, to the effect that such transparency or revisability is possible or actual, then it is a metaphysical speculation with little evidence. If it is a normative claim, then it merely restates the norms of neutralist liberalism. It is utterly without demonstrable support to say as a matter of fact that each of my beliefs and values "can be" revised by myself. Indeed, it is implausible to say that all my beliefs and values are *even known* to myself, although they may all be know*able*. A lot of what we would be hard pressed to deny as free action does not presuppose such self-awareness at all.[16] One must guess that human beings differ vastly in their ability to revise themselves. Self-knowledge is a variable, contingent capacity. The notion of an utterly self-revisable, self-transparent human being is fantastic enough; to claim that *everyone* is utterly self-revisable is fantasy, as Bentham said of natural rights, "upon stilts."

That we cannot *name* any such non-revisable element of any particular self – that is, draw a line between the revisable and the un-revisable – is no disqualification; presumably the inability to thematize or draw such a line is connected to the inability to revise. What would make sense to say is that we do not know *a priori*, with respect to any person, what is the limit on their potential self-awareness and self-revisability. But this no more justifies the assertions above than the fact that I don't know what my limits are justifies my saying that *I have no limits*. Possibilities are determinate traits of things; each thing has its own limited set of possibilities. That we fail to know precisely what those are, or how copious they are, for any given thing or person no more means that possibilities are unlimited, or worse, equally unlimited for all persons, than our failure to know all the actualities of a thing or person means that those actual traits are unlimited. Here the communitarian attack on the "liberal self" and the conservative object to a liberal "myth" of freedom is no exaggeration: the liberal remarks quoted above posit a mythically plastic and transparent self, a self that does not exist, but belief in which is very stubborn among liberal theorists.[17]

Among egalitarians, as we saw, this mythical self is often combined with the claim that an individual's un-chosen characteristics are not the individual's moral responsibility, and so cannot rightly be the basis of the person's social advantages or disadvantages. Such "morally arbitrary" features of my status are open to political removal. But no one really believes this. The idea that my responsibility ends with my choices would imply that I have no responsibility to care for or support a child I have fathered if I did not "want" the child; that I have no responsibility to my aging parents or other family members; that patriotism and concern for the community, including paying taxes for egalitarian distribution, cannot be assumed since I didn't choose to be born into this society, etc. If most Americans actually lived this way our social welfare system would collapse under the weight.[18]

In closing this section we can say that the conception of the free self that many contemporary liberals employ is seriously defective in two senses.

First, it fails to recognize the inner complexity of the notion. Liberty is both negative and positive, both a matter of latitude and propriativity. Neither independence nor autonomy honors this complexity. (We will see later that the third notion of liberty, authenticity, has a right to be included, but it too is merely partial.) Second, its conception of the self, to which it predicates liberty, is likewise too simplistic. The self is dependent, embedded, and contextual. In Philip Selznick's phrase, it is "implicated" in complex networks. It is to that point we now turn.

The Implicated Self

The conservative anthropology insists on the socio-cultural and temporal-geographical embeddedness, hence the dependence, of the human self. Family, social groupings, and culture, themselves geographically located, with their practices, institutions, and artifacts, form the networks of dependence. Mind emerges from, and remains logically dependent on, these networks, which are historical, that is, largely traditional or inherited. Thus, the self which is the subject of individual liberty is a creature of tradition, family, neighborhood, history, and authority. Here is where conservatism in political theory in the past two decades has had its strongest innings. For the development of communitarianism in American political theory – in the work of Michael Sandel, Alasdair MacIntyre, Amitai Etzioni, Charles Taylor, Philip Selznick and many others – is *prima facie* a turn to a conservative anthropology.

Dependence

In everyday usage what we mean by "independence" is relative to what we regard as constituting a normal adult life in our society. We know what dependence in the conventional, contemporary, pejorative sense looks like: someone unable to get through the day without cocaine, or the affection of a lost love, or who is physically or mentally unable to dress him or herself, or who must survive on charity, or cannot decide whether to go to the toilet unless told, is badly dependent. But not all forms of dependence count for us as indicating a pathological lack of independence; it "depends" upon the thing depended upon. What is often called the "independence" of adults actually refers to transient dependence on interchangeable others, rather than on particular others. If I am unmarried and have a series of intimate relationships am I less dependent than if I am married? I would rather say that the dependency of the former is simply less focused and less formal. We do not regard the need for love, or company, or advice, or medical or legal services, or for truckers to ship food from rural areas to one's local market, as dependency, because none of these preclude the physical, social, and intellectual maneuvering among the kinds of choices that constitute a conventional day for an "independent" person in our society.

Individualism, as we saw earlier, wants to conceive of my life as a series of choices, and in so far as those choices involve others, free agreements or contracts. But un-chosen relations form the permanent and virtually inescapable scaffolding of the individual's life. The most powerful relations on which our lives most obviously depend are usually those not chosen at all: one's birth family, neighborhood, culture, and country. And even chosen relations, of course, create dependency. As a modern citizen of a liberal republican society I would regard it as a truncation of my freedom if I were forced into marriage. But once I freely chose marriage I am no longer free, that is, independent, if I was before. I have chosen to yoke myself to another, indeed, if children are desired, to an undetermined number of others, not to mention that – paraphrasing the popular public health phrase aimed at terrifying people into celibacy – when I enter into a quasi-permanent relation with someone I thereby enter quasi-permanent relations with everyone to whom that person has quasi-permanent relations, e.g. his or her family.[19] I marry not only a person but a network of family and friends, some of which will only be acquired by my spouse after my decision to marry him or her. Even divorce, after all, does not by itself eliminate the set of constraints and claims that may be made on the now "free" former spouse. Even death cannot unmake some obligations, e.g. in the case of inheritance.

In Sandel's terms, the "unencumbered" liberal self was a non-existent independent self, a self whose freedom was not conditional on social networks.[20] In particular, he emphasized that the "formative" project, the communal and traditional constitution of the self, is a condition of what passes for independence. Formation is the process of producing what counts conventionally as an "independent" self out of networks of dependency. Human infants and small children are utterly dependent, and only a very long process of formation, if it is performed well enough, can create conventional independence.

But I would add this: the formative period *never ends*. Childhood does not end, but is merely incorporated into adulthood, and remains present in the deepest layer of our emotional life. Adulthood merely alters, and does not overcome, dependence. Some never achieve even the conventional sense of independence. Some achieve it, but lose it for brief periods. Eventually we all lose it. Even if we construe independence in the conventional sense, a certain percentage of people lack this quality much of the time in crucial respects, just as all of us lack it under special circumstances, like recent loss or illness. Non-contractual dependency never ends. The contractual, competitive and contingent enterprise associations into which independent adults freely enter, and which do indeed constitute a central aspect of liberty, remain parasitic on conditions which, if they are not maintained, lead quickly and easily to the devolution of an "independent adult" into a non-functional blob. It does not take too much to do this. For the average person, the collapse of a marriage, the loss of employment or a child, or even the rupture of other family relations, is enough to rip out the wiring of functional independence for at least a time, and sometimes permanently. There is an enormous amount of stage-setting that must occur, and be maintained, before two "independent" adults can emerge under the right conditions able to engage in a free exchange or contract with one another. Independence is dependent on dependency.

Now, Charles Taylor speaking in favor of communitarianism once admitted that the truth of communitarian anthropology has no clear implications for social policy.[21] That we are communally-created beings does not logically require that, for example, we object to liberal policies, restrict individual liberties, etc. But Taylor was, I think, being a bit too generous: the communitarian anthropology does indeed have normative implications, albeit *vague or mediated*, rather than precise and deductive, ones. After all, it claims that neither society nor individual liberty can exist without background conditions that themselves cannot be rightly understood on the model of the contract, conditions that may themselves require communal promotion and even coercion to be maintained. What happens when in public policy we treat dependent persons as independent, hence non-contractual relations as contractual? It means such relationships get treated as: contingent on individual free and informed assent; relations among equals; having been selected from among other options as best fulfilling individual self-interest, given resources and options (that is, as judged by the party making the selection); capable of annulment by failure to uphold terms, or by mutual agreement; and subject to public legal adjudication, in which evidence must take certain forms, e.g. written statements, witnessed verbal statements, witnessed behavior, etc. Clearly not all human relationships can be analyzed this way "without residue." As I noted earlier, Sandel makes the valid point that dependency itself is disadvantaged in such a system.[22] That is, under neutralist social policies persons who choose to live frankly and openly dependent lives pay a price for doing so. This is made more poignant by the fact that all of society *depends* on such persons, e.g. stay-at-home parents. As Sandel argues, and as the feminist political theorist Susan Moller Okin would agree, in the current climate of divorce, and with the presumption of the equality of marriage partners after divorce, women (or men for that matter) who choose to work primarily as child-rearers open themselves to terrible economic danger.[23] Currently, the royal road to poverty in the United States is to be a woman, marry, stay home with the kids, then get divorced. Thus it is irrational from the point of view of self-interest for anyone to choose perform that role which society desperately needs to be performed, and performed well, namely, raising children. A legal and cultural climate of "equality of independence" disadvantages such persons.

Far from being independent, some people are consistently self-destructive, while others become self-destructive during critical periods in life. Conservatives are willing, in Galston's terms, sometimes to prefer the coerced pursuit of the good to the uncoerced pursuit of the bad. The neutralist response is to rest on a deontological bottom-line: we cannot be permitted to coerce even self-destructive people, absent threatened harm to others, because such violates liberal moral principles, and puts us on the slippery slope to an unfree society. No abridgement of deontically recognized liberty is morally acceptable. In reaction, those who have consistently lacked the level of combined self-control and perspicacity to make good choices for themselves may well say to the neutralist at the end of the day: "It was evident to anyone who cared to look that I was out of control, that I needed help, even though I denied that I did. If you had taken action, part of my life might have been salvaged. But you chose to honor my 'liberty,' which in fact did not exist, and so I destroyed the best things in my world and my whole life has come to nothing. Thank you very much."

Of course, coercion is not the only means at hand. There is also promotion or discouragement, that is, community or government persuasion that one form of life is superior or inferior to another. Galston argues that while liberal polities must minimize coercion, they must more commonly resort to promotion and discouragement, which are morally distinct from coercion.[24] But besides coercion and promotion/discouragement there is a last, middling strategy at society's disposal: *construction*. The existing forms of community and cultural life during an individual's childhood and youth construct the conditions of the individual's life, and this is the most powerful form of public or communal formation. Society, in which government plays a role, constructs the conditions of life in such a way that most people's wants and values will develop in predictable and desirable directions, such that there will be little need to coerce or persuade, since recalcitrant desires and values will be rare. Very few people grow up knowingly to desire a form of life that is not available in their environment. Society does this, by and large, "spontaneously," that is, without planning coordinated by a single agency. This is actually how most societies and cultures work; few people feel either coerced or persuaded to follow the well-worn paths. There is nothing insidious about all this, unless the existence of that thing we call "society" is itself insidious.

Institutions

Whatever one's view of morality, it is difficult to argue that it does not involve an ability, acquired in an adequate childhood, of identifying with others, an identification that arises in the course of activities governed by rules, like games, and through communication, which presumes an inherited language. If thought is largely linguistic, then it is both social and traditional, since language is a social inheritance. Nor can we utterly separate the contents of our thought, our meanings, ideas, and philosophies, from the grammar and vocabulary of our language (which is not to endorse a Whorfian global relativism).[25] Furthermore, there is a strong argument that rationality is internally related to learned language and is dependent on communication. Rationality is an ability to order speech and action to make it publicly comprehensible. Very diverse movements in twentieth-century philosophy, psychology, and linguistics, from very different points of view – e.g. Wittgenstein's later philosophy, hermeneutics, the American pragmatic tradition, structuralism and post-structuralism, the discourse ethics of Jürgen Habermas – have in effect argued for the social basis of rationality, morality, and thought, and hence, of the self. To this the conservative political philosopher must add that institutions, enduring human organizations, are what compose and influence this social inheritance. We saw that Hegel famously made family, the institutions of civil society, and the state constitutive for the self, in addition to arguing for the superiority of the *sittlich* or customary morality of an historical community over the supra-cultural commands of universal, *a priori* reason. Contemporary communitarians, like Taylor, have emphasized this part of the Hegelian legacy.

The conservative self is a self of offices and stations, in the spirit of F. H. Bradley's "My Station and its Duties" (although without his metaphorical equation of society to organism).[26] One might say that the conservative self is the *institutionalized* self.[27] My offices or stations obtain wherever my self functions in an institutional order. An institution is a "socially integrating pattern," a practice or association, with a distinctive character, that endures across generations.[28] This conception is reflected in Henry Sumner Maine's version of modernity, that "the movement of progressive societies has hitherto been a movement *from Status to Contract.*"[29] The "law of persons" in Anglo-American legal tradition refers to laws attendant on "status," like wife, master, child, king, etc. The status carried with it rules, obligations, and entitlements, not to mention, social standing and identity. There can be no definitive listing of what counts as an institution in a complex society. Certainly the state itself, its various levels, as well as many businesses, schools, etc. – in short a series of enduring agencies – are institutions, but so are the family, neighborhood, religious groups, and some kinds of voluntary associations.[30]

Knud Haakonssen has argued that the Enlightenment did not yet make a decisive break with status. The eighteenth century continued the older natural law tradition even as it developed the political language of rights, consent, and contract. Its concept of "implied," as opposed to "tacit," contracts referred to rights and duties attaching to positions which people occupied not necessarily through choice, but that were "naturally" attendant on situations. In such cases – for example, finding myself a father – a series of obligations are undertaken as a whole, and I am not free to pick and choose among them. Not that choice plays no role, but the point is precisely that its role is variable and not decisive. Describing implied contract situations, Haakonssen writes that, "Within a range of voluntariness that cannot be specified a priori for all cases, once a person signals that he or she is playing a certain role, the performance is judged in terms of the obligations that generally pertain to that role."[31] This "signaling" may not be the subject's choice. And the particular account of what duties and rights the office implies is largely granted by tradition. This conception, and not the notion of "subjective" rights attaching identically to individual humans and their will without reference to custom, was the dominant Enlightenment conception; contractualist and voluntarist radicals like Rousseau and Kant were the futurist exceptions. Haakonssen points out regarding the implied status contract, "It is of course a moral philosophy which was tailor-made for a conservative Enlightenment."

Building on this conception, the conservative position involves a tripartite claim. First, largely inherited social networks have value and deserve attention because they are the means by which society is cared for and preserved. Second, the individual self that liberalism is concerned to defend is thoroughly dependent on these networks. Lastly, the very features of the human self which liberalism, even in its minimal anthropology, is concerned to emphasize – rationality and liberty – are themselves constituted and maintained by such networks. Without institutions there is no individuality, rationality, or liberty.

Tradition

Liberalism is arguably anti-traditional. It typically understands *traditum*, the inherited, as an obstacle to freedom and individuality. Since most of culture is at any one time inherited, this makes liberalism suspicious of culture itself. J. S. Mill called "custom" a "despot" against which individuality must constantly struggle. This is a remarkable statement, for Mill is in effect saying that *culture itself is a tyrant*. One is led to imagine what it would mean to regard all custom as primarily an obstacle; this would have to include not only religious and moral strictures, but all the inherited elements that go to constitute the self, and are utterly necessary for it to do anything, including fight for its own liberty. After all, language itself is custom; we speak and think in patterns and through a medium that is, in the case of English, more than a millennium old, the result of the interactions of vast numbers of now dead people.

In contrast, conservatism famously likes tradition. The conservative or holistic perspective insists that at every moment the self is embedded in something larger on which all the phenomena of the self are *in some sense* dependent. The foreground has a background, and the background is relevant for, is partly constitutive of, what the foreground *is*. We could argue for a long time about whether "novelty" can mean utter novelty or must instead mean a novel arrangement of previously existing elements, or whether individuality can mean great or merely relative uniqueness. The conservative need only say that novelty and individuality are always set against and dependent on a background of the common, the inherited, the stable, the social. In Wittgenstein's figure for the relation of language use to grammar, the river must flow in the riverbed.[32] But didn't the river make the riverbed? Yes, but at each moment any particular volume of water was and is bounded, has been made part of *this* river, by the constraints of an already existing riverbed.

Thus the iconoclast, the bohemian intellectual, and the political revolutionary reject some parts of what is inherited on the basis of other parts of the tradition that continues to form the basis of his or her self and activity. The inventor creates a novel form by refusing to accept inherited and common ways of thinking *about something*, but pursues this invention with inherited social, cultural, and economic resources, including an inherited work ethic. The social critic needs to find a language, which cannot be, as Wittgenstein argued, private; pure idiosyncrasy has no voice. The revolutionary needs a grammar of rebellion; she may attack capitalism or a form of government, but on the basis of a sense of community life, of classes left behind in industrialization, or a romantic notion of primitive democracy. The attack on society and tradition, if it is to be intelligible at all, must be stated in a socially inherited language. The Students for a Democratic Society embodied in their anti-capitalist rhetoric the well-worn American tradition of populism and participatory democracy. On what radical, anti-traditional basis did the civil rights movement reject legalized racial segregation, and thereby revolutionize American life? On the basis of a two-hundred year old Constitution and a two-millennium old New Testament.

A *significant* departure from the dominant culture must itself be sociable. If I seek to rebel against the majority's plan for my life, I must go somewhere, do something; find a bohemia or subculture, become a writer or artist, join a political cell or counter-cultural group. There must be a *place prepared* for my choice. The margin is culturally defined too. Bohemias, biker gangs, avant-garde artist colonies, and parts of academia are socially prepared places for those who do not "fit in." If there is no bohemia to join, I cannot join it. The alternative would be the rebel's utter idiosyncrasy, which can be, of course, civically permitted, but entails complete isolation, not only from the mainstream but from any sub- or counter-culture. The rare circumstances in which individuals or minorities change the institutions or cultural options of society means finding an existing cultural niche first, which can then be bent and expanded to accommodate the self.

Now, liberals may respond that they know all of this. Of course the self is dependent on tradition. Egalitarian liberals can argue that it is they who have most sought to preserve certain of traditional networks against the market through governmental action. Our point, they will say, is not to oppose these anthropological claims, but to avoid the communitarian coercion of individuals while nevertheless permitting community. Citizens of liberal societies are free to be communitarians or individualists; liberals merely oppose *enforced* community.

But the conservative can rightly answer that liberalism is not "neutral" with respect to the balance of community and individuality. In at least three ways it takes sides. First, in practice, when individual and network conflict legally, morally, or politically, the liberal almost invariably takes the side of the individual (the only exception being egalitarian liberal restrictions on property rights). Second, as seen, in practical ways liberalism disadvantages openly dependent, symbiotic lifestyles like child-rearing. Third, the rhetoric, hence the culture of politically liberal societies is, we cannot deny, efficacious in promoting individualism. Can we imagine or name non-liberal societies in human history that have, or could conceivably, equal contemporary liberal societies, especially America, in their at least negative individualism, their separation of the individual's life path from a particular community or locale and a single family? If we cannot, are we then to imagine this combination of actual individualism and political liberalism is a *coincidence?*

Here the liberal may take a different tack and respond that liberalism is *itself* a tradition. In this she would clearly be right. Liberalism is a constellation of values, ideas, practices, and institutions passed on from generation to generation. We teach it to our children, privately, in school, and in our cultural media. But liberalism is a remarkable, paradoxical tradition: an "anti-tradition," a generationally transmitted cultural belief that what is generationally transmitted is less important than the ahistorical decisions of living members.[33] *It is a tradition whose traditional message is that traditions do not matter.* We train our children, directly and through a thousand messages embedded in our social and cultural institutions, to believe that tradition is primarily an obstacle to the highest value, individual liberty and self-actualization, and something it is the task of each generation to overcome.

The conservative point is, whatever our views about liberty, the notion that inherited culture and institutions are the enemy of the individual is *absurd* and *dangerous*, although its danger has fortunately been mitigated by its absurdity. While a characteristic sobriety may lead the conservative to downplay this mitigated danger, we should not be surprised if that absurd rhetoric should have some effect on the way Americans feel, think, and act. In logic can we be assured that nonsense is ineffectual, but not in society.

Authority

Conservatives famously like authority, and nothing could make conservatism more repugnant to liberals than this. Authority has a bad reputation in modern times; "authoritarian" is our name for an illiberal regime. But a few contemporary thinkers have pursued a more nuanced conception.

Hannah Arendt clears a space for authority. Authority, she says, can only exist in the absence of both force and persuasion.[34] Force is violence: "where force is used, authority has failed." Persuasion is argumentation among equals who need to be convinced; it is the sphere of discourse and politics. Historically, Arendt argues that in the Western tradition authority is a predominantly Roman notion, although Plato had tried to introduce it into Greek politics. Plato continually sought to find an alternative to force and persuasion in the "self-evident," hence compulsive, nature of truth, or in narrative myth, or in his many examples of an "intrinsically compelling relation," e.g. of patient to physician, seaman to helmsman, child to parent, the ordinary person to the expert. Authority was connected for the Romans to the founding of the state or political community by the *maiores* or greater ones, our ancestors, whose tradition then must be continued. The Latin *auctoritas* most basically meant "augmentation" of the founding, not the actual power of building or making society, but the advising, hence the completion, of the task of founding.

Richard Sennett has pointed out some of the deep ambiguities and problems in the modern liberal attitude toward authority. He defines authority as the image of the conditions of power or strength. In premodern, feudal society dependence on and deference to authority did not provoke shame; one adult obeying another was "no more shameful than a child obeying its parent."[35] But in the modern age, we tend to conceive of freedom as self-mastery, hence the *absence* of masters or authorities other than ourselves. Authority is at the same time depersonalized by what Max Weber called rational legitimacy or law (versus charismatic and traditional authority). Authority under this modern condition becomes expertise, rational knowledge, and is embodied by the manager. Psychologically, for Sennett, this leads to the rise of "shameful dependency." Not to be one's own master, to do what others say, to be needful of direction, is shameful. Yet, Sennett insists, psychologically we continue to need authority. Thus the modern view leaves us with a dilemma. Sennett writes that, "The dilemma of authority in our time, the particular fear it inspires, is that *we feel attracted to strong figures we do not believe to be legitimate*" (Sennett's emphasis).[36]

Samuel Fleischacker has argued that authority is essential to tradition. Authorities always speak for traditions, and are trusted for this reason. Authority without tradition is very dangerous, since then there is no canonical good, nothing to which the authority is beholden, before which he/she must be humble. Furthermore, authorities must embody *phronesis*. The merely rational application of rules is not what we mean by authority. Rather, authorities are those we recognize as legitimate interpreters of the tradition, achieving an interpretation that cannot be understood as the application of rule. Authority is intrinsically hermeneutic. The authority thereby represents the ultimate good of the tradition in its obscurity. Judgment or *phronesis* is conceived in terms of cultural tradition: it is the application of authority and a canonical narrative about the ultimate and obscure good to a particular case.[37]

Fleischacker tries to explain the difference between authority and expertise by saying that I can imagine trading places with the expert, not with the authority.[38] I would put it differently. In expertise, which I would say is a kind of rational–legal authority in Weber's sense, I understand the procedures by which the expert became an expert, and so "imagining trading places" means I could, upon reflection, say what I would have to do to trade places – even if this would be outside my control. I know I could not hit major league pitching, but I understand the genetic abilities and processes of training that would lead to that capacity. There is nothing in the process that, so to speak, transcends my understanding. Following Fleischacker's lead, authority beyond expertise entails something other, something whose process of acquisition I do not understand. I might indeed imagine myself as the authority – but if asked how I would get to that point, how I would acquire those abilities, or even precisely what those abilities are, I could not say. This does not mean authority is mystical, but that it is more than the product of manipulable routines and procedures. We may characterize, but not explain, the authority in the way Aristotle understands the person with *phronesis*: the authority is someone who *habitually gets it right*.

The kinds of things that have authority or are authoritative, are people above all, but also the offices they inhabit, and certain utterances. The authoritative text in a field sets the standard, is the last word (for now). Authority *speaks*, and does not merely *show*. The saint is not an authority unless he or she chooses to speak to the people. Michael Jordan, perhaps the best basketball player who has ever lived, is not an authority, because his excellence is not that of a decisive office which tells us what to do. Authorities do not, strictly speaking, do. The great achiever may be an authority, but these two roles are distinct; *qua* authority, she must speak rather than do. Authority is a social, public station. Often it commands, but it might be more accurate to say we take *as commands* what it says.

Authority is not intrinsically non-consensual. Philip Selznick argues that authority in fact presumes consent.[39] This is plausible depending on how we conceive consent. I do consent, submit to authority. But if I meet someone, view her skeptically, quiz her aggressively, and after a long negotiation, say, "Alright, I'll take you as an authority," then authority is not what I have taken on. Rather, I have been persuaded. That is, the acceptance of authority points to a notion of consent akin to what Haakonssen describes as the consent to un-chosen duties implied by a station or office. My consent flows directly from the kind of person the authority is and the kind of person I am, not from a set of justifying reasons I am offered.

Authority is pervasive and profound. It is intrinsic to our notion of an *ideal self*. When we imagine our version of the "great souled" person, we understand that person serving as someone whose *phronesis* can be trusted by others because of the kind of person he or she has become. A world without authorities would be a world where we did not believe anyone has answers to our questions. It would be a world in which parents, teachers, respected relatives, and leaders of all kinds – not only governmental, but academic, cultural, spiritual, etc. – did not bear within themselves the wisdom to guide. And if no one has an answer to my questions, then *I cannot answer them either*! Some proponents of individualism seem to want to say that I alone can answer my questions. But we ought to think about this concretely. If it is the case that my personal traits are so unique that no one can advise or answer questions for me, then how can I possibly come up with any answers either? Indeed, how can there be "answers" at all, that is, wisdom regarding the best ordering of my desires or aims? Just as there is no science of the particular, and no private language, *there is no wisdom of the idiosyncratic*. If answers are possible, the search for them will take the form of reviewing the answers others have given, that is, a search among authorities. Absence of authority would mean absence of guidance, hence decision without reason.

One may counter by accepting this, but insisting that what makes an answer to my questions an answer is not *that* a particular authority gave it. It is the subject matter, the reality judged, not the judge or the judge's office, that makes the answer valid. But this objection imagines a straw version of authority. What makes the authority's answer right is not the *nature* of the authority. In that case the being of the authority would be prior to its meaning; the meaning's validity would be *caused* by its speaker, making the advice-giving utterance a performative utterance (like saying "I do" *makes* the marriage). That would indeed be an ancient, pre-civil, Pharonic answer: it would make the authority God. In contrast, a sub-divine authority is one in which we find the sign and its meaning, speaker and utterance, to be *indistinguishable*. The utterance is valid independent of the speaker's being, but in the order of knowing the nature of the authority tells us that its utterances are valid.

The equality of liberal republican society ought not be interpreted as a "world without authorities."[40] Rather, it is a world in which there is widest possible operation for authority in the true sense, which excludes coercion, hence allows freedom of officially unrecognized authorities to be so recognized, which is also to say, the freedom to discover authority. A liberal republican society permits each citizen to find his or her place or context of authority, however great or limited. What would be anti-republican would be to determine that classes of adults are unfit for authority, to foreclose *a priori* their chances of fulfilling this ideal human task. The liberal republican rejection of royal and aristocratic "authoritarianism" meant, not the rejection of authority, but the insistence that no one stand beyond legitimate authority.

Liberty in Context

The foregoing was a rehearsal, albeit brief and incomplete, of the conservative account of the self. It is to such a self that freedom must attach, if there is to be freedom. But what is this freedom? What is the free versus un-free state of the implicated self? After describing some of the naturalistic background conditions for liberty, we will examine authenticity to understand the sense in which propriativity or "mineness," along with latitude, is essential to liberty. Then we will gloss liberty through the concepts of agency, judgment, and meaning, concluding that liberty is the agent's judgment in so far as it contributes to a meaningful or valuable life. This will make liberty intrinsically social; that is, not only is the self social, but what counts as freedom must also be. The problems this raises for liberal institutions will be less daunting than might first appear.

Selective response

Human freedom has its place in the context of the unique underdetermination of human judgment by its genetic inheritance, which is to say, the mediacy of the connection of genetic inheritance to environmental cues. The use of signs, hence memory, imagination, and expectation, vastly increases the size and complexity of the human experiential world, the set of possibly relevant considerations for any response. The staggering breadth of the environment for the individual human mind puts a premium on choice or, in John Herman Randall's phrase, the "power of selective response." Selectivity is always present. Delay, difference, absence, and selectivity are consequences of our biological under-determination. There is thus a growth in complexity of self and environment, inner and outer, that betokens the relative narrowing of the power of *presence*, of the dominant sensation of present environmental cues. Humans encounter a broad world of actualities and possibilities beyond the this-here-now of perception. Presence is taken up into a flowing system, hence rendered less than overpowering.

In this process self and environment are distributively correlated; each salient piece of the self is connected to salient pieces of the world, and vice versa. That is, a set of interests, desires, habits, and organs may be connected to certain things or events in the world that may or may not be attended or responded to. As Dewey argued, sensation and motor response are part of a circuit, not discontinuous. Every selection, in perception or action, takes place in the context of a prior selection. The prior selection may be unconscious, or as Peirce suggests, uncontrolled. This is not necessarily to say, uncontroll*able*. It only means that at every moment the area of control is smaller than the total area of salience. The controlled selection is a standing on, a judging with respect to, a set of uncontrolled saliencies of self and world. To choose is to choose in the context of a pre-selected set of environmental considerations and a pre-selected set of personal considerations, pieces of the self, connected to the former. Each successive act of choice can be based on a distinctive set of world- or self-considerations. Each selection reinforces that part of myself most continuous with what is selected, and subordinates other parts of myself. Where this is captured by reflection, as Charles Taylor suggests, some choices are significant enough to be determined by, and have consequences for, the self's interpretation of itself.

A human being is a history. This is not true of all things in the universe; all things *have* histories, but not all things *are* their histories. We can fully describe the being of a stone, its physico-chemical composition and location in its environment, hence fully understand what is entailed in the events involving it at this moment, without attending to its history. We cannot do this in the case of human beings, except when our interests are utterly rudimentary (e.g. understanding the trajectory of a human plunging off a cliff). Events *mean* for humans, and this meaning is intrinsically related to what has gone before. Human experience is compulsive, it must drive itself into the future. The need actively to maintain itself, the necessitous nature of human existence, has existential priority, because personal existence is tenuous and fragile. I more or less must eat every day, and have shelter every day in harsh climates, and act without major conflict with social members; these are only the most general of a long list of "musts" that place unrelenting demands on me. We are born, in Justus Buchler's admirable phrase, in a "state of natural debt," and while that debt may be rolled-over or re-financed, the books never balance.[41] Short of nirvana or death, periods of minimal or zero needfulness are brief. Thus human latitude exists within the joint context of history and compulsion.

The immense and manifold forces, internal and external, that burden the moment of selection would seem to blow through the agent without affording the possibility of choice; thus philosophers have wondered whether ultimately there really is freedom. Perhaps greater clarity comes from examining the most obvious cases of unfreedom. The victim of torture, as noted, may be said in some philosophically extravagant sense to be still "free" to name names or die silently. This is a matter of degree; the victim's latitude has been restricted to a socially anomalous extent. This sounds rather undramatic, as if the torture chamber were only marginally worse than standing in line at the Registry of Motor Vehicles. But there is, I think, a qualitative difference that emerges from the massive quantitative reduction of latitude in this case. There is a visceral sense that, while some people in that frightful situation may be so constituted as to remain in control of their response – to answer or die silent – others may reach a point where their experience is flooded by a sensation, e.g. pain or panic, such that their world shrinks to one with nothing in it *but* pain or panic, hence their blurting out information was not "free." Selection has been lost through the *simplification* of the normally complex human world, tunneled down to a simple plus or minus: pain or no pain. The person in an anxiety attack or addictive longing may be in a comparable situation. Some people describe the threat of imminent drowning in similar terms, which, unlike some forms of mortal danger, generates an "animal panic" to go on breathing or find something to hold on to.[42] What is absent here is more basic than the ability to – in the rationalist metaphor – "reflect" or gain "distance" from the moment. It is the collapse of a world of diverse necessities with latitude attached to each of them to one overwhelming necessity bearing down on one tiny power to respond "yes" or "no." This collapse is simultaneously a collapse of the self into the digital: pain continues/pain stops. Thus freedom rests on the experience of latitude, which rests on the experienced complexity of the world, itself coordinated with a complex self.

My suggestion is a horizontal, rather than a vertical, notion of liberty. Liberty is made possible not by the subject's or agent's possessing some faculty that transcends the level of empirical determinations, which "acts" outside the temporal chain of causes, but rather by the experiential complexity of those determinations; that is latitude. But of course there is more to freedom than opportunity or possibility: there is the self's *appropriation* of some subset of possibilities. That is "mineness." How it can be that this particular organism is capable of this appropriation is not the job of the political philosopher to say. It suffices for my purposes to suggest that it is a matter of fact that some combination of uncontrolled elements of self constitutes a collection that itself is able to exercise some control over subsequent selection, to "deflect" the energies that pass through it, and to do so over – compared to other Earth species – an immense range of semiotically constructed possibilities. The underlying fact is one of fantastically increased *breadth* due to *mediation* among the phases of the sensori-motor circuit (presence-sensation-response).[43] There is something by which we choose, a power of selective appropriation of possibilities provided by the psycho-biological organism under a broad but not endless spectrum of socio-cultural conditions, which gives us our sense of continuity in time and space, that is, which makes our temporal world more than the present moment and makes our synchronic or spatial world a tolerably open and secure space. Human liberty is the emergent form of the power of selective response of such a being in such a world, a being with the power to appropriate, not merely to occupy, possibilities.

Authenticity

As we saw earlier, authenticity is a conception of freedom derived from the root notion of mineness, the relation of appropriation and hence expressiveness holding between agent and choice. It bears an interesting and ambivalent relation to both liberalism and conservatism. Liberals fear authenticity, particularly when it is applied collectively, as in nationalism. When Isaiah Berlin rejected positive liberty in the name of liberalism, he was in part attacking the "jargon of authenticity" that began with Rousseau, was reflected in Kant's notion of autonomy, and which Adorno found so dangerous in Heidegger's existentialism.[44] Yet, as Charles Taylor, and in different ways, Nancy Rosenblum and George Kateb, have shown, the Romantic notion of authenticity is a crucial part of modern liberalism, both as individual expressive liberty and as national self-determination. Conservatism, reputedly happier with nationalism, might seem fond of authenticity as well. But conservatism is not more nationalistic than liberalism; both liberalism and conservatism, and most modern political conceptions, are nationalistic, since the modern polity is nationalistic. At any rate, for conservatives the collectivization of authenticity evident in twentieth century Fascism was the ideological cathexis of worldly realities by transcendental impulses. It was idolatrous. Conservatives also have little patience for the individual "search" for authenticity where this implies an asocial self mystically hidden beneath "inauthentic" social institutions. Authenticity has discomfited many masters.

Certainly Romanticism placed new significance on the particular, the idiosyncratic, hence the individual. But an important distinction must be made here. It is one thing to value the particularity of the individual as having universal significance. Renaissance Republicanism saw universal significance in the historical particularity of the great individual. Likewise, later Romanticism did not negate the universal; it grasped the particular in a new relation to the universal. It is yet another thing, however, to regard the particularity of the individual as having *ultimate significance in itself*, regardless of the universality of its meaning. With this part of the Romantic legacy the conservative is not sympathetic. For it would be to say that the particular is ultimate, not as the site of a universal meaning, but merely *qua* particular. Occasionally the liberal tradition, where it waxes in positive rhetoric about that which negative liberty defends, in effect endorses this particularism. Hence idiosyncrasy is defended and valued independent of any relation to the universal, simply because it *is*. Conservative authenticity, in contrast, values individual biography as a particular chapter embodying the Great Drama.

What then is individual authenticity, and how is it constituted? Here the conservative makes an expected contribution: the "mineness" of my life is historical and social. Authenticity must include a recognition of the limits and context of the self, a recognition of place, station and duty. Like the dead king Mufasa in the Disney film *The Lion King*, the conservative enjoins individuals to "Remember who you are." This intonation can be a call to return to the place or network, the "proper" role or status of the self, where that station is one's *own*. It is a call to be true to oneself, where the self is historical and institutional. Unlike Kateb's expressive individualism, conservatism claims that the modern individual must find what it can regard as its proper place *in* society. What some conservatives fear in authenticity is that its pursuit leads away from the social to some mystical, asocial core – or emptiness – within the self. But once we accept the implicated, socialized self that conservatives typically endorse, that fear is misplaced. *For when we go deeply into the self we find others.*[45]

The modern conservative accepts social mobility, choice, and liberty as attempts, not to achieve an asocial and ahistorical selfhood, but to choose among my complex social inheritance those strands most true to my best self-interpretation; not to *escape place* but to find the *right place*. As Berger and Neuhaus claimed, "Liberation is not escape from particularity but discovery of a particularity that fits."[46] But what if my search finds no such place, threatens to take me beyond the *polis*, physically or metaphysically into an unsubdued outland, an antinomian existence, where there are no social markers? Is it the conservative position that I simply *am* my manifold social position, and that, philosophically speaking, is that? Ought I accept what *feels* wrong because others expect it of me?

The initial answer to this question is that there is no general, that is, no philosophical answer. The conservative can accept that the ability of others to ascertain what social place is appropriate for the individual is limited, as is the ability of the individual. We cannot say in general and in advance who will be right. But this initial response is the leading edge of a subtler methodological point. Conservatism neither denies the legitimacy of the philosophical search for the self beyond one's social being, nor does it allow social and political arrangements to be predicated on the completion of such a search. If I try to discover a philosophical, which is to say, an ultimate answer to the question, "Who am I?," I must engage in a quest. Conservatives welcome the seeker. But they caution, for the sake of society and the seeker, that life cannot await the completion of that quest.

Self-formation is not mystical, but it is dialectical. Who I am influences my choices, and my choices influence who I am. A fork in the road comes. A series of considerations appear, pressures from the outside, fears and desires from the inside. I go down one path, even though I could have gone down another. Part of what I want gets fulfilled on this road, part gets thrown away, or more accurately, part of me atrophies. As time passes I become increasingly comfortable with my choice, or increasingly uncomfortable. If the former, the parts of the self not pursued fade in the light of the satisfied parts of the self that have coagulated around the choice made. Good choices are those around which the self can grow; bad choices open up a fissure that gets worse with time. If the latter, I increasingly live with an internal crisis which may someday boil over, or may remain as the cross I have to bear to maintain the parts of my life I cannot give up.

If I am lucky, then at some point in life I can say one of the following, both of which represent versions of an "authentic" life: either I say that I *did* it, I made a rational, self-conscious choice and through enterprise brought about the current conditions of my life, which I affirm as expressing my self; or, I *retrospectively affirm* who I am and my life as *mine*, as an expression of me, even if it was arguably *not* the intended product of my choices. The later is just as authentic as the former. Rationally made choices and actions that achieve self-consciously desired ends are not the only way for my life to be mine. We are lucky enough if the self as it becomes through its choices in necessitous contexts comes to "match" its environment as that environment has become through the self's choices. This match implies that the ongoing cycle of reconstruction of environment and accommodation to environment, the dialectical circuit of self and world, is characterized by a *working* fit, balance, or harmony. If I cannot make either statement, if my life is not what I want, then it can either be because of accident, necessity, or because I was subject to someone else's will. Civil society attempts through procedural rules to minimize this last. Because liberty is a goal for a modern republican *civitas*, it rightly attempts to minimize accident and necessity, e.g. through scientific advances, social opportunity, etc. But the achievement of authenticity remains a limited and contingent project. The state of being "free" is always relative; I am never "free" *uberhaupt*, free generally and in all respects. I am always only "free with respect to" some conditions of the environment or some parts of myself – free of some environmental constraint, free to be or express or actualize some part of myself. And, as in most other things, luck matters. Consequently, there never has been and never will be a society in which freedom or authenticity is either complete or guaranteed.

So conservatism thinks that in my philosophical search for my authentic self I would do well to begin with a deep meditation on the meaning and coherence of my social roles – citizen, teacher, wife, mother, etc. – and that I could do worse than to discover myself in those roles and other social institutions, hence call off the search. What if I persist and ask, "But what am I *beyond* that social being? Don't the manifold phenomena that I sense within, the hidden crevasses, the fringes of my awareness, the bowels of my self, indicate some deep and ultimate divergence between that social being and the real, authentic me? Should I pull on this thread, though it may unravel everything, or put it away with childish things?" To this the conservative says, with an empathetic smile, "The quest for ultimacy is very interesting, but it is the philosopher's job, not the political theorist's. Good luck on your search. I am due at home."

Agency, judgment, and meaning

A helpful perspective is brought by Charles Taylor's analysis of agency. Taylor views human agents as "strong evaluators," who have not only "first-order" desires, but "second-order" desires as well, desires *to* desire or *not* desire certain things. Second-order desires form attitudes about the "worth" of first-order desires, hence are in effect desires to be a certain kind of person.[47] We do not simply "weigh" our desires, we evaluate them, entangling us in a "struggle of self-interpretations." This leads to an interesting distinction among ways of conceiving what I do when I choose which takes my earlier discussion of the relation of rationality and liberty further.

Taylor criticizes Sartre's conception of "radical choice" or absolute freedom, that every decision in some way entails an ultimately groundless or "criterionless" choice. Taylor claims that such a conception essentially denies the existence of choice. Taylor considers Sartre's example of a young French student during the German occupation who must decide whether to join the Resistance or stay with his mother. Taylor objects to Sartre's conception that it,

> brings us to the limit where choice fades into non-choice. Do I really choose if I just start doing one of the alternatives? And above all, this kind of resolution has no place for the judgement "I owe it to my mother to stay", which is supposed to issue from the choice . . . The theory of radical choice is deeply incoherent, for it wants to maintain both strong evaluation and radical

choice. It wants to have strong evaluations and yet deny their status as judgements.[48]

What must hold if we are to speak of the student making a choice is that there are different moral self-interpretations that in fact *have a hold* on him, that are pressing him. Sartre's absolute freedom severs the pressures that make the dilemma compelling. There must be personal continuity, an existing "horizon of evaluation" that characterizes the chooser before, during, and after the choice, for us to speak of an agent "making a choice" at all. As Anthony Appiah writes, if freedom is literal self-invention, then there is no continuity through the moment of choice.[49] Then the choice can never be an achievement; achievement implies that something is overcome, and if there is no continuity, no resistance, but simply *de novo* creation, nothing is "achieved."

We can extend Taylor's claims in the opposite direction as well. What if we imagine choice as the application of pre-existing principles or rules, hence as automatic, deductive, or causal. Suppose I have a system of principles from which my choice in a particular situation could be simply derived. Here too there would be no strong evaluation and no achievement. In effect, there would be no "choice" at all, but simply the application of a rule. It would be, not the initiation of a process of action, but simply a point in an ongoing process whose initiation was the achievement of that system of principles in the first place. Just as the absence of any continuity between self and choice eliminates choice in Sartre, if the continuity of self and choice is too strong, there is no "free choice" either. The insight to which Taylor's analysis leads is that *neither an absence of relation* between the choice and the identity the agent brings to the choice, nor *a mechanical or deductive relation* between them, qualifies as a choice at all. Free choice, hence agency, operates in the middle ground between discontinuity and derivation.

This has what may appear a counter-intuitive implication. What of Luther's, "Here I stand, I can do no other"? We normally regard his choice as an exemplar of noble, Stoic freedom, the adamantine self determining its acts in the face of overwhelming force. But that is because we take Luther's self-description with a grain of salt. If he meant he was unable to act otherwise in the same sense, for example, that a drug addict asserts an inability to kick the habit, Luther's would not be a free choice. Instead we take Luther's own self-interpretation, in Taylor's sense, to be the source of his "inability," which means it is something he is actively affirming. In fact he could have done differently, although to him this would have meant denying his vision of truth, hence his self. He could do no other *and* remain himself.

The example of the drug addict is open to the objection that it concerns something external to the self, a biological or neurotic compulsion. Hence we might say that Luther's inability to do otherwise is a real inability, but one internal to the self, hence still a case of free self-determination. We may ask, though, is an adamantine self, a self that "cannot do otherwise," actually free? A self that lives in a rut, unable to imagine alternatives or to encounter novelty, is not free even though its life is its "own," that is, even though it is, given the qualifications we must make to this term, "self-determining." Surely the self could be such as to eliminate latitude, just as external events or biological necessities or neurotic compulsions can. Here we would have perhaps *free acts* but an *un-free self*.

Once we consider it, however, this paradox is merely terminological. For the insight that lies behind Taylor's critique of Sartre is not only that freedom is impossible with either too much or too little continuity across the moment of choice. It is also that freedom is a bivalent condition requiring both an "internal" and an "external" qualification. Freedom obtains in the *meeting of latitude and propriativity*; the absence of either undoes freedom. Self-determination, or mineness, without latitude, for internal no less than external reasons, is not free, just as latitude or open possibility without a continuously acting self, without that self's appropriation, is not free either. Freedom presupposes an *owness that operates in and through experienced latitude*.

To be an agent is neither to be a point in a process, nor is it to be an origin, an uncaused cause. It requires that the self be sufficiently integral that external forces, and internal impulses stimulated by those forces, do not sweep through it unaltered by its substance. It requires that the self be not a point but a *mass*, absorbing energy and reflecting back energy *due to its own character*. The degree of self-determination is proportional, to use an ocular metaphor, to the degree of refraction, to the potential of the self to deflect, alter, add to, influences that pass through it. A self that is not self-determining is a tube or a transparent glass, through which inputs flow directly into outputs with minimal alternation. A self that is self-determining has sufficient substance to absorb inputs, which are then subject to distinctive interpretation. Thus its outputs are its *own*. At the same time, it requires that this owness be historically maintained and evolve through appropriated environmental possibilities, that is, latitude. A self that cannot learn from experience, cannot avail itself of novel opportunities, is not free, for while its environment may, objectively speaking, present it with possibility, unperceived possibility cannot be appropriated.

Another clue comes from the etymology of "choice," which links the term to the Old German *kiesen*, to taste. To choose is to perceive and to judge, to examine, to test or taste, which then leads to action or utterance or belief. If we cannot speak of a judgment being made, we cannot speak of a choice being made. Agency is that condition of self-determination in which the agent's judgment, taking up a position, makes a difference. To say this is to imply that *choice is judgment*. We must, I think, liberate our notion of choice from the abstract model of a transcendent mind, somehow floating above both options for action and its own desires, motives, traits, etc., equidistant from all of them, investing will in one of them – or in a less lofty version, the donkey standing equidistant from two carrots.

Samuel Fleischacker has recently interpreted liberty through the concept of judgment in order to move beyond the contrast of negative and positive liberty toward a "third concept of liberty."[50] He argues that the complex notion of judgment from Kant's aesthetic philosophy, if informed by Adam Smith's moral and economic philosophy, provides a modern version of Aristotelian *phronesis*. With the recent work of Charles Griswold, Fleischacker's claim represents another step in the current return of some political theorists to the Scottish Enlightenment, and to Smith in particular, as forming the basis of a superior liberal republican notion of freedom.[51] Fleischacker rightly points out that the liberty that modern liberal republicanism claims to respect must be something *positive*, *particular*, and *immanent*, that it cannot be a purely negative liberty, a rationality whose job is the formulation of principle independent of circumstances, or a self that transcends desire, experience, inheritance, community, etc.[52]

Note that to speak of judgment is not to talk of deliberation, cognition, self-criticism, discourse, or rationality. These are important human processes and traits, and in some degree they are almost ubiquitous; virtually everyone deliberates sometimes, is rational much of the time, etc. But these qualities do not make *the* difference between a free act and an un-free act. One must imagine that some of the most free persons who have made distinctive contributions to the arts or who act heroically in crises, are acting out of an immediately effective sensibility that is distinctively theirs, not rationally and deliberatively weighing alternatives. The *intellectualization of freedom* is a result of philosophers projecting their own highly deliberative and reason-considering habits onto their anthropology. Rather, we can import Justus Buchler's notion of judgment as the taking of a position, the perspectival appropriation of the world, the adoption of a stance, whether it be linguistic and representational, or active or exhibitive; running for a bus or arranging flowers in a vase is as "judgmental" as the pronouncements of a magistrate.[53]

Last is the most controversial component of the conservative notion of liberty. Intrinsic to Taylor's notion of agency and all of the foregoing is that the agent is, as we saw, self-interpretive. As Taylor writes, an agent is a "subject of significance," a thing to which things matter, and must therefore have a view of the world and of the self, a view embodied in judgments. "Moral agency," he writes, "requires some kind of reflexive awareness of the standards one is living by (or failing to live by)."[54] This means that agency is linked to *meaning*. A refraction of energies that has no meaning for the agent's life is not indicative of the kind of freedom civil society exists to permit and encourage, any more than the fact that I may have a unique neurological twitch is indicative of my individuality. Liberty is not only judicative agency, but *meaningful* judicative agency. The liberty on which liberal republican society rightly places a high value is the individual's self-determination of a meaningful or valuable existence. Liberty is the liberty to live a life that has meaning.

Such meaning is *social*. The individual's judgment of the meaning of its life is no more independent of social institutions and cultural inheritance than is its judgment of the meaning of phrases in a natural language. The individual must judge with resources garnered from society. Only this makes the individual's judgment intelligible to others *and* to itself, intelligibility being social. But these interpretive resources are enormously complex, capable of reiterated and recursive application. Consequently, how these cultural complexes are combined, hierarchized, and applied is the realm of individuality. Individuality is thus a process of *re-interpretive appropriation*, the capacity of the individual's judgment to contribute to the meaning of its social existence.

This is disturbing to liberals, for it presumes that society will have to judge the meaningfulness of the individual's choice, and may prohibit what it thinks insignificant. But society must inevitably weigh the *meaning* of an otherwise dubious choice in deciding whether to permit it. Denying someone the "right" to destroy themselves with drugs is a legitimate cultural decision about the meaninglessness of such a life-path. There is no way to avoid these judgments, the "harm" principle being, as I have argued, itself too vague to be employed without a cultural view of the Good. We must be honest: if we say it is legitimate to prevent risks to self in cases, for example, of drug use but not bungee-jumping, we are doing so because we share a sense of the meaning and value of human existence under which getting high chemically makes little or no contribution, but getting high vertically may. We can see, if not share, the meaning-constructing value in bungee-jumping, but not in heroin. If we then can easily imagine regulating bungee-jumping in a way that decreases risk but does not obliterate what we regard as the possible meaning of the experience, then we feel little compunction to regulate. Nor should we. As Walzer argues in matters of distributive justice that the meaning of a good is crucial to determining its just distribution, so it is also true that in determining the limits of freedom the meaning of acts matter to their permissibility. What distinguishes modern liberal republican freedom from that of other social and historical forms, thereby increasing individual liberty despite continued social judgment of meaning, is novel social conditions, cultural valorization of individuality, and a particular set of civic norms about how and when to discriminate. The liberal republican society recognizes that to judge meaning it must engage in dialogue with the individual. Its liberality rightly leads it to accept that extant notions of what is meaningful may be inadequate, and it waits to be convinced.

When liberals reject any such talk of "meaningfulness" or "value" of a life-path within political debate they sometimes deny the cognitive adequacy of such social judgments. It is here that skepticism or relativism regarding human knowledge and reason enter into liberalism with powerful effect. For it is skepticism and relativism, rather than any political doctrine, which justify the move from the claim that no one should be coerced out of a potentially meaningful course of life that doesn't harm others to the claim that no one should be coerced out of *any* non-harmful course in life, potentially meaningful or not, since we *cannot trust our considered judgments* about meaningfulness. The neutralist liberal retort is often: "But who are you to judge what is meaningful for me? You, society, have no right to decided that my chosen course is implausible."

But why ought we be skeptical about society's judgment of the limits of what might lead to a meaningful life? Taking this relativism or skepticism seriously means also disbelieving the validity of the *individual's* judgment. In the real world, of course, society may be wrong; but is there any source of judgment more likely to be right? Certainly not the individual. The claim that each individual knows what is best for him or her self is factually ludicrous.[55] Some individuals know what is best and some most decidedly do not. Society, or more properly speaking, culture is the historical repository of working notions as to the limits of meaning. The best we can do is be sure we have a relatively open, hence liberal, culture, and then let it make its judgments. We are condemned to condemn; we might as well do it self-consciously by our best lights.

Civil Liberty

In the civic context, to be free is first of all to be a *citizen*, that is, a full social member. The ancient use of "free" was primarily an indicator of a status, the status of the freedman. It was an intrinsically social term, tied to love and friendship, which could exist in their complete form only among free persons. The ancient notion of "liberality" as generosity is part of this history. Liberality is the attitude proper among freedmen in their mutual relations. "Political liberty" is a narrower term than civil liberty, referring to liberty to engage in politics, to think and speak in political life, to associate for political purposes, to vote and hold office, etc. Political liberty at some level is part of civil liberty, that is, part of the liberty of citizens in a civil society. Thus the kind of liberty or freedom that civil society ought to recognize is by nature a civil and social thing, a status. It implies, among other things, the availability to the individual of the degree and kinds of latitude that the *civitas* considers necessary. It also means that, whatever the philosophical definition of freedom, the actually requisite conditions of freedom are always socially defined. In this sense, freedom is socially and culturally conventional. This civic conception has something in common with Hobbes's *silentia leges* and Berlin's negative liberty, in the sense that whatever the *citizen* does, whether it expresses self or is "autonomous" or any other "positive" condition you like, *is free*. The philosophical burden has thus been transferred, in effect, from "free" to "citizen."

Liberty in modern liberal societies is unthinkable without the social, economic, and cultural vicissitudes of such societies. Socially and economically, modernity presents a vastly widened division of labor, giving, in a civil society where coercion is reduced, vast latitude. A complex society increases the possibility of liberty, a simple society decreases it. Likewise, "careers open to talent," social mobility, and the establishment of a middle class are all as necessary to what we today regard as a free society as limits on governmental power and rights guarantees. Modern citizens are used to an unprecedented level of social opportunity, which is to say, functional complexity. Culturally, starting in one sense with the Renaissance but expanded by nineteenth-century thought, modern society has come to regard the individual *as* an individual. This is to say, it has come to understand the particularities of the self as potentially essential to the self's *meaning*. We expect some of the unique or idiosyncratic elements or orderings of elements within the self to be expressed, effective, and the object of sustained attention. But it is simultaneously the emergence of a kind of *realism*. The modern tendency is to see the individual, not ultimately through the normative concepts or "descriptions" or roles of social tradition, but as the individual *is individually*.

Regarding political and civil norms, three principles stand out as forming the basis of liberal republican society's uniquely expanded domain of liberty.

First, such societies incorporate a realistic recognition and valorization of judicative individuality. Individuals make *novel yet meaningful* judgments. People are different, and need and seek different things. Liberal republican society accepts that it is no small matter for society to prohibit an individual from pursuing a course of life that the individual regards as necessary to its life's meaning, given the context of its particular endowment of needs, abilities, interests, and environment. The reason we rightly feel apprehensive about limiting individuals' liberty is not that the sheer interference in individual will or desire is immoral, but that the prevention of the individual from constructing a desired and meaningful course of life is a serious matter.

Second, and related, such society is rightfully alert to the limits on its own omniscience. It recognizes that it can be wrong. It does not commit the idolatry of assuming its political judgments to be divine. This is not the same as a global skepticism or a relativism that makes all judgments equally true or false. It is the reticence of modern civil society. This means we are open to change, to regarding a practice tomorrow as plausibly meaningful and valuable, or at any rate as not antithetical to our meaningful goods, which yesterday we regarded as anathema or simply meaningless.

Third, and dependent on the foregoing, this reticence is itself morally valued as civility. Civility entails an inhibition of the idolatrous urge, an acceptance that the social world is never ideal. So a limited amount of vice and disorder, at certain levels, is accepted as part of modern life. That acceptation is entirely plausible for a modern conservative; the Puritan Revolution, which aimed to utterly moralize society, was not a conservative revolution.

The collective effect of these considerations is that liberal republican society, conservatively understood, must be relatively, not absolutely, permissive. It accepts a series of relevant considerations in deciding to permit or discourage forms of life, not the simple yes/no of the harm principle (or of how it is rhetorically stated, if not applied). Its conception of the Good is complex, and recognizes the need for balance among goods. Thus the individual whose failure to embody one recognized good seems to be the condition of her embodiment of another recognized good may be judged holistically. Actions or lifestyles that fail to conform to recognized goods may be permitted if they either are not egregious or cause little trouble for others, or little long-term impact on the self. These can be discouraged, and their antonym encouraged, without literal prohibition. Even practices that are seriously noxious to society, incapable of being recognized as valuable, as adding anything to life, *may* be permitted, especially if they remain private. But if we add to this that such practices are destructive of the individual's ability to, at some time in the future, redeem the meaning of his or her existence in a return to recognized goods, they may be prohibited, even if they do not cause obvious harm to others. The point is that there are multiple goods, multiple considerations, and multiple forms of community response, which means both that there is much to decide and discriminate, and many resources with which to do so, certainly more than is dreamt of in the neutralist philosophy.

In conclusion, we may rightly ask, is modern liberal republicanism *the* society of freedom? The answer can only be that our society is *relatively* more free than other societies in human history in respects that *we* consider meaningful. There is no universal definition of a "free society" that is not vague. Any more precise notion will presuppose a set of social and cultural considerations that are internal to traditions and that are logically independent of the concept of liberty, a complex that not all "free" societies need presuppose. Holism implies that we cannot specify what "free" means to us in a way that does not implicate a set of social, cultural, and economic conditions. What makes a society a free one is both a matter of degree and a matter of socio-cultural definition.

Thus we cannot claim that modern liberal republican society is the only model of a free society. We are arguably freer in religious membership and ideological commitment, in choice of occupation, mate, locale, lifestyle (within certain limits), etc. We are not freer in our daily lives in all respects, those being largely determined by the complex forms of discipline imposed by every choice of occupation we make and the bureaucracies they today entail. We cannot, like the subsistence farmer, hunter, or island fisherman, take the afternoon off; we cannot even be minutes late for an appointment without potentially significant consequences. Or differently, if ours is a society of greater freedom, it is also a society of greater and more complex forms of necessity.

The kinds of social and political liberties most people in modern liberal societies have come to expect are primarily four.[56] First there is freedom from arbitrary or unjust social, legal, and governmental power, which requires equal treatment by law and government. Second is freedom of belief, assembly, and expression relating to religious and other "high cultural" matters, concerning the meaning of one's life and the content of one's mind, which freedom requires non-interference by social and cultural groups as well as law and government. Third is the freedom to find one's way in civil society, in cooperative economic and non-economic organizations and activities, without concerted effort to deny opportunity or subjection to arbitrary rules or personally targeted edicts. Even this is highly qualified, for, as we have seen, the competition of self-interested groups can as easily block my maneuvering as could a religious *Gemeinschaft*, clan, or King. Last, we expect a region of "privacy" or non-interference in lifestyle and home by social or legal-governmental power, which is also qualified. What we call our "free" society is a society that has increased, perhaps even maximized, these kinds of freedom in certain contexts or dimensions of life. A very different society might be free in different senses. Note that this does not presuppose that freedom is "relative," that it is whatever a society says it is. It presupposes only that freedom is complex, making it possible, perhaps even necessary, to expand or diminish kinds of freedoms in kinds of contexts, rather than believing that freedom is one thing to be expanded or diminished monolithically.

From a conservative perspective, then, it is entirely reasonable to regard a high degree of freedom in these four dimensions most typically valued by our tradition as primary values. Operationalizing these freedoms in law, with their mutual conflicts, in the context of a changing social, economic, and cultural reality, is prone to endless difficulty, of course; nothing said here changes that. But we ought not employ as a criterion of freedom a single, monadic conception which we then, making freedom the ultimate value, try to purify and extend to utter independence, complete autonomy, or ideal authenticity, claimed as the universal standard of social good. That is a fantasy even with respect to our own society, let alone others. And if we employ a fantasy to correct and critique our kind and degree of freedom, we will reap a political theory that is fantastic.

Notes

1 That my chapter title is a paraphrase of Nancy Rosenblum's book on romantic liberalism, *Another Liberalism*, is not meant to imply that that liberal tradition, or her conception of it, are conservative.

2 Scruton, *The Meaning of Conservatism*, p. 73. Liberalism is not, in my view, a "myth," but its typical notion of liberty is, in the true sense of the word: a posited ideal narrative, anchored by something indemonstrable, that endows life with meaning for those who accept it.

3 My use of the later term, admittedly unwieldy in English, bears no particular connection to Heidegger, who used it (*Jemeinigkeit*) as a technical term in *Being and Time*.

4 I should add that none of these three concepts that I will criticize is Samuel Fleischacker's "third concept of liberty." See his *A Third Concept of Liberty: Judgment and Freedom in Kant and Adam Smith* (Princeton: Princeton University Press, 1999). I will discuss Fleischacker later.

5 See Arendt, *The Human Condition*, p. 177ff.

6 Jean-Paul Sartre, "The Flies," in *No Exit and Three Other Plays* (New York: Vintage, 1973).

7 Eric Fromm, *Escape from Freedom* (New York: Rinehart, 1941).

8 Kris Kristofferson, "Me and Bobby McGee," Columbia Records, 1973.

9 See Robert Pippin, *Modernism as a Philosophical Problem: On the Dissatisfactions of European High Culture* (Cambridge: Blackwell, 1991). For an historical account of the development of the notion, see J. B. Schneewind, *The Invention of Autonomy: A History of Modern Moral Philosophy* (Cambridge: Cambridge University Press, 1998).

10 As Richard Sennett, one of the few social theorists willing to criticize autonomy, argues, autonomy in practice would mean complete self-possession, self-control or self-mastery adopted as an ideal, and the elimination of dependency of any kind. If taken seriously, this would require "indifference, withdrawal, a willful numbness to others." See Richard Sennett, *Authority* (New York: Knopf, 1980), pp. 117–18.

11 Although this is not the case with what Knud Haakonssen has called "implied contracts," to be discussed later.

12 Michael Sandel, *Liberalism and the Limits of Justice* (Cambridge: Cambridge University Press, 1982).

13 Will Kymlicka, *Liberalism, Community, and Culture* (Oxford: Clarendon Press, 1989), p. 50.

14 Ibid., p. 63.

15 Avishai Margalit, *The Decent Society*, trans. Naomi Goldblum (Cambridge, MA: Harvard University Press, 1998), p. 117.

16 Part of the view I am expressing does indeed rest on an acceptance of what psychoanalysis has called the unconscious – although it does not *have* to accept this. Still, I confess to being an unreconstructed Freudian sympathizer in this regard. I also confess to being unable to understand the animosity of a sizable percentage of the social scientific and philosophical academy to this notion. To deny the unconscious is to insist that the two categories of *consciousness* and the *body* exhaust what I am. The burden is on that position, it seems to me, to justify itself. It seems to me very unlikely to be true, and certainly very hard to show, that *mentality* – my being, excluding a complete description of my neural-chemical-physical self – is exhausted by what is available to my consciousness at any given time.

17 It would be hard to imagine a transcendent, metaphysical concept like this – that the present state of some real world entity is sufficiently free of all of its past states that every member of the class has an equally unlimited power of revision and hence self-recreation – holding much currency in any field of contemporary philosophy except for political philosophy.

18 Again this is a case of liberal neutralism in practice resting on the existence and continuation of layers of social obligations that it does not recognize.

19 If one really took seriously the claim that when I have sex with someone I am having sex with everyone that person has ever had sex with, then no one would

have sex with anyone other than themselves. Sex would be intrinsically perverse.

20 Sandel, *Liberalism and the Limits of Justice*.

21 Charles Taylor, "Cross-Purposes: The Liberal-Communitarian Debate," in Rosenblum, *Liberalism and the Moral Life*.

22 Sandel, *Democracy's Discontents*, pp. 111–15.

23 Susan Moller Okin, *Justice, Gender and the Family* (New York: Basic Books, 1989).

24 This distinction – of the permissibility of promotion/discouragement versus coercion – is in fact virtually the definition of a non-neutralist liberal; for the non-neutralist, government or community must be able to promote or discourage, thus act on a notion of the Good, and yet, coercion must be minimized. Neutralist liberals, in contrast, typically deny that promotion or discouragement can be distinguished from coercion, and so make both equally illegitimate.

25 Benjamin Whorf was a famous exponent of the kind of relativism of linguistically-based conceptual schemes that Donald Davidson later undermined. See Whorf's *Language, Thought, and Reality: Selected Writings* (Cambridge, MA: Technical Press of MIT, 1956).

26 F. H. Bradley, "My Station and its Duties," in *Ethical Studies* (Indianapolis: Bobbs-Merrill, 1951), pp. 98–146. The chapter of Bradley's 1876 book is a case of communitarianism *avant la lettre*. Idealism has always had a communitarian bent, of course, if one wants to call the relevant portions of Hegel's views communitarian. Classical American philosophy is also communitarian, and to a degree arguably coincident with its relation to idealism – noticeable in Peirce's convergence theory of truth and Dewey's neo-Hegelianism, but more socially in Josiah Royce and Ernest Hocking. It is also interesting to remember how much Oakeshott was influenced by Bradley.

27 I recognize the infelicity of the phrase, namely, that liberals no doubt think that conservative selves *ought* to be institutionalized.

28 The definition comes from Philip Selznick, *The Moral Commonwealth: Social Theory and the Promise of Community* (Berkeley: University of California, 1992), pp. 232–3. The following paragraphs are partly inspired by Selznick's discussion.

29 Henry Sumner Maine, *Ancient Law: Its Connection with the Early History of Society and its Relation to Modern Ideas* (Gloucester: Peter Smith, 1970), p. 165.

30 The last categorization is from Peter Berger and Richard Neuhaus and their influential 1977 essay, "To Empower People," and remains felicitous. See Berger and Neuhaus, *To Empower People: From State to Civil Society*, (Washington, D.C.: American Enterprise Institute, 1996).

31 Haakonssen, *Natural Law and Moral Philosophy*, p. 317.

32 Ludwig Wittgenstein, *On Certainty*, trans. Denis Paul and G. E. M. Anscombe (New York: Harper Books, 1969), e.g. statement 97.

33 Shils, *Tradition*, p. 290. The same concept is implicit in MacIntyre's *After Virtue*.
34 Hannah Arendt, "What is Authority?," chapter three of *Between Past and Future*, p. 93.
35 Sennett, *Authority*, p. 71.
36 Ibid., p. 26. Sennett makes the interesting connection that the decline in the American "work ethic" is related to a decline in authority. Work can be made meaningful in several ways. Certainly sheer need valorizes work; work for pay makes private life for the self and the family possible. There is as well the value of the work itself and its products, and the social life of the work place, to which employment and job performance is the price of admission. But, Sennett argues, this is impossible without recognizing the legitimate authority of manager or owner. Respect for that authority is a powerful motivation, and loss of a respectable authority to valorize one's work can fundamentally de-legitimate work (p. 109).
37 Samuel Fleischacker, *The Ethics of Culture* (Ithaca: Cornell University Press, 1994), ch. 4.
38 Ibid., p. 85.
39 Selznick, *The Moral Commonwealth*, p. 266ff.
40 Paraphrasing Jessica Benjamin's sexist hope for a "world without the father." See her "Authority and the Family Revisited: or, A World Without Fathers," *New German Critique* 13 (Winter 1978), p. 57.
41 Justus Buchler, *Nature and Judgment* (New York: Grosset & Dunlap, 1955), p. 3. The passage reads: "Man is born is a state of natural debt, being antecendently committed to the execution or the furtherance of acts that will largely determine his individual existence. . . . From first to last he discharges obligations."
42 I think it might be that the combination of struggling for breath and falling in space, having neither anything to stand on, which is frightening enough, nor anything to fill one's insides (one's lungs), may be a peculiarly overwhelming form of panic.
43 See Hans Jonas, *The Phenomenon of Life: Toward a Philosophical Biology* (New York: Harper, 1966). Jonas used the unfortunate metaphor of "distance" for this mediation. Dewey described the sensori-motor circuit in his crucial 1896 essay, "The Reflex Arc Concept in Psychology."
44 Theodor Adorno, *The Jargon of Authenticity*, trans. Knut Tarnowski and Frederic Will (Evanston: Northwestern University Press, 1973).
45 This is what Kateb claimed about the heights of democratic individualism, but, unlike the conservative, he regarded the solidarity discovered within the self as unrelated to social institutions and cultural traditions, which he regarded negatively as the source of "conformity."
46 Berger and Neuhaus, "To Empower People" (1996), pp. 205–6 (italicized in original).
47 Charles Taylor, "What is Human Agency?," in his *Human Agency and Language*.
48 Ibid., p. 31.

49   Anthony Appiah, "Liberalism, Individuality and Identity," *Critical Inquiry* 27 (Winter 2000), pp. 305–32.

50   Samuel Fleischacker, *A Third Concept of Liberty: Judgment and Freedom in Kant and Adam Smith.*

51   See Charles Griswold, *Adam Smith and the Virtues of Enlightenment* (Cambridge: Cambridge University Press, 1999).

52   While sympathetic to Fleischacker's treatment, I have two tentative objections. First, his claims for judgment are expansive; at various times judgment is the ground for liberty, is liberty itself, is core of the self, etc. At times he crosses from recognizing that the turn to judgment places the problem of freedom in the proper locale, to implying that this turn solves the problem of freedom. Second, he remains excessively individualist. He consistently tries to hold the individual's identification with community or tradition at arm's length (e.g. see his p. 256). Thus, while he, I believe, makes the right move on the question of what the faculty of liberty is, he continues the liberal conception of the free operation of this faculty as "independence."

53   See Justus Buchler, *Nature and Judgment* (New York: Grosset and Dunlap, 1966). I should say that Buchler did not deny the cognitive or rational nature of judgment; rather, he conceived of its "cognitive" and "rational" nature widely enough to apply indifferently to doings and makings, as well as sayings. But my point is the same; a linguistic or discursive notion of rationality and cognition are not presupposed by judgment as the locus of freedom.

54   Taylor, "The Concept of a Person," in *Human Agency and Language*, p. 103.

55   As Charles Taylor writes, that the individual is always right would have to mean that there is nothing to be right about. See his "What's Wrong with Negative Liberty," p. 223.

56   The same number as F.D.R.'s, but a different list.

6

Civil Society

We have seen that the modern liberal republican tradition is more complex than is often credited, hence that there is more than one way to value and maintain the key liberal institutions that help to define that tradition. I have criticized neutralist, and some "affirmative," liberal attempts to simplify that tradition, to read it as the application of one or two philosophical principles or goods, encouraging instead a conservative conception of politics and liberty. Conservatism, properly understood, is the perspective most congenial to an acceptance of the complexity of our political inheritance. In particular, it is the political methodology most able to abide the core concept and structural component of that tradition, namely civil society.

Civil society is a normative conception, but it is more, or less, than that too, for it is a conception of society as a set of interlocking institutions and practices that cannot be philosophically simplified by principle. It is, if you will, a form of life. Not that "civil society" refers to everything going on in contemporary liberal republican societies. Rather it is the most crucial component of their socio-political structure. Thus I claim that liberal republicanism cannot be adequately defined by reference to popular sovereignty, democracy, markets, rights, or freedom – these are pieces of the puzzle, aspects of the whole, which have to be modified and contextualized by civil society. It is the task of this and the following chapter to say what civil society means and what are the political implications of putting it first among our political notions. But before proceeding, we must begin by defining politics.

Politics is first of all something that characterizes and obtains in *society*, that is, in human associations. Politics is a dimension of a human society. But controversy arises already. What exactly is a society? Are all human associations societies? Must all politics be *within*, not between, societies? And might we not conceive of politics as the active "institution" of society, as Claude Lefort would say, hence something logically prior to the notion of society?[1]

But we are already going too fast. We have to start with a purely nominal definition of politics, without which we cannot decide even which topics to discuss and which to leave out. The nominal definition I offer is this: "politics" refers to the *process of social decision-making and decision-enacting*. The social is that about which decisions are made and enacted, not who is doing the making and enacting. Even if one person decides, a decision that stands for a society is collective in meaning and effect, hence political in this nominal sense. By "enacting" I mean not the entire process of making the decision effective, but the initiation of that process. The technical details of the achievement of a policy may not be political, but the power that initiates that achievement is. Now, not everything political is decisive; a debate about elected officials is a political debate even if nothing is in the end resolved. But a dimension of social discourse and thought which at no point touches action, which cannot link up with enactments, is not political either. In this sense politics is indeed about power, the ability to produce effects in a human group. This is the kernel of Carl Schmitt's view that we must accept: politics is *socially decisive*. This is not to endorse "decisionism," the idea that such decisions are non-rational or extra-legal.[2] It is only to say that if a society has endless discussions about social matters which have no prospect of affecting decisions that bind action, then those discussions are not political.

While the most fundamental decision of any association is, one might say, the decision to found it or maintain it – hence politics makes and establishes association – here we face a problem more terminological than real. Humans always find themselves in associations. Already associated humans can change their mode of association, and can initiate new associations. The decisions to do so, and the manners of bringing such associations about, are indeed political in the same sense as the decisions of an ongoing association.

Are the relations among associations political? The answer is yes, but in two senses which each involve qualifications. Let us say that any set of persons sharing some trait constitutes a human *order*. Association is a special type of order, namely, an order of interaction, whether direct or indirect. To associate is to participate in an interactive whole, which, again, does not mean either that associations are intrinsically "organic" or that each member must immediately interact with each member. Members of associations know that they have interests in common, and affect each other by what they do or fail to do. Any such association can involve politics, so we commonly in English refer to the politics of any human organization;

behind the scenes maneuvering to get the International Olympic Committee to choose the site of the next Olympics is "political," as are the intramural strategies of aspiring CEOs. This wide use of the term is often a disparaging way to indicate that an association's decisions are made not on considerations of "substance," but through the influence of powerful members to achieve their factional, corporate, or individual interests. When the first violinist of an orchestra is chosen, and the choice seems not to have been based on ability, but on the personal connections of the violinist to influential officials, we say that the decision was "political." This too is politics, in the sense that *associational power*, a power itself based in the social relations of that or other associations, affects the outcome. If the violinist paid off the officials, or slept with them, or blackmailed or threatened them with physical violence, then the decision was corrupt but not political. It was political only if *social* power – not financial, sexual, or physical power – the mutual assistance of some clique within the larger association of actual and potential influential people, is involved.

But while legitimately political, such is not the kind of politics that forms our concern in this book. We are here concerned not merely with any associations in which there can be politics, but in *political associations*. The Olympic Committee is an association with politics in it, but it is not a *polis*. And this matters, for it will turn out that, whatever various orders and associations the members of the Committee belong to, each of them also belongs to a *polis*. To qualify as a *polis*, an association must be a society. A society is a horizon of interaction and interdependence. Consequently, societies are geographically continuous associations whose members are open to regular interaction in the tasks that constitute living, hence responsible to one politics.

A military battle between states is not a political association (although it is presumably a conflict between political associations). First, thrusting a sword under my ribs is not political; it attains "decisiveness," one might say, but not through a process of decid*ing*. Political processes may have brought me and my killer together, and our fight may have political consequences, but it is, as fight, not a political fight. But it also fails to be political because, simply, fighting is not "associating." Political decisions, however they are accomplished, must be decisions that hold across a society. It is the mark of a political association that the association across which such decisions hold is characterized by the mutual dependency of living together. Is there international politics? Yes, if the decision-making holds across several societies that are now "associating," that is, engaged in living together. To be sure, this togetherness is not the togetherness of intra-*polis* relations, the relations among fellow citizens. But it is perfectly reasonable to accept that relations among political associations can be political in a derivative sense.

So there are two ways in which human groups can *fail* to be political in the primary sense. They can associate around issues that are not that of a political association, which means their civil belonging or living together is not the dimension that subtends their interaction and which, directly or indirectly, is at stake in the decisions in question. Or, while what brings them to the interaction is indeed their civil association, the aim of their interaction may not be to place themselves under a joint political process of decision. An example of the first is all manner of human associations in science, business, recreation, etc. An example of the second is war.

We need not go further down this road. For our concern is with the common features of political association, whatever its social basis. Particularly important among these features are *unity, necessity, dominance, exclusivity, plurality,* and *place.*

Political authority is a *unitary* authority operating over a *unitary* association. I do not mean political authority is intrinsically indivisible, or that the association it governs is undivided, or that its members fail to exhibit connections with extra-association groups. I mean that to say the politics of a society is the process of decision-making is to say that it is *the* process, leading at least potentially to decisions that hold for all members. A political process that claims legitimate authority over only *some* members of a locale is not that locale's political process. One hundred people living adjacently but each making his and her decisions and enforcing them solely on him and herself is not a political process. That we call private life, not politics.

Contra Hannah Arendt, politics is based in associations of mutual interdependence, hence matters of *necessity*. Political decision-making is primarily concerned with the ongoing life of the civil association, a life constituted by economic, cultural, and social conditions. As such, necessities are relevant to the *polis*. Politics is always *about something*. Politics about economics is no less politics than politics about culture, religion, or public morality. Dealing with necessity need not relegate us to meaninglessness, as Arendt feared; the meaning of existence is largely determined by *how* we deal with its necessities. A politics that avoids matters of necessity would mean a politics unconnected to some of the most profound realities of people living together in a place. Dealing with such realities, as well as ideals and aspirations, *is* politics in the actual, human world.

The political association is potentially *dominant* regarding all other forms of association. Politics trumps, by definition. A society's political form can be based in its customs, laws, religion, ethnicity, its science, its economic needs or anything else at any time. But if one of these "trumps" all others, then it trumps because it has become political. When the final trump is played, *that* is politics. The reason for this trumping is straightforwardly Weberian: the state has a monopoly on the legitimate use of force in a society.[3]

As inherently territorial and necessitous, a political association is spatially and socially *exclusionary*. It cannot include everyone. Michael Walzer suggests that "to tear down the walls of the state . . . [is] to create a thousand petty fortresses," since exclusion would simply be shifted to the level of provinces, counties, towns, or neighborhoods.[4] If all forms of political exclusion were somehow prohibited, people would predictably spend an increasing amount of their time and identity in voluntary associations where exclusion is permitted. The human self requires a limited horizon for interaction and interdependence.[5]

As Arendt points out, politics is characterized by *plurality*. While any form of decision-making for a group is political, nothing like the normal problems and considerations of politics arise unless decision-making and -enacting is open to a multiplicity of members characterized by differences, primarily, different opinions. We may, strictly speaking, share with a being from a society without any such internal disagreements or differences the trait of being political or being members of a political association, but we could learn nothing of any practical or normative import from a conversation with such a creature.

The final feature deserves extended comment, given its significance for what will follow. The political association is tied to a *place*. It occupies a territory. This does not mean that a *polis* is self-consciously linked to a particular piece of turf – e.g. the state of Israel – but rather that a *polis* is always rule over some people who are spatially contiguous, even if the association changes turf. Borrowing Edward Casey's term, it is "placial."[6] This is true even for nomadic societies; the circle of hogans is on any given night in some place and not another. Not to mention that polities assume legitimate power over the inhuman resources and characteristics of a geographical place.

It is true that sometimes non-contiguous spaces are part of one *polis*, but in each such discontinuous place there is a plurality of people in *a* place, and they ambiguously regard the places of their polity, or nested polities (locale, province, imperial city, etc.), as linked places. Far-flung places constitute one political place or *polis* in a derivative sense, as in various forms of protectorates and colonies, and this derivative status has, as we know, complex consequences in the real world. It is also true that membership often fails to coincide with territory – there may be resident aliens, temporary visitors, and members travelling "off-shore." Also, many polities have considered as "citizens" only residents with a certain status. But this only means that residence is a necessary but insufficient criterion of membership. Where classes of residents are not considered citizens, "citizen" has the narrow sense of possessing full political rights. Note that those of lower status are not automatically members of *another* polity outside the authority of the full citizens. The more problematic cases are where the political association or individuals regard the criteria of membership as permanently including spatially far-flung groups. But this is "the exception that proves the rule" – an old saw that means that the exception shows the right way to interpret the rule. An *emigré* community that feels its true home is elsewhere, or which plans on returning, will not be regarded as full citizens by themselves or others in their new home. Nor does their "home" polity consider them identical to spatially present members. Israel may open its doors in principle to Jews living anywhere, but Jewish Americans are not invited to vote in Israeli elections.

The test case for such off-shore identification arises when the non- or supra-territorial identification competes with the territorial *in the political realm*. Some Muslim members of a non-Islamic polity may well determine their political action by religious identification with each other and with Muslims in other polities, or with a dominantly Islamic polity somewhere. But their political situation is entirely different depending on whether they are Muslim families scattered among non-Muslims versus residents of an Islamic enclave within a non-Muslim polity. The later is placial, hence has potentially an utterly different political force than the former. If the scattered Muslim families claimed not to be bound by local rules, whatever they could invoke as justification they could not claim to constitute a polity. For that they would have to live together in a "Muslim" place.

For a polity not to be placial in the sense that I mean would imply that the criteria of who is and is not a member, who is obligated by its laws and empowered by its institutions, have nothing to do with location of residence. It would mean that *where* I am is not a significant matter in determining to *which polity* I am obligated, e.g. if in my locale each person were a member of and obligated only to distinct, super-imposed non-spatial polities – the polity of African-American-retired-people, the polity of auto workers, the polity of female handicapped people, the polity of Hindus, etc. This would only make sense if residence were not significantly correlated with the kinds of life phenomena that polity must often be concerned with, if *where* I do most of my living, hence my relations to others in the same locale, were not particularly important *for* that living. This would have to mean both that neighbors did not interact – that is, that there was no pressing need for common rules governing neighborly relations – and did not use common resources in living.

Notice that I have presumed that the political place is primarily, although certainly not exclusively, a place of *residence*. For most agricultural societies, hence for most larger human societies of the last 10,000 years, no serious distinction need be made between the politics that holds for residential space and politics holding for other social spaces; each home abuts agricultural land, and other social functions take place at the center of a space defined by farmed land. In a hunting society, however, the hunters may have to move to locate game, separating residence from point of acquisition of food. Certainly the political relations of the home area remain in force on the hunt; that is, hunters on the hunt are still members of the *polis*, even if the *polis* recognizes distinctive rules for the relations among hunters in the field and neighbors at home. The center is still the collection of hogans to which the hunters return, where food is prepared and eaten, where one can sleep in the safety of numbers, where dependents live, where public ceremonies among beloved objects can occur. War parties also may have special rules, but these are, if the warriors remain members of a polity, subject to "home rule." Residential space has a primacy even when it is disjoined from "economic" space, as it is both in hunting societies and in contemporary industrial and post-industrial societies (in this sense commuting reproduces the pre-agrarian condition).[7]

A Brief History of Civil Society

Like so many stories, this one starts with Aristotle.[8] In the first chapter of his *Politics*, Aristotle described the city as *the* political community or partnership (*koinōnia hē politikē*).[9] The *polis* is that partnership that is "most authoritative of all and embraces all others." It is an association of persons who "cannot exist without one another." It is a geographical locale, but residence alone is not the definition of membership, since the *polis* contains aliens, slaves, women, and children. The *polis* is distinct from the household and the village: the household (*oikos*) is a partnership constituted by nature for "daily" needs, and is properly ruled by a "lord;" the village (*komē*) is the partnership of several households for "nondaily" needs and as such is an extension of the household. The city then arises from the partnership of several villages. It is the smallest partnership that is fully self-sufficient. It exists by nature and for needful, mortal rational beings, not beasts or gods. Its purpose is not merely for members to live but to live *good* lives. It is not an alliance by "contract" for mutual self-protection, nor a nation or *ethnos*. It is characterized by reciprocal equality, by friendship or fellowship, and by justice. As such, political rule is properly over "free and equal persons," who "share in decision and office," unlike the other two stages of partnership. Aristotle implies that there are upper limits on the size of a *polis*. Babylon, which was so large that its fall was not known to all citizens for three days, had the "dimensions of a nation rather than a city."[10]

Aristotle's is not an inevitable conception. As Luhmann points out, it is wedded to the notion that human society is what humans make of it, is the object of action, hence subject to moral legitimation.[11] The political order is something people do; it is dictated neither by gods, pre-given rules, or nature. This does not gainsay Aristotle's, or anyone else's, notion that it is human nature to be political, just as it does not imply the absence of tradition or divine reference or "natural" law. But this notion of the *polis* is fundamentally humanistic or anthropocentric; the *polis* is a human circle, which gods, tradition, and nature condition but do not determine. If they determine it, then there would be society without the need for politics.

Aristotle's *koinōnia hē politikē* would eventually be translated into Latin as *societas civilis* in the fifteenth century, a term with its own intriguing history.[12] The ancient Roman *civis* meant citizen, and *civitas* referred to the independent state, that is, the state or province governed more or less independently from Rome. For the Romans and much of the medieval tradition, "civic" was the antonym of rude, natural, ecclesiastical, military, and familial. Roman law distinguished "civil" law, which governed legal conflicts among citizens, from the "criminal" law which covered crimes against and punishable by the state. Special social organizations, like the military, and much later ecclesiastical orders, stood outside the civil. So, civil refered above all to the association of citizens, in distinction from special institutions – army and eventually church – and in its legal use it related to property and private obligations. At this point, "civil" was understood as concerning state, but not state as *government*. Rather, it refered to the state as governed citizens, sometimes emphasizing their place under government, sometimes emphasizing their status independent of government. At the same time, "civil" was the antonym of rude or barbarous. Barbarous meant to the Romans and the Greeks before them simply, "foreign," and bore a relation to language; its Greek root meant "stammering," unable to speak *our* language. Civil has retained to the present day this connection to being civilized and "refined." Thus the term "civil" has always functioned to two related but distinct orders: the status of the citizen in civil society, and the constrained behavior of the civilized.

Following for a moment the latter strand, in his seminal work *The Civilizing Process* Norbert Elias demonstrates that the modern meaning of *civilité* had its origins in the French *courtoisie*, courtesy, the kind of behavior required at court.[13] Courtesy or courtliness becomes important during the rise of absolute monarchy in the sixteenth and seventeenth centuries. According to Elias, this standard of behavior was one of increasing restraint, self-consciousness, "drive control," "affective neutrality," the heightening of shame and repugnance, and the concealment of a range of bodily functions. Thereby, at court especially, a "good" society was created. The feudal warrior nobility was transformed in the late medieval and early modern period into a courtier nobility. With this new standard of behavior, which was constantly evolving in the direction of greater restraint and con- cealment, a new distinction between adulthood and childhood arose. For children were, as opposed to the medieval period, to be prevented from seeing a range of behaviors. Self-restraint exacerbated the distinction between proper adult and child behavior. One of the first definitions of civil- ity in this sense was Erasmus' 1530 *De civilitate morum puerilium (On Civil- ity in Children)*. Civility was thus a pedagogical issue. All this presupposed as well the development of the modern state, for civil society was likewise understood as a "pacified space," which must be protected by an ultimate authority with a monopoly on the use of force.

As noted, *civilité* and *civilization* were in early modern Western Europe primarily French terms, that is, developed in their early modern importance by the French, and even in translation regarded as connected to French society by others, e.g. the Germans. Kant himself denigrated mere *civiliza- tion*, as the external adoption of artificial, contrived manners, in contrast to culture (*Kultur*), which for Germans of the eighteenth and early nineteenth centuries was the more important concept, referring to the inner formation of the spirit.[14] While the rising bourgeoisie and its intellectual representa- tives came to regard courtly manners as affected, after the German attitude, they nevertheless took on their own version of self-control, which became the nineteenth-century bourgeois standard, and continues, Elias claims, through the twentieth century. Until very recently "civil" carried with it the opposition to the low, the peasantry or workers, the *internal barbarians* if you will. Civility and civilization came retrospectively to be understood as a continuous, developmental process, whose most advanced version was, of course, Western. In the mid-nineteenth century "civilization" became what Western imperialism thought it was bringing to the rest of the world.

Returning to the notion of civil society, seventeenth-century social con- tract theory, most influentially in the work of John Locke, made "civil" syn- onymous with "social" and opposed to natural, hence aligned with the Greek *nomos* as opposed to *physis*. Civil society is society as we know it, that is, with political authority. The opposite of civil society was the state of nature. But Locke conceived of such authority, and society itself, as the product of agreement or convention (albeit convention restrained by divine law). Thus civil society includes government, but as the product of citizens. This continued to be the dominant usage of the term until the nineteenth century, as we shall see.

Habermas points out that it was in the late Middle Ages and early modern period that formerly unseen household economic activities emerged into the public space of town life through the rise of the "burghers," including new merchants, guild craftsmen, and officials.[15] The emergence of the town and its members now freed from legal subservience to, and devoid of the protection of, the manorial lord, was the precondition for the modern experience of a public, civic realm of equal members. By the eighteenth century "public" indicated as well a new reading public, through which "public opinion" emerged as both a political force to be taken into account by power and an ongoing sphere of debate carried on independently of the state. And this was of course connected to the rise of commercial society in the eighteenth century. The public space was forced open by the success of the market economy and the various social structures it encouraged. Together the free, now increasingly commercial cities, with their reading publics, and the new conception of society as the product of human agreement, promoted the view that, according to Elias, "Society and the economy have their own laws, which resist the irrational interference of rulers and force." Here, "men, for the first time, [come] to think of themselves and their social existence as a process."[16] This is what Karl Polanyi called "the discovery of society," the breakthrough into the consciousness of the time that Church and King were not the emanating center of the structures of life. Those structures had their own weight. Thus commercial society was the leading edge of the new notion of *the autonomy of the social*. And this provoked, as we have already seen, a profound inquiry especially on the part of Scottish thinkers into the moral plausibility of such an autonomous society.[17]

It was in this context that Adam Ferguson initiated the modern discussion of civil society with his *Essay on the History of Civil Society* (1767). Ferguson remained closest to the older republican model; as Pocock remarked, Ferguson's book is the "most Machiavellian" of the Scottish Enlightenment.[18] He insisted that a public spirited citizenry was essential to maintaining the good society. He saw such republican virtue in the unrefined, martial attitudes of Highland culture.[19] For this tradition, inheriting as it did Ciceronian Stoicism, the cultural refinement in the arts and sciences that Montesquieu and the more "liberal" Enlightenment thinkers encouraged was suspect because of its necessary connection to luxury and the valuation of sensibility over action. Ferguson's quasi-Rousseauian reaction was also connected to a kind of proto-Romanticism or -nationalism, in that the distinctive, less "civilized" culture of Scotland was thereby honored, in contrast to the developing commercialism and cosmopolitanism of more "modern" thinkers. For Ferguson civil society is the polity itself, although a republican polity whose character derives from the citizen, not the government. Citizen here means the propertied free male.

Ferguson's book was still well-known when Hegel redefined the term early in the next century. For Hegel civil society or *bürgerliche Gesellschaft* was distinct not only from family but from the state as well, hence from the private and biological realm on the one side and the public and political realm on the other.[20] In his *Philosophy of Right* (1821), the development of *Recht* (Right) takes place through three levels of will: immediate or Abstract Right, the rights of the individual with respect to other individuals and things, e.g. via contract; will mediated through these externals, hence as the demands of Universal Morality (*Moralität*); and finally "Ethical Life" or "Customary Morality" (*Sittlichkeit*), hence the concrete embodiment of right in the institutions of the moral community. These institutions are themselves developmentally ordered into three: the natural piety of family life, civil society, and the state. Civil society has three moments: first of all the system of interdependent relations based on needs; then the "administration of law;" and two loosely connected forms of unification, the "police" or governmental authority, and the commercial "corporation."[21]

Hegel gave special importance to autonomous economic entities within civil society. This way had been prepared by Kant, who had recognized the "unsocial sociability" of the modern competitive town. James Schmidt points out that Hegel's economistic revision of the meaning of "civil society" was literally perplexing for his readers.[22] For the first time the term was used to mean something entirely distinct from the state. Here we need to be clear. The tradition understood the status of citizen as *staatlich*, even where government, rule, and kingship were understood as dependent on the association of citizens. There was a counter-tradition, of course, namely, royalism. Royalism regarded the political community and its territory as the kingdom, the *domos* or household of the king. Hegel was the first to break the connection of civil society and state, hence in effect to render civil society independent. The way he did it was to render it primarily economic. But notice as well that civil society for Hegel is a moral (*sittlich*) and a pedagogical notion, if a deficient one. Civil society educates the subject away from the family toward a conventional, competitive association of economic actors, preparing it for the final step, the fulsome moral association of membership in the state. Marx of course took the Hegelian usage further, making civil society equivalent to capitalist society, hence intrinsically a society of alienation and oppression.

There is one more piece of the historical puzzle, associated with the name of Alexis de Tocqueville. In his *Democracy in America* (1833), Tocqueville saw American egalitarianism as the civilized world's future. It was his aim to say what lay ahead on the road. According to Tocqueville, equality is first of all more powerful than liberty. Americans "will want equality in freedom, and if they cannot have that, they still want equality in slavery."[23] For equality's benefits are more immediate and common; equality "daily gives each man in the crowd a host of small enjoyments." But in this improvement all extremes are "blunted" toward the average, which average is indeed above that of most traditional peasants, but lower than that of the aristocratic elite. As a result, Americans "have abolished the troublesome privileges of some of their fellows, but they come up against the competition of all. The barrier has changed shape rather than place."[24] Tocqueville's most important and counter-intuitive claim is that *equality isolates*. Aristocracy provided daily contact and a sense of obligation across classes. While concerns for "humanity" are weak in aristocracy, there is loyalty to those above and below, outside family and friends. Each belonged to his or her station, hence to a moral network. Democracy "breaks the chain" of the interdependence of isonomic classes in hierarchical society. In democracy there is no "devoted service." Tocqueville feared that, absent traditional bonds, Americans would tend toward "individualism," by which he meant privatism, the restriction of one's concerns to a narrow circle about the self.

Tocqueville noted, however, a variety of social forms that had grown up to protect Americans from this weakness. His worry was that paternalistic government would provide the sense of connection.[25] But he noted an alternative with more hopeful prospects: the cultivation of voluntary associations. Tocqueville wrote, "In democratic countries knowledge of how to combine is the mother of all other forms of knowledge. . . ." Americans have honed the "art of association." Such associations take the place of hierarchic patrons. This is Tocqueville's remedy to the evils of egalitarianism, that "associations of plain citizens can compose very rich, influential, and powerful bodies, in other words, *aristocratic* bodies" (my emphasis).[26] The remedy to the aristocracy of lineage is a network of voluntary "aristocracies," institutions that thicken the social bond and social diversity simultaneously. Theoretically speaking, if pre-Hegelian civil society is primarily political or governmental, and Hegelian civil society is economic, Tocquevillian civil society is sociological.

Here we may conveniently, if unfairly, conclude our history lesson. For it happens that the Hegelian notion, economized even more thoroughly by Marx, became the dominant meaning of civil society in modern political thought. Whatever the virtues of this approach, the interpretation of civil society through economic life led to its amalgamation to the argument between advocates and enemies of capitalism. From the 1930s through the 1970s, the opposition between Marxism, with various "progressive" forms of liberal egalitarianism – the party of the state – and libertarians, commercial conservatives, and status quo liberals – the party of the market – seemed to absorb all the energies of political thought. To the left "civil society" was an obfuscatory name for the interests of capital, the social forms dictated by the ruling class; for free marketeers it was a suspicious mystification of what really mattered, namely, markets and individual rights. Talk of civil society had little relevance to the only issues that counted, helping the poor or protecting property rights from government.[27]

The Return of Civil Society

The story of the recent return of civil society to the center of political discussion has been told elsewhere.[28] It was adapted by Central European dissidents in the 1980s, soon to be leaders and state-builders after 1989, as a name for the complex non-governmental "social capital" required for liberal society. It was then adopted by theorists from many parts of our ever more interconnected world, particularly by Anglo-American theorists. In their hands it served several related but distinguishable purposes. Economic conservatives used it as a counterweight to egalitarian liberal "statism." Worried egalitarian liberals turned to it as a partial explanation of the recalcitrance of poverty to their policies. Some communitarians adopted it as a less loaded, less intimate name for the solidarity they sought in excessively individualist liberal society. Some became primarily concerned with civility as an increasingly lost virtue in America. Civic republicans emphasized the "civic" and "citizenship" connection within civil society. Others expressed specific concern for the health of American "mediating structures" and "associational life." It is true, as some have complained, that a term regarded as so wholesome by so many different thinkers is naturally suspect.[29]

But our suspicions can, I think, be allayed. "Civil society" has a small set of distinct but related and rather stable meanings that answer to two creditable intellectual and political motives of recent decades: disenchantment with and then the need to replace the totalistic statism of European–Soviet communism, as well as worries about the moderate statism of liberal republican societies under pressure of late or "post"-modern social conditions. If it is true that distinct groups are fudging their differences a bit by hitching their placards to a single slogan, nevertheless, as slogans go "civil society" is a pretty good one. There are four themes that go under the name in current, as opposed to historiographical, usage, although some of them permit further interpretive differences.

First and most reliably, civil society refers to the social complexity required for liberal republicanism and democratic capitalism, which Central European theorists recognized as a precursor to a functioning liberal republic, and which Western theorists recognized they had ignored in their overweening concern with the battle of State and Markets. This statement already contains controversy. There is a division between civil society theorists who see State as the overwhelming threat – thereby tending to collapse their view into libertarianism or economic conservatism – and those who regard big capitalism equally as troubling. Note that this use of the term contains an implicit critique of certain features of modernity. States and markets are, with science and bureaucracy, arguably the driving forces modernity.[30] The dominant ways of being modern have generally entailed replacing what in earlier eras were the ongoing practices, institutions, and traditions of society by market forces or by government. Alan Wolfe argues that our dominant social discourse in recent decades has been determined by the hegemony of these categories, hence the disciplines of political science and economics. What then is ignored is society itself, "the process by which individuals construct together with others the social meanings through which they interpret reality – including the reality of moral obligation itself."[31] Wolfe argues that the dualism of States and Markets cannot do the analytical job; we need a third, sociological turn in political economy and cultural critique.

Second, "civil society" functions as the name for a level of solidarity, community, or moral commonality putatively lacking or eroded in liberal polities. One form this takes is attention to the role of mediating institutions, e.g. family, neighborhood, church, and voluntary associations. This brings with it an emphasis on pluralism and localism. Some regard political activity itself as the missing form of relation, thus turning toward civic republicanism or discourse theory or participatory democracy. Others interpret civil society as socially and morally thick, in effect making it the successor term to "community" in the hands of communitarians. Yet others read it as a *civil* society, a society characterized by lawfulness, order, and civility or civilized behavior, in contrast to contemporary society, marked by incivility, rudeness, a lack of proper restraint.

Third and more theoretically, some thinkers find civil society to be an intrinsically non-foundationalist concept. Perhaps reacting to the foundationalist and universalist interpretations of liberalism – egalitarian or libertarian – they believe that civil society is characterized both by a recognition of limits and a commitment to institutional pluralism rather than philosophical principle. One could call this postmodern; at any rate, for these thinkers something about the commitment to civil society is a rejection of modernism. Thus, John Gray has argued that civil society is the "living kernel" of an historical "foundationalist" liberalism that is now defunct.[32] Civil society for Gray is marked by tolerance, the rule of law, limited government, and private property, the necessary conditions for a free society. Liberalism ushered this social form into existence, but philosophical liberalism's ultimate commitments to individualism, universalism, progress, and egalitarianism are unsustainable. Civil society is the better term for a social order that eschews foundational narratives.

And of course the concept has been subjected to critique. Three in particular can be mentioned.

First, where civil society implies a hope for the reinvigoration of solidarity or civility, the cry of "nostalgia" will not fail to be heard.[33] The historically most sophisticated version of this criticism comes from Adam Seligman. He argues that the modern notion of civil society was dependent on a particularly Scottish moral theory, which made the human desire for approbation or approval fundamental. The rational pursuit of personal advantage, then, was in service of, *and limited by*, the former. As naturally sympathetic creatures, we are not capable of indifference either to others' suffering or to others' opinions of ourselves. Thus self-interest and altruism can be harmonious.[34] Seligman argues that this "naive" moral theory can no longer be maintained. In a related vein, Alan Ehrenhalt points out that the solidarity of earlier civil society hinged upon authority; you can't have one without the other. Unless we are willing to reinstate a pre-critical trust in authority, civil society is a pipe dream.[35] In either case, a solidaristic civil society presupposes anachronistic conditions. Second, certainly many students of the left continue to regard "civil society" as a depoliticized name for a capitalist-driven reality that sorely needs political control. Civil society is for them the mythologization of an economic–historical construction, a structure of domination. The contemporary use of the term betokens a reactionary political movement that seeks to ground social order in a non-political and non-economic concept, making of capitalism as a kind of "natural" social order. And last there is a simple historical objection against those who trace civil society to the eighteenth century: none of the Scottish Enlightenment thinkers, including the only one who features the term "civil society" (Ferguson), took it to mean a purely sub-state phenomenon. That usage began with Hegel (or in a sense, with Kant). Thus contemporaries who use "civil society" as a label for sub-state society are in the odd position of using Hegel's term, but not his meaning – namely, a non-autonomous, morally suspect realm of economic relations that needed to be completed by the *Rechtstaat*. Instead, they read Hegel's term retrospectively through the social theory of Mandeville and the Scotts, expanding it to include the whole arena of "autonomous" society.[36]

Dealing with the last criticism first, I will plead guilty in the Hegel kidnapping case, but nevertheless assert the honor of thieves. Civil society has been stolen so many times that its title is no longer clear. The Hegelian and then Marxist translation of Ferguson's "civil" as first "*bürgerliche*" and then "bourgeois" are jarring enough appropriations. Having been the medieval translation of Aristotle's political community of citizens, traveled through the Roman distinction from the criminal, military and then ecclesiastical, always maintaining its orderliness and refinement against rudeness, and functioning as a label for humanly-constructed republics out of the ultimate rudeness (the state of nature), civil society was used by Hegel as a label for the commercial society that Mandeville and the Scotts recognized as the new social order of the eighteenth century, an order the Scotts saw as having its own non-transcendent morality, which the Germans found sorely lacking. Hegel's definition actually is the most modern one, and the current discussion continues it, while largely rejecting his evaluation. Contemporaries who critique civil society accept both Hegel's definition and his evaluation. Those who admire it accept his definition but take it as a label for something of which English and Scottish thinkers gave the better, more modern account.

Civil Association

A civil society is first of all a form of social-political organization rooted in a particular form of association, the association of citizens according to civil rules. The most complete theoretical account of civil association without moral *Gemeinschaft* comes from Michael Oakeshott.[37] In *On Human Conduct*, Oakeshott defined civil association as an association of *cives* or citizens according to procedural rules or laws, which have no end other than the maintenance of a just association. Government is the juridical agency that adjudicates, interprets, and applies the laws; politics is the discussion among *cives* and government aimed at changing the laws. Oakeshott's main aim is to deny that civil association is or can be an "enterprise association," an association with goals whose activities must be managed toward the collective achievement of an end. The replacement of civil by enterprise association through yoking civic and political life to the management of economic life is for Oakeshott the great political sin of the twentieth century.

Given collective acceptance of an end, it is legitimate to discipline members toward its achievement. Entrance to or exit from such an association may be free, but behavior within it is not. "Management" is the proper name for running an enterprise, but an improper name for the governance of citizens free to decide their own ends.

Thus for Oakeshott civil society is not united by a solidarity of purpose or worldview or even a common morality, beyond the moral procedural rules of civility itself. While I will reject the notion that any civil society can be *purely* non-enterprising, purely procedural, Oakeshott is right that civil society is at least *primarily* non-enterprising. Civil society cannot be yoked to rationalization or progress, even toward moral goals. A unity of purpose is outside of, and threatening to, civil society.

Civil association is, in my definition, a quasi-independent association of households, equally subject to primarily procedural rules in which public life and politics are open to action from any household or member, and in which government, the agency charged with maintenance of the association through the adjudication, interpretation and application of law, is responsive to this discussion. Readers of Oakeshott will notice two respects in which his definition has been mangled. First, the subject of civil association is not primarily individuals but households. This may seem odd. The implication is not that individuals *qua* individuals are not members, do not carry rights or obligations as members, or have no legal independence of family. It is that, following, in somewhat different respects, both Aristotle and Hegel, we must regard the civil association as an association among individuals that are *already embedded in social networks*. Individuals come to the civic table already dressed, relationally speaking, bringing with them their household station. The household is, I think, the preferable term for the most important costuming worn by citizens, because it is the primary – although not the sole – locus of the private life. This model places its emphasis on the liberty of private life as well as the liberty of members of each household to appear and pursue interests in public, and to participate in political discussion and thereby to impact governance, as well as the responsibility of governance to all households.

Most important for issues to come, I have qualified Oakeshott by making the independence of households only "quasi" independence and law only "primarily" procedural. As said earlier, independence in human society is an unattainable and only ambiguously desirable condition. By primarily procedural rules I mean something that straddles the distinction between substantive and purely procedural rules. Quasi-procedural rules are those that, like Oakeshott's procedural rules, serve no other purpose beyond the *civitas*, yet, unlike his rules, they explicitly have a *telos*, namely, the maintenance of the *civitas*. The maintenance of the *civitas* cannot be distinguished from the maintenance of the *civitas* and its goods *as they are understood* by citizens. This is a *telos* which may from time to time require that citizens engage in joint enterprise, in order to maintain the civility and liberty they commonly enjoy. Such an admission is a denial of the rigidity of Oakeshott's most important distinction, that between civil and enterprise association. I am accepting that there can be no such thing as a purely civil, absolutely non-enterprising, state. In other words, while the *civitas* is primarily a procedural association without a goal that transcends itself, it is the kind of association which, under certain conditions, must *become an enterprise association*. If it does not, then it is no longer a civil association. Civility both entails a thick interpretation of what its survival requires, and can mandate collective enterprise for the sake of that survival.[38]

Despite this, Oakeshott has certainly seen part of the truth.[39] We cannot make sense of a free society that is *primarily* an enterprise association. The requirements of enterprise are in tension with civil freedom of members. But the point is, not that enterprise is the great evil of modern states, but that it is one pole, the other being procedural civility, between which we are always forced to find a balance.

If we are to understand civil association, we must clarify its relation to government. The etymology of "government" indicates direction, as in that component of a mechanical device which directs the device's operation. In the political sphere, government has four functions, the last two of which are sometimes not distinguished since they are usually assigned to the same agency: adjudication, legislation, execution of the law, and the management of external relations. It must be said, however, that this list is itself an abstraction from the fulsome social role of government. In reality government serves cultural and psychological functions in addition to those listed; in effect, the "direction" of society cannot be fully analogized to the direction of a machine. But for the moment we will restrict ourselves to the purely political functions in exploring the relation of civil association and governance.

Civil association is self-ruling in the sense that it is and regards itself as that for which government exists, and to which government is responsible. Its politics must have an effect on government. But self-rule is not the aim or end of civil association, and there are a variety of mechanisms for ensuring government responsiveness that could be compatible with civil association. Self-rule there must be, in some form or another, because to deny self-rule is to deny dignity to the *civitas*. To put self-rule first, however, as do participatory democrats and civic republicans, is to understand the *civitas* through governance rather than the other way around.

If we abstract the logically primitive structure of the *civitas*, it has rules, largely but not exclusively adverbial, by which members are to control their dealings with one another as they live their quasi-independent lives and pursue their particular goals. These rules need not be explicit, that is, formally stated in public. Conflicts will arise among members. Occasionally this will involve someone clearly and knowingly and without provocation violating a rule of association. More commonly it will involve a difference in interpretation of the rules, or action claimed by the actor to be a response to previous unpunished violation of the rules. In either case, adjudication must occur. This may well occur informally, that is, among members, with those so moved taking a leading role in adjudicating and punishing and resolving. But this may as well require interpretation and revision of rules. When all this is accomplished without the establishment of special offices, this is the most fundamental form of self-rule or democracy. It is comparable to the Aristotelian notion, recaptured by Dewey, Arendt, and Walzer, according to which the only truly political form of rule is self-rule. But in my version, it is not quite so profound. What is crucial is that it is informal; it is the form of rule intrinsic to the *civitas*. So, if the question is, Is the *civitas* self-ruling by nature?, the proper answer is: if it has to be. What matters in the *civitas* is the continuity of an association of free members over time. Self-rule is a means and not an end.

The creation of formal authority, or civil offices, with official procedures of the exercise of authority, is the creation of government. There is, as said earlier, virtually no such thing as "self-government." To *be* governed is *not* to rule oneself. Whether these formal offices are the installment of a ruler, or a committee of rulers, or the establishment of special meeting times when all citizens can jointly adjudicate cases, the creation of formal procedures and the definition of who and when decisions are made is the end of *purely* civil rule. This cessation of purely civil rule is not an unhappy fact for the *civitas*, Rousseau and Arendt to the contrary notwithstanding. Since active self-rule is not a primary concern of the *civitas*, ceding such activity to an agency responsible to the civil association is not unwelcome.

Now, there are certain relatively timeless norms that define what government must be or do, at least from the viewpoint of citizens. Government must be *legitimate* and *good*. Legitimacy is dependent on cultural criteria inherited from the past, and as such are widely variable. But there are conditions of good government that both exceed legitimacy – a bad government can still be legitimate – and are universal.[40] These minimal conditions of good government are: assurance of the survival of society, hence prevention of widespread premature death and excessive misery; the enforcement of law; prevention of conquest; and avoidance of tyranny, corruption, the intentional punishment of the innocent or the intentional reward of the guilty. Survival as an internally ruled society requires the first three; justice requires the last four. Justice is part of the validity of governmental authority, which is not to say that it is the only test of governmental validity. I am claiming that these values or ends are internal to governance, and more or less universally recognized as necessary. How they are to be *interpreted* is, of course, widely variable. The reasons that government must do these things are two, or rather, derive from the consideration of government in two different contexts. First, like anything human, government has its own status as a moral entity. Hence it ought not be corrupt or unjust. Second, it serves the *civitas*. This is inherent in the notion of civil association, or more precisely, it is inherent in the view that within the civil–legal–political–governmental sphere, the civil has logical priority.

Where there is government, that is, official or formal rule, the interests of the *civitas* in government are threefold: that government be legitimate and good, as described; that it act in such a way as to maintain or restore the conditions of a good civil life; and that members are free to participate in a public discussion which affects governmental action. The last is not, as it is normally understood, a right to self-government, or more intensively, a right of the people to have their will put into force. It is rather political liberty, one of the three forms of liberty that free citizens must have, along with private and public liberty. Must formal authority be formally dependent on the formal consent of members? Not necessarily. That is, it is not a necessary condition of the *civitas* that government be based in explicit or formal consent. What is necessary is that members are free to participate as they wish, hence, to inject their views into the process of decision-making.

Given this description, what is the relation between the political form called liberal republicanism and what I have called the *civitas*? First, all but the most minimal, simple and short-lived forms of human society are in fact governed. Historically, rather than logically, any civil association exists under government. In this light, the Enlightened republic, the creation of the eighteenth century, was an attempt at creating a political society of "free citizens," that is, an independently governed society modeled on the *civitas*. Famously, in its historical context, this involved *reducing* government, as well as the introduction of a variety of innovations necessary to make a modern state as civically tractable as possible. This entailed the establishment of legal and civil equality, the differentiation the identity of person as citizen (hence legal and governmental subject, and political discussant and actor) from his or her social, cultural, and economic identity, and the rejection of Burke's "equal rights but not to equal things." Furthermore, Enlightenment Republicanism introduced what may be called *formalism* into civic affairs. That is, formal procedures and offices were to be constructed for popular sovereignty, rights guarantees, lines of authority, etc. Rule is by law, not personality, and government powers are limited to those explicitly granted to government, hence constitutionalism. This is arguably a form of what Weber called modern rationalization. Rational decision of the people is here understood to mean that law is to rule power. More subtly, power is to be *spoken*, spelled out in public so all can hear and see it, so that it can be weighed and measured by the *civitas*. This is a pragmatic decision that, without such formal constitution, power cannot in fact be controlled. It is, along with many other characteristics of modern liberal republican politics, extrinsic to the model of civil association, but nevertheless justified as necessary for a modern civil society to be maintained.

Conditions of Civil Society

Modern civil society has a series of distinctive characteristics, features that must be in place for it to obtain. Six in particular are of concern: the autonomy of the social, the expansion of *civitas* to society, spontaneous order, institutional pluralism, market economy, and a particular relation to culture. Discussion of the last of these will be postponed until the following chapter.

The autonomy of the social

First and most important, civil society is the name for the worldly autonomy of the social, the notion that social life is existentially self-sustaining and generates its own norms of validity, distinct from the directorship of any special, supra-social agency.[41] Society gets its norms from the inside rather than from institutions outside or above it. The phrase is telling; a *civil society* is first of all a *society*, and one that is civil. Civil society declares the moral and political autonomy of a society of citizens. Earlier I defined politics as logically dependent on society. A civil society recognizes that dependence; it recognizes the priority of society as given to political processes and political power. Historically, those institutions which have dictated to society from above or outside are government and church. So a civil society is one in which the social is understood as having its own "substance," its moral reality and weight, independent of government and church.

Clearly, social autonomy requires certain political conditions, we would could roughly call republican and even, in a limited sense, liberal. Consistent with Aristotelian usage, civil society refers to an association of citizens. To speak of the citizen is implicitly to refer to political and governmental society, and to impute equality to those members. That is, the civil society notion accepts a politicized conception of membership. But the point is that civil society refers to a politically sovereign social group in which government and politics do not constitute the group, in which the group and its norms impose themselves on government and politics. Further, governmental power must not be sacralized, it must be responsive to the dialogue among citizens, and must be limited. Government must not violate social norms. Likewise, there must be limits on Chuch power.

In this sense we can say that civil society is not characteristic of the "Axial Age" or "agro-literate" or stratified societies which dominated civilization from the Neolithic invention of agriculture to the dawn of the industrial age. For those societies were typically hierarchical and ordered in reference to King and Church understood as the sources of power and legitimacy. But the autonomy of the social was arguably true of some commercial, trading cities, like the Greek city states, including Athens. Hence Aristotle's original meaning of civil society is bound up with the idea of social autonomy.

Expansion of civitas to society

As mentioned, the Enlightened republic, the creation of the eighteenth century, was an attempt at forging a whole political society of "free citizens," that is, to extend the ancient notion of the *civitas* uniformly to an entire horizon of interdependence and interaction that we call "society." What this rejected was isonomia, the existence of hierarchically arranged geographically coincident social orders. The state, the sovereignly governed territory, is to be treated as one *civitas*. To be a subject is to be a citizen; "no subjection without citizenship" could be its motto, even if it was not fully implemented until the twentieth century. It is probable, as argued separately by Gellner and Liah Greenfeld, that the development of nationalism was crucial to this equation, for nationalism elevated the pleb, the populus, from a denigrated status ("commoner") to that by which sovereignty was justified. Politically or civically, what the aristocrat and commoner share – e.g. their "Frenchness" or "Englishness" – mattered more than what differentiated them. This does not mean that nationalism is a necessary trait of modern civil society; that remains to be seen. It means rather that, paraphrasing Greenfeld, nationalism was the "cocoon" from which modern civil society emerged.[42]

Spontaneous order

Also unlike the ancient model, any modern civil society must be a society of *spontaneous order*. As seen in chapter 1, spontaneous order is the uniquely modern conception of unintentional good, of a whole whose virtue is not the result of mind or *telos*. It is a commitment, explicit or implicit, to the superiority of a social process in which nobody is in charge. In Claude Lefort's figure for democracy, the "throne is empty." Negatively defined, spontaneous order refers to social order that emerges out of social interactions not coordinated by command or by democratic will. That leaves several different avenues for social control. As noted earlier, at least three distinct kinds of restraints or ordering mechanisms can be included in a "spontaneous" social order: social norms embodied in interpersonal approbation and disapprobation; constitution of personality by cultural institutions; and the self-interested free choices of other individuals (the last being the libertarian ideal). Modern civil society is characterized by spontaneous order, but its social, economic, and cultural spheres largely obey *distinctive forms* of spontaneous order. A spontaneously ordered society does not lack order, but exhibits plural and conflicting forms of order.

Institutional pluralism

Two aspects of spontaneous order are important enough to be considered distinctive traits of modern civil society. The first of these is *institutional pluralism*. No single agency dominates social life or is the sole arbiter of norms. Institutional pluralism comes in two forms: a pluralism of kinds of institutions, or spheres of life, and a pluralism of similar institutions within each kind. In a modern spontaneously ordered society commercial, political, familial, recreational, associational, and religious institutions become distinct from each other, and at the same time there are many, sometime competing, political institutions, many recreational institutions, etc. I can join rival political clubs, each of which understands itself as distinct from religious or commercial associations. Social institutions and associations carry their own particular social norms; hence, as noted, spontaneously ordered social life carries its own constraints. This double process of pluralization is driven by another feature of modern civil society which we will encounter in a moment. A modern society is crisscrossed by institutions of all kinds – religious, political, voluntary interest associations, commercial corporations, nationalistic groups, etc. – and none of these has unquestioned control over the others. There is meaningful individual liberty in a civil society because the individual has a variety of places to go, associations to join.

Market economy

The second, and most famous, aspect of spontaneous order is economic: civil societies must have market economies. If, as Robert Heilbronner long ago noted, economies can only be organized in three ways – by tradition, command, or markets – then civil modern society must have a market economy. Tradition is ruled out by modernity – not in *toto*, but as the dominant organizing principle – and command would require vast state control. Historically, it was the development of commercial society which led the way to a society of spontaneous order. Commercial society proved to be the crucial means of "buying off" power, as Gellner puts it. It led to unprecedented prosperity and technological power, making populations and governments willing to accept spontaneous order; populations, because of the prosperity, governments because of the relative advantage such prosperity and the attendant technological power granted them over other governments. Furthermore, one can argue that the shift of work, construction, for profit to the center of social life was necessary to make civil society the society of all the people, not merely a civil society of land-rich and/or martial aristocrats and/or wisdom-and-grace hoarding elites. The majority must work to live; hence a society whose center of power is either martial or prayerful cannot include the majority as equals.

We cannot exclude economic activity from civil society or its local, mediating institutions. But this raises the basic disagreement, mentioned earlier, between those who include the economic sphere in civil society and those who see civil society as a distinct member of a trinitarian social conception along with Markets and State. Must we make civil society synonymous with that oxymoron, the "market society"? I think not. While it was indeed the economic order that began the differentiation of social life from the directives of power – it was the thin end of the wedge that pried society away from Church and State – this does not mean that the society thereby released was or is purely economic, or that all economic institutions are civil institutions. Markets are a necessary but insufficient condition for modern civil society; a civil society must be partly constituted by markets, but it *is not* those markets. But where then to draw the line?

From the perspective of the late or "post"-modern era, we can distinguish the economic *system*, or more precisely, subsystem from economic life in general. Economy, in the sense of economic activity and the products and effects of such, is ubiquitous. The various institutions of society are difficult to distinguish from the economic; it is hard to find social agencies, even in the premodern era, that do not function economically as well as in other dimensions. But, with Habermas and others, we can distinguish the systemic level of economic activity from non-systemic levels. The system is that realm of activities, properties, and their effects that are tightly bound up in the "logic" of the market, the non-local network of functional economic agencies and their forms of regulation that increasingly dominates local economic life. It is highly rationalized and progressive; every entity in its highly competitive environment must rationalize to maximize profits. And this level of market activity is part of an interlocking system with governmental administration, law, and the media-culture.

Civil society is thus distinct not from economics *per se*, but from that level of economic life, the system. Civil society is a dimension of public social existence and experience which is relatively unintegrated by, uncoordinated by, the system. Whereas the market's single-stranded or functional rationalization leads to the constant revolutionizing of social conditions, civil society does not "lead" anywhere, although it permits progress. The dimension of life in which social members act and experience themselves as living together according to civil rules is a different dimension from that in which they act to increase marginal advantage and volatilize existing institutions and practices by placing them on the functional scale. Civil society needs its markets, and it benefits from (and suffers from) market rationalization; it needs to *abut* the market. Nevertheless, the rules of civility are not the rules of the market. Non-systemic agencies and actors – or better, agencies and actors in their non-systemic dealings – are indeed part of civil society. So the corner *bodega* can be an important civic meeting place, whereas the conference room of IBM's executives is not.

Notes

1 Claude Lefort, "The Question of Democracy," in *Democracy and Political Theory*, trans. David Macey (Minneapolis: University of Minnesota, 1988).
2 See for example Carl Schmitt, *The Concept of the Political*, trans. George Schwab (Chicago: University of Chicago Press, 1996).
3 More precisely, the state is the dominant repository of the legitimate use of force and the final arbiter of the legitimacy of the use of force by others. I should add that this dominance need not imply the "tyranny of politics," by which Michael Walzer characterizes single party rule, say, in communist societies. Walzer's tyranny of the political arises when the political order not only

rules all, but in its ruling *listens to no other sphere*, refuses to countenance the relative autonomy of spheres. It is because politics by nature trumps that the liberal republican tradition evolved to *limit* the use of that trump. See Walzer, *Spheres of Justice: A Defense of Pluralism and Equality* (New York: Basic Books, 1983), chapter 12.

4 Ibid., p. 39.

5 Now this may seem problematic for any political theory that endorses localism, as mine will in the following chapter. For clearly in a modern state locales cannot be granted very significant rights to exclude fellow state members. However, as we shall see, political or civil membership is plural and graduated. The social individual is simultaneously a member of a series of associations or orders, some of which are civil or political. While I will argue that the locale or neighborhood must be the primary civil or political order of membership, each member of a neighborhood is simultaneously a member of city or county, province (or state in the American sense), and independently governed state (or "nation-state"). Each level of membership, if it is to matter, must have its own duties and privileges, and its own form and level of exclusion.

6 Edward Casey, *Getting Back into Place: Toward a Renewed Understanding of the Place World* (Berkeley: University of California Press, 1995). See also Casey's *The Fate of Place: A Philosophical History* (Berkeley: University of California Press, 1997).

7 We could imagine militaristic or hunting societies that regard the domicile as culturally unimportant. Or to update the fantasy, some have suggested that the postmodern telecommunications society will cause residential locale and political life to diverge, that my most important political affiliations will be with persons I contact via the Internet. But if so, we would then live in an environment that begins not to look to us like a political society at all. If the "living together" that matters to politics is in fact only hunting or fighting together in the field, or the communicating-together of members of an Internet "chat" group, while residential living-together is irrelevant to collective decision, then what we are calling the "politics" of that group is really only the politics of warriors or hunters or telecommunicators and not the politics of *a society* at all.

8 For a summary of the history of civil society, see Krishan Kumas, "Civil Society: An Inquiry into the Usefulness of an Historical Term," *The British Journal of Sociology* 44, no. 3, September 1993, pp. 375–96. For an important critique of common uses of the notion, see also James Schmidt's essays: "A Raven with a Halo: The Translation of Aristotle's Politics," *History of Political Thought* 7 (Summer 1986): 295–319; "Paideia for the 'Bürger als Bourgeois': The Concept of 'Civil society' in Hegel's Political Thought," *History of Political Thought* 2 (Winter 1982): 469–93; and, "Civility, Enlightenment, and Society: Conceptual Confusions and Kantian Remedies," *American Political Science Review* 95 (June 1998): 419–27. Schmidt rightly points out that our contemporary attempt to recapture ancient versions of the concept must take into account the historical differences of the societies in which the term appeared, on which their conceptual and linguistic resources to some extent depend.

9   Aristotle, *Politics*, trans. Carnes Lord (Chicago: University of Chicago Press, 1984), 1252a6.

10 Ibid., 1276a130. The criterion Aristotle employs is interesting. While the size limit on the *polis* would imply that most modern states fail to be political in his sense – they might be nations, linguistic–cultural entities, but not political communities – Aristotle uses the speed of communication as the criterion of excessive size. Modern electronic communication could re-qualify highly modernized societies as political communities, despite their size.

11 Niklas Luhmann, *The Differentiation of Society*, trans. Stephen Holmes and Charles Larmore (New York: Columbia University Press, 1982), pp. 332–44.

12 The translation was in 1438 by the Florentine, Leonardo Bruni. See James Schmidt's fascinating study of the problems of this translation in his "A Raven with a Halo: The Translation of Aristotle's Politics."

13 Norbert Elias, *The Civilizing Process: The History of Manners and State Formation and Civilization*, trans. Edmund Jephcott (Oxford: Blackwell, 1994).

14 Immanuel Kant, "Idea for a Universal History with a Cosmopolitan Intent," trans. Ted Humphrey, in *Perpetual Peace and Other Essays on Politics, History*, and Morals (Indianapolis: Hackett, 1983), p. 26.

15 Habermas, *The Structural Transformation of the Public Sphere*, p. 19ff.

16 Elias, *The Civilizing Process*, p. 36.

17 Although this question had been prepared by James Harrington in the preceding century, when his *Oceana* (1656) made landed property, rather than arms, the basis for republican political personality, thereby modernizing the ancient model.

18 Pocock, *The Machiavellian Moment*, p. 499.

19 See Fania Oz-Salzberger's "Introduction" to Ferguson's *An Essay on the History of Civil Society* (Cambridge: Cambridge University Press, 1995). As she points out, Ferguson took etymology seriously: "virtue" and "virility" share the Latin root, *vir*, man, which he took in a gendered sense.

20 G. W. F. Hegel, *Philosophy of Right*, trans. T. M. Knox (Oxford: Clarendon Press, 1945).

21 The state then has three moments for Hegel, only the first of which is relevant for our discussion. The "constitution of the state" that succeeds civil society is: first of all, the sovereignty of the Crown itself; then the bureaucratic executive or administrative branch; and lastly the legislative, which means an assembly of the three Estates or classes (*Stände*), to which Hegel adds the element of "public opinion."

22 James Schmidt, "Paideia for the 'Bürger als Bourgeois': The Concept of 'Civil society' in Hegel's Political Thought."

23 Alexis de Tocqueville, *Democracy in America*, trans. George Lawrence, ed. J. P. Mayer (New York: Harper and Row, 1969), p. 506.

24 Ibid., p. 536.

25 Government, he wrote, "gladly works for [citizens'] happiness but wants to be the sole agent and judge of it. It provides for their security . . . necessities . . .

pleasures. . . . Why should it not entirely relieve them from the trouble of thinking and all the cares of living? Thus it daily makes the exercise of free choice less useful and rarer, restricts the activity of free will within a narrower compass, and little by little robs each citizen of the proper use of his own faculties. Equality has prepared men for all this, predisposing them to endure it and often even regard it as beneficial." Ibid., p. 692.

26   Ibid., p. 697.

27   Few thinkers turned to the notion during this time. Exceptions are Antonio Gramsci, Edward Shils' work on "civility," and most important for this study, Michael Oakeshott's analysis of civil association.

28   See Jean Cohen and Andrew Arato, *Civil Society and Political Theory* (Cambridge, MA: MIT Press, 1992) and John Keane, *Civil Society: Old Images, New Visions* (Stanford: Stanford University Press, 1998).

29   The "new wave" of civil society literature is extensive, but for example see: Peter Berger and Richard Neuhaus, "*To Empower People: the Role of Mediating Structures in Public Policy*" in *To Empower People: From State to Civil Society* (Washington, D.C.: American Enterprise Institute, 1996; orig. 1977); Ronald Beiner's edited, *Theorizing Citizenship* (Albany: State University of New York Press, 1995); E. J. Dionne's edited, *Community Works: The Revival of Civil Society in America* (Washington, D.C.: Brookings Institution, 1998), particularly Michael Walzer, "The Idea of Civil Society;" John Ehrenberg, *Civil Society: The Critical History of an Idea* (New York: New York University Press, 1999); Robert Putnam; *Bowling Alone: The Collapse and Revival of American Community* (New York: Simon and Schuster, 2000); Alan Wolfe, *Whose Keeper?: Social Science and Moral Obligation* (Berkeley: University of California Press, 1989); John Gray, "What is Dead and what is Living in Liberalism, " in *Post-Liberalism: Studies in Political Thought* (London: Routledge, 1993), pp. 283–328; and Ernest Gellner, *The Conditions of Liberty: Civil Society and its Rivals* (New York: Penguin, 1994).

30   See Peter Berger et al., *The Homeless Mind*.

31   Alan Wolfe, *Whose Keeper?: Social Science and Moral Obligation*, p. 208.

32   John Gray, "What is Dead and what is Living in Liberalism." There are a number of points at which I would disagree with Gray, but the spirit and formulation of his most basic claims is, in my view, entirely right.

33   See Jean Bethke Elshtain, "Not a Cure All: Civil Society Creates Citizens, It Does Not Solve Problems," in Dionne, *Community Works*.

34   See Adam Seligman, *The Idea of Civil Society* (Princeton: Princeton University Press, 1992). Seligman is one of the few to notice that this is George H. Mead's conception of the social self a century early. See p. 28.

35   Alan Ehrenhalt, "Where Have All the Followers Gone?", in Dionne, *Community Works*.

36   The exception, of course, being Adam Ferguson, but he never separated civil society from republican politics and the state.

37   The key work is Michael Oakeshott, *On Human Conduct* (Oxford: Clarendon Press, 1975). The virtual absence of Oakeshott's work from the current debate

is, I think, unfortunate and telling. One of the few current civil society theorists who use Oakeshott is John Gray.

38 Oddly enough, while Oakeshott wishes more than any other theorist to maintain a distinction between civil and enterprise association, hence politics and economics, his purely procedural notion of civil association is, I suggest, derived from a particular model of human production, namely *agriculture*. In a hunter-gatherer society, particularly those dependent on large, fast herds of game (e.g. the Buffalo for the plains Indians), the hunt was inherently collective. Where the survival of the society is based on a single activity that is most effectively carried out in concert, it is entirely natural and reasonable for the civic association and/or government to manage and direct that activity. This may well lessen, or rather, prevent the development of more extensive forms of liberty, but it is nevertheless inevitable and generally desirable. Agriculture presented the possibility – and only in some of its wealthier versions – of individual households being largely economically independent. A family can run a farm. To be sure, this independence is still relative and a matter a degree. But my point is, the picture of economically independent households united by procedural rules, in which enterprise need not, under normal conditions, be the concern of the *civitas*, and in which politics involves the more or less equal participation of each household via one (or more) of its members, is an agrarian picture. In this sense, modern libertarianism – with which Oakeshott has an ambiguous, but not negligible, relationship – attempts to extend an agricultural or agrarian picture to industrial capitalism. Industrial society is, like the hunter-gatherer society and unlike agriculture, a collective enterprise to which households must contribute together, under collective management, or production simply ceases. I do not suggest that civil association is incompatible with the modern industrial age; quite the contrary. But I will suggest that we cannot hinge our notions of civility and politics on an economic model that has little application in the late or "post"-modern world.

39 One could go further, if the aim were a more comprehensive encounter with Oakeshott, to find in his distinction between civil and enterprise association precisely that sort of abstraction found in modern rationalism. For rationalism's greatest sin is its willingness to split the legal-political-governmental order from culture, to impose political rules on society independent of all other social and cultural considerations. Oakeshott's sin is lesser, but not dissimilar in kind. Where in history – a history he knew so well – could we find a purely civil state, with no enterprising concerns? Nowhere, he would have to agree. But then, whence the legitimacy of the normative division of the two, given conservative grounds?

40 Whether the reverse is possible is more tricky. If a government were to be good but not legitimate, presumably this could only occur in a transitional situation in which a prior legitimate but bad government is replaced by something better through violating what had been the criteria of legitimacy. But one imagines that in this situation society pretty quickly comes to find a form of legitimacy

that is applicable to the new, superior government; people change the criteria, or discover in their political tradition previously unnoticed complexities of legitimation, so as to legitimize what is good. This is precisely what most English political thinkers, including Burke, did regarding the Glorious Revolution of 1689.

41   I say "worldly" to indicate that civil society is compatible with transcendent, e.g. religious, beliefs.

42   Liah Greenfeld, *Nationalism: Five Roads to Modernity* (Cambridge, MA: Harvard University Press, 1992), p. 10. See also Ernest Gellner, *Nations and Nationalism* (Ithaca: Cornell University Press, 1983).

7

Civility, Neighborhood, and Culture

In the preceding chapter we defined civil society in a macroscopic sense as a type of political–social order distinct in human history. In the present chapter I will in a microscopic sense distinguish the manner of relationship and experience that is civil association – as opposed to other types of social and communal association. Civil society is a kind of order; civility is proper to it; it is lawful; and it evinces a kind of solidarity. But I will argue that it is not primarily a form of "community," moral or political, if that term is meant in its usual fulsome sense. If civil society indicates a kind of community and morality, it is a limited, minimal, and not very warm sort of community. It is neither *Gesellschaft* nor *Gemeinschaft*. I will present the goods intrinsic to civil society. But first some remarks are in order about what is *not* morally embedded in the civil society conception.

Oakeshott approvingly refers to Aristotle in forming his notion of civil association. But Aristotle famously made ethics derivative of politics.[1] Politics was for him the master inquiry dealing with what is the greatest good for human beings living together, since those beings are always members of a *polis*. The inquiry into how life should be lived must presuppose political society. This is in sharp contrast to much recent Anglo-American political philosophy, which, inheriting the social contract tradition, tends to derive political norms from ethical norms worked out independent of any social account. Liberal neutralism is a particular offender here. Most of the works mentioned in chapters 1 and 2 begin by formulating ethical principles, then decide what civil or political society ought to look like. To do so is part and parcel of what Oakeshott attacked as "rationalism in politics." Indeed, it is arguable that the conservative tradition is deeply Aristotelian in putting politics in the broad sense of civic life, before ethics, and not the other way around.[2]

We must add, however, that the fact that morality evolves within and must base itself on the civil experience does not mean that it is bound by that experience. Civil society does presuppose rules that are morally obligatory, but this is only a part of morality. Politics in the broad sense, which includes the civil, is tied to a place, hence a particular society. Morality is not thus restricted. Morality both under-determines and exceeds civility and politics, for its concern is with the individual and the world, or the species *homo*. As Lon Fuller argues, we must distinguish the "morality of duty" from the "morality of aspiration."[3] Civility is not the morality of aspiration. Crucially, it is the proper job of civil society *not* to answer all moral questions.[4] Civil society is, if you will, metabolic or vegetative; its function is continued life as members. Its morality is horizontal, not vertical. Morality as a set of concerns that transcend membership exceeds the *civitas*, just as the personal concern with the achievement of a meaningful and good life under-determines it. Even if ethics recognizes my special obligations to my particular community, it is still, *qua* ethics, addressed to any fellow *animal rationale*. The perfectly civil individual can fail morally in the pursuit of the Good.

As mentioned, Adam Seligman makes the interesting criticism that the notion of civil society is wedded to an ethics of natural "sympathy" characteristic of the eighteenth-century Scotts. For sympathy was a way of making altruism and egoism compatible: if the primary human social desire is for approbation, approval, and status, then egoistic desire must honor other-regarding moral strictures, including benevolence, because otherwise approbation suffers. Seligman argues that with this "naive" fusion of private with public good goes the whole project of finding a socially autonomous, non-transcendent moral sphere.

I would argue that it is by no means clear that civil society rests on the kind of moral Archimedian point Seligman questions.[5] But even if it did so rest, the argument for sympathy is far from naive. The conservative anthropology presented in chapter 5 implies that the social and institutional self is constructed to connect altruism and egoism, public and private, at *some* level. The vast number of socialized persons regard social status and approbation as essential to self-regard. Socialization is hardly conceivable otherwise. Now, it is certainly true that the confluence of altruism and egoism is a contingent, historically and institutionally established connection, not an *a priori* one. The connection can be broken. And it need not hold at all social levels. It is possible for society to tolerate or even promote the *limited* de-linkage of the two, so that, for example, the pursuit of personal interests utterly without regard for social approbation is permitted or tolerated, at the cost of social esteem, or that approbation at one level, e.g. national celebrity, could be compatible with the ruthless abuse of family, neighbors, professional associates, etc.

Some would argue in contrast that civil society can be identified with the moral sphere if the right conception of morality is employed, namely, a "communitarian" as opposed to a universalistic or cosmopolitan approach to ethics. Such views hearken back to Hegel's distinction between *Moralität*, the universal and abstract moral rules meant to be independent of place and people, and *Sittlichkeit*, translated as "customary morality," hence a morality rooted in particular social institutions and cultural traditions.

But there is an ambiguity in Hegel's notion that affects morality's relation to civil society. Despite the meaning of *Sitte* (customs), Hegel's analysis places the emphasis on *institutionalized* morality, not on tradition or custom as we normally understand it. Custom or tradition is histocially particular; institutions need not be – the family, after all, has existed in many different cultures. The claims that moral life (here using "moral" vaguely to include both *Moralität* and *Sittlichkeit*) is institutional and that it is historical, hence based in a local inheritance, are distinct. If *Moralität* is the universal name for an ethics whose obligations hold for moral individuals independent of social institutions or historical inheritance, *Sittlichkeit* can be *either* the universal name for an ethics that is dependent on social institutions *or* the universal name for the fact that ethics is locally, culturally conditioned. *Sittlichkeit* in the former sense, as an institutional morality, is indeed part of civil society. Every civil society must have inherited social institutions, and for it, these are indeed morally obligatory and morally meaningful. But the other possible meaning of *Sittlichkeit*, the morality of a particular culture, is not the morality of civil society. Just as civil society is not a contractual *Gesellschaft* serving interests, neither is it a *Gemeinschaft* of shared thick or full morality or a common culture. Indeed, to have a civil society is to have an association of citizens who deny that their association is a community in that sense.

Connected with this, there is a pronounced popular tendency in our political culture to make law the medium of political and civic existence. For some, the only substantive or decisive political process is one that culminates in the creation or modification of a legal statute; likewise, public morality is for many a discussion of hypothetical rules that ought to be imposed. Whereas twentieth-century French and German political philosophy have a history of connecting politics to sociology, anthropology, and history, the recent Anglo-American tradition has consistently seen politics through ethics, and conceived both legalistically. Oakeshott himself makes a morally significant legal structure essential to the *civitas*. I would object, however, that normatively speaking civil society is the *source, not the result, of law*. To be sure, civil society is inconceivable without rules. But these rules can be tacit, while positive law cannot. Positive law is a *formalization* of the restraints built into the practices and institutions of the civil association. Civil society evolves law out of its *substance*, to use an Hegelian figure, like the spider spins its web. At any rate positive law is not the medium of civil association. Civil association is the out-of-which and the for-which of law.

Lastly, while it absorbs a politicized conception of membership, as I have defined it civil society is *not primarily a political concept*: it is not constituted by political activity. The common identification of the civil with the political suffers from several intellectual tendencies noted earlier, e.g. the cult of activity and agency, the identification of the political with the *staatlich* or governmental, and an overvaluation of the public realm which is connected to progressivism. Civil societies, to be sure, always have governments, networks of offices that are the agencies of political authority. But in its narrow or proper sense, the political is a more restricted dimension than the civil.[6] "Civil" refers to the relations and conditions of fellow citizens *qua* citizens, who are members of the *civitas* or civil association; politics, properly speaking, is the decision-making and -enacting process. In a free society politics takes the form of an open discussion among citizens, but such "discourse" does not exhaust, nor is it even the center of, their civil existence. Two strangers sitting silently on a part bench are having as much of a civil experience – both in the sense of civility and, more to the point, in the sense of living as fellow citizens – as they would in a political demonstration. This means that the moral commitments of civil republicanism, discourse theory, and participatory democracy are *not* the moral commitments of civil society. Civil society is primarily a matter of living-with, not talking-with. This reversal is important. For the notion that civil society is primarily political makes of the citizen primarily a political being, and this makes the tail wag the dog. And this in turn deprives the tail, that is, politics, of its rightful context of operation.

Bivalence and the Civil Goods

There are four main goods internal to the notion of civil society: membership, freedom, civility, and dignity. Civil society must value and promote them. Of course they can be differently interpreted and applied; that is a matter of culture. Their requirements will vary from society to society. Also, civil society is not restricted to promoting only these four goods. That too is a matter of culture. But the implication is that if it is to remain a civil society, society may not, in promoting other goods, violate the civil goods. So these four goods put a limit on what a political society may promote, as well as how it may promote.

The householders who constitute civil society have the primordially bivalent status of *free members*. In civil society members are not first free, then members, nor are they first members, and then free. They are primordially both. This distinguishes the concept of civil society from both the social contract tradition, which presupposes free persons who choose membership, and collectivist–organicist versions of nationalism or communitarianism, which presuppose membership and then, in some cases, try to evolve a version of freedom within it. Freedom and membership are jointly fundamental to the individuals of civil society. Differently, civil society is that form of association committed to balancing liberty and membership. Liberty having been discussed in chapter 5, we will focus for the moment on membership.

Membership is a powerful notion. To be a member is to belong, and to be treated as belonging, hence treated differently from non-members. Being a member requires living in the *civitas*, which means, at minimum, having a domicile in the *civitas*. It carries with it duties, and it obligates the *civitas* to respond to each member in certain ways.[7] The condition of being a member, with some few intermediate exceptions (e.g. resident aliens), is not a matter of degree. This then entails equality before law, equality of duties and rights of membership, etc.

Members are associated, at the minimum, through civility. Now, civility cannot but sound in contemporary English like a meager and superficial value. Until recently few theoreticians have deemed it a worthy topic. Today it is enjoying a renaissance as object of theoretical attention, due jointly to the resurgence of civil republicanism and to the emergence of interest in civil society. Some contemporary writers, like Stephen Carter, have noted a decline in civility in American life, and have tried to rehabilitate it.[8] Historians have recounted, in somewhat different terms, the development of American views about manners.[9] Political theorists, like Richard Dagger, have developed accounts of the virtues of citizenship that are embedded in the notion of a liberal republican society.[10] Others have seen a dangerous nostalgia in this project.[11] These analyses have significance for our current investigation, but only where they connect civility with the notion of civil society. For civility is not merely politeness or manners, although it must include these as well. It is nothing less than the rules and habits that sustain the association of citizens. It is shared acknowledgment of moral rules without which we cannot live together, and it includes within it a recognition of the liberty, membership, and dignity of each citizen, and attention to the conditions that make that possible.

As mentioned in the last chapter, civility is connected not only with civil society *per se*, but also to commerce and to civilization. The connection with commerce is not misplaced, even when considering civility as a moral virtue. Civilized people countenance the private interests of their fellow citizens, as long as their fellows are civil. Civil life is largely composed of those "private" interests, that is, of individuals pursuing their interests in public and civil ways. Further, civility does indeed require that members be "civilized." But it would be a mistake to claim that refinement of the arts and sciences, or sophistication of taste, or education, is requisite for the kind of civilization that is essential to civil society. The only civilizing required is whatever is necessary to make fellow citizens feel that the civility of the public sphere, and their own dignity therein, is protected. "Civic education" is another matter. Learning how to respect civility is different from learning the theory behind elections or the history of one's government.

As Nancy Rosenblum emphasizes, civility is distinct from feelings of community in that it includes significant distance or looseness.[12] Edward Shils points out that ideology and political radicalism, the determination of the association by thick metanarratives, are incompatible with civility. Civility treads a subtle line between requiring a collective self-consciousness on the part of members – which, as noted, sometimes implies collective enterprise – and yet limiting that sense of membership to guarantee its "thinness," hence tolerance. Civil society never loses sight of the fact that it does *not* constitute the meaning of human life for its members. It recognizes that it is a dimension of life, not the whole of life. No one can be *only* civil. Thus civility means that the whole can never abuse the part and the parts cannot seek to dominate the whole. Civility, for Shils, is virtually the virtue of balance, circumspection, and moderation in all things involving others. As such, it does not claim to be the supreme virtue; such a claim would violate civility.

Before turning to the final good, dignity, something must be said about two core political norms and their relation to civil society, namely, equality and justice.

The kind of equality that obtains in the civil association is particular. It is *civil equality*, recognized recently by Mickey Kaus.[13] To be equal before the law, to be counted equally as a citizen, to be treated with respect by fellow citizens as a fellow citizen, to limit the spheres in which forms of inequality – achievement, luck, wealth, job status, desirability – reign, so that they do not spill over into determinging one's status as citizen; these are what matter most in a civil society. This is distinct from material equality which is *not* presupposed by civil equality. Being socially insulted in a ritzy neighborhood is a greater violation of civility than having to wear an old suit. I can stand seeing my car next to that of a wealthy man as long as the wealthy man speaks to me with a recognition of the dimensions in which we are equals: individuals facing the demand to organize our lives in the knowledge of approaching death, each with a destiny made profound by its unrepeatable and limited course, each bearing the rights and duties of membership in the polity. It is citizenship that registers this equality. To fail to distinguish this form of equality from material equality is not only, as libertarians object, to require selective coercion and hence unequal treatment by law and government, but to muddy the case for civil equality.[14]

Civil equality is indeed a value in the context of the history of politics, and its achievement is a strong argument for the modern liberal republican tradition. That the wealthy and the poor, the female and the male, the physician and the janitor, the genetically fortunate and the handicapped, and members of all races and ethnicities each receive one vote and equal treatment before law and its courts, that each is counted and considered by government – and further, that the advantaged may not cut ahead in a line at the movie theater, that forms of address and manners look beyond supra-civil distinctions, barring individual misbehavior, so that each citizen is worthy of decent respect – all this is essential. However, to argue for a more-than-civil equality, to condemn morally undeserved non-civic inequities, is to slip into our civic attitudes the view that money and social status are essential to civic respect. Ironically, that conflation is shared by many egalitarians and elitists. They share the idea that the janitor and the physician *cannot* be equals, that they can only be equals if they have equal wealth, with only morally justified exceptions. Hence the egalitarian tries to equalize the wealth, and the elitist treats each in accordance with his or her wealth. This is to grant too much civic weight to money and status. Like Walzer and Kaus, I accept that the task is to ensure not material equality, but that civil equality is distinct from money, job status, etc.

But that the distributions of civil status and material wealth do not have a one-to-one correspondence does not mean they *never* touch, that they are wholly independent. Certain employments of wealth and certain extremes of poverty do undermine civic equality. Civil society does have a characteristic position on distributive justice: *decent equality*, or a common minimum, is implied by the very notion of membership. If my neighbor's child is dying of a disease curable at a cost of a few thousand dollars which that family does not have, and I blithely complete the construction of my new swimming pool in time to attend the funeral, then my neighbor would rightly conclude that she and I share no greater sense of membership than two people living on opposite sides of the earth. We would not be fellow members, which is to say, if we *are* members of something, that something has now been shown to have *no moral importance*. As Walzer argued, membership requires that what can be done must be done, not to achieve sheer outcome equality, but to achieve decent equality regarding issues that are crucial (like the life or death of a child). If a household is sacrificed without its consent, or has lost the conditions necessary for membership, liberty, or dignity, or is violated at the hands of another, or is allowed to suffer what social members regard as an ultimate loss, where the *civitas* could have prevented such, then those householders have been treated as non-members.

Again, regarding wealth material *decency*, not material equality, is the essential qualifier.[15] What matters is ensuring, where we can, that no one fails to have the resources that we take to be necessary to a normally good, that is, decent existence in our society. What counts as a decent existence is an historical and cultural matter, as Walzer argues, but not therefore impossible to determine. For post-World War II Americans it means something like income sufficient to provide the necessities for oneself and a family in a domicile, including medical expenses, that does not require one to sacrifice too much to work (e.g. health, safety, all of one's time), with a reasonable expectation that one's children will have educational and economic opportunity, within an economy that makes it possible for the talented and ambitious to move into higher status and/or more profitable positions, within a social milieu that is reasonably safe and pleasing. This is decency, and in so far as all have it, there would be equal enjoyment of such decency. But this means neither equal nor even *near* equal holdings. Nor is decency "equal opportunity." Opportunity could conceivably be equal only negatively, that is, through outlawing illegitimate discrimination. A positive notion of equality of opportunity is unrealizable; even without monetary inheritance, the fully-abled, talented, beautiful, well-adjusted, adequately-parented, and lucky will always have more real opportunity than the handicapped, untalented, ugly, miserable, dysfunctionally-reared, and unlucky. *Fortuna*, genetic or historical, is enough to derail the fantasy of equal opportunity. The sports image of the "level playing field" and everyone leaving the "starting blocks" at the same time has no social application. But decency does.

Ronald Dworkin is quite right that equality requires that we may not regard the disadvantages of or harm to some minority as irrelevant to social policy. That a minority be forced to pay for, or suffer the consequences of, the *largesse* of the rest of society without consideration, compensation, or consent, is indeed civically intolerable. We may not keep their pain off the books, leave it as a non-consideration. But this is not to say that material equality of circumstances is the only way to avoid this lack of consideration, or that choice and talent are the sole legitimate sources of material advantage. The greater propensity of the American political system in the last forty years to acknowledge and give voice to those who disproportionately are disadvantaged is a gain in morality and in realism that strengthens civil society. But the next step in realism would admit that there is no policy or program that harms no one, thus rather than allowing harm to some to paralyze the political system, we must balance what kind of harm, for how long, with what prospects for future compensation or recovery.

Justice and equality are indeed internally related; to treat equals as unequals is unjust, and so is, as Susan Moller Okin points out, to treat non-equals as equals. There is an ancient metaphor according to which justice is the *moral equilibrium* in which each is granted what is his or hers. Although as Nietzsche suggested in his *Genealogy of Morals*, the primitive creditor–debtor experience no doubt was a prime example, justice was not merely a commercial relation. Not only money or property was owed, but also respect, fidelity, etc. The most basic meaning of justice is then *suum cuique*, to each his or her due. Justice is offended whenever one thing oversteps its bounds and correspondingly another fails to receive its proper measure, whether this involves thievery, failure to receive political rights, or mistreatment by *fortuna*. The ancient Greeks took this as a cosmic principle applying even outside the human realm, as when the presocratic philosopher Anaximander interpreted the becoming of any thing or quality as an offense against *dike* or order, requiring its opposite to be "compensated" by succeeding the former in existence (e.g. as the winter succeeds the summer).[16]

The *polis*, which is to say the *civitas*, must be just. Justice is implicit in civility; for citizens to treat each other unjustly is inherently uncivil. Here, oddly enough, I side with neutralist liberals like Rawls and against Michael Sandel, who in his critique of Rawlsian proceduralism argued that justice is not the first principle of the polity. Justice is a – admittedly not "the" – fundamental principle of the polity as such, that is, a constitutive rule the *civitas* imposes on itself and its members. It is, with equality, a condition of the goods civil society seeks. But Sandel's critique is still right in spirit. The *civitas* does indeed have an end that is prior to justice: living together. That living together is what determines the value of justice. Furthermore, the idea of *suum cuique*, to each what is owed, is intrinsically thin. Any application of justice, any determination of what is owed, presupposes a thick notion of the Good which must be culturally inherited, as Walzer has argued.[17] Sandel's critique was lodged against a notion of justice that claimed to be able to exclude thick notions of the Good. He was right that such is impossible.

One kind of violation of justice is unfairness. As I argued in chapter 2, there are three kinds of unfairness, beyond the obvious unfairness of a lack of equality before the law: that some individuals are uniquely made to bear the burden of social policy without consideration, compensation or consent; that some individuals, because of their idiosyncratic notions of the Good, are in effect penalized by policies not aimed at harming them; and that some individuals regard themselves as harmed because others are benefited but they are not. As I argued, the first is crucial; civil society must aim to avoid such unfairness, although even here, sometimes there can only be recognition and not compensation. But the latter two kinds of unfairness are, civically speaking, extravagant. That I must never be differentially affected because of my conception of the Good is *not* an obligation of civic justice. Some conceptions of the Good will be discouraged, even if permitted. Toleration may require that I not be coerced away from my choices, but that does not mean the community is required to benefit everyone equally in all circumstances. Lastly, worsening my situation for a reason can be unfair while failing to improve it for the same reason may not be. Civil society is not obligated to correct such unfairness. Indeed, in most cases it is obligated not to try.

We now turn to the concept of dignity, or "worthiness." I suggest an equation: *under conditions of civility, membership plus freedom equals dignity.* To say this is to make two important and distinct claims: first, that dignity is in some respects *the* ultimate value the individual enjoys in civic life, which is enabled by civic life; and second, that it results from the combination of freedom and membership under the condition of civility. Dignity requires two complimentary conditions: a self and a social background. The self with dignity is, minimally, one whose personal resources and achievements are valued by others. But this approval has a particular aspect in a modern civil society: it is approval as a free judicative agent pursuing a meaningful course of life. Dignity is recognizable worthiness; a worthiness that is not recognized or is not potentially recognizable is not dignity. That is, dignity is social. The identity of the citizen – which, to be sure, is never a purely civil or political identity – is that of a member, accorded civic respect and place, whose identity as manifested through social roles is recognized as a free one. Without freedom, the maintenance of my roles is not mine; it is what "they" do *to* me.[18]

Now, reflections on the historical meaning of dignity complicate this picture. Peter Berger has pointed out a change brought by modernity in the "obsolescence" of the concept of honor.[19] In his analysis, honor is a value in traditional societies that depends on the linkage of identity and social role. The place honor occupied in traditional societies has been taken by the modern notion of dignity, a valuation placed on identity independent of social role, hence capable of universal and egalitarian application. This exchange gains universal freedom at the cost of a "permanent identity crisis," the result of the loss of social role as a defining context for the self. So, the claim is both that the very concept of dignity, at least in its widespread application, is a recent historical phenomenon, and that it is individualistic in a way that subjects it to an essential indeterminacy.

While Berger is identifying a real historical shift, I question his label. First, dignity is certainly a premodern notion. It was linked with honor and, true to Berger's analysis, with role and class. The Latin *dignitas*, merit, comes from the root *decet*, what is fitting or seemly, even gracious, and is related to *decor*, what is beautiful. Dignity is what is aesthetically proper, what makes a worthy whole. Honor, on the other hand, was linked more directly to office and award, as well as honesty. Honor is the more purely moral term in our modern sense, more fully relating to social duty. It is true that modern politics does attempt to universalize premodern dignity (thereby, to be sure, changing it in the process) in a way that honor *cannot* be universalized or modernized, hence honor has arguably become anachronistic while a modified dignity has been retained. Berger is right that the concept of identity as utterly independent of social role is problematic. But it is a different matter to say that modern identity, hence dignity, must be found in the continuity, the combined meaning, of such roles. Identity comes *through* social roles. The essential indeterminacy or identity crisis of which Berger speaks is more properly the result of liberal voluntarism – the view that the individual life-path is of ultimate value, and its value is dependent on choice – not republican egalitarianism. It is a mistaken notion of liberty, and not equality or the distinction of social spheres, that necessarily undermines identity. Hence dignity need not be an indicator of identity crisis, absent that mistaken notion.

Civil Association as Neighborhood

I suggest that neighborhood is the paradigmatic form of human civil association. By "neighborhood" I mean what I think neighborhood means in contemporary America, urban, suburban, or rural: an association of adjacent and nearby households whose fortunes are relatively independent, but who accept civility, the collective concern for the survival of the neighborhood, and the concern for the decent life of members. I am suggesting that, when we search for practical alternatives to the *Gesellschaft*, or voluntary contractual association, that modern American society seems increasingly to have become, we ought not to look to *Gemeinschaft*, to communities of virtue, but rather to what we call neighborhoods. I am also implying that civil association, which has never ceased to exist, now is perceivable most clearly at the level of neighborhood, not at the level of enterprise, religious, ethnic, familial, or political associations, nor large cities, regions, states, or nations.[20] Other forms of desirable political association are normatively parasitic on the neighborhood. Civility is essentially "neighborliness."

Let us review some of the characteristics of the neighborhood. It is a face-to-face local association, usually with shared streets and other shared public space, and common and informal, although not universally regular or frequent, contact among members. The degree of involvement with others in the neighborhood varies. Its spaces are of various kinds: communally owned and public; privately owned; and legally private spaces that are in fact public because typically or regularly open to members without formal permission. Its members live under like conditions. Certainly not all conditions are shared (e.g. economic fortune) but very important conditions that affect the lives of any member will affect all, e.g. weather, local economic cycles, shortages, infrastructural changes, festivals, crime, etc. It is an association through *civility*, not intimacy or love, nor contract; each must treat each other according to rules which count each as equal, on pain of neighborly punishment at least; and these rules are mostly adverbial, that is, they limit how each may pursue personal aims. Nor are common outlooks, tribal membership, or religious homogeneity necessary features, although such may have been causes of the constitution of the neighborhood; cause of residence and basis for continuing association can be distinct. There are limits on power, hence rough equality of power; it must not be the case that the public space of the neighborhood is controlled by a few. Lastly, there is broad latitude for what the adverbial rules are, what degrees of obligation and interference are justified, and no formal procedure for deciding these.

The neighborhood is thus the landscape of persons with whom one habitually deals, or with whom one may well have to deal. These are the people to whom one *must*, with rare exceptions, be civil. Failure to do so will not only be seen as a moral failing by others, but will threaten to make one's life unhappy, perhaps even dangerous, given the proximity of mechanisms of social sanction. It is not restricted to friends; it need not generate similar feelings of affection and loyalty in all members; some may follow its rules out of a moral sense, and some out of practical self-interest. Many of us either live in such neighborhoods or try to construct their equivalents. Even if we do not know our neighbors, we come to regard our co-workers, fellow commuters, local retailers, insurance agents, etc. as comprising our *civitas*. But a purely functional context of relation is not a *civitas*. The neighborhood is a contiguous residential space, a locale or place.

When I lived in Brooklyn in the mid-1980s, on a racially and ethnically mixed street of three-story houses, when commotion would occur on the street at night, a scream for example, by the time I scrambled downstairs there would be women leaning out of windows in every building, and one or more men standing on each stoop, some with baseball bats. Niceties aside, *that is neighborhood*. I was almost never invited into others' homes in that neighborhood; nor did I normally invite others to mine. Clearly some long-time residents were friends, but the block had too much diversity – of ethnicity, language, religion, educational background, and occupation – for most people to feel comfortable each other in their private spheres. But the public spaces, the street, sidewalk, and stoops, were very friendly. Hence it was not a *Gemeinschaft* of feeling, and belief; nor was it a mere contractual association of contingent interests. When my ancient vehicle needed work, or worse, a push, men on the street always helped. I would have done the same for them. Yet we were not friends in any real sense, and did not know what to say to each other beside the American Esperanto of weather, sports, complaints about local bureaucracy, and tellingly, worries about the neighborhood. *That* is what we shared, even when we shared nothing else, and that sharing was crucial. This sharing, whenever a crisis loomed, *actualized temporary community*. We all knew that a community of action subsisted in potency.[21]

In more recent times I have lived in a small city on the edge of a cosmopolitan area, a working and lower-middle-class town. After living here a few years, I became acquainted with the joys of neighborhood again. With sufficient neighborly and local experience the walk home from the bus stop is a constellation of familiarities: in this house my children visit to play, in that house lives a beer-drinking friend, over there lives my son's soccer coach, in that home the lady with the adorable dogs, and in many others neighbors with whom I exchange friendly greetings. I know them, they know me. Of course they do not know the full or intimate me; but that is not required. Nor is great similarity necessary; my neighbors come in all races, many different classes and educational backgrounds. But we all have to raise our children, make mortgage payments, bring home paychecks, find local recreation, etc. Even a neighbor I have never spoken to is familiar to me; I know who she is, share the neighborhood with her, am bound on pain of potential suffering to treat her civilly. She at least does not block my driveway or litter in front of my stoop, and nods hello; this is enough to lead me to believe that she feels the obligations of civility. So, in a confused crowd of strangers, she and I will recognize each other, and constitute a *we*. We will feel obliged to help each other if needed. Even if not needed, we will discuss the public situation from the standpoint of a shared life. In contrast, with strangers there can be no certainty that favors will be returned, that interaction will be civil, no way to judge that we share important concerns.

Conservative analysts theorize about, and average citizens recognize, a loss of something public, something common, something communal in contemporary society. But our tendency is to think that recapturing the communal requires enterprise association, joint projects, a renewed spirit of political activism. Others retreat into ethnic or religious nationalism. Civil association, exemplified in neighborhood, is different. It is the sharing of quasi-independent households, with no pretense to more-than-civil similarity or unity. We do not need to look further for civic glue than the living-together of the neighborhood.

When the survival of the neighborhood or the membership of any member as minimally decent is threatened, *and* the threat can be averted by action, failure to take action shows that this association is no longer a neighborhood. If private households or other neighborhood spaces are be allowed to fail, to fall below the decent minimum, or are characterized by a failure of the rules of civility, then the neighborhood develops "holes," non-places or sites that are not considered part of the neighborhood by neighbors. The existence of such holes, and their proliferation, is the decay and death of neighborhood. All households must count, both in occasional decision-making and in contributing to the sense of well-being of all members: not to count is not to be a member. Under special historical circumstances, for example dealing with such potential holes, the neighborhood *becomes* an enterprise association. If it does not then it is not a neighborhood.[22] In fact, of course, when holes develop in the contemporary world, the responsibility of repairing them is normally placed on non-local institutions. That necessity is a sign of the decline of neighborhood.[23]

Neighborhood and the Modern State

Now, the obvious problem with any attempt to place the local *civitas* or neighborhood at the normative center of our political theory is that the central facts of the modern state appear to be incompatible with it. As Robert Nisbet and Anthony Giddens, two thinkers separated by generation and political coloration, both argued, modern society above all shifts the center of social order away from kin/local relations to the unmediated opposition of individual and state.[26] In the modern world sovereignty belongs to a very distant and powerful state, which provides resources that cannot be provided locally. That state has also been nationalistically invested with cultural functions: today the political *we* is normally a state *we*. The delocalizing nature of modernity seems to preclude the integrity and relative independence of the local *civitas*, to relate me more fundamentally to networks outside the local *civitas*. What chance does a placial, localist conception of the *civitas* have in this environment?

My point is not a simplistic anti-statism. On the contrary: it is apparent that in the contemporary world of states, markets, and technology, a state is a necessary condition for the survival of the neighborhoods within it. The point is simply that we pay a very significant cost whenever we neglect to maintain *some* version of localism, whenever we allow modern centralization to proceed without compensation or limit. "Tip O'Nealism," the view that all politics is local, is a *phenomenological* truth. The experience of being a free member, hence the dignity of the citizen, is fundamentally a local experience. Public liberty and political liberty, both of which are essentially positive – as opposed to private liberty, which is primarily negative – need the neighborhood. Membership obviously does. State membership is phenomenologically derivative of neighborhood membership. Whatever the benefit or the necessity of increasingly supra-local and even supra-national government, if such government exhausts politics, that is the *end of the politics of the citizen*.

The disadvantages attendant on the evisceration of local politics do not have to be repeated here. But one aspect of the problem does deserve special mention: the political replacement of the multi-functional *civitas* by unifunctional political enterprise associations.[25] The latter are normally called "special interest" or "single-issue" associations or lobbies. However beneficial, political enterprise associations – enterprise associations whose substantive goal is the exercise of political influence – are necessarily associations whose most active members are *professionals*, that is, professional politicians, not only electoral politicians, but professional political actors like lobbyists.[28] It is in the rational self-interest of these professionals and their organizations to promote a single issue at all costs. By contrast, the *civitas* is multi-functional, because what unites the civic association is proximity, shared fate, and civility, not one particular substantive end. The result is that civic associations, while they certainly might be inclined to favor their own interests over those of other locales, cannot favor one aspect of life over another. For example, they may be concerned both about the liberty to defend oneself with a privately owned gun, *and* with threats to public safety from widespread gun-ownership, unlike the National Rifle Association, whose members by fact of membership have declared the greater importance of the former over the latter. Even if the latter is not true, the NRA will act as if it *were* true. What we call politics today is largely a contest among the professional politicians that run and staff state government and the professional politicians that represent major enterprise associations, in a forum constructed and operated by professional media operatives. Between these political behemoths, the *civitas* is squeezed. This further encourages citizens to abandon the *civitas* as a basis for political activity and concern. If any particular study were necessary to document this evident fact, the masterful analysis of the ill-fated Clinton health care initiative by David Broder and Haynes Johnson serves to make the point.[27]

Contrary to our cosmopolitan prejudices, local political discussion tends to be *more reasonable* than non-local politics, the later being dominated by uni-functional associations. For reasonableness in its normal usage (unlike rationality, or Rawls' version of 'reasonable') implies the recognition of a variety of competing values and the need for balancing them. In contemporary mediapolitics, which is our national and even state-level political forum, recognition of a multiplicity of legitimate countervailing concerns, like need for self-protection and need to regulate firearms, is anathema. Any such recognition merely supplies the opposition with ammunition. Compromises are, of course, worked out, but only in the "back room." This model of adversarial advocacy may have its benefits in courts of law, but not in the "court" of public opinion. It is not the model of neighbors. The reason is not that neighbors are sweet and kind, but that, not being uni-functional professionals, neighbors cannot be so clear, so "rational," so limited, so "on-message".

But as Benjamin Barber has argued, beneath the national media radar there is more going on out there.[28] While modernity may not be friendly to the political locale, more neighborhoods than ever before have educated and prosperous people, and access to the enhanced technologies that are the fruit of non-local progress. Sophisticated information is no longer the province of the few or the city. A revived localism could employ powerful means to press its interests.[29] Perhaps the majority of Americans continue to live in local civil societies about which they are concerned, in which they participate and live. The measure of civic health is not voter turnout or the attendance at town meetings, although these things certainly matter. More important is that people live together in a civil fashion, that the crucial functions of child-rearing, schooling, working, recreating, buying and selling go on, that people regard fellow members as members, known or not, and that the locale's overlapping social networks of neighbors and friends are sufficiently viable that when communal problems arise a majority is able to attend to those problems and deal with them as members.

Given my concept of neighborhood, the political problem is this: since the neighborhood is intrinsically local, how to arrange non-local state conditions so as to, at the least, avoid maiming, and at the most, harmonize with, support, or extend the neighborhood? We know that there is a competing movement within Enlightenment Republicanism, called in America *federalism*, which argued for the rights of provinces (in America, "states") against the sovereign capital. Clearly the current proposal shares the federalist spirit, although in America "states" are far too large to be local. If the fundamental, concrete form of liberal republican political life is to be maintained, then somehow we must manage to channel the delocalizing forces of modernity so as to permit the maintenance of local civil society. Neighborhoods must increase their ability to deflect the supra-local forces – economic, cultural, and governmental – that increasingly sweep through them. The aim is not for them to subsist against or independent of such forces, which would be unimaginable, but to subsist *through* them. Toward this end, I can only offer a way of thinking about the role of state *vis-à-vis* neighborhood. The sovereign state must be conceived both as a *meta-neighborhood* and a *mega-neighborhood*. These two functions must be balanced.

In its role as a meta-neighborhood the state is a framework for the collection of civil associations. As such the state must enforce the legal equality of every locale with every other. It must print money, manage the financial system of credit, etc. It must coordinate or manage the interaction of civil associations, e.g. of interstate crime, trade, etc. It does all this by way of providing an open space in which neighborhoods can subsist and interact. This is, speaking generally, the federalist version of the state. The state is in this respect the last of a series of nested forms of association, starting from the most local, the neighborhood, proceeding in serial order through county, "state" or province, to sovereign state. As a meta-neighborhood the state accepts that it is not analogous to primary, local forms of civil society, and seeks only to be the right kind of place for civil associations to flourish. As such, when it looks out of its offices in Washington, the state sees not individuals but local civic associations, cities, counties, and "states" or provinces.

In its role as mega-neighborhood the state must be a pseudo- or metaphorical-*civitas*. That is, it must be *like* a neighborhood. If being a member of a state is to matter, if citizens are to feel they are its members, are to identify with other state members, then to that extent the state must act like one mammoth civil association. Of course, it can do so only in a metaphorical sense. But this means the state must act on limited analogy with the primary form of civil association, which is local. It is as a mega-neighborhood that state can call upon me to die for it in war. I cannot feel patriotism for a framework, for the meta-neighborhood; to feel loyalty I must regard the state as the semiotic representation, the sublimated form, of my local *civitas*. Likewise, only as mega-neighborhood can the state call upon me to send money to fellow citizens, that is, *potential neighbors*, in far-off domestic locales. It is also under this function that state must guarantee that every domestic *civitas* acts like a *civitas* with respect to minorities and individuals within it, which is merely to say that no local majority may pervert the *civitas* into an enterprise association. When, as mega-neighborhood, the state looks out on the country it sees not civil associations but individual citizens that are its members.

Of the two notions, the mega-*civitas* has increasingly had the upper hand. The direction of modernity is toward the integration all local communities, the evisceration of locale. Due to many factors – the most prominent being nationalism, the development of a state-wide mediaculture, and the necessity of state-wide economic management – it is the nature of the late modern state to magnify this sense of itself as a Big We, a big neighborhood, hence a collective actor. Neutralist liberalism, at least in its egalitarian version, removes the power of locales, hence is in league with the mega-*civitas*. Even in its libertarian version, it is a framework for individuals, not civil associations. My argument is not that national and state governments are to devolve all authority to local government, or that our increasingly national (or global) culture and economy can be shrunk to fit locale. Rather it is that if the Big We is to be a *civil* We, then it must be a We that encourages and recognizes the importance or the locales that form our most immediate, lower case "we's," and the forms of connection and dependency that constitute the local structure of life. The state as mega-neighborhood must be balanced by the state as meta-neighborhood or differently put, as mega-neighborhood it must recognize its parasitic, metaphorical, constructed status with respect to the place most people still live, their neighborhood.

Liberal Anti-Localism

Before proceeding it is necessary to reiterate a rejoinder to the dominant liberal antipathy to locale. Intellectually rooted perhaps in Richard Hofstadter's attack on the Populist tradition, and animated most obviously by a reaction both to American racism and Fascist anti-Semitism, liberals tend to see locale as synonymous with jingoism and prejudice. Local people are not to be trusted. We ought to call this what it is, namely, a fear of democracy, indeed, a fear of politics *per se*. Oddly enough, however, particularly among egalitarian liberals, the fear does not extend to the national *polis*. That is, egalitarians typically act as if the national *polis* is inherently more trustworthy than the local political communities that compose it. Hence the way to affect political change is to "go national," either by creating a media-recognized movement that will lead to legislation by Congress, or by legal action that will hopefully lead to a Supreme Court decision, hence circumvent politics entirely. Neither are libertarians particular friends of locale, since locales sometimes attempt to restrict the local activities of supra-local corporations.

In contrast, distance, disengagement, ignorance of local conditions, and absence of loyalty to the institutions and historical life of a community, are *not* by themselves indicative of superior political judgment, of a higher objectivity or rationality or morality. There is no reason to believe that non-local wisdom intrinsically is superior to local wisdom; we have plenty of experience with the stupidities of distant expertise. Certainly locales are not always right. Locale is to be limited and corrected when it reveals a local divisiveness that leads it to treat some of its members uncivilly, or when it fails to deal civilly with fellow locales within the national polity. The national polity was right to oppose the states' rights argument of Southern leaders earlier in the 1960s in their attempt to deny the rights of some of their own citizens. But the memory of their being wrong should not tempt us to extend that historical metaphor to all times and situations. Learning from history also means learning when not to "learn" too much, when not to make false analogies. As Constant argued, Paris of the 1790s was not ancient Rome or Athens; as many argued in the 1960s, Vietnam was not Czechoslovakia. By the same token, not every contemporary American town is Birmingham.

The current renewal of economic globalization, based both in the eclipse of communism and burgeoning telecommunications and informations technologies will no doubt extend the modern prejudice against locale. What Alvin Gouldner called the New Class of professionals whose claims to status hang on context-free communications skills, for whom delocalization is a mark of status, will become more prominent, not less.[30] The non-local classes will increasingly have power over, and be separated from, those portions of society whose lives are rooted in locale. But at the same time, we must say, the new round of modernization is increasing the sophistication of locales. It is not an insignificant matter that rural Americans now frequently are connected to the Internet and cable and satellite television, hence have access to news and other information identical to that of the educated urban elites. Rural Americans can get the same up to the minute news on CNN that George Bush senior watched during the Gulf War. Local communities are now more pluralistic and better informed than ever in American history. Anti-localism was always elitist. Now it is increasingly anachronistic too.

A prominent social commentator on the economics of poverty and race, whose work I admire, once responded to my discussion of neighborhood by saying that he did not believe that a return to neighborhood would lead residents of, let us say, the largely white, upper middle-class town of Brookline, Massachusetts, to care about the children of nearby black, impoverished Roxbury. Localism will do nothing, he suggested, to solve the deep problems of poor minority neighborhoods. If anything, I think he meant to imply, it would do the reverse, lead Brookline to neglect its external obligations.

This objection is fair enough: there is nothing automatic or osmotic about such a spread of concern. That Brookline cares about itself does not mean it will care about Roxbury. Notice two things, however. Negatively, the two forms of concern are not inversely related: the loss of neighborhood does not release wider and more inclusive forms of concern. That is, if Brookline fails to care about itself, that failure to generate local civic concern would not magically lead it to care about Roxbury either. Local concern is the last form of concern that extends beyond my home or person. The loss of locale is not normally replaced by universal citizenship, but simply by no citizenship at all. As Burke claimed, to love the "little platoon" is "the first link in the series" of nested circles of membership.[31] Positively speaking, I defy anyone to get the residents of Brookline to care about Roxbury's streets and children *if* they are not even willing to care about their *own*, if they retreat behind locked gates or fail to pay child support or respond to local problems with the indifference born of the careerist belief that they can pull up stakes and move higher up the economic ladder of choice towns of residence. A Brookline that does not care for itself will not care for Roxbury either. Neighborhood is not a sufficient condition of wider concern, but it is a *necessary* condition.

Michael Sandel rightly refers to the irony that George Wallace and Robert Kennedy appealed to many of the same white voters in the late 1960s.[32] Both politicians were aware that power, governmental and economic, tends in the modern age to be non-local, and powerlessness to be local. That is, those at the lower rungs of the economic ladder tend to be most tied to locale. For the upper rungs of the ladder, and the national culture and political debate that swirls around it, locale is of diminishing importance. Of the portions of American society hooked into economic success, and the culture that speaks mainly to them, Kennedy rightly said, "We live in many places and so we live nowhere."[33] Concern for neighborhood becomes more crucial as we descend that ladder; unfortunately, power to do anything about that concern decreases proportionally. Whatever Kennedy's virtues and vices as a political figure (and he had both), he recognized powerlessness in its multiple colors and forms – black and white, market-induced vulnerability and government-induced dependency – something that could not be said of many contemporary egalitarian liberals.

The loss of neighborhood is the loss of the fundamental political experience, of living as a citizen, a free member, and its replacement by the experience of being a freestanding non-member, or a client, or a partner in self-interest-promoting enterprise associations, or most likely, a patron siting in the back row of a very large political theater, related to fellow audience members only through joint witnessing of the spectacle on the national media stage. The point is not merely that the audience is largely passive, but that audience members are largely unrelated to each other, that the theater experience is designed so that their only relation comes through the passive reception of a common spectacle, and, of course, their joining in the sole act of expression and participation that is encouraged, voting "yea" or "nay."

Now many thinking and well-intentioned people, of all political stripes, both those in power and activists trying to "speak truth to power," are evidently comfortable with this image. They are concerned to get the drama on stage right, to focus their efforts on the mechanisms of power, to send their messages and try to influence the players by mobilizing the audience to applaud and hiss at the right moments. Much political activism in the contemporary world accepts this direct-mail, media-oriented, mass-semiotic methodology, in which the way to influence policy is to seek to raise poll numbers by a few percentage points by elbowing one's way into the national media-stream, then get those points into the minds of national political and corporate leaders and their organizations.[34] The people's opinions matter as data with which to frighten and cajole the real players at the margins.

Such advocates could care less what audience members really have to say, which is often complex and subtle, or even less, how they live outside the theater. On the stage side of the footlights they see and hear only an anonymous mass, not the plights or opinions of the individuals whose real lives in the million pockets of America are invisible to them, an America that is at one level not so different from the India that Gandhi once called "ten thousand villages." Worst of all, when the opinions of ordinary people do filter through, they are often frustratingly non-ideological or "irrational," that is, they do not fit nicely into the black and white strategies of uni-functional political enterprise associations. Some of the activists want ticket prices reduced, some want them raised, some want to improve parts of the theater, re-upholster the seats, do some good: but all *dramatis personae* want the audience to stay in the theater and just keep listening and watching the stage, the only activities on the part of the audience they value. When people get tired or this form of entertainment and start leaving the theater, the players accuse them of apathy and lack of compassion, of retreat and retrenchment, of loss of idealism, of niggardly self-interest.

I am suggesting that the theater is an unsatisfactory civil experience, and that it brings with it costs that the actors and the director and even the writer are loathe to acknowledge. A visit to the theater is a fine thing, but one need not be a Rousseauian to recognize that *real life is outside, in the locale*. A political culture that increasingly accepts as its only officially recognized form of civil interaction the passive witnessing of the stage becomes less and less real.

The Dialectic of Civility and Culture

As noted in the preceding chapter, the last determining trait of civil society is its peculiar relation to culture. We may begin its analysis with an historical example. Ernest Gellner argued that the precondition for the emergence of civil society in the modern West was the stalemate of Puritan reform in seventeenth-century England. The upshot of the Puritan revolution was neither its success, nor its destruction, but a stalemate leading to a demand for toleration and co-existence, the presence and the restraint of religious "enthusiasm," hence its routinization and "hyprocritization." Western modernity required the secularization of religious, soteriological enthusiasm – Weber's "Protestant Ethic" – the application of "*askese*" (ascetism) to the "*innerweltliche*" (inner-worldly) sphere, albeit an *askese* that had to be compromised and routinized, hence, disappointed. The centralized state, more powerful than ever, then found its interests *enhanced by restraint of its own power*. As in Hume's history of England, Gellner finds the secret to Western free societies to be no particular principle at all, but a contingent collection of institutions, practices, and principles whose consequences were too salutary to be replaced with something theoretically consistent.

Compromise and stalemate, the inability to consistently apply principle across society, is the hallmark of civil society. It is in this spirit that Edward Shils identified civility or the rules of civil association as the midpoint between *Gemeinschaft* and *Gesellschaft*, the "consensual pluralism" that is necessary to support social and political unity while mandating tolerance and permitting looseness. Civility is all about limitation; for Shils civil society is the society of "nothing too much," of the partial inhibition of every impulse. "Civil society," he writes, "permits neither the single individual nor the total community the complete realization of their essential potentialities . . ."[35] Civility inhibits any tendencies within a culture toward "ideology," the totalization of social life according to one value or one value hierarchy. "What is so malign" about ideology, for Shils, "is the elevation of one value, such as equality or national or ethnic solidarity, to supremacy over all others, and the insistence on its exclusive dominion in every sphere of life."[36]

Yet, at the same time, Shils denies there can be a "pure" civility, a civility completely unconnected with ideology, or in the present case, substantive culture. That would mean a purely procedural, neutralist polity without substantive values or a sense of supra-civil legitimacy. For "neither religious freedom nor intellectual freedom could be maintained unless the beneficiaries of toleration and freedom accepted the rules imposed by their own traditions and by their membership in a loosely consensual society."[37] Civility requires the collective self-consciousness and the substantive inheritance provided by cultural tradition.[38] After all, civility must be interpreted to be applied, and must be valued by members. Culture is the meaning-inheritance, the generationally transmitted interpretive repertoire, of a society, embodied in practices, artifacts, and beliefs, which form the hermeneutic resources of individuals. The minimal rules of citizen relations and behavior, which condition membership, liberty, and dignity, must be interpreted, and, if they are to be cathected as good, there must be shared accounts of the Good to support that cathexis. Shils remarks, "Civility requires respect for tradition because the sense of affinity on which it rests is not momentary only but reaches into the past and the future."[39] Tradition encourages the sense of connection. It provides contact with the sacred, that is, it allows the ultimate rightness of the social order.[40] Shils wrote that "the system of freedom . . . can flourish only if it is permeated with a largely unreflective acceptance of [the] rules of the game of the free society . . . [and] must, at least to some extent, be based on" tradition.

This means both that civility is informed by, and must restrain, cultural tradition. Culturally transmitted civility can limit and oppose other parts of the cultural tradition, thereby promoting toleration and liberty. There is nothing strange about this, unless one believes that "a culture" is monolithic, a logical hierarchy of values that never conflict. We are familiar with the fact that parts of a cultural tradition exist in tension; civility exists in tension with other elements of culture.

Philip Selznick has made the analogous point that civility and *piety* are jointly required for a "moral commonwealth," despite the fact that they conflict. He recognizes that "Their reconciliation is a prime object of theory and policy."[41] Quoting Santayana, he understands piety as an individual's "attachment to the sources of his being," the "spirit's acknowledgment of its incarnation." Piety is essential to what Selznick calls the "implicated self," the self that emerges "out of the meshing of lives and activities . . . whose obligations are neither wholly voluntary nor wholly imposed."[42] This piety, in Selznick's hands is, like Dewey's notion of "natural piety," primarily a reverence for the social and natural sources of the self, including loyalty to family, love of country, duties to institutions, etc.[43] The objects of piety are "relatively unconditional bound[s]." They include "customary" or "conventional" morality, which, while not exclusively traditional, is significantly composed by traditional culture; the contemporary practices that "take on symbolic meaning" become objects of piety. All critical or reflective morality, with which civility is more closely tied, rests in part on traditional culture. The civil order cannot do without piety, hence reverence for the perceived sources of social life.

This forces us to distinguish between, on the one hand, the cultural interpretation of civility and any activities and aims associated with the *civitas*, and, on the other hand, the supra-civil areas of culture, values that transcend the *civitas*. The former includes the rules of civil association, civility or neighborliness, as these are culturally interpreted. A civil culture must distinguish between the rules of association, culturally interpreted, and supra-civil cultural aims, in order to tolerate wider deviance in the latter than in the former. This is, among other things, a deformation or limitation on any culture that includes liberal civility within itself. A liberal culture is a culture that must *limit itself*, must draw a line between quasi-adverbial rules of civility, themselves including whatever is necessary to civility, dignity, liberty, and membership, and the task of maintaining and reproducing its supra-civil values.

If this appears analogous to the neutralist distinction between the political and the cultural, that impression would be correct. But only "analogous." The difference from neutralism is twofold: the line here is drawn *within* the non-neutral realm of culture, within a culturally embedded politics; and the line is porous, not rigid. Holism does not require that civic or political life be merged with culture, or more precisely, with all other cultural zones, for example, religious traditions. On the contrary, such a merger would be idolatrous for the conservative. The problem with neutralism was not that it drew a line, but that it drew a rigid, absolute line and drew it in the wrong place, or better, in a place that does not exist (a "non-cultural" place). The division of labor here is ambiguous; the cultural valorization of membership and civility is unstable unless it is informed by and connected to supra-civil cultural values. Thus, *civil life cannot mean without culture*, and *culture cannot be the culture of citizens*, free and equal members, *unless it restrains itself* from treading on its culturally valorized civility.

There is as well a global and historical story in which the dialectic of civil association and culture fits. Modernity appeared in the joint development of the market, civil society, and nationalism.[44] The escape from hierarchical and absolutist polity was made possible by the prosperity released by the market and civil society, and by the retention of political unity henceforth underwritten by an egalitarian, culturally-identified domain of communication created by modern nationalism. Modernity compensated human beings for releasing them from their cocoon of feudal caste, kin and locale, into the maelstrom of free, commercial society by encasing them linguistically–culturally homogeneous sovereignties. The meeting of polity and culture gave the polity a strength that the market and civil society would otherwise have threatened. Ever since, there has been a creative tension between civil association and culture. A relatively homogeneous cultural space provided a realm of context-free communication necessary to markets, supporting the polity whose administration was likewise necessary to those markets. This cultural unity was necessarily more "thin" than that of local folk cultures. At the same time, the rationalist–progressive activities released by an open, civil society constantly threatened the cultural unity of the polity; they threatened to break through any established, thick, cultural metanarrative. Over time, in the "advanced" societies, culture continued to thin out. Globalization pushes this process further. The result has been a series of different ways of balancing culture and civil society, ordered as points along a spectrum. At the extremes, a polity that underwrites membership with a thick and determinative metanarrative ceases to be a civil society (e.g. communism, fundamentalism, ethnic nationalism), and one that utterly eviscerates cultural metanarrative with a purely civil society undercuts political membership and meaningful political–moral discourse (e.g. neutralism, libertarian or egalitarian). The point is to find a place in between.

The position of modern civility with respect to culture is not mere meliorism, nor is it an easy-going compromise. It is a profoundly disturbing acceptance of cognitive and moral incompleteness. It is here that some supporters of civil society sense its deeply "anti-foundationalist" nature. In modern civil society *I must accepts as a condition on the comprehensive Good the relative independence of the partial good of civil life which is nevertheless a part of the former*. The civil or political must relate to the ultimate or moral–soteriological–aesthetic as part to whole, and yet the wisdom bequeathed by the vision of the whole that is in question – that is, the particular view embodied by accounts of the Good that endorse a civil society – indicates that the relative autonomy of the civil *is itself a necessary condition of* the social achievement of the Good. This is connected to the crucial eighteenth-century notion that the goodness of the whole is actually predicated on the whole's failure fully to determine the parts. Just as no "one" is running the show, no authority, institution, or good is ultimate; all must accept the inadequacy of any notion of the whole. Berlin's value pluralism and Weber's "polytheism" of value-spheres are alternative formulations of this deep acceptance of compromise. This is a significant cultural deformation: to those who oppose it, modern civil society is experienced as a *discipline of laxity*, a *straightjacket of freedom*, constituted by the multiplicity of institutional language-games, and continually reinforced by the dominant rationalizing, progressive sectors of society – big business, bureaucracy, science, and technology – which inhibit our ability to imagine the world as governed by a single metanarrative, as comprising one context of contexts. We are each left with a deep loyalty to the transcendent value of what explicitly refuses to be transcendent, which permits but also prevents from complete realization our salvific hopes, a situation we cannot rationalize except through looking at its beneficial consequences. A profound superficiality, a wise hypocrisy, a sense of the transcendent importance of denying the transcendental determination of the immanent, the real ideality of the society that refuses to remake the real to match the ideal. This is not, as some claim, irony.[45] It is rather, as I will suggest in the final chapter, the distinctive implication of the primacy of practical to theoretical reason.

This means that civil society is rational in the sense of distributively permitting and encouraging a rationality that it denies collectively: it retains enough of what Gellner called "Durkheimian rationality," the particular's instantiation of an ideal form or whole, to valorize its "Weberian rationality," the particular's differentiation from the whole in service of progressive improvement, with the latter in turn limiting the former. The refusal to rationalize the whole, fully to subordinate the civil and all other social life to a rational formula, hence to permit their at least quasi-independence, encourages the spheres of social life and the agents and agencies that work through them to rationalize their activity, to differentiate and create progress and change. Yet the whole is not dispensable, for the valorization of civil society, not to mention life itself, hangs on it. The parts (both individuals and spheres of activity and value) are driven forward by the endorsement of projected cultural values, accounts of the Good, which cannot be fulfilled without overturning pluralism and liberty.[46] So the whole that is projected by culture must simultaneously see itself as merely partial with respect to a "greater whole" – a second-order "whole" consisting of the first-order whole and the parts that the first-order whole permits to outdistance it, e.g. civil society – which is then endorsed, perhaps tacitly, as the best form of human social order. As Niklas Luhmann puts it, in modern society the whole is less than the sum of its parts.

Normatively, then, in a modern civil society we must accept the mutual dependence of civil rules and cultural tradition, each of which affect and limit the other. This symbiosis is not a "civic culture," a culture that contains and values nothing but civic phenomena.[47] My claim is rather that the viability of civil society requires that tension must be maintained between a substantive, not purely political or "liberal" culture which limits itself because it values civility, and a liberal or civil society which recognizes its embeddedness in culture, so that while culture is limited by civility, cultural consensus legitimately informs public and political decision-making.

Here the objections come quickly. Neutralist liberals may regard such as the "establishment" of particular cultural or comprehensive doctrines, potentially resulting both in endless controversy over their interpretation and employment, and, worst of all, publicly sanctioned intolerance of cultural minorities and individuals who diverge from the cultural majority. And we may wonder whether it makes sense to speak of "a cultural consensus" at all in a pluralistic society like America.

First, in a diverse liberal society "cultural consensus" takes a special form. Here, oddly enough, a Rawlsian conception is helpful. Rawls' notion of the "overlapping consensus" allowed him to avoid saying that commitment to political liberalism is external to citizens' comprehensive doctrines. Given his neutralist purposes, Rawls made the overlapping consensus purely political, the relevant intersection of reasonable comprehensive doctrines being their common commitment to liberal procedure, tolerance, fairness, etc. But arguably liberal societies require as well an *overlapping cultural consensus*, the joint endorsement of an account of the human Good and key social practices and institutions, each on the basis of distinctive cultural traditions. To speak only in terms of some "ultimate" religious or philosophical conceptions, many American Catholics, Jews, secular humanists, Baptists, and Hindus share a host of cultural commitments, among which is a set of culturally valorized political and civil institutions, as well as supra-civil metanarrative elements, institutions, and practices. Civility requires that this consensus be, in Martha Nussbaum's term, "thick but vague," substantive but formulated in non-sectarian terms.[48] Not everyone's worldview or commitments intersect in the consensus; some fall completely outside (like the holders of "unreasonable" comprehensive doctrines in Rawls). Some of the overlap is constituted by the "thin" or political and economic valuations of individual liberty and progress, to which we can now add a commitment to civil society itself. But other cultural elements of the consensus are thicker; they determine the meaning of human existence. Arguably in contemporary America there is an overlapping cultural consensus on, among other things, faith in God, commitment to family, and belief that employment is an essential component of dignity. Many different cultural groups have values which coalesce about these, however else they differ. So the cultural majority of a pluralistic liberal society is already pluralistic.

Still, the empowerment of an overlapping cultural consensus would authorize the inequality of minority cultural values and practices that fall outside the overlapping consensus. Some people's cultures will be more fully reflected in public policy than others. Here a culturally valorized civility provides the limit on what the consensus may encourage or require of all members. Civility requires tolerance of those who do not share the dominant cultural values and practices, since it requires the liberty and dignity of all members be respected. This is why civility is in conflict with other cultural values. The liberal society's repertoire of strategies for reproducing its dominant cultural values is complex, ranging from legal requirement or prohibition through government promotion or discouragement to extra-legal social approbation and disapprobation. The overlapping consensus is certainly open to negotiation, as Bhikhu Parkeh argues; civility requires that cultural minorities not only be tolerated, within limits, but be free to try to change the consensus.[49] What makes society liberal is, as Galston argues, not the absence of officially promoted or required notions of the Good, but that the strategy of coercion be held to a minimum.[50] And what constitutes the minimum is itself a matter of cultural interpretation.

Neutralist critics are right about on thing: any step away from neutrality permits greater limits on individual and minority liberty. But both the implausibility of neutralism as theory and the consequences of neutralism as practise leave us with no alternative. Liberals must recognize that the political force of an overlapping cultural consensus *is a fact* in any democratic society. Culturally-neutral or -anonymous law and government is inconceivable. What do we call that set of social meanings that interpret the requirements of civility, liberty, and membership, which allows social members to know how to be civil, tolerant and respectful of others, except the intersection and accommodation of a finite set of cultural traditions varying in pervasiveness and dominance? Except for libertarians, most neutralists seem unperturbed by the fact that our significantly, if not predominantly, European heritage leads us to condone liquid intoxicants while banning the smoken intoxicants prevalent in other cultures. To take a more crucial issue, policies of distributive justice cannot ignore the cultural meanings of the goods that need to be distributed; as Michael Walzer writes, "Every substantive account of distributive justice is a local account."[51] Culturally diverse Americans constantly negotiate these matters, striking a shifting balance, both in mass politics and culture and in local publics. As in all negotiations, the outcome at any moment will tend to be closer to the intersection of the interests or traits of the most dominant groups.

There is nothing profound or unusual in these observations; the point is simply that the political–legal–governmental sphere cannot be understood as devoid of cultural partiality. All societies have texts and margins, predominant narratives and subdominant ones, norms and exceptions. It is not a legitimate objection to civil society that its overlapping cultural consensus marginalizes the cultural commitments of some persons within it. Such persons cannot demand a supra-political declaration of equal validity for their distinctive worldview, nor to have their vision uncluttered by the dominant cultural consensus. The fact that the group with which one identifies and is identified is a minority cannot be drained of *all* significance and consequences, only of *uncivil* consequences.[52]

To summarize, civil life cannot mean and be valued without culture, and culture cannot be the culture of citizens, free and equal members, unless it restrains itself from treading on civility, itself part of the complex of cultural values that gives life in the *civitas* meaning. Society as civil is society understood as a moral association of free members. Culture is the interpretive-inheritance of those members. Thus cultural reproduction must not be allowed to overwhelm civility, and civil rules must not be allowed to eviscerate its own cultural cathexis. In a land-locked paraphrase of Oakeshott, civil society and culture engage in a kind of dance which has no end outside itself. But dancing, when it is well-done, often kindles hopes whose realization would end the dance. The point, however, is to keep dancing. So neither dancer can dis-embrace its partner, nor can the two retire from the dance floor in hopes of a more complete merger.

Notes

1   Aristotle, *The Nicomachean Ethics*, trans. David Ross (Oxford: Oxford University Press, 1980), I.2.

2   On this point I differ with John Kekes' recent *A Case for Conservatism*.

3   Lon L. Fuller, *The Morality of Law* (New Haven: Yale University Press, 1969).

4   Just as Nancy Rosemblum argues that a civil society must not require access to my true or complete self, and my true and complete self cannot expect to gain civil recognition. See the Conclusion to her *Membership and Morals: The Personal Uses of Pluralism in America*.

5   Seligman is careful to say that his critical target is only a concept of civil society that rests on this faith in moral fusion. I would suggest that his very interesting analysis is meant as an answer to a question that the concept of civil society, in my understanding, does not have to answer, namely, How is it philosophically plausible to assert moral order without transcendent legitimation? The complex relation of social morality to transcendence will be explored more fully in my final chapter. For the moment, I might say that civil society is just the kind of social order that does not need that kind of justification.

6   I am following Oakeshott here.

7   My notion of membership is inspired by Michael Walzer's *Spheres of Justice*. I do not claim that I am here using the concept in a way consonant with his.

8   Stephen Carter, *Civility: Manners, Morals, and the Etiquette of Democracy* (New York: Basic Books, 1998).

9   See, for example, John Kasson, *Rudeness and Civility: Manners in Nineteenth Century Urban America* (New York: Hill and Wong, 1990), and Rochelle Gurstein, *The Repeal of Reticence: A History of American's Cultural and Legal Struggles over Free Speech, Obscenity, Sexual Liberation, and Modern Art* (New York: Hill and Wong, 1996).

10 Or, as Richard Dagger prefers, a "republican liberal" society. See his *Civic Virtues: Rights, Citizenship, and Republican Liberalism* (New York: Oxford University Press, 1997).

11 See James Schmidt, "Is Civility a Virtue?," and Alan Wolfe's, "Are We Losing Our Virtue?," both in Leroy Rouner's *Civility: Boston University Studies in Philosophy and Religion*, vol. 21 (Notre Dame: University of Notre Dame, 2000). See also my response to Wolfe's lecture in the same volume.

12 See the Conclusion to her *Membership and Morals: The Personal Uses of Pluralism in America*.

13 Mickey Kaus' *The End of Equality* applies the notion of "complex equality" worked out by Walzer in his *Spheres of Justice*, although, as I argued, Kaus overrates the equity implied in civil society, making it into a *telos*.

14 The danger of careerism is its anti-egalitarian quality. Simply put, the more our culture imagines the meaning and value of life to be constituted by one's career, and less by private family life or personal relations, the more inegalitarian our attitudes become. Career is about status; the private life of family and friends is about networks of dependency. The later is, as available to a far greater percentage of persons, egalitarian, the former inegalitarian.

15 I should mention that the exploration of this metaphor by Avishai Margalit, in his *The Decent Society*, really addresses a different point. Margalit desires a society in which no one is humiliated. Well, one could say that the level of decent opportunity and a decent existence does indeed work against the humiliation of poverty. But freed from that interpretive connection, the idea of a society without humiliation is too broad and vague. People can be quite effectively humiliated by failure in a fair competition, by the refusal of friendship or

love, by all sorts of situations that arise from the free interaction of individuals. Such cannot be the subject of political regulation.

16 I would guess this idea was itself a later rationalization of an earlier notion of justice. Most primitively, justice was likely the way of life, with its rules and taboos, laid down by ancestors or gods. Injustice breaks those commands. Injustice is then primarily a violation of supra-human will. Eventually such will's were regarded as principled and rational, so that we humans could fully understand the meaning of their commands, which contributed to the eventual notion of a moral order or equilibrium.

17 See Michael Walzer, *Thick and Thin: Moral Argument at Home and Abroad.*

18 Civility and free membership are only the *political* conditions of dignity. Dignity is dependent politically on civility, freedom, and membership, but it is also utterly dependent on the development of a self, which is in turn dependent on social, cultural, and economic life. That is, it is here, in the consideration of dignity above all that we face the shading off of purely political or civil considerations into the economic, social, and cultural considerations in which, as holism claims, the civil association must be embedded.

19 Peter Berger, "The Obsolescence of the Concept of Honor," in Peter Berger et al., *The Homeless Mind.*

20 Here is where I depart somewhat from the civil society advocates of "mediating structures," with whom I am otherwise in agreement. I fully accept the social importance of religious and voluntary associations. But civil society as I define it is properly and primarily families in neighborhoods. Local is the center. We may say then that those voluntary associations tied to locale, and especially what I will call "multi-functional" associations, are virtually civil. But non-local and/or "uni-functional" associations (e.g. political lobbies) are not.

21 As noted, neighborhood is not solely urban. It can as well be rural, and yes even suburban. The last deserves emphasis because of the common antipathy of many liberal theorists, who tend to be concerned with cities and their problems and to have some distant sympathy for rural life (a sympathy actually misplaced, given the common rural suspicion of liberal values), but seem on personal grounds to regard the suburbs as a politically apathetic, ethnically homogeneous, and privileged form of blight. Suburbanites are people too, and many suburbs have vibrant neighborhoods.

22 This echoes what Robert Neville called the Principle of Universal Responsibility in his *The High Road Around Modernism* (Albany: SUNY Press, 1992), ch. 10.

23 I do not mean that non-local institutions ought not be involved; that would be absurd. On the contrary, that repairs be carried out is the most crucial need, and effective governmental action is almost always welcome.

24 Robert A. Nisbet, *The Quest for Solidarity: A Study in the Ethics of Order and Freedom* (orig. 1953; San Francisco: Institute for Contemporary Studies, 1990), and Anthony Giddens, *Consequences of Modernity* (Stanford: Stanford University Press, 1990).

25 I do not mean these terms to be synonymous with Gellner's "multi-" and "single-" stranded thinking. But there is a connection. Multi-functional political thought must be less "rationalizable" than uni-functional thought because it must juggle incommensurable values.

26 It is rather odd that we restrict the meaning of "politician" to electoral candidates, as if we had still not gotten used to the idea that the vast majority of persons paid to be involved in political matters never would consider running for office.

27 Haynes Johnson and David Broder, *The System: The American Way of Politics at the Breaking Point* (New York: Little, Brown, 1996).

28 Benjamin Barber, *Strong Democracy: Participatory Politics for A New Age*.

29 I should mention that there is a tradition of attention to neighborhood politics in empirical political science. See for example: Roger Ahlbrandt, Jr., *Neighborhoods, People, and Community* (Pittsburgh: University of Pittsburgh Press, 1984); Matthew Crenson, *Neighborhood Politics* (Cambridge: Harvard University, 1983); and less recent, Milton Kotler, *Neighborhood Government: The Local Foundations of Political Life* (Indianapolis: Bobbs-Merrill, 1969).

30 Alvin Gouldner, *The Future of Intellectuals and the Rise of the New Class* (New York: Seabury, 1979).

31 Edmund Burke, *Reflections on the Revolution in France* (Indianapolis: Hackett, 1987), p. 41.

32 Sandel, *Democracy's Discontents*, p. 304.

33 Robert Kennedy, in testimony before the Subcommittee on Executive Reorganization, in Edwin O. Guthman and C. Richard Allen, *RFK: Collected Speeches* (New York: Viking, 1993), p. 179, quoted by Sandel, *Democracy's Discontents*, p. 302.

34 One thinks here of the claim made during the American involvement in the Persian Gulf during the Iran-Iraq war – I have no idea whether it was really true – that all that would be necessary for the Iranians to choke off the flow of oil was, not actually to control the Gulf militarily, but to sink a couple of ships in order to cause insurers to raise their rates. The analogy is that the way to affect the situation on the ground (or water) politically is get some major, risk-averse organizations to flinch, rather than actually proposing sensible reforms to voters and trying to convince them that they would work.

35 Edward Shils, *The Virtue of Civility: Selected Essays on Liberalism, Tradition, and Civil Society*, edited by Steven Grosby (Indianapolis: Liberty Fund, 1997), p. 49.

36 Ibid., p. 59.

37 Edward Shils, *The Constitution of Society* (Chicago: Unversity of Chicago Press, 1982), p. x.

38 Edward Shils, *Tradition* (Chicago: University of Chicago Press, 1981).

39 Shils, *The Virtue of Civility*, p. 51.

40 Ibid., p. 110.

41 Philip Selznick, *The Moral Commonwealth*, "Civility and Piety," p. 387.

42 Selznick, p. 205.

43 John Dewey, *A Common Faith* (New Haven: Yale University Press, 1934), p. 25.

44 See Ernest Gellner, *Conditions of Liberty: Civil Society and its Rivals* (London: Penguin, 1994), *Plough, Sword, and Book: The Structure of Human History* (Chicago: University of Chicago Press, 1988), and *Nations and Nationalism* (Ithaca: Cornell University Press, 1983).

45 As is claimed by Rorty, political theorist William Connolly, and in a different way, Leo Strauss.

46 This picture is in a sense Leibnizian, or akin to the point that the cosmological thesis of the expanding universe means that *every point* in the universe is expanding. Modern, or if you will, postmodern society – which is nothing but the advanced course in the modern society of spontaneous order – expands from, not every point – there being non-progressive, metabolic spheres – but from every *rationalizing* point, that is, every progressive "language-game" or practical–discoursive social context. Each is both self-directing according to inner principles and dependent on, affected by, networks formed by other points.

47 See Gabriel A. Almond and Sidney Verba, *The Civic Culture* (Princeton: Princeton University Press, 1963), p. 13. For the authors civic culture refers to "the specifically political orientations [of citizens] – attitudes toward the political system and its various parts, and attitudes toward the role of the self in the system. We speak of a political culture just as we can speak of an economic culture or a religious culture." So their concern is, unlike mine, with the culturally prevalent interpretations of political life and patterns of civic behavior.

48 Nussbaum, "Aristotelian Social Democracy," in Douglass et al., *Liberalism and the Good*, discussed above in Chapter Three. I am admittedly using the term differently than Nussbaum.

49 Bhikhu Parekh, *Rethinking Multiculturalism: Cultural Diversity and Political Theory* (London: Macmillan, 2000).

50 William Galston, *Liberal Purposes: Goods, Virtues, and Diversity in the Liberal State* (Cambridge: Cambridge University Press, 1991).

51 Michael Walzer, *Spheres of Justice: A Defense of Pluralism and Equality* (New York: Basic Books, 1983), p. 314.

52 As both Andrew Sullivan and Richard Rodriguez attest. See Rodriguez's *Hunger of Memory*. In *Virtually Normal: An Argument About Homosexuality* (New York: Vintage, 1995), Sullivan writes, "No homosexual child, surrounded overwhelmingly by heterosexuals, will feel at home in his sexual and emotional world, even in the most tolerant of cultures. . . . Anyone who believes political, social, or even cultural revolution will change this fundamentally is denying reality. . . . It is definitive of homosexual development" (p. 13).

8

Politics and Truth

We have criticized the attempt intellectually to reconstruct the normative features of liberal republican society through a small set of theoretical principles. Our modern civil society cannot be thusly simplified. Rather, that form of life hangs on multiple institutions, practices, and principles which exhibit their own inconsistencies and conflicts that theoretical reduction would imperil. Its civil complexity becomes visible when we accept a meta-theoretical conservatism that eschews rational simplification.

Certainly this very approach raises philosophical questions about the status of political inquiry, about what are the rightful aims of a *theoria* of *politikē*. That is, occasionally explicit but always implicit in the foregoing has been a notion of what philosophical intelligence can and ought to do with (and within) our political form of life. Of what kind of justification are political accounts, like that presented herein, susceptible? Critical questions have been begged throughout. It is now time for begging to come to an end, and honest work to make a place for the present account in the context of the philosophical search for truth.

Four questions arise about philosophy's relation to politics. First, is truth, or the search for truth, compatible with politics? I refer not to the alleged mendacity of politicians, but to something stranger and more confounding: Is there something about even a good political life that is violated by the concern for truth, especially the philosophical search for truth? Is there something anti-democratic or anti-liberal, something authoritarian about philosophy and truth? Second, must politics violate truth? Most famously, does the good *polis* need some untruth, or at the least, beliefs which philosophical inquiry tends to put in doubt? Further, these questions raise the issue of what is the proper aim, and what are the proper limits, of philosophy about politics, that is, political theory.[1] Last and most obviously, can philosophy justify the validity or superiority of liberal republicanism, and in particular, the notions of civil society and holism through which I have interpreted it? We shall take the last question first.

Justifying Liberal Republicanism

There are a variety of ways of trying to provide a philosophical justification of liberal republicanism. The usual approaches can be divided into the moral and the methodological. The moral ways argue that liberal republicanism is uniquely consonant with the best way of life for human beings. These can be divided into positive and negative approaches. The former vary with the version of ethics that is used: deontologists, who accept an ethics of duty, may claim ultimacy for individual rights, and argue that liberal republicanism is the only regime consonant with such rights; utilitarians can argue that liberal republicanism maximizes the social good; and a virtue ethics approach could claim that liberal republicanism embodies, encourages, or permits virtue, or the best virtues, to the greatest extent. The negative approach argues that liberal republicanism is the least bad regime, that it minimizes the *summum malum*, the greatest evil, for example, coercive violence.

The methodological justifications argue that, given certain views about the limits of human knowledge, like skepticism or relativism, the least governmental power, the most morally neutral regime, or the regime allowing the greatest liberty of individuals and groups is the least objectionable. In effect, these are negative in that they argue that any non-liberal regime rests on objectionable epistemological or methodological views, presuming to know a truth that in fact cannot be known. Notice that the negative political and the methodological approaches, and as it happens, sometimes the positive political approaches too, are comparative. That is, they argue that liberal republicanism is valid because it is superior to alternatives. This mode of argument presupposes a practical orientation, that since in practice we *must* decide questions of validity, even if an ultimate or non-comparative decision cannot be justified, we can still justify a decision on comparative grounds.[2]

I will make no attempt to survey all of these approaches. Most are familiar, especially the positive ethical approaches. Proceduralist liberalism especially has favored the Kantian version, which justified liberalism as based in the duty to recognize individual rights. I will only call attention to other arguments that have received less attention in the present volume.

Utilitarianism has been out of favor in English language political philosophy for more than a generation, largely due to the great success of neo-Kantian political theories since the early 1970s. It has been criticized on two grounds. First, it seems not to be able to rule out majoritarian violation of individual rights. This is the practical motivation for the Rawlsian diagnosis that utilitarianism does not respect the differences among individuals, substituting a mega-subject, regarding whom happiness can be said to increase or decrease, for the plural moral subjects of the deontological conception. Second, utilitarianism's explicit grounding of political norms in a particular good, happiness, as well any particular qualitative weighting of goods, has seemed to some unable to withstand questions about justification. Utilitarianism must make a host of empirical, hence fallible and changeable, judgments relevant to moral decision-making, something which always disturbs the Kantian meta-ethical mentality. For example, John Stuart Mill's utilitarian defense of individual liberties rests on the claim that those societies who best defend individual rights are, in point of *fact*, arguably those with the highest levels of prosperity or happiness. Kantians can retort that, while this may be largely true at this point in time, we could imagine a society with little liberty yet great happiness of some kind, e.g. Aldous Huxley's *Brave New World*, which provides "soma" to all citizens. (More realistically, we have the oil-rich Islamic fundamentalist societies.)

Without offering anything like an adequate defense of utility, I would soften these criticisms. Political anti-utilitarianism seems rather unfair. First, the argument from consequences ought not be so lightly dismissed. From the view of what we might call *bio-values* – health, longevity, beauty, sensual pleasures, etc. – which always matter, and are universally treasured, modern liberal societies usually are superior, at least at this point in time, by virtue of a higher standard of living, lowered infant mortality, better health care, etc. This is a very significant argument for real human beings. Add to this the relative freedom from political repression, and contemporary liberal republican societies are comparatively speaking very attractive polities. Given the choice, more human beings seem to want to live in them than in traditional societies. They are sometimes ambivalent about this choice, but they make it anyway. And they presumably do so not on deontological grounds; that is, they do not face the rigors of the *emigré* life and personal cultural revolution because of a conviction that liberal societies are deontologically superior. They presumably reason on the consequentialist grounds that, with the trade-offs, *life seems better here*. Again, this argument does nothing for those who are willing to accept lower standards of living and lesser longevity in exchange for ethnic purity or theocracy. It presupposes a kind of biotic pragmatism, hence by nature excludes personality types who are willing to sacrifice all for cultural homogeneity. While we needn't accept the reasoning of the mass of consequentialist liberal republicans, we ought not disrespect it either.

Regarding the deontological fear that utility threatens individual liberties, I suggest that while theoretically apt – nothing in the utilitarian *principle* rules out trading some individual's rights for majority happiness – it is less clear that when combined with secondary considerations, applied utilitarianism is really so dangerous. Mill's belief that as an empirical matter maximum liberty promotes social happiness is, hard cases aside, arguably right. The argument between utilitarians and deontologists then seems to hang on the aforementioned Prince Faisal dilemma regarding mercy as a passion versus mercy as good manners: "You may judge which motive is the more reliable." Which is the more reliable, an absolute commitment to rights that must inevitably quality them to make room for utility, or a commitment to social happiness that regards liberty as the *de facto* road to that happiness? In the real world, as opposed to theory, the answer is not so clear as some deonotologists would have it.

Lastly, regarding the alleged difficulty of a philosophical justification of an ultimate *telos*, i.e. social happiness, the plausibility of this charge hangs on believing that deontological justifications of liberal republicanism are better candidates for fulfilling our justificatory hopes. I would argue that this is not the case. If deontological and other justifications of liberal republicanism fare just as ill, then the malign view of utilitarianism is unjust. If utility fares no better, it also fares not noticeably worse.

The virtue-oriented approach has been tried explicitly by Martha Nussbaum, but can be found implicit in a variety of utilitarians and others (including Dewey). It claims that liberal republicanism makes for more or better virtue than other regimes. Now this can immediately be qualified into several options: that liberal regimes make possible the greater actualization of virtues by an elite few of its members, or what Rawls called "perfectionism" (not to be confused with affirmative or non-neutralist liberalism); that liberal regimes make for the most virtue in society as a whole; and that liberal regimes, either with respect to the majority or an elite, make virtue more possible, if not actual.

While this way of justifying liberal republicanism is not as common in political theory as the utilitarian and deontological, we are familiar with popular versions of it. Liberalism is often viewed as that regime whose freedom and open competition encourage hard-work, expression of talent, self-reliance, creativity, and independent thought, all arguably virtuous. These virtues may indeed be more widespread in a liberal society than in any other. Some may be primarily concerned with the few creative geniuses that this system permits, arguing that, whatever the level of virtue in the general population, a free society contributes more to civilization by freeing the few to make new culture. Few political theorists make this elitist–perfectionist argument openly, but it is hard not to hear it lurking behind justifications of aesthetic freedom and governmental support for the arts. Certainly admirers of aesthetic modernism have often prided liberal republicanism in this sense. Or more globally, holding the moral view that behavior must be freely chosen to be virtuous, one can argue that our free society alone makes truly virtuous behavior *possible*, while the apparently virtuous behavior of people in non-liberal societies is in fact un-free, hence not truly virtuous.

Whatever the virtues of the virtue argument, all of these options themselves presuppose some specific account or ranking of virtues, i.e. one in which self-reliance, for example, ranks above filial piety. There certainly are virtues that are *not* maximized in modern liberal society, e.g. loyalty, constancy, simplicity of heart, faith, etc. So the virtue justification of liberalism hangs on the even more daunting philosophical problem of deciding which are the best virtues. As noted earlier, I respect the heroic attempt to arrive at such a decision. However, it is hard to see how it can ever be non-circular, that is, how it can avoid justifying modern liberalism on the grounds of the fulfillment of a moral theory modern liberals are likely to hold. It would thus return us to the holism I have encouraged, the admission that our ultimate political norms are not independent of our particular cultural inheritance. This would be fine, but it does not help us to find a non-circular justification.

Moving on to the negative moral justifications, the most famous version in recent theory was offered by the late Judith Shklar.[3] She argued, in a Hobbesian vein, that liberalism is the least bad regime, hence the best regime, because its aim is to minimize cruelty, primarily violence. While all regimes seek to control criminal violence among citizens, liberalism seeks as well to limit violence by the state or sanctioned by the state, making it the least cruel of regimes. Liberalism is willing to live with elevated levels of other vices, like hypocrisy, in order to minimize cruelty. Thus, the *summum malum* approach, while it liberates the political theorist from what may seem to be a more onerous task, that of defining the *summum bonum*, nevertheless cannot avoid the controversy over which evil or vice is the worst. Its problems of justification are analogous to those of the virtue approach.

The problem with all of the moral approaches, negative or positive, is that they employ presuppositions which themselves seem rather difficult to justify. A deontological ethics of individual rights, basing all political authority on consent; a liberal utilitarian calculus, which must assign relative values to the material prosperity resulting from individualism over, for example, the pleasure of conformist *Gemeinschaft*; the valuation of the critical and individualistic virtues over, for example, filial piety and loyalty; and the, as mentioned, view of cruelty and coercion as greater evils than, for example, disharmonious competition or an individual freely ruining her life – all these ways of justifying liberal republicanism rest on values or principles that not only are themselves in need of justification, but are linked to liberal republicanism in the first place. It is no more clear that they can be justified in a non-circular way than can liberal politics. What modern liberal republicans use to justify liberal republican politics are the modern values that normally are held in liberal republican societies, e.g. individualism, prosperity, concern for autonomy and independence, all in a secular context. These might indeed be adequate if the alternative to liberal republicanism were only, say, Marxism, or some other modern Western, but non-liberal, alternative, whose proponents might share the aforementioned tendencies. But for justifying liberalism *uberhaupt*, including justifying it against premodernist, religious, or authoritarian options, this will not do. It is like, as in a Wittgensteinian example, trying to justify the reliability of a newspaper story by pointing to another story in the same newspaper.

Hence the appeal of the methodological approach. Here the field of battle is not politics, but the possibilities of knowledge. And, like the negative political approach, a deflationary posture is taken to be less open to attack. This strategy has the appeal of stealing its opponent's thunder. For if the liberal faces an opponent who adopts a relativist or skeptical position toward the possibility of justifying liberal republicanism, the liberal asks, What would be the least offensive political regime from the perspective of skepticism or relativism? That is, which society would *you* skeptical –relativist types find least troubling personally? Presumably it would be a liberal republican society, in which power is most circumscribed and individuals are maximally free to doubt in public. Furthermore, the best form of liberal republicanism, on this view, would be proceduralist liberalism, a society which denies any official theory of the Good. If all such theories are in doubt, let us have a regime that presupposes none of them. So those who doubt the validity of liberal republicanism are thereby invited on board.

This methodological justification says that liberal society is in fact not a particular form of life at all, but a framework in which all forms of life are allowed. In other words, liberal republican society is more inclusive, not only of individuals, but of lifestyles, theories of the Good, and even communal forms, so that, *if qualified* in certain ways, non-liberal forms can be included in a liberal society. The strategy is the same as that used by some in the philosophy of science who argue that a scientific theory which, as well as explaining what a predecessor theory cannot explain, also explains everything the predecessor *did* explain, may be called rationally superior to the predecessor theory. In an analogous sense, a form of political life may be called superior if it permits opposing, and in this case, more traditional forms of life within it, at least to a greater degree than opposing or traditional societies would permit "liberal" lifestyles. Immigrants from traditional, religious societies, the story goes, are more able to maintain continuity with their former lifestyles in America than the contemporary American could maintain his or her lifestyle in, for example, a theocracy. So liberalism is more inclusive and less objectionable.

But, as we have seen, this neutralism is troubled. Brian Barry has pointed out that liberalism cannot claim to be compatible with all ways of life; liberal society in fact presupposes a liberal way of life.[4] It has an official view about the value of toleration, critical thinking, tradition, freedom, public criticism of all ends, etc. In practice this means that more traditional, homogeneous, and dogmatic subcultures are always *under threat* within a liberal society. They can indeed exist, understood as based in contract, free consent – a monastery is fine if it has unlocked exits. But, as Barry and others have noted, this view that consent must subtend all lifestyles is itself incompatible with the views of some of those subcultures. Any non-liberal community has great difficulty maintaining itself against the onslaught, keeping its younger generation down on the farm once it has seen MTV.

There is much to be said for the argument that, on the whole, liberal society permits more illiberal lifestyles than illiberal societies permit liberal, or any anti-official, lifestyles. But this is matter of degree, hence a utilitarian or consequentialist matter. The superiority it would ascribe to liberalism would be not the deontolgical and neutralist claim that liberal societies are tolerant, but that liberal societies are *relatively more* tolerant. This is in fact true, and a perfectly legitimate reason for preferring liberal regimes. But the intolerance of liberal societies is not thereby easy to dismiss. Thus if a person or group happens to consider that of which the liberal society is intolerant to be the *summum bonum*, liberalism's relatively greater tolerance is not for them a reason to accept its superiority. And this form of argument against liberalism is not that unusual. Some liberals believe that the pro-choice position on abortion is intrinsic to liberalism, hence that liberal societies must accept abortion. They may say that the permissive society, which permits those who want abortions to get them, and those who do not to avoid them, is more inclusive and so superior. But some who take the pro-life, anti-abortion position regard the permissibility of abortion to be so heinous – the killing of unborn innocents is an absolute evil – that it de-legitimates the entire liberal regime.[5]

My point here is that there can be no philosophical justification of the superiority of liberal republicanism that does not itself presuppose some of the values epitomized by liberal republicanism, values presumably embedded in those societies that have evolved or are likely to evolve liberal polities. This is what Richard Rorty has claimed, and he is right.[6] In other words, no attempt at justification avoids begging the question. There is no justification without important, value-laden presuppositions; no justification from zero.[7] (I should add that the existence of universal norms of a minimally good regime, mentioned earlier, does not help here, because those norms are too vague to dictate the kind of regime.)

Rorty's own response to the impossibility of fundamental justification is to commit himself to liberal republicanism on what he calls a "frankly ethnocentric" basis.[8] He endorses the superiority of liberal republicanism on a "circular" basis, one that does not try to imagine justification on grounds other than its own. In effect, this is to accept that liberalism is justified, but *not philosophically*. His conventionalism, then, is not so much a philosophical justification of liberalism as a refusal to regard such justification necessary. Applying Thomas Reid's figure to the current issue, when Philosophy calls Liberalism to its bar to demand justification, Liberalism, on advice of counsel Rorty, refuses to recognize the court's jurisdiction.

Rorty's position is at this level akin to the conservative view, on which Oakeshott, as we have seen, is the most clear.[9] The possibility of deriving the rules or values of our polity from some set of principles that either themselves need no justification, or are transparently justified, or are necessary and universal for human beings, is nil. The conservative, holist response is that there is no such thing as "justifying the tradition." Alasdair MacIntyre is here entirely right; if I seek to abstract from everything I value and believe, and then ask, how can I justify my values and beliefs, in principle I can get no answer, for the process of abstraction is precisely the process of deactivating, bracketing, everything that could give an answer. If a tradition is to be argued for, it will always be in terms of principles or values shared or accepted without argument. (This does not imply, however, that traditions are solipsistic. For the notion of a tradition that *shares nothing* with other traditions is also nonsensical. As MacIntyre has shown, traditions can understand each other even when their languages are incommensurable, and may even rationally decide *on their own grounds* that another tradition is in some respects superior.)[10]

This does not make philosophical justification pointless, but limited, the establishment of a relation of necessity or plausibility between one set of principles or ideas and another. Justification reveals the relations, positive or negative, among families of ideas. The value of any argument here can only be a matter of degree. No argument will presume nothing, that is, fail to presuppose certain basic value-laden principles, like the value of liberty and equal membership. The better or more useful argument is one whose net of presuppositions, by virtue of being least specific to that which is to be justified – liberal republican society – thereby provides the rationale for seeing that a larger set of possible first principles implicates the legitimacy of liberal republican society. The better argument shows how wide is the set of distinctive values which ought to lead their holder to endorse liberal republicanism. This is no mean achievement. The least valuable argument is one that takes individualism or progress or self-rule as ultimate values, that is, the implicit or explicit ends of liberal republicanism, and shows that liberal republicanism is justified based on them. Such an argument is true but trivial. It is in this sense that the arguments from utility, virtue, and the *summum malum* are good and useful arguments; they indeed point out the web of values that crowd around liberal republicanism, whose pursuit leads to liberal republicanism. In this sense as well, the deontological arguments are similarly good but less useful, given their reliance on the values embedded in liberal republican rules (e.g. "rights"). The methodological argument is in a sense a good and useful supplement to a deontological, proceduralist version of liberal republicanism, but by its very nature can speak only to a narrow range of views, e.g. skepticism, relativism, etc. In other words, the conservative view of the task of justification is not that, absent ultimate justification, nothing can be said, but rather that *lots* can be said, none of it final. All the ways of attempting to justify liberal republicanism mentioned above have their limited, philosophically indecisive but practically significant place in our reasoning about what is a better and a worse regime.

Now, all this applies to the study which is, in this chapter, coming to a close. I have accepted the commitment to liberal republicanism through two notions, civil society and holism. What justification can, or ought to be given of these ways of interpreting liberal republicanism, or rather, of liberal republicanism as viewed through these lenses?

Civil society can be justified only through the premises that liberty and membership must be combined, hence that the dignity of all members is to be maintained. But there is no non-circular rational argument for why civil society ought to outweigh other considerations. Free membership has in fact been shown to be the condition for unprecedented social prosperity, itself highly valuable, but again, without a non-circular justification. Forms of political order that violate civil society would most obviously include totalitarianism, Fascist or Marxist, forms of authoritarianism, or the merger of social and religious orders, as in contemporary Islamic fundamentalism.

If some such society were to prove more resilient or prosperous over the long-term, especially if in non-idiosyncratic conditions, that would constitute a significant threat to the legitimacy of civil societies, there being no presuppositionless, hence universal, philosophical justification of the superiority of civil society, or a regime consonant with it. But in the modern world we have yet to see such a development. Of course, even in such a counterfactual situation our culture could continue to endorse civil society on its own peculiar grounds.

What of my avowal of holism? Holism relates to the project of justification in two distinct ways, a fact which is itself troublesome. First, the holist position insists that politics be viewed as a part of a social whole, so that political norms must take into account and cohere with social, cultural, and economic realities. So we may first ask, Why ought one accept this embeddedness rather than insist that politics be investigated autonomously, that political norms be grounded in political considerations alone? Isn't it essential to the great normative achievements of modern life to differentiate spheres, and isn't that differentiation the condition of social progress? What then is the philosophical justification of the superiority, with respect to truth, of holism over the autonomy of the political?

In response, we must clarify that holism does not imply a wholesale de-differentiation of spheres. It merely denies that such differentiation is ultimate, that it "goes all the way down." Holism insists that the spheres are permeable, that they sit within a context that is the collection of them all. This implies not a foundational metaphor – which would mean that the context is more than the sum of the parts – but that the collection of parts is a reality and an influence on its parts, in contingent and shifting ways. The relation of spheres is a contingent matter; their degree of mutual involvement changes. So a holist can insist, as I did in the preceding chapter, that some version of the liberal distinction of politics and culture ought to hold, i.e. in the tension of civility and culture, while nevertheless denying the absoluteness of that distinction.

Even if this clarification reduces the force of the objection, the question remains, why accept holism over the autonomy of politics? Here the only "answer" is embedded in the concept of civil society itself. To regard our politics as the business of civil society is to make politics intrinsically *social*. As I suggested in the Introduction, the dominant concern of the modern Western political tradition, both liberal and conservative, is to prevent political power from violating society, by grounding and locating political power in society. I am suggesting that holism is embedded in the social assumptions of the modern civil society tradition, hence even in earlier (pre-neutralist) liberalism. Neutralist liberals who make politics autonomous of society and culture are violating their own tradition. If one accepts that politics exists in service of, is a function of, social existence, then the door is open to holism. The burden is then on anti-holists to show why politics ought nevertheless to be rendered autonomous.

This is the only kind of philosophical justification of which holism is capable. Holism is obviously prohibited from attempting a justification of itself from zero. Its justification can only be a depiction of its coherence with a variety of ideas and realities that are held to be interpretatively salient, which purports to show its superiority to alternatives. This is to argue that the view in question is valid because it is the best current view. As noted above, this form of justification is not philosophically unobjectionable; showing one view comparatively and practically better than others does not show that it must be *true* (otherwise, the best current view at every moment in history regarding any topic would be true, which is false).[11] In first philosophy, such a justification would be inadequate. But in ethics and politics, such justification can be adequate *from a conservative viewpoint*. That is, if we accept that practical reason has different standards than theoretical reason, since ethics and politics are those areas of philosophical inquiry meant to guide action, and since action *must* be guided, it is legitimate to endorse the best view, even if no ultimate philosophical justification of its truth is available. This means that as philosophers we must retain a level of uncertainty even while we endorse holism and civil society.

This may seem like sleight of hand. I claim that it follows from holism that the justification of a form of political life will not be solely political, that is, will entail reference to a variety of social and cultural elements. The justification of this holism is then supported by that very view of the place of theory in social and cultural life. For to accept holism is to accept that the bar of justification is lowered, which then allows the justification of holism. This is, admittedly, a case of "closing the circle." Conservatism makes the doing of political philosophy, and implicitly any form of philosophy, emergent within and dependent upon historical social reality. *Conservatism denies that Reason is the basis of social life; rather, social life is the basis for reason.* This is to accept the primacy of the practical over the theoretical. In deciding where to stand, how to "set out," or what questions to ask and what presuppositions to endorse, the philosopher must, as Peirce claimed, set out from where he or she is. That does not mean philosophy cannot abstract from social conditions, but that this abstraction is an achievement performed with the resources provided by society, a sublimation of society. Inquiry arises within a social, cultural, and historical setting, and, in order to solve the problems arising within that setting, tries to abstract or prescind from a variety of thematized presuppositions embedded in it. "Freedom from presuppositions" – which is always freedom from *some* presuppositions – is a goal, not a starting point. Eager to reach conclusions valid not only for myself, my kin, my co-religionists, etc., I progressively prescind from or bracket in thought what I take to be the presuppositions embedded in those shared identities. There is nothing impossible about such abstraction. It takes place in real-world political and cross-cultural negotiation, as well as in the quiet internal dialogue we call philosophic thought. What is impossible is for it to be complete or final.

Legislating Truth: Indiana and *Pi*

In "Truth and Politics," Hannah Arendt presents an historical survey of the relation of different kinds of truth to the political realm.[12] She points out that since the Greeks, politics has been understood as a realm neither of philosophical or "rational" truth, nor of factual truth, but of opinion. Power is the realm of opinion. As we will see later, truth, whether rational or factual, is "compulsive," it precludes the debate that is the soul of politics. Furthermore, Arendt insists, the philosophical valuation of truth above all else, "*Fiat veritas et pereat mundus*," "Find the truth though the world perish," is utterly improper for the political sphere.

Now, human existence requires truth, especially factual truth. So lying, while itself an indicator of the uncanniness of human freedom, eventually undermines human existence. Tyranny has always been secretive, has always attempted to restrict truth. But in modern totalitarianism, Arendt argues, we see for the first time regimes that make it their business systematically to lie about factual truth. Totalitarianism returns facts to the status of mere "potentialities" and so undermines the very fabric of life. In non-tyrannical regimes there are in fact a number of specifically truth-guarding institutions set up independent of the political sphere: the judiciary, the academy, sometimes the press, and ultimately the poets and historians. In totalitarianism these are colonized by politics. Thus Arendt warns us against the governmental invasion of the realm of truth.

Let us take a milder, non-totalitarian example. In 1897 the lower house of the Indiana state legislature voted to change the mathematical value of *pi*. An Indiana physician and amateur mathematician named Edwin Goodwin had worked out an alternative (and false) value. He wrote the bill, the opening line of which read "A bill for an act introducing a new mathematical truth. . . ." It was proposed in the House by his county representative. The stated incentive for legislators was that, if passed, Goodwin would then allow the state to use his mathematical demonstration in its

textbooks without royalties. Despite the fact that some thought it bizarre –
one newspaper account was compelled to note that the bill "is not intended
to be a hoax" and another pronounced it the "strangest bill that has ever
passed an Indiana Assembly" – the lower house adopted it unanimously!
When the bill arrived in the Indiana Senate it was laughingly referred to the
Committee on Temperance, but the committee returned the next morning
with a vote of approval! In the meantime, by sheer luck it so happened that
a mathematician named C. A. Waldo had been in the lower house on the
day the bill was first read, lobbying for an appropriations bill for the Indiana
Academy of Science. He later "coached" the senators on the proposed bill's
absurdity. When the Senate committee returned its approval the senators
present made merry at the bill's expense. One senator lamented the ridicule
the bill had brought his state in Chicago and the East. The Senate postponed
decision indefinitely, the matter being, as one paper reported, "not . . . a
subject for legislation." Yet remarkably, almost ten days after this dismissal,
one local paper still published an entirely laudatory front-page story on
Goodwin's historic mathematical achievement.[13]

Exactly what is bizarre about this case? After all, public works bills must
include or presume mathematical truths. When a legislature makes a declaration honoring an inventor or an explorer, it officially recognizes the
scientific value of the invention and the facts of the discovery. The contemporary state also funds the sciences, so must decide what is and what is not
a promising avenue of research. Legislatures cannot do their job if they are
supposed to remain neutral on or indifferent to the truth of empirical and
scientific claims. Not to mention that in far less "objective," that is, more
contentious arenas like the arts, government often makes judgments of
validity, e.g. which artist shall receive a grant. Wherein, then, lies the absurdity of legislators explicitly deciding a truth which their other legislation
must implicitly presume anyway?

There is no record of the Indiana Senate's discussion except for newspaper accounts. In those accounts the critical reaction circled around
several points. One Indiana paper put it plainly enough: "The Senate
might as well try to legislate water to run up hill as to establish
mathematical truth by law." Papers outside Indiana did not spare Hoosier
pride. A *Chicago Tribune* editorial, under the title, "Indiana's Finger in the
Pi," commented:

> The House has therefore decided that hereafter in the State of Indiana Pi shall
> be 3.2. . . . The immediate effect of this change will be to give all circles when
> they enter Indiana either greater circumferences or less diameters. An Illinois
> circle or a circle originating in Ohio will find its proportions modified as soon
> as it lands on Indiana soil.

After its defeat, the *Tribune* reported that "The bill was about to be passed when the point was raised that the Legislature had no power to declare a truth . . ."[14] A *New York Daily Tribune* editorial referred to "Vaudeville Legislators." Another *Daily Tribune* editorial writer dryly noted that:

> From the time when Euclid first passed the laws of geometry up till recently, no legislator has sought to amend it. . . . In these democratic times, however, it is not unnatural that a legislative body, duly representing the people, should proceed to the enactment of other similar geometric laws.[15]

I think our perception of absurdity in this case hangs on several elements, some of which these writers have articulated. First, the proposed result was *wrong*. If the wrong value of *Pi* were to be accepted, and that acceptance were to have any practical effect – e.g. be required to be used by engineers contracting with the state – then bridges would fall down. That is, part of our perception of the Indiana bill's absurdity is that we take the accepted value of *Pi* to be well-established and not open to dispute. But that very assumption, and with it the perception of absurdity, hangs on additional factors. As one writer expressed, the situation of one state holding a different mathematical value for *Pi* than all other states would indeed have been bizarre. Practically, it would have been endlessly troublesome. On the other hand, iconoclasm is neither amiss in inquiry nor in American federalism. The absurdity of mathematical truth changing at the Indiana state line itself presupposes the belief that the majority must be right after all.

But additionally, we are unused to legislatures legislating truth so nakedly. While legislation presupposes all manner of truth claims, this bill explicitly presents itself as the official *proclamation* of a truth. In modern liberal societies we regard legislation as practical, aimed at doing something, or making a value judgment of something, not sharpening (in this case, clouding) our cognitive picture. The *Daily Tribune* expressed this by saying that the legislature had "no power to declare a truth." But we would have to refine this point. The Supreme Court, the sole arbiter of the legislature's power, did not speak on the matter, but one could argue that legislature *did* have that "power." If "declare" is supposed to have a performative meaning, then many of us would agree that the legislature has no power to *make* truth, to make the value of *pi* 3.2 – although much of the force of even this objection hangs on accepting a mathematical *realism*, on believing that mathematical values obtain independently of human decision, which is philosophically controversial. Short of this, the legislature does arguably have the power to "declare" truth in the sense of officially recognizing something whose truth is independent of legislative action. We do accept legislative declaration on other occasions, e.g. the truth of the equality of males and females, the sanctity of a human life, the superiority of science to magic, etc. We may deny the legislature the power to be the primary agent of such truth, its sole authority. But if the legislature merely announces and codifies, for public and governmental and educational purposes, a truth it neither manufactures, nor over which it is the ultimate authority, then it can indeed "declare" truth.

All this points, I think, to a last and fundamental belief: we believe that mathematical truth is something to be determined by mathematicians. Unlike premodern, theocratic, and totalitarian polities we accept a division of labor that narrows the political task. Politics may presume and may apply scientific or mathematical truth, but it is not its job to establish that truth, to wade into disagreements among mathematicians or physicists or art critics. Truth-authority, the authority over truth, belongs to distinctive groups, not to government. What lies behind the perception of absurdity in the Indiana case is a specifically modern view of the separation of norms, like truth, goodness, justice, beauty, etc., such that particular non-governmental social institutions – professional organizations of scientists and inquirers – are uniquely responsible for such truths.

Is Truth Anti-Political?

Certainly there is a view that denies the divergence of truth or inquiry from the right kind of politics. One may say it is the dominant, although not the sole, legacy of the Enlightenment to see truth as a friend both to social progress and to the public life of a free society. John Stuart Mill, John Dewey, and Jürgen Habermas are at one in holding both that the search for truth leads to liberal republicanism, and that liberal society is the proper home for the search for truth. All believe that a community of inquirers must, after all, proceed by roughly liberal principles, principles that allow open and inclusive debate among equally respected members in order to attain true agreement. One could almost say that "promodernism," the defense of the Enlightenment in contemporary discussion of modernity, is this very position, which understands freedom and inquiry as natural partners in social progress.

Less familiar are those liberal and democratic theorists who articulate, not the fear that political power will colonize the groves of truth and inquiry, but the contrary fear that truth or philosophy will subjugate the political forum. Benjamin Barber, in promoting his notion of "strong democracy," claims that politics is circumscribed by the condition of the necessity of public choice "in the absence of private or independent grounds for judgment."[16] This formulation means that the "ultimate political problem is one of action, not Truth . . ." Politics is, he writes, "the search for reasonable choices . . . choices that are something less than arbitrary even though they cannot be perfectly Right or True or Scientific."[17] More forcefully, "Politics concerns itself only with those realms where truth is not – or is not yet – known. . . . Where consensus stops, politics starts."[18] Barber here is reminiscent of Rorty, who follows the Pyrrhonic tradition in believing that philosophical skepticism is in fact morally superior to foundationalism, as discussed by David Hiley.[19] Likewise, contemporary political postmodernism, in the work of William Connolly and Bonnie Honig, suggests that the philosophy of politics as normally practised is an attempt to tame politics, that philosophically "founding" or "grounding" the political in effect colonizes the political.[20] If, after all, philosophers decide that Reason by itself demands and justifies what the *polis* ought to do, then all forms of citizen debate ought to be superfluous.[21] Any reference to nature, natural law, *archē*, *telos* or principle is a decision to shut down decision, and for these writers, actually undermines the normative human sphere, which is located in a contentious struggle. They accept with Barber that politics is to be "epistemologically autonomous" of philosophy, a kind of "knowledge" that is provisional, artificial and non-representational. The implication is clear: there is something *authoritarian* about truth.

Just what are the differences between politics and inquiry into truth? In the order of truth or inquiry, no value is ascribed to recalcitrant, idiosyncratic, or false views, except in so far as they serve as spurs to further inquiry, foils that stimulate the achievement of truth. In inquiry the false opinion has only a hypothetical and consequentialist value, if it eventually leads to truth. In democratic politics, views can be honored independently of their truth-value; we often say that diversity of opinions is valuable in itself.

Compromise is a crucial political process and virtue. Not that there must be compromise on everything. One could perhaps say that *normal* politics, on analogy with Thomas Kuhn's "normal science," is all about compromise, whereas extra-normal politics, *revolutionary* politics, is the attempt to change the rules within which compromise is arrived at. But revolutionary politics is full of compromise too, even if only among the revolutionaries. Compromise is at the heart of politics; it keeps the ship afloat. But compromise has *no* place in inquiry. In a convention of cosmologists, the disagreement between one group that thinks the universe is ten billion years old, and other that has discovered evidence they believe to show the universe is fourteen billion years old, will not be resolved by accepting a compromise of twelve billion.

As touched on earlier, the bar of cognitive acceptance is placed differently in politics and inquiry. It can be a virtue in theoretical discussion to adopt a stance of skepticism regarding a question, to decide that all options for belief are, at the time being at least, inadequate, and to withhold assent. A witty and insightful essay that debunks a position and leaves us with a theoretical *aporia* is in philosophy a welcome addition. But *aporia in practice* simply returns us to the status quo. In politics, this can be a vice. To fail to make the leap of faith, to fail to judge, hence act, in an atmosphere of uncertainty may sometimes be a great evil. In theoretical decision, it almost never is, or, whether it is will be a controversial matter. But there is no controversy on this matter in politics: to say "I don't know yet, I am waiting for more evidence," can in politics be the height of irresponsibility. The obligations of political and theoretical decision are very different.

History plays a distinctive role in politics. Michael Walzer writes that philosophy – or I would rather say, the kind of philosophy that Oakeshott called rationalism – is particularly unhappy with the historical nature of politics. Political conditions are the result of an historical hodgepodge, where it is not clear that any one principle rules, where policy X is now dominant because a century ago Y was favored by group A, and Z by group B, then Q compromised with R, then the war came, then . . . etc. At the end of an historical process of compromise and accident, the philosopher turns his or her attention to the normative question that "should have" been asked at the beginning of the process, and is, from the philosophic viewpoint, still the only question: is policy X right? Walzer argues that this ahistorical philosophical approach is incompatible with politics, especially democratic politics, which must honor the history of contingencies and compromises that constituted the present.

For democracy makes will, not reason, the basis of political authority. Whereas the philosopher is committed to the view that it is never right to do wrong, democracy is committed to the view that the people have the *right to act wrongly*. Walzer criticizes philosophers who try to make democracy more palatable to the logic of philosophy. One way is by emphasizing the role of the judiciary – the Supreme Court in particular is the closest thing in American public life to a philosophical discussion that has power. The creation of "rights" in particular is a way to limit democracy through the judiciary. Walzer responds, "As soon as the philosophical list of rights extends beyond the twin bans on legal discrimination and political repression, it invites judicial activity that is radically intrusive on what might be called democratic space."[22] A second way is to employ fictions like "ideal speech situations" and "original positions" (Habermas and Rawls) to try to discipline the popular will into a more philosophical form. These strategies are part of the philosopher's attempt "to capture the city."

Connected to its distrust of the historical nature of political validity, philosophy as it is usually performed fails to respect the particularity of a given *polis*. The universalist philosopher seeks a validity independent of membership, the validity of the "outsider" meant to apply to all polities. Walzer accepts that Wittgenstein correctly exhibited the implications of the "heroic," "outsider" view of the philosopher when he wrote that the philosopher belongs to no community, and *that* is what makes him a philosopher.[23] Walzer responds that this is also what makes him unfit to give political advice, for only an insider can give advice to the inside; a knowledge that can only be found outside this particular place "yields no rights inside."[24] Walzer's alternative role is the "particularist" or "inside" philosopher, the philosopher who accepts the sovereignty and the form of his or her political community. The philosopher must make herself "a fellow citizen," make herself "local," if he or she is to have anything to say to fellow citizens. This means "forsaking the prerogatives of distance."

There are, of course, limits to the virtue of partiality; not all partiality is good. But partiality is a necessary, if not sufficient, condition for the legitimacy of political advice, whereas for inquiry particularity and partiality are dangers, threats to truth. For many philosophers reflecting on what is true or false, considerations of time, place, role, and status are supposed to disappear – not, to be sure, as characteristics of the *object* of study, but rather as characteristics of the *inquirer* and his or her inquiry. The philosopher debates with Confucius and Quine, Plato and Gandhi, Nietzsche and Maimonides, as equals and contemporaries. Even without the foundationalist aims of traditional, "perennial" philosophy, which are now under suspicion, the contemporary philosopher who announces that the results of her inquiry are meant only to be valid for her locale, country, or philosophical school invites irrelevance. Richard Rorty's critique of foundationalism leads him to say that our cognitive picture of the world may rightly be ethnocentric or conventionalist, but he does *not* say that the critique on which it is based is only valid for Americans, or Westerners, hence would not hold as a critique of, for example, the metaphysics of non-dualist Vedanta.

We might add that another disparity between inquiry and politics is that the political sphere is intrinsically *procedural*. This may seem at odds with my critique of proceduralism, but it is not. My point has been that politics cannot be *solely* procedural, as liberal proceduralism would have it. But politics is indeed partly procedural, that is, it concerns what is the proper way for a society to make a decision. Whatever else it is, politics is the endorsement of a method and agency of judgment. Consequently, as a citizen I may accept a policy I believe to be wrong as nonetheless *politically valid* if I accept the constitutional authority and process that legitimates it. This is distinct from the merely prudential or pragmatic advisability of obedience. Hence there is always the possibility of objecting on grounds of truth or rightness to the result while nevertheless accepting its binding nature. In politics I can judge to be "right" – legitimately binding – what I judge to be "wrong" – a policy I disagree with. Thus politics is normatively doubled; the norm of rightness applies twice – and potentially in contrary ways – to a political judgment, once to its process and a second time to its claim or goal or effect.

Now, one may object that scientific inquiry also endorses a "method" or process. This is true; inquiry is, in the broadest possible sense, a method. But *truth* is not. Truth norms the method's *output*. The only virtue the method claims is its likelihood of achieving true output; only as goal can we say that truth norms the process.[25] Consequently, while inquirer and citizen each have a method, the relation of method or process to outcome is different. The inquirer's aim is truth, toward which inquiry is his or her chosen method, and the method has *no value* independent of the promise of eventually achieving the truth. Truth is valued for its own sake; inquiry is not.[26] But in politics the method has value and validity even if the outcome is wrong. A polity unable to organize or enforce compliance around what will eventually be shown to be bad and false decisions is in trouble. Of course, the independence of the value of the procedure is not absolute; bad choices result in bad effects, and enough of them, or a sufficiently bad choice in a crisis, will undermine the polity. Being right matters in politics *and* in inquiry. But the rightness of a decision-procedure in politics also matters.

The contrast of politics and inquiry, especially philosophy, is not the product of contemporary anti-foundationalism or postmodernism; it is an old story, one we have already heard in Oakeshott's critique of political rationalism. Oakeshott's view, along with that of Hans-Georg Gadamer and Leo Strauss, reflect the Aristotelian distinction between theoretical and practical reason. For Aristotle *phronesis* or practical wisdom and *theoria* or theoretical reason differ in aim – goodness versus truth – in method, and in legitimate criteria of adequacy. In a related vein, the Scottish Enlightenment thinkers accepted that the ultimate source of social virtue is pre-theoretical, partial, or sentimental, something that cannot be captured by or derived from the principles that theoretical reason might hope to achieve, and indeed, may be harmed by any such attempt. Our moral life is rooted in parts of our nature that fund and are recalcitrant to the glare of reason; too much light may kill the plant. As Charles Griswold recently noted in his analysis of Adam Smith's complex moral method, the moral theorist must inquire, as an impractical observer, into our pre-philosophical moral sentiments which cannot be philosophically justified, while not undercutting them as "the main source of light," at the same time embodying and encouraging the virtues in his readers as a practical, partisan participant.[27] The theorist must face the dilemma that his or her work can be threatening to the source of virtue which it hopes to enlighten and preserve.

The modern age exacerbates the problem. On the one hand, as Weber and others have argued, modern cultures differentiate inquiry and truth from other social concerns. Modernity renders dubious the status of any context that would integrate these value-spheres; this rendering is apparently the condition of our rationality and our progress. As Weber suggested, like the gods of a polytheistic religion, they battle for supremacy. At the same time, the explosion of scientific knowledge provides enormous power to political institutions. Thus government funds science. Cognitive advance is politically required. This spills into all of our discourse; we often employ a cognitive style akin to scientific inquiry in our public discussion of political, moral, and aesthetic questions. Ours is, in historical terms, a highly educated and literate polity.

What can be said is that there are particular traditions or schools of thought about inquiry, truth and reason, which since the Enlightenment have tended to make the complex relation of truth and politics intractable. First, there is *cosmopolitanism*, the view that the ultimate norms of human life, and truth in particular, are the same everywhere on Earth, thus inquiry and moral norms ought to be independent of locale, class, status, etc. The enemy of the good life and social progress is prejudice, partiality, and tradition. The urge to achieve truth can be interpreted through the "prerogative of distance." The notion is that prejudice, rooted in involvement, veils the truth, is a smudge on the "mirror of nature." It is this "prejudice against prejudice" that Gadamer criticized, this partiality against partiality, that Walzer rejected above.[28] Second, there is *rationalism*, which accepts the rightful determination of practical decision by theoretical reason. This is distinct from the ancient Greek view that *theoria* is superior to the political life. Here I refer to the attempt of theoretical reason to arrive at formulae that hold without exception for ethics and politics, as in mathematics or physics. The good society is designed according to principle, hence explainable and controllable. This is the supremacy of single-stranded inquiry, "Reason."[29] Third and last is what we could call *democratic scientism*, the Enlightenment model of inquiry, characteristic of Mill, Dewey, and Habermas, according to which relations among members of the scientific community are characterized by toleration, equality, and liberty. From this perspective, science is not only continuous with, it is a *model for*, the good *polis*.

These three components of the modern tradition do indeed tyrannize the political with the philosophical. They are inadequate views of political life,

and do not help us in our political tasks. Regarding rationalism and cosmopolitanism, the whole of this volume has been an argument against
them, although their mistakes are of different orders. Cosmopolitanism is
politically viable, that is, it is a legitimate political view, but a bad one. Ironically, cosmopolitanism fails in its epistemology and its anthropology, and
hence its politics; it is a faulty account of the *cognitive* mission and method
of political life. Rationalism however violates politics *per se*; as we have seen,
it attempts to substitute mathematics or engineering for politics. Democratic scientism is at once the most naive and the least politically objectionable
of the three; it is actually a social view, although it is based in an analysis
of a sub-society of a very peculiar type. To presuppose the scientific community as a model for the messy world of politics, where all kinds of
decision may be called for and any value-consideration may come up, is
no more or less parochial than to propose a *monastic community* as the
model for the polity. Society is not a community of inquirers. Such a community would not be a *polis* at all, and would not face the problems of a
polis, rooted as they are in the project of plural persons trying to live
together well, rather than, as Peirce rightly said of the aim of inquirers, to
converge.

But the Mill–Dewey-Habermas position will not go gently. It regroups for
one last stand. It is possible to make a strong argument for the real social-
political advantages of importing theoretical reason into the *polis* on the
latter's *own* terms. That is, *the political realm might vote for the supremacy of
the theoretical.* Hasn't it been shown to be the height of political or social
reason to make way, to yield, at least somewhat, to theoretical reason? Is
this not the great achievement of Enlightened civilization? Doesn't every
child of religious parents who surfs the net and watches MTV show this?
That is, people are in fact today voting with, if not their feet, then with their
keyboards, for the scientifically-and-truth-governed society and its combined benefits of technological–material progress and personal liberty.

My modern conservative retort is that the modern *polis* has indeed discovered the political advantages of the relative autonomy of truth, hence
its ongoing responsibility to truth and inquiry. But this can be honored
without idolizing inquiry, without taking inquiry to replace politics and
social norms. A modern conservatism accepts the primacy of practical
reason, or better, the dependence of Reason itself on social conditions. That
Reason, the child of social–practical life, comes to oppose its birthright
generates a permanent familial tension. Conservatives accept the necessity
of living with this tension, of giving to Caesar what is Caesar's and to
Socrates what is Socrates'. For the conservative never expected consistency
from life. *Theoria* must recognize its dialectical relation to the *polis*, hence its

limited dependence on the latter. One may say that here Zion outweighs Athens, that the Judeo-Christian portion of our tradition is qualifying the Greek supremacy of contemplation, but in fact each of these strands has acknowledged the dialectic of truth and goodness in its complex history. A particularly famous example of that recognition follows.

The Noble Lie

One aspect of the question of truth in the *polis* is nicely summarized by a reference to Plato's *Republic*: Is the noble lie necessary? We must acknowledge that the existence of any such issue hinges on one's view of inquiry as well as politics. If one believes that inquiry, or philosophy, or science, or theoretical wisdom, by nature culminates either in beliefs that are antithetical to the conditions necessary to a good *polis* or in a denial of beliefs necessary to a good *polis*, then and only then does it become necessary to face the question of whether the *polis* ought to be protected from inquiry, whether what is from the viewpoint of inquiry a lie ought to be promulgated in the *polis*. In twentieth-century political theory this question is associated above all with the work of Leo Strauss.

In *Persecution and the Art of Writing* Strauss famously argued that many important philosophers, from Plato through Hobbes, wrote in such a way as to hide their full meaning from most readers, due to constraints on freedom of expression.[30] This led Strauss to careful and, for many philosophers, frustratingly complex readings which paid attention to the dramatic setting and form of such writings. In the most prominent case, the simple question, Why did Plato write dialogues?, led to the hypothesis that the character of Socrates cannot in the dialogues be regarded as a simple mouthpiece for Plato's views. In a Wittgensteinian figure, Plato wrote dialogues to *show* what he could not straightforwardly *say*. The Straussian distinction of an "esoteric" and "exoteric" layer of the work of pre-eighteenth century writers has been disturbing to many philosophers, as was the possibility that Strauss himself was disguising his "esoteric" views behind an exoteric writing.

But Strauss' view is deeper than this. The esoteric–exoteric distinction was the expression of a philosophical and not merely hermeneutic problem, the conflict, again, of *theoria* and *phronesis*, philosophy and politics. For Strauss philosophy's ideal search for the truth about the whole is incapable of satisfaction; he believed philosophy is *zetetic*, that it ends in uncertainty. It nevertheless is, and here is Strauss' classicism, the highest of human occupations. In his account the ancient and medieval writers of the "Great

Tradition," practitioners of "classical," as opposed to modern, rationalism, recognized that social goodness, ethics, politics, and religion were undermined by such *theoria* for all who were not philosophers by nature, that is, those who did not gain moral strength from this unending search, but rather were morally weakened by it.[31] The philosophers of the Great Tradition consequently sought to protect themselves from society *and* to protect society from themselves. They recognized the conflict of political goodness and philosophy, real virtue and ideal knowledge, and the constraints each must accept to live together. Part of the insight of the philosophical attempt to grasp the whole is that it is in conflict with at least one of its parts, politics. Ultimacy must respect the rights of the non-ultimate, the urge to truth must recognize the *truth of the importance of the untrue*. Totalitarianism, for Strauss, comes from the attempt to merge ideal and real, to create the philosophical "republic."[32]

We can take a more modest and concretely political version of the Straussian argument. As noted earlier, William Galston argues that philosophical education is in conflict with civic education.[33] The function of public education, in so far as it is civic, is to inculcate the habits necessary for civic life in a liberal society. This includes the use of "noble, moralizing history," and the suppression – at primary and secondary school levels – of revisionist histories of, for example, the American Founders. Galston's point is that civic education should be independent of philosophy; its job is not to train future Ph.D.s or social critics. "Critical thinking" is an ambiguous virtue in liberal democracies, just as in other polities, for Galston accepts that we have no philosophically adequate justification of the ultimate commitments of liberal democracy. Rights, equality, and popular sovereignty would fall before the scythe of critical thinking just as would the principles of theocratic or authoritarian regimes. We should, he suggests, admit this and the finitude of our aims in educating our fellow citizens. Philosophical education, education unyoked from civic concerns, is to be permitted but not required.

A related point was made in the controversy surrounding the crucial Supreme Court decision in *Wisconsin v. Yoder* (1972), a case which has been called America's leading "legal hymn to pluralism."[34] In it the Court decided not to require Amish parents to send their children to public schools. The Amish argued on the grounds of freedom of religion; Wisconsin argued on the grounds both of the state's interest in future citizens and the children's future interests. Warren Burger's majority opinion affirmed that the Amish in fact educated their children to achieve the state's substantive aims of producing hard-working, lawful citizens. But Justice Douglas argued in dissent that the children's liberty was thereby abused, that their future opportunity to make a "free" choice among life-options was hampered by the inculcation of their parents' worldview. For Douglas the state had an interest in children being educated to "diversity," hence freedom. Many have commented on this case, but of particular relevance is Christopher Lasch's criticism of Douglas' dissent. Douglas' response was, for Lasch,

> a classic example of the sentimentality of liberal humanitarianism, which invokes "diversity" to support a system of uniform compulsory schooling and proposes to rescue the child from the backward culture of his parents by delivering him into the tender care of the state. . . . [it assumes] that the state can spare the child who does decide to break from his parents' traditions the pain, suffering, and guilt that such a break necessarily exacts – the confrontation with which, however, constitutes the psychological and educative value of such an experience.[35]

Expanding on Lasch, I would say that in Yoder the court made the right decision for the wrong reasons, and Douglas raised the right question but took the wrong side. The Court was right to permit the Amish to educate their children, not because that education in fact serves legitimate state interest – although it does matter that their education did not *violate* such interest – nor because the state should be neutral and permissive, but because the state has a legitimate interest both in family and moral tradition, on the one hand, and diversity on the other. America is, in short, served by the strength of Amish community. Douglas raised the right question, of whether the values embodied in Amish education are conformable to what he regarded as the values of the American polity. But his notion of the latter was misguided. For he makes the primary value to be served by civic education the moral emptiness of the person, the absence of strong commitment, the lack of constitutive community. In contrast, as Galston writes, "the greatest threat to children in modern liberal societies is not that they will believe in something too deeply, but that they will believe in nothing very deeply at all."[36]

The belief in the necessity of the noble lie hinges on three claims, one about philosophy, one about citizenship, one about the relation of the two. First is that philosophy is ultimately skeptical. For complex reasons that cannot be given here, I believe this is correct: inquiry when pursued ultimately leads away from any conclusive validation of value principles.[37] The second is that the imaginative requirements of good citizenship include ultimate beliefs, that is, beliefs about the final validity of the practices of one's society, or what Lyotard called their "metanarrative" justification. I think this is right too, although within certain limits to be explored shortly.

Third is that the skepticism of the few will have an impact on the many, or more generally, that theoretical skepticism is a danger to practical wisdom.

This is the problematic claim. *Phronesis* is not incompatible with theoretical skepticism or relativism. To believe otherwise is to give too much credit to philosophy, to fail to see that philosophy may, in its very skepticism, recognize its own limits or bounds and the need for a *phronesis* that transcends *theoria*. Philosophy can recognize that – insofar as it pursues the end of truth without heed to the other ends of human query or production – it is, in a different use of the Wittgensteinian phrase, "a wheel that plays no role in the mechanism." In other words, to believe the *skepsis* of *theoria* must undermine the *phronesis* of *praxis* is already to presuppose that *phronesis* is somehow based in *theoria*.

The philosophical–political problem is usually formulated as the disjunction between citizens or statesmen and philosophers, between those whose practices manifest ultimate beliefs and those whose entertain a certain internal skepticism. But this disjunction occurs *within the philosopher's life as well*, between the philosopher *qua* philosopher and the philosopher *qua* citizen, moral actor, human being. The philosopher, after all, loves, strives, hates, obeys the laws, etc., just like everyone else. It is not a question of the philosopher versus the *polis*, but of *theoria* versus all other components of human experience and activity, which, to employ a classical categorization, means *theoria* versus *poiesis* or making, *praxis* or doing, and the wisdom which attempts to manage the relation among *theoria*, *poiesis*, and *praxis*.

What is the source of this *skepsis*, or hidden knowledge of the absence of knowledge, that the philosopher has? It is the release of inquiry from practical aims to *theoria* of the whole. If we may say for the moment that the norms of validity to which human judgments aspire are truth, goodness or success, and beauty, the respective norms for cognitive, practical, and aesthetic judgments, then *omnivalence* refers to the fusion of the three, or non-differentiated validity. Judgments intended to be valid indifferently with respect to the norms of truth, goodness, and beauty are omnivalent. Premodern thought is characteristically omnivalent. Cultural progress, especially in modernity, entails the differentation of these norms; what Weber called "rationalization" certainly hangs on a progressive differentiation of validity. The separation of *praxis* from truth is comparable to the release of *poiesis* from practical or scientific aims, or *praxis* from aesthetic aims. That is, what makes philosophy a threat both to the *polis* and to the practical unity of the philosopher's own life would be true of *any* of the fundamental aims of human activity, abstracted from all others, hence released from all external constraint, or, what is the same thing, released from the governance of *phronesis*. The "divine madness," or erotic dimension of *theoria*, its willingness to burst all bounds, is fueled in the same way as the erotic or "mad" expansions of *praxis* or *poiesis* toward the unencumbered and total possession of Success or the Good, or the Beautiful or Sublime.

Fortunately, omnivalence makes cowards of us all, most of the time. The philosophical skeptic still steps out of the way of the runaway truck, fights against totalitarianism and lawlessness to preserve the liberal republican regime he cannot justify, tries to get her children enrolled in the good school which teaches ideas she ultimately doubts, etc. But, also fortunately, a few exceptions assert themselves, for, as noted earlier, progress in human society is often the doing of "unreasonable" persons who are willing to accede to the demands of one ultimate value at the expense of all others. This is not a problem as long as it takes place within limits, as long as we can usually keep them from destroying us. Recalcitrant geniuses are welcome, especially after they are dead. The purifications of human ends or concerns, the assertion of the supremacy of truth or goodness or beauty over the other two, is acceptable in human society as long as it does not try to actualize itself across the polity. To repeat Nietzsche's remark, and it should be repeated again and again: "There are actually some things to be said in favor of the exception, as long as it does not try to become the rule . . ."

The Straussian error is an over-valuation of philosophy and its role. In making philosophy a threat to moral order it regards philosophical beliefs as the basis, the foundation, of moral and social order. It excessively cognitivizes, intellectualizes, the basis of social life. One must add here that if philosophy is skeptical then it must be skeptical about, among other things, the value of philosophy. To regard philosophy as the ultimate human endeavor is a judgment which is incapable of philosophical demonstration. The dogmatic assertion of its superiority is deeply unphilosophical. As a form of faith it is no worse and, probably, better than, many others. But philosophy isn't faith. I am suggesting that Strauss, who more than any twentieth-century thinker was sensitive to the claims that practice can make against philosophy, nevertheless, in his endorsement of the ultimate value of the philosophical life, betrayed a conception of *theoria* as the foundation of *praxis*.

But, as the Scottish tradition argued, practice does not rest on theory. Philosophical beliefs articulate and culminate the values embedded in social practices in a certain register, a kind of language, namely the conceptual. It may indeed be true that modern society, especially in its contemporary, or as some would have it, postmodern version, makes these culminations unavailable or ineffective. That would indeed be a significant fact. But the absence of a cognitive *summation* of the values of social practices is not the same as the absence of a *basis* for such practices and their values. To believe otherwise is to engage in what Oakeshott called rationalism, to make theory unambiguously the basis of practice.

So, is the noble lie, or more broadly, *myth* necessary for the modern liberal republican *polis?* As indicated in chapter 4, I would argue that myth is compatible with but not necessary to our political order. Myth is an expression of, a coagulated and articulated form of, the commitments and modes of interpretation embedded in social practices. To make myth necessary is to endorse the view that a highly specific narrative, as suggested earlier, a particular "name of God," is required for moral life. This puts the cart before the horse. Myth is the product of social and cultural life, the cognitive expression of a form of life, not a set of beliefs that makes social and cultural life possible. Failure to assert an official myth, or any myth, is compatible with continuing the dominant practices of society. The absence of myth does not *undercut* our social life. Rather it *unhinges* it, makes it less internally coherent, puts a certain level of its cognitive system at odds with its form of life. It is thus entirely reasonable for a liberal republican society, conservatively understood, to regard myth as a respectable contributor to its structure among others without regarding it is as the linchpin of social order.

What would not be an exaggeration, however, is to insist that *faith*, the commitment to what cognition cannot validate, is crucial to modern liberal republican polities. Faith is a name for the emotional commitment to the furtherance of life. This faith sometimes voices itself in a narrative, that is, a myth, but the faith, the felt commitment, is more essential than the myth. We may not need, in Dewey's phrase, a "common faith," but we commonly need faith. And in fact few human beings lack this faith. No special indoctrination on the part of governments or philosophers is required to ensure that most people sustain sufficient faith to continue living, to raise their children, to find things to hope for. The liberal republican societies, like all others, need faith, or faiths, but not agreement on the name of God.

Berlin famously ended his essay on the two concepts of liberty by quoting Joseph Schumpeter's remark that "To realize the relative validity of one's convictions and yet stand for them unflinchingly, is what distinguishes a civilized man from a barbarian."[38] Rorty quotes this remark approvingly as an expression of what he considers an "ironic" stance.[39] In a Kantian vein Berlin allowed that to desire more certainty and unity is deeply human, but to permit such desire to guide one's practice is political immaturity. Still, we must worry, as Gellner wondered, that while men will indeed die for their faith, will they die for their "faith," that is, for what they recognize to be a hypothetical self-construction, a heuristic?[40] Why should they die for an "as if," given that their deaths are not "as if," but *as is*? To be willing to stand unflinchingly, to be willing to die for, beliefs one takes to be only "relatively" valid may indeed be the mark of a certain liberal–rational version of the "civilized man." However, keeping in mind Samuel Butler's remark, which inspired Charles Peirce's pragmatism, that belief is that on which one is prepared to act, the distinction between acting or dying without irony, and doing so with ironic distance or a recognition of relativity, seems rather precious. In this matter I would side with the pragmatists and the existentialists: the proof of the spiritual pudding is in action, and the significance of a distinction too profound to find expression in action is dubious. I suggest an alternative to the Schumpeter–Berlin–Rorty line: To be willing to die for beliefs is *by definition* to take them to be *absolutely* valid. Thus, to stand unflinchingly for one's beliefs, and nevertheless to tolerate with civility those who reject them, is the true mark of the civilized *believer*, which is to say, the faithful citizen.

The Place of Political Theory

As we have seen in this chapter, there is something odd about a *theoria* of *politikē*. The political theorist or political philosopher lives a divided life, obligated to *polis* and *theoria*. The conflict is implicit in the distinction between political validity and truth. Further, if multi-stranded rationality is typical of premodern societies, and if multi-strandedness in effect means, as I have suggested, the supremacy of the social, then this problem arises wherever truth or inquiry or morality or artistic value are claimed to be autonomous from social norms. There is inherent in the modern condition, which gives greater autonomy to inquiry and truth, a discomfort stemming from the fact that we must make and abide by political decisions, especially in a democracy, which cannot be validated as "true" by an autonomous inquiry that is recognized to be independent of social tradition. If we say the political decision is valid because it is the will of the people, expresses their preferences, or survives their political procedures, then we are uttering what is for us a tautology: such is political validity. Yet we also recognize inquiry or science as in some sense the standard of truth, whose results, however dynamic and changeable, nevertheless form our official picture of reality (if one that under-determines life's choices).

Theory, of any kind, seeks truth, and does so through inquiry. Political theory is no exception. Now, the philosophical vetting of a position as true, meaning justifiable by rational inquiry, would seem to short-circuit the political process. At least, it must *want* to do so. There is something bizarre about a political theorist trying to answer all the questions that the *polis* may need to answer while simultaneously endorsing democracy. This becomes most obvious in what we could call *constitutional politics*. I refer not to any particular way of interpreting the constitution, but rather to the habit of turning to the constitution as the desideratum of virtually all current political issues. To claim a policy's rightness on constitutional grounds is to insist that the nature of the *polis*, its identity, its form of life, dictates the policy. Hence it is to claim that no *phronesis* is required, no balancing of legitimate goods, no steering among inherited values, is necessary. In effect, this means no politics is required, but merely the application of rules or the unfolding of the collective identity embodied in the constitution. This style is tempting to the theorist, since a constitution – particularly, as in the American case, a written constitution – can serve to provide secure foundations, that is, justification, with which the theorist is always concerned. The political philosopher is often very at home in the constitutional style of politics.

Given the understanding of politics presented herein, the political theorist ought be wary of such habits. This does not mean that constitutional rules and the nature of the polity can be absent from political debate; political decisions always imply some sense of who or what the polity is. But such decisions are not simply to be read off that constitution or that identity.[41] The endorsement of democracy requires that on occasion the political theorist, asked for his or her conclusion regarding a contentious issue, respond by saying, "Whatever the polity decides." The theorist as citizen may of course encourage fellow citizens to balance inherited values in a particular way, to come to see a particular course as the embodiment of practical wisdom. But to assert that rightness or wrongness is *never* dependent on political will or decision-making or the current balance of interests is to deny the validity of democratic politics *per se*.

Thus the political theorist is condemned to straddle a fence. Her bivalent identity suggests that two warnings ought to be posted on the door to political theory.[42] The first is: *Beware the hegemony of politics*, which would renounce forms of validity that escape political determination, and subject all of social and cultural life to the rules of politics. Politics must recognize its embeddedness in a social tradition, and its vulnerability to the manifold values and norms of that tradition, including truth as sought by inquiry. But the second is: *Beware the hegemony of truth*, the attempt by inquiry to dictate the principles of politics, and through them, to de-legitimate extant forms of social life. The notion of civil society has built into it the refusal to merge the norms of validity, truth, goodness, and beauty.

This may sound like I am endorsing, at one level, liberal toleration, or more deeply, the modernist differentiation of spheres, or perhaps even postmodernism. Each would be partly true. Toleration is a crucial part of the modern North Atlantic tradition, for conservatives and liberals, and differentiation is intrinsic to modernity and to what is called the "postmodern" condition. But I am suggesting something more problematic: the need for *both* respect for the differentiation of norms *and* the desire for unity. A value-pluralism which leaves each sphere of social life solely obligated to its distinctive norm is not tolerant either. That was the mistake of the neutralist segregation of politics and culture. Differentiation without the urge to relation or mediation leaves each context *tyrant in its own house*. The tendency of rational differentiation is to divide life and society into distinct contexts whose constitutive rules determine all behavior within; freedom then becomes solely the freedom to enter or exit. In contrast, a *balanced* pluralism combines the differentiation of spheres with the drive to synthesize, relate, and violate such differentiation. Hence each field is determined by at least two forces, centrifugal *and* centripetal. The centripetal drive is essential to modern rationalization and progress. The centrifugal drive to synthesize the diverse value spheres of human life is a faith in the ultimate omnivalence, the fusion of the true, good and beautiful. This faith is the necessary discipline for each sphere, the spur that keeps us from resting content with a goodness that is not true, a beauty that is not good, or a truth that is neither; or more to the current point, with a political validity that violates truth or moral goodness, or a morality or a cognitive picture that makes politics obsolete. Without the centrifugal drive, each would deny the need to moderate its claims in its own sphere.[43]

This means that, while we can inquire into the validity of political systems as much as we like, we cannot assume that what inquiry cannot validate ought to be dismantled. Nor can we hold up our lives to wait for the kind of ultimate knowledge we seek as philosophers. This is as true for the individual as for the polity: we must decide in advance of the knowledge, necessary for knowingly choosing aright, that can only come after the experience decision will unlock. As Milan Kundera once wrote, the problem with life is that it is not a repeatable experiment: ideally we ought to be able to go through for a trial run before doing it for real.[44] Sadly this is not the case; we don't get to practise living before it counts. Neither can we run through political history first and see how it ends before doing it. The real is not the ideal, and so we must in effect chose not only *avant le connaissance*, but often *avant la lettre*, before we can even name what, in later hindsight, we will know to have been crucial to our decision.

To ask more than this would be to ask that the decision as to the political good be dependent on answering *the* ultimate question of philosophy, What is the whole? Now, in a sense it is legitimate to say that, absent the answer to that question, *theoria* must remain discomfited in political life, recognizing its political commitments as only hypothetically valid. But one may say, again from the viewpoint of a *theoria* that recognizes its own incompleteness, that the good political life is attainable nonetheless, even given this infirmity. It is this recognition that is embodied in civil society. Alasdair MacIntyre once wrote that the good life for man is the life spent searching for the good life for man.[45] I would rephrase this to apply to politics: *the good political life for humanity is the life that is good for those who are still searching for what the good life for humanity is.* That means both a society which aims for the Good – which rejects the neutralist assumption that the search for the Good is irrelevant to political life – and which recognizes its inability adequately to state what that good life is – hence a civil society of finite creatures trying to live together while always guided by an incomplete vision.

So, purged of rationalist *hubris*, the philosopher's search ought to recognize its own embeddedness in the whole. But the discomfort rightly remains. For philosophy's role in that whole is to seek to represent the whole, committed as it is to the view that true judgments of the parts may well hang on that vision, that only in reference to the context of contexts could we *reliably* decide the proper limits of each context. That ultimate referent would be God, or if one prefers a cooler language, "Being," or "the Good," or "the Event," or "the Unnameable," etc. Whatever one calls it, for the conservative it *is* but *is unspeakable* except in the form of myth which itself is omnivalent, thus incapable of reduction to inquiry or politics or poetry and the rationalization such reduction would permit. With this fallible and incomplete statement of what seems to be true about our predicament the modern conservative must be content to rest.

Notes

1   We have already opened this question in the critique of "rationalist" political theory for failing to understand the place of theory in political life. In what follows we will not engage the deeper philosophical question of whether truth and politics are fundamentally related. There are historical and etymological connections between, for example, "justification" and "justice," implying that our conception of truth may already presuppose a moral-political conception of what is "owed," as Nietzsche claimed, and as Heidegger explored in "The Anaximander Fragment." Interesting though this may be, my concern is at a different level.

2   I have argued elsewhere that this pragmatic, comparative, or "vindicatory" form of validation is not inescapable (see my *The Ends of Philosophy*). In theo-

retical philosophy we might reject it (as I have), but it is arguable that it is more defensible in practical philosophy – e.g. ethics and politics. I will assume that here, without argument.

3　See, for example, Shklar's *Ordinary Vices*.

4　Brian Barry, "How Not to Defend Liberal Institutions," in R. Bruce Douglass, *Liberalism and the Good*.

5　As a pro-life advocate – a philosophy professor no less – once said to me, if you accept that the fetus is fully human and that abortion is the murder of the most innocent and helpless victims, then no action, including violent action, aimed to prevent abortions is morally illegitimate. I happen not to agree with the premises, or that the conclusion *strictly* follows from the premises – some other possible views, including pacifism, would derail it – but given the premises the inference isn't incomprehensible.

6　See Richard Rorty, *Contingency, Irony, Solidarity*, and "Solidarity or Objectivity," in *Objectivity, Relativism, and Truth*.

7　It might appear that Rawls, in *Political Liberalism*, has taken the hint and offered, like Rorty, a "non"-justification of liberalism, making no attempt to convince non-liberals to be liberals. But he has, I have tried to show, done a bit more. He has tried to make the very essence of the political to imply liberalism; whatever diverges from liberal politics is a divergence from politics itself into the domain of the comprehensive. Nevertheless, since this view of politics is itself notoriously liberal, he has not actually expanded the circle.

8　Richard Rorty, *Essays on Heidegger and Others* (Cambridge: Cambridge University Press, 1991), p. 168.

9　The two are not unconnected. Rorty's conception of non-foundationalist philosophy as having its proper place in the "conversation of mankind" borrows from Oakeshott's essay "The Voice of Poetry in the Conversation of Mankind," in *Rationalism in Politics and Other Essays*.

10　See Alasdair MacIntyre, *Whose Justice? Which Rationality?* (Notre Dame: Notre Dame University Press, 1988).

11　See my *The Ends of Philosophy*, chapter four.

12　Hannah Arendt, "Truth and Politics," in *Between Past and Future: Eight Exercises in Political Thought* (New York: Viking, 1968).

13　Published documentation of this episode is based in three separate essays in the *Proceedings of the Indiana Academy of Science*, by C. A. Waldo ("What Might Have Been," 1916 volume, published 1917, pp. 445–6), Will Edington ("House Bill No. 246, Indiana State Legislature, 1897," Volume 45, 1936, pp. 206–10) and Arthur Hallerburg ("House Bill No. 246 Revisited," volume 84, 1974, pp. 374–99). It should be noted that Waldo, himself a principle in the affair, gives the wrong year for the episode (1899) in his brief account; Edington gives the essential facts pretty completely; and Hallerburg gives a full analysis, especially of Goodwin's background. My quotations are all from the Edington account. I have had to use these essays as sources for the newspaper accounts from the *Indianapolis Sentinel*, *Indianapolis News*, and *Indianapolis Journal* because of the condition of the extant microfilmed copies, with the exception of the Sunday Morning, February 21 issue of the *Indianapolis Journal* ("Squaring the Circle"). I thank David Lewis, Reference Librarian of the Indiana State Library, for all his help. The case, including its mathematical merits, or demerits, is also discussed in Petr Beckmann's *A History of* π (Boulder: Golem Press, 1977), pp. 174–7, and in Web postings by Mark Brader and Allan Adler at www.urbanlegends.com/legal/pi_indiana.

14 From Hallerberg, "House Bill Revisited," p. 391.

15 Ibid., p. 393.

16 Benjamin Barber, *Strong Democracy: Participatory Politics for a New Age*, p. 120.

17 Ibid., p. 127.

18 Ibid., p. 129.

19 See David Hiley, *Philosophy in Question: Essays on a Pyrrhonian Theme* (Chicago: University of Chicago Press, 1988), and my *The Ends of Philosophy*, chapter nine.

20 See for example William Connolly, *Identity\Difference: Democratic Negotiations of Political Paradox* (Ithaca: Cornell University Press, 1991), and Bonnie Honig, *Political Theory and the Displacement of Politics* (Ithaca: Cornell University Press, 1993).

21 See also Thomas Thorp's comparative study of the politics of Jacques Derrida and Jürgen Habermas, *Politology*, doctoral thesis, State University of New York at Stony Brook, 1992.

22 Michael Walzer, "Philosophy and Democracy," *Political Theory* 9, 3:379–99 (August 1981), p. 391.

23 Ludwig Wittgenstein, *Zettel*, trans. G. E. M. Anscombe (Berkeley and Los Angeles: University of California Press, 1970), remark 455.

24 One thinks here of the Talmudic rebuke to God Himself for interfering in a Rabbinical dispute, arguing that such matters have been ceded by God to the community for decision: "Whereupon a Heavenly Voice cried out: 'Why do ye dispute with R. Eliezer, seeing that in all matters the *halachah* agrees with him!' But R. Joshua arose and exclaimed: '*It is not in heaven*.' What did he mean by this? – Said R. Jeremiah: That the Torah had already been given at Mount Sinai; we pay no attention to a Heavenly Voice, because Thou hast long since written in the Torah at Mount Sinai, *After the majority must one incline*" (*Hebrew–English Edition of the Babylonian Talmud*, trans. H. Freedman, ed. J. Epstein [London: Soncino Press, 1962], Baba Mezi'a, vol. 17, Folio 59b) Walzer is no doubt familiar with this passage, although I do not know whether he had it in mind in the present context. It was brought to my attention by the late Burton Dreben, who often referred to it. Jonathan Klawans kindly helped me track it down.

25 It is true that a particular philosophical view, pragmatism, attempts to define truth in terms of method, but I have suggested that this is inadequate (see my *The Ends of Philosophy*). At the very least it is controversial, which shows that most inquirers, and not only Gadamer, separate "truth and method."

26　Some philosophers value inquiry despite the fact that they do not expect a "final" or ultimate truth to be achieved. Most of these nevertheless think some truth, some cognitive gain, results. Some grant philosophy aesthetic or moral value independent of cognitive gain, but they thereby give up truth as aim.

27　See Griswold, *Adam Smith and the Virtues of Enlightenment.*

28　Hans-Georg Gadamer, *Truth and Method* (New York: Continuum, 1975), p. 240.

29　Notice that rationalism and cosmopolitanism taken together regard truth in essentially the same way as modern science.

30　See Leo Strauss, *Persecution and the Art of Writing* (Glencoe: Free Press, 1952).

31　See for example, among the many collections of Strauss' essays, Thomas Pangle's *The Rebirth of Classical Political Rationalism: An Introduction to the Thought of Leo Strauss: Essays and Lectures* (Chicago: University of Chicago Press, 1989).

32　The comparison of Strauss with Alexandre Kojève is particularly relevant here. See, *On Tyranny: including the Strauss-Kojève Correspondence,* ed. Victor Gourevitch and Michael Roth (New York: Free Press, 1991). See also Stanley Rosen's discussion of the two in his *Hermeneutics as Politics* (New York: Oxford University Press, 1987).

33　William Galston, "Civic Education in the Liberal State," in Nancy Rosenblum, *Liberalism and the Moral life,* pp. 89–101.

34　Martha Minnow, *Not Only for Myself: Identity, Politics, and the Law* (New York: New Press, 1997), pp. 111–12.

35　Lasch, *The Culture of Narcissism: America in an Age of Diminishing Expectations* (New York: W. W. Norton, 1979), pp. 381–2, footnote.

36　Galston, "Civic Education in the Liberal State," p. 101.

37　See my *The Ends of Philosophy.*

38　The original appears in Joseph A. Schumpeter, *Capitalism, Socialism, and Democracy* (New York: Harper, 1942), p. 243.

39　Richard Rorty, *Contingency, Irony, and Solidarity* (Cambridge: Cambridge University Press, 1989), pp. 46 and 61.

40　Gellner, *Plough, Sword, and Book: The Structure of Human History* (Chicago: University of Chicago Press, 1988), p. 208.

41　There is a relation between constitutional politics and the so-called "politics of identity," which roots politics in cultural-ethnic identification. In each case action or policy is derived from identity, either constitutional identity or cultural-ethnic identity. This suggests that the problem with what is called identity politics is not merely the apparently antiliberal role of cultural group membership, but a tendency, shared by some liberals, to want to derive political decision from something *beyond the reach of political decision*, from the certainties of the identity of the agent – individual or social – in question. Like Leibniz's attempt to derive all the traits and relations of a monad from its essence, this tendency would leave no space for the contingent validity of judgment, *phronesis*, or for freedom itself. If all decisions are dictated by my, or our, identity, then there is nothing to decide.

42   As Peirce posted "Do not block the road of inquiry" on the door of philosophy and science.

43   This necessary combination of differentiation and the urge to synthesis is part of the perception of Bruno Latour's *We Have Never Been Modern*, trans. Catherine Porter (Cambridge: Harvard University Press, 1993).

44   Milan Kundera, *The Unbearable Lightness of Being* (New York: Harper & Row, 1984), p. 8.

45   Alasdair MacIntyre, *After Virtue: A Study in Moral Theory* (Notre Dame: Notre Dame University Press, 1981), p. 219.

Index